The Future of Work

Inka Knappertsbusch · Gerlind Wisskirchen
Editors

The Future of Work

Shaping New Work with Flexibility and Legal Certainty

Springer

Editors
Inka Knappertsbusch
CMS Deutschland
Köln, Germany

Gerlind Wisskirchen
CMS Deutschland
Köln, Germany

ISBN 978-3-658-45149-3 ISBN 978-3-658-45150-9 (eBook)
https://doi.org/10.1007/978-3-658-45150-9

This book is a translation of the original German edition "Die Zukunft der Arbeit" by Inka Knappertsbusch and Gerlind Wisskirchen, published by Springer Fachmedien Wiesbaden GmbH in 2023. The translation was done with the help of an artificial intelligence machine translation tool. A subsequent human revision was done primarily in terms of content, so that the book will read stylistically differently from a conventional translation. Springer Nature works continuously to further the development of tools for the production of books and on the related technologies to support the authors.

This Springer imprint is published by the registered company Springer Fachmedien Wiesbaden GmbH, part of Springer Nature.
The registered company address is: Abraham-Lincoln-Str. 46, 65189 Wiesbaden, Germany

Contents

Introduction

Introduction

Gerlind Wisskirchen

"It is the beginning of a new era of work—where the focus is on flexibility and previously unknown forms of work that integrate ever smarter technologies into our daily work.

The future of work is a fascinating topic. Technological advances, demographic changes, and a globalized economy have already had profound effects on our world of work and present us with challenges and opportunities that need to be mastered. How will we work in the future? How will we organize our work? How will we use the technologies available to us? How will we regulate our wages and salaries? What responsibility do companies have for society, the environment, and the digital future?

This book attempts to find answers to these questions. The focus is on the work of the future, working hours, the organization of work, the use of technologies, remuneration, corporate social responsibility, and the digital responsibility of companies and co-determination in the workplace.

For companies, dealing with the future of work is essential for their competitiveness. In a fast-paced world where technological progress is advancing ever faster, companies must invest significantly to remain competitive. One of the biggest challenges is to attract and retain sought-after skilled workers. This requires an attractive working environment that meets the needs and desires of modern workers, such as promoting lifelong learning to keep employees "employable" within the company.

This book is therefore aimed at all decision-makers who want to deal with the effects of the future world of work. It offers perspectives on how we can prepare for the challenges and opportunities of the future of work. It is a call to actively shape the future of work and to adjust to the changes that lie ahead."

Stop: This foreword was written by ChatGPT/OpenAI. Perhaps the next edition will be written entirely by AI? The question that all employers must therefore ask themselves is what the consequences of technical, economic, and social change will be. The aim of this book is to contribute to the discussion about the future of work. It is intended to develop new ideas on how we can work successfully and satisfactorily in the future. This includes both short-term solutions and long-term strategies.

G. Wisskirchen (✉)
CMS Deutschland, Köln, Germany
e-mail: gerlind.wisskirchen@cms-hs.com

I. Knappertsbusch and G. Wisskirchen (eds.), *The Future of Work*,
https://doi.org/10.1007/978-3-658-45150-9_1

The world of work is currently presenting employers and workers with ever new challenges. Already foreseeable and initiated developments, such as increasing digitalization, the desire for mobile work, a shortage of skilled workers, and constantly changing job requirements, are leading to long-term changes.

This book aims to describe these challenges and show how employers can shape the future world of work.

1 The Labor Market of the Future

The German and European labor markets will undergo profound changes—due to a shortage of skilled workers, demographic change, and the growing use of AI and increased digitalization.

1.1 Shortage of Skilled Workers and Demography

The shortage of skilled workers is already having a negative impact on almost half of the companies in Germany.[1] For many companies, filling vacancies has become a major challenge. The situation is particularly critical in the MINT professions, where there is a gap of 320,000 people.[2] Given the demographic development and the associated decline in the workforce, this is likely to intensify in the future unless there is a significant influx of skilled workers.

1.2 Digitalization

At the same time, technological progress also has a significant influence on the world of work. It is foreseeable that the further implementation of software and AI will change the working world. Indicators of this are the use of multi-dimensional technologies that are neither physically nor geographically limited and whose development is exponential. According to a study by McKinsey[3], up to 50% of today's activities can be automated. The OECD estimates that 14 to 20% of jobs in Germany are at high risk of being replaced by technology.[4]

All employees will be affected by this development, regardless of their level of qualification and salary. Some professions will disappear completely as a result of this development, while others will change significantly or new ones will emerge. For all activities, routine tasks carry a high risk of being automated.

---

[1] *Ifo Institute*, press release from August 2, 2022.

[2] *IW*, MINT Spring Report 2022, p. 92.

[3] McKinsey Global Institute, A Future That Works, January 2017, p. 6.

[4] *OECD*, Job Creation and Local Economic Development 2020, Figure 2.1.

Jobs in industry will become increasingly replaceable due to the increased use of smarter robots and networked machines.[5] Although automation in manufacturing in Germany is already well advanced due to high costs, the complexity of tasks that machines can perform will increase significantly. The goal is a Smart Factory, an automated factory hall that operates largely without humans. In the future, human workers will only control the machines and perform those work steps that are technically difficult to automate. This development can even be observed in countries with low wages; for example, Apple supplier Foxconn replaced 60,000 of its factory workers in China with robots as early as 2016.[6]

White-collar jobs will be changed primarily by the introduction of AI applications. Here too, routine tasks in particular have a high potential for replacement. Initially, this will affect back-office activities, such as secretarial and administrative tasks.[7] Data collection and analysis is relatively easy to automate.[8] However, even highly paid and complex tasks can be replaced. For example, Goldman Sachs has reduced the number of traders in the stock trading sector from 600 to 2 and replaced them with algorithms.[9] Researching complex information and then summarizing it in a continuous text is also already possible as a field of application for AI.[10]

The least affected will be professions that require a high level of education, a lot of social interaction, as well as skills in leadership, planning, and coordination of complex environments.[11] This will lead to a changed employee profile where critical thinking and problem-solving skills are at the forefront and creativity and technical expertise are required. The professional knowledge that has been learned is thus fading into the background.

1.3 Consequences for the Labor Market

Highly qualified employees, especially those with MINT skills, will be in even greater demand than they are now. The shortage of skilled workers in this group will therefore continue to be a major problem. Professions with a medium requirement profile, such as skilled industrial and administrative workers and middle managers, will be less in demand, as their tasks can be largely automated.[12] They will be replaced by AI applications and highly qualified employees who monitor

---

[5] *McKinsey Global Institute*, A Future That Works, p. 43f.

[6] *Wakefield*, bbc.com.

[7] *Brzeski/Burk*, The Robots are Coming, p. 2.

[8] *McKinsey Global Institute*, A Future That Works, 2017, p. 6.

[9] *Brynes*, technologyreview.com.

[10] See the recent application ChatGPT by OpenAI: *Roose*, nytimes.com.

[11] IOE, Artificial Intelligence and Robotics, p. 19.

[12] *OECD*, Job Creation and Local Economic Development 2020, Chapter 2.

the applications. On the other hand, low-skilled jobs in the service sector will be in higher demand, such as in household-related services and, due to the aging population, in nursing professions.[13]

A consequence of this development will therefore be a further polarization of the labor market with a "squeezed middle".[14] High unemployment in some areas cannot be ruled out as a possible scenario, as there will be a mismatch of jobseekers despite a shortage of skilled workers.[15]

2 The Work of the Future

To keep up with technological progress and remain competitive, companies need to invest heavily. Recruiting and retaining sought-after professionals is crucial. Young workers are often no longer attracted by a good salary alone, but also desire flexibility in terms of location and time of their work, and a good work-life balance. To achieve this, an attractive working environment must be created. This book contains many suggestions for this.

2.1 Lifelong Learning

For employees who are already working for a company, lifelong learning is becoming a must in order for them to remain "employable". This applies to all professional groups in view of the changing world of work in all areas. Companies face the challenge of having to constantly develop further training courses. The skills that will be in demand in the future need to be taught, especially soft and digital skills.

2.2 Attractive Working Environment

One of the most important things for many young people is flexibility in terms of where and when they work.[16] This allows them to better balance their professional and private lives and work where and when they are most productive.

In light of this, the office will continue to lose importance as a workplace in the future. Work in the future will often be hybrid. The days when the entire workforce spent their entire working week in the office are already over. Many employees have gained experience of working from home since the coronavirus pandemic

[13] BMAS, White Paper Work 4.0, p. 52.

[14] *OECD*, Job Creation and Local Economic Development 2020, Chapter 2.

[15] *IBA*, AI and Robotics, p. 33.

[16] *Zenjob*, Gen Z or Generation All in, p. 4.

and want to continue doing so in the future. In a survey, 78% of all employees questioned stated that they want to work from home at least part of the time in the future.[17] The "Work from anywhere" concept promises even greater flexibility. In its most generous form, employees are free to choose their place of work, anywhere in the world.[18] Shorter periods can also be spent at another location as part of a workation. If the work is performed abroad, social security and tax law often pose a challenge. An employer may be obliged to pay social security contributions or taxes abroad. In addition, the laws of the place of work, such as laws on permissible working hours or leave entitlement, often have to be observed. It is unlikely that the office as a place of work will disappear completely. Only 13% of workers want to work exclusively from home.[19] In a hybrid working world that combines both location-independent working and working in the office, the office must also adapt and be an attractive meeting place that highlights the advantages of personal collaboration.

In addition to a flexible workplace, flexible working hours are also essential for an attractive company. As a determining factor in work, time is increasingly losing importance, while performance and ("output") are moving to the fore. This offers workers the advantage of a better work-life balance. In addition, they can work at the times when they are most productive.

As early as 2019, almost half of workers had a strong influence on the start and end of their daily work.[20] However, the legal situation is a major obstacle to more flexibility here. Documentation obligations[21] and daily maximum working hours and rest periods[22] under the German Working Hours Act make it difficult for employees to freely organize their time.

In addition to the more flexible organization of daily working hours, a four-day week can be introduced and more freedom for employees can be created with sabbaticals or essentially unlimited leave (trust-based leave).

2.3 Organizational Adjustments

In the new world of work, the deployment of the workforce must also be adapted. Collaboration will increasingly take place in matrix structures and agile work in project-related teams.

[17] *Eurofound*, Living, working and COVID-19, p. 34.

[18] In this direction Air-bnb: *Kelleher*, forbes.com.

[19] *Eurofound*, Living, working and COVID-19, p. 34.

[20] DeStatis, press release No.026 2021.

[21] See: BAG, decision of 13.9.2022 – 1 ABR 22/21, juris; ECJ, judgment of 13.5.2019 – C-55/18 "CCOO", NZA 2019, 683.

[22] Sections 3, 5 ArbZG.

This presents managers with new challenges. Given the shortage of skilled workers, a corporate culture that is inclusive and utilizes potential regardless of gender, sexual orientation or origin must be created for economic reasons alone.

External workers will also be increasingly involved. It may be attractive to focus on the company's core competencies and outsource other tasks.[23] This allows companies to respond flexibly to the workload and the competencies demanded of the respective project. Digitalization creates new opportunities through crowdworking and the facilitated employment of freelancers.

For employees, this offers the great advantage that they enjoy a lot of flexibility and freedom in their time management and in the organization of their work. This also enables them to work from anywhere, including abroad. Crowdworking and freelancing are becoming particularly attractive. At the same time, however, they are no longer protected by employee protection regulations and mandatory social insurance. One major uncertainty is the question of whether and at what point crowdworkers are employees. There is often a risk of pseudo self-employment. Due to the lack of legal regulation in most European countries, the classification of platform workers poses great challenges to European courts.[24]

When adapting to the changed conditions and especially when introducing new technologies, the co-determination rights of works councils must also be taken into account. This creates new problems, because the detachment of work performance from a specific location and modern matrix structures often make it a challenge to determine when and where a company exists. In modern corporations, there is often no longer a single point of contact where co-determination can be easily located. If employees are at the workplace less often or not at all, the question also arises as to how trade unions can recruit members digitally and whether they also have a "right of access" to the physical workplace.

3 Outlook

Like any change, the future of work presents opportunities and risks. Those who fail to adapt risk losing their competitiveness in the long term. At the same time, the developments also offer the potential for significant increases in productivity.[25] Employees can benefit from being relieved of monotonous tasks and being given a higher degree of flexibility.

However, the legislator is also called upon to utilize this potential. The shortage of skilled workers must be tackled by further simplifying skilled immigration. Visa procedures still take too long and the fact that foreign degrees are not recognized prevents people from working in Germany.

---

[23] IOE Brief 2017, p. 22.

[24] *Wisskirchen/Haupt*, RdA 2021, 355.

[25] *McKinsey Global Institute*, A Future That Works, p. 94.

The desire for more flexibility should also be reflected in working time legislation. Here, exceptions for larger groups of employees, who in any case determine the content of their work themselves, could meet the realities of life and the wishes of highly qualified employees. Possible models would be an opt-out, as in the United Kingdom,[26] or the Dutch model,[27] in which those who receive three times the minimum wage are largely excluded from the scope of working time legislation. In the area of crowdworking, clear standards for distinguishing pseudo self-employment would be helpful. It is also worth considering making certain groups of solo self-employed persons subject to social insurance obligations.[28]

References

Brynes, Nanette, As Goldman Embraces Automation, Even the Masters of the Universe Are Threatened, MIT Technology Review, 2017, (https://www.technologyreview.com/2017/02/07/154141/as-goldman-embraces-automation-even-the-masters-of-the-universe-are-threatened/) – 12.12.2022.

Brzeski, Carsten/Burk, Inga, Die Roboter kommen: Folgen der Automatisierung für den deutschen Arbeitsmarkt, 2015, (https://www.erc.de/wp-content/downloads/texte_tools/ING-DiBa_Economic-Research_Die-Roboter-kommen.pdf) – 12.12.2022. (zitiert: *Brzeski/Burk*, Die Roboter kommen).

Bundesministerium für Arbeit und Soziales (Herausgeberin), Weissbuch Arbeiten 4.0., 2017. (zitiert: BMAS, Weissbuch Arbeiten 4.0.).

DeStatis, 9,7 % aller Vollzeiterwerbstätigen arbeiteten 2019 mehr als 48 Stunden pro Woche, Pressemitteilung Nr. N026 vom 30. April 2021, (https://www.destatis.de/DE/Presse/Pressemitteilungen/2021/04/PD21_N026_13.html#:~:text=Vor%20Ausbruch%20der%20Pandemie%20im,%2C%20weitere%2028%20%25%20zumindest%20teilweise) 21.11.2022. (zitiert: *DeStatis*, Pressemitteilung Nr.026 2021).

Eurofound, Living, working and COVID-19, 2020, (https://www.eurofound.europa.eu/publications/report/2020/living-working-and-covid-19) – 12.12.2022.

IBA Global Employment Institute (Herausgeberin), Artificial Intelligence and Robotics and Their Impact on the Workplace, 2017. (zitiert: IBA, AI and Robotics).

ifo Institut, Fachkräftemangel steigt auf Allzeithoch Pressemitteilung, 2022, (https://www.ifo.de/pressemitteilung/2022-08-02/fachkraeftemangel-steigt-auf-allzeithoch) – 12.12.2022.

Institut der deutschen Wirtschaft Köln e.V. (Herausgeber), MINT-Frühjahrsreport 2022: Demografie, Dekarbonisierung und Digitalisierung erhöhen MINT-Bedarf – Zuwanderung stärkt MINT-Fachkräfteangebot und Innovationskraft, 2022, (https://www.iwkoeln.de/studien/christina-anger-enno-kohlisch-oliver-koppel-axel-pluennecke-demografie-dekarbonisierung-und-digitalisierung-erhoehen-mint-bedarf.html) – 12.12.2022. (zitiert: *IW*, MINT-Frühjahrsreport 2022).

International Organization of Employers, IOE Brief: Understanding the Future of Work, 2017, (https://www.ioe-emp.org/fileadmin/ioe_documents/publications/Policy%20Areas/future_of_Work/EN/_2017-02-03__IOE_Brief_-_understanding_the_Future_of_Work__full_publication__-_web___print_version.pdf) – 12.12.2022. (zitiert: IOE Brief 2017).

[26] Regulation 5 Working Time Regulations 1998.

[27] Art. 2.1:1 Working Time Regulation (Arbeidstijdenbesluit).

[28] As in Spain Solo Self-Employed: Art. 24 Law on Self-Employment (Ley 20/2007).

Kelleher, Suzanne Rowan, Airbnb Triples Down On 'Work From Anywhere' As The Permanent Normal, Forbes, 2022, (https://www.forbes.com/sites/suzannerowankelleher/2022/05/11/airbnb-work-from-anywhere-permanent/?sh=419283dc36e2) – 12.12.2022.

Lock, Samantha, What is AI chatbot phenomenon ChatGPT and could it replace humans?, 2022, (https://www.theguardian.com/technology/2022/dec/05/what-is-ai-chatbot-phenomenon-chatgpt-and-could-it-replace-humans) – 12.12.2022.

McKinsey Global Institute, A Future That Works: Automation, Employment, and Productivity, 2017, (https://www.mckinsey.com/~/media/mckinsey/featured%20insights/digital%20disruption/harnessing%20automation%20for%20a%20future%20that%20works/mgi-a-future-that-works_full-report.pdf) – 12.12.2022.

OECD, Job Creation and Local Economic Development 2020: Rebuilding Better, 2020. (zitiert: *OECD*, Job Creation and Local Economic Development 2020).

*Roose, Kev*in, The Brilliance and Weirdness of ChatGPT, 2022, (https://www.nytimes.com/2022/12/05/technology/chatgpt-ai-twitter.html) – 12.12.2022.

Wakefield, Jane, Foxconn replaces 60.000 factory workers with robots, 2016, (https://www.bbc.com/news/technology-36376966) – 12.12.2022.

Wisskirchen, Gerling/Haupt, Jan, Crowdworker: Arbeitnehmer oder Selbstständiger? Zugleich eine Besprechung des Urteils des BAG v. 1.12.2020 – 9 AZR 102/20, RdA 2021, 355ff. (zitiert: *Wisskirchen/Haupt*, RdA 2021, 355).

Zenjob, Generation Z oder Generation All-in, 2022.

Factors Influencing the Future Job Market

Historic Turning Point in the Labor Market in Germany—How Demographic Change Slows Down Growth

Thomas Obst

"Demographic change should also change our thinking."

(Helmut Glaßl)

1 Introduction

The German labor market is facing major challenges in this decade due to demographic change. On the one hand, the economic dependency ratio,[1] is increasing because the baby boomer generations are retiring and hence the proportion of retirees in the population is rising. This poses not only major challenges for the stability of the social security systems and their financing. Shrinking labor supply also reduces the medium-term growth potential of the economy and exacerbates the shortage of skilled workers. Thus, shortages of skilled workers already hampered the German economy in the 2010s (Geis-Thöne et al. 2021). Meanwhile, the number of employed persons (self-employed and employees) reached a record high in 2019 (Hüther et al. 2022). This so-called demographic dividend, which was still effective until the beginning of this decade, has been exhausted. The shift in the age structure will even accelerate in the coming years. The main reason for this is that a large part of the approximately 13 million baby boomers in Germany—the birth-strong cohorts between the mid-1950s and mid-1960s—are reaching retirement age (GD 2021).

[1] Ratio of benefit recipients to contributors.

T. Obst (✉)
Institut der deutschen Wirtschaft, Köln e.V., Berlin, Germany
e-mail: obst@iwkoeln.de

I. Knappertsbusch and G. Wisskirchen (eds.), *The Future of Work*,
https://doi.org/10.1007/978-3-658-45150-9_2

Demographic change is a complex phenomenon. It essentially describes the development of the population composition with regard to the age structure. The migration balance (difference between arrivals and departures of people), the number of births and deaths contribute significantly to this. The change in the age structur, e.g. due to a decline in births and increased life expectancy, is a societal phenomenon in many industrialized countries. In Germany, demographic change is characterized by the fact that since 1973 the birth rate has been lower than the death rate. Without immigration from abroad, the population would have been declining for almost 50 years. Between 2013 and 2019, the population even increased slightly, as the positive migration balance overcompensated for the negative difference between births and deaths (birth deficit). Demographic change, therefore, involves changes that have an effect over a long period plays a crucial role in determining the future labor supply.

In order to correctly assess the effects on the labor market, definitional differences must be clarified in advance. First, the employment rate must be distinguished from the unemployment rate. The number of working persons (L) results from the sum of the employed (N) and the unemployed (U):

$$L = N + U \tag{1}$$

The unemployment rate (u) is thus the quotient of the number of unemployed and the number of working persons:

$$u = \frac{U}{L} \tag{2}$$

The employment rate (n) is the number of employed divided by the population of working age (P):

$$n = \frac{N}{P} \tag{3}$$

The labor force participation rate[2] (E) takes the sum of employed (N) and unemployed (U) persons and divides it by the population of working age (15 to 74 years or 20 to 64 years). It is also called the participation rate:

$$E = \frac{N + U}{P} \tag{4}$$

In this article, we focus on the group with the highest proximity to the labor market—the employed—and thus primarily consider the employment rate from equation (3) when it comes to possible approaches and strategies for dealing with an aging and shrinking working population.

The question of the effects of the shrinking labor force potential is frequently pursued in research (GD 2021; Hüther et al. 2022). The search for the right approaches leads to heated discussion in public debate at times. However, within the political discourse, concrete answers are hard to find despite the great

[2] The term 'labor force potential' is even broader: This is the sum of employed, unemployed, and hidden reserve.

relevance of this problem. The issue of demographic change has been known for some time, but is currently gaining in relevance again. The economic impact of the Corona pandemic in the education sector and labor market, as well as the supply-side tensions exacerbated by Russia's war of aggression on Ukraine, bring this structural issue back into focus. Both events require high fiscal expenditures and cause the debt ratio in Germany to rise, from which politics hopes to be able to grow out. However, this requires economic dynamism in the coming years similar to the developments of the last decade.

Looking back at the time after the financial crisis, it becomes clear how essential the creation of new jobs has been in supporting economic growth and enabling the consolidation of the state budget through dynamically increasing tax revenues and social security contributions. The increase in the employment rate significantly contributed to reducing the debt ratio from 80% after 2009 to below 60% in 2019 (Hüther et al. 2022). Since the Hartz reforms, Germany has been able to increase the employment participation rate—with an interruption due to the financial crisis—to over 80% by the beginning of 2020. Before the Hartz reforms, between 2000 and 2004, the employment rate was significantly lower, averaging below 70%. Even though there has also been a significant increase in part-time employment, the increase in the number of employees subject to social security contributions and the simultaneous decrease in the number of marginally (remunerated) employees since 2010 indicate stable employment relationships. At the same time, it becomes clear that there are still opportunities for further labor market mobilization in terms of working hours when it comes to increasing the volume of work—despite increasingly exhausted potentials in employment participation.

2 Expected Developments

Based on the expected population development and the employment behavior of households, the Federal Statistical Office (2020) forecasts the future labor supply. We present three scenarios for a possible development of the working population aged 15 to 74 years in Fig. 1. The gray line indicates the actual development of the working population up to 2019. Thus, the number has increased from just over 40 million working people in Germany in 1991 to almost 43.5 million. The increase has been particularly dynamic since 2011.

Variant 1 assumes a low positive migration balance of 147,000 people per year and continues to assume that the employment rates will remain at the average level of 2017 to 2019 until 2060. If the positive development in the increasing employment participation of women or the elderly from the last decade thus does not repeat itself in the future, the potential working population could shrink by up to 5 million, from 43.5 in 2019 to 38.5 million working people in 2035. By 2060, the German labor market would have 10 million fewer workers available. Variant 2 maintains the constant employment rates but assumes a significantly more positive migration balance of 311,000 people. This would somewhat dampen the shrinkage of the potential working population. However, between 2019 and 2035, there

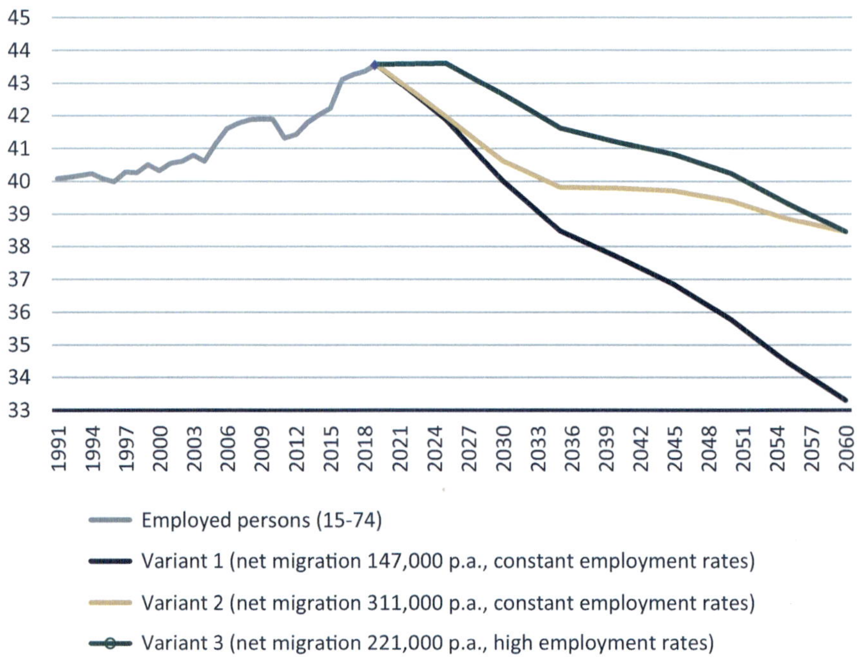

Fig. 1 Decline of the working population by up to 10 million by 2060
Three scenarios of the development of the working population aged 15 to 74 years, in millions of people Note: Gray line represents actual numbers; forecasts after diamond (2019) *Source* Federal Statistical Office, Own calculations

would still be 3.7 million fewer people in the German labor market. In Variant 3, a moderate migration balance of 221,000 and high employment rates (continuously increasing until 2060) are assumed. So if we manage to continue the very positive developments in the German labor market with increasing employment participation in the future, the potential working population would "only" shrink by just under 2 million people between 2019 and 2035. By 2060, both Variant 2 and 3 would have reduced the number of working people by just over 5 million people.

All three variants thus show a uniform direction. The potential working population is decreasing despite a continuation of the positive dynamics in employment participation in the next decade. With the retirement of the baby boomer generation, the potential working population will significantly decrease, and no major leaps are expected in immigration or in the development of labor productivity in the next decade in Germany (Geis-Thöne et al., 2021).

The developments presented hence support the argument that the real lever lies in the volume of work (average annual working hours per employed person) and not in a further increase in employment participation (more persons in the labor market). However, an increase in the working life has already been anticipated with the decided increase of the age limit to 67 by 2030. In their own forecast, Hüther et al. (2022) therefore expect a shrinking working population (20- to 64-year-olds) of 3 million workers by 2030. Taking into account the average annual working hours, the demographic effect on the total labor volume leads to a loss of 4.5 billion working hours. This needs to be replaced first if we want to maintain the current growth potential. Potential output gains are thus largely exhausted and will restrict growth in the future. The demographic change is therefore not only a decisive determinant for developments in the labor market, but also for economic growth.

3 Positive Impacts of this Factor on the Labor Market

Positive effects of a shrinking working-age population and an associated shortage of skilled workers are mostly expected for workers. We have already seen during the pandemic how increasingly open vacancies could no longer be filled. In October 2022, the number of unfilled reported open positions is around 820,000. The total number of job offers in the third quarter of 2022 is even higher at 1.8 million positions. The cyclical increase in short-time work to roughly 6 million from spring 2020 could be significantly reduced to 453,000 in spring 2022. All of this indicates an imbalance in the German labor market, but also means that people in involuntary part-time work or without any employment have good chances of either extending their working hours or taking up new employment.

However, demographic development is highly likely to be accompanied by structural changes. Even if the gap between the available labor force potential and labor demand seems to be closing, a move towards full employment is by no means certain. In this context, the so-called qualification *Mismatch* must be taken into account, i.e., a divergence between the existing qualifications of job seekers and the sought-after qualification requirements of companies. Thus, despite increasing labor demand, a group of workers may not benefit from a tight labor market due to a lack of qualifications. On the other hand, particularly well-qualified individuals should receive higher wage premiums in the future. Indirectly, a shortage of labor can have a positive effect on overall economic productivity if companies manage to automate processes or simplify labor-intensive steps through technological progress.

4 Challenges of this Factor for the Labor Market and Economy

The domestic working-age population is expected to shrink significantly in the coming years. This is likely to result in labor and especially skilled labor shortages that could jeopardize future economic growth, the sustainability of social security systems, and the transformation towards a climate-neutral economy. Demographic change affects the economy through several channels. First, the available labor supply decreases as fewer people of working age are available. The Joint Economic Forecast (2021) predicts that by 2030, economic growth could be about one percentage point lower than in 2020. Demography thus dampens economic growth by leading to a decrease in labor volume. Second, a multitude of studies show that an aging society negatively affects labor productivity. By 2030, demographic change could further reduce labor productivity (GD, 2021). Third, demographic change directly affects companies by exacerbating the shortage of skilled workers in the German labor market (Geis-Thöne et al., 2021). Fourth, the investment rate decreases with an increasing proportion of people over 64 (GD, 2021). Fifth, demographic change could trigger further inflationary effects as retirees no longer produce but continue to consume, thus reducing the supply of goods and expanding the demand for goods.

5 Solutions and Practical Tips

To discuss the negative effects of an aging society and ultimately also concrete solutions in the German labor market, it is helpful to present the influencing factors on total labor volume (AV). AV is calculated as the product of the number of employed persons (N) and the average working time per employed person (AZ):

$$AV = N * AZ \tag{5}$$

The following Table 1 for determining the labor force potential shows the essential levers to counteract demographic change and the associated shrinking labor volume. Thus, the AV is determined by participation in the labor market, but also by the time effect, which in turn is composed of the two factors annual working time and the proportion of employment in part-time.

Hüther et al. (2022) consider the levers shown in the table to develop possible strategic approaches to compensate for the shrinking potential of the working population:

Table 1 Determination of the Labor Force Potential

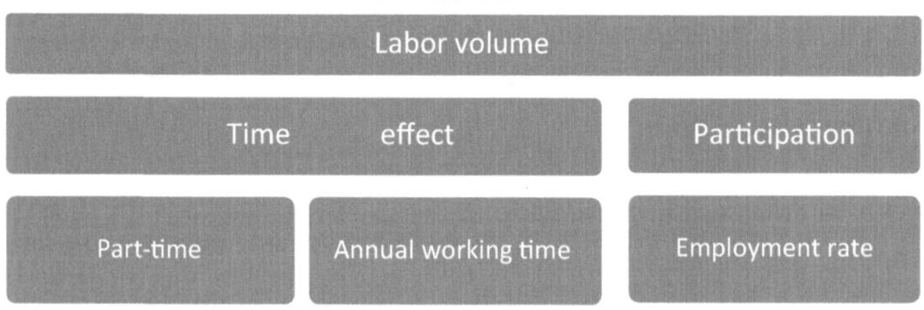

Source: Own representation

Conceptual overview of the influencing factors of the total economic labor volume
Source: Own illustration

(1) Increase the number of actual workers by increasing the employment rate (increase in labor force participation[3]);
(2) Expand the volume of work by increasing the working hours per week and per year given the part-time rate (increase in annual working hours);
(3) A shift in employment towards more full-time work among those employed part-time (increase in annual working hours).

Generally speaking, the labor force participation rate is already very high in international comparison, especially among women and older people. The employment rate of older people (55 to 64 years) increased by 30 percentage points to 73% between 2003 and 2019 (Hüther et al. 2022). This could be seen as a pull effect of various pension reforms since the 1990s. But it is also a reflection of the fact that the shortage of skilled workers has become increasingly pronounced over the past decade. Early retirement is proving to be less and less of a viable strategy. In Germany, the labor force participation rate of women has increased far above average in international comparison. In 1998, the country was in the European midfield with around 59% among 20- to 64-year-olds, but by 2019 it had reached a top position with 76% among EU countries. For comparison: in the euro area, this was only 67%. For the labor force participation rate of the 20 to 64 age group (men and women), the rates increased to over 80% between 2005 and 2019. This puts Germany in fourth place in Europe behind Iceland (87%), Switzerland (83%) and Sweden (82%) and well above the average in the euro area (72%). This means that further increases in the labor force potential through labor force participation are rather limited.

The strong increase in the employment rate in the German labor market was accompanied by a significant increase in part-time work. With a part-time rate of 27% of total employment in 2019, Germany is significantly above the euro area, where part-time employment only accounts for 20% of total employment. This leads, among other things, to the situation that Germany ranks last in measured working hours in the OECD comparison. The average annual working hours in this country were 1349 hours in 2021, while in the EU27 they were 1566 hours and in the OECD on average 1716 hours. Even though the OECD data have some weaknesses, Hüther et al. (2022) show with an improved database that in Germany the annual working hours fell significantly by more than 160 annual working hours between 1999 and 2019. For comparison: In relative terms, the Swiss level in 2019 was about 11% above the German level, the Swedish level almost 7%.

Thus, the second and third approach promise more impact through an increase in annual working hours and the expansion of employment from part-time to full-time. In fact, Hüther et al. (2022) show that, under ceteris paribus conditions, an increase in the weekly working hours and the number of working weeks to the average level of Switzerland and Sweden could increase the volume of work by 4.8 billion hours by 2030 and thus compensate for the demographic loss of 3

[3] We only consider those in employment, not the unemployed.

million working people and 4.5 billion working hours. Further potentials exist in reducing involuntary part-time work and expanding part-time work to full-time positions. Kolev and Obst (2021) have shown significant growth potentials for the German economy in this context based on macroeconometric model calculations. Adjusting the average weekly working hours in Germany (34 hours in 2019) to the Swiss level (36 hours in 2019) would result in a GDP level in Germany in 2030 that is more than 3% higher and would lead to a reduction in the debt ratio of 6% points.

The mobilization of further employment is anything but self-evident in an aging society. At the company level, a bundle of measures is recommended to be able to attract skilled workers in the future and to counteract the shrinking potential of the working population. In principle, even if individual companies succeed in recruiting suitable skilled workers, the macroeconomically relevant problem of a shrinking labor supply is not solved. Continuing professional development (see the article "Continuous Learning—The Importance for Companies and the Approaches of Continuous Learning in an Ever Faster Changing World of Work") plays an important role in qualifying the domestic labor force for the changed requirements. Part-time work plays a much larger role for women than for men. Therefore, it would be advisable to expand childcare facilities on the employer's side. However, better childcare, e.g. through the expansion of all-day schools, remains primarily a state task. Corporate health management to employ older employees will increasingly play a role. The targeted recruitment from third countries, also of non-academics, as regulated in the Skilled Immigration Act, will have to increase. Further use of flexibility in working hours at the maximum working time, as recently proposed in Bavaria and long demanded by employers, is recommended.

Suggestions such as the 4-day week (see the article "The Four-Day Week") are not effective, as they are far from sufficient to replace the predicted shrinkage in work volumes, even assuming increased labor productivity. It is unclear how reducing one day per week (20% working time) should ignite corresponding productivity increases of the same magnitude. In recent decades, labor productivity in advanced economies such as the USA, Japan, or Germany has been declining. While labor productivity growth in Germany was still at 4% in the 1970s, at 3% in the 1990s, it is now only at 1%. Full-time-like working time models already exist and can be freely chosen by employees. In Belgium, a 4-day week was introduced—however, without reducing working hours, which increases the problem of existing work intensification. In other words: Existing proposals to solve the demographic problem in the German labor market through the 4-day week are at best wishful thinking.

6 Summary and Outlook

The brief overview of the developments of demographic change in Germany has shown significant expected changes in the German labor market. While the working population continued to increase until 2020, the demographic dividend seems to be exhausted. The retirement of the baby boomers leads to an accelerated decrease in the potential workforce. Various forecasts for the expected population development show a uniform direction. The potential workforce is decreasing significantly—despite an assumed future positive migration balance and a continuation of the positive dynamics in labor force participation from the last decade. The volume of work could thus decrease by 4.5 billion hours by 2030. This presents the German labor market and the German economy with a variety of challenges. The shortage of skilled workers will accelerate, labor productivity will tend to fall, and the growth potential will be restricted. Wage premiums may arise for employees. Employers will need a bundle of measures to retain good staff and attract qualified applicants. However, it is not certain that full employment will be achieved in this decade. The structural change triggered by the energy transition requires new knowledge and skills. Thus, despite a robust labor market, structural unemployment may occur. A special lever in the strategic solution to the problem lies in working hours. Empirical research shows that most potentials lie in increasing the weekly working hours and extending part-time to full-time.

References

Geis-Thöne W et al (2021) Wie lässt sich das Produktivitätswachstum stärken? Gutachten im Auftrag der KfW Bankengruppe, Berlin Köln

Gemeinschaftsdiagnose (2021) Gemeinschaftsdiagnose Frühjahr 2021: Pandemie verzögert Aufschwung – Demografie bremst Wachstum, Gemeinschaftsdiagnose im Auftrag des Bundesministeriums für Wirtschaft und Energie, Essen

Hüther M et al (2022) Wachstum durch Beschäftigung: Potenziale der deutschen Volkwirtschaft. In: Zeitschrift für Wirtschaftspolitik, Band 71, Heft 2, S. 95–123

Kolev G, Obst T (2021) Schlummernde Wachstumspotenziale im deutschen Arbeitsmarkt, IW-Kurzbericht, Nr. 37, Köln

Statistisches Bundesamt (2020) Erwerbspersonenvorausberechnung. https://www.destatis.de/DE/Themen/Arbeit/Arbeitsmarkt/Erwerbstaetigkeit/Erwerbspersonenvorausber echnung-2020.htm (abgerufen am 04.10.2022)

Skills Shortage—Myth or Reality?

Christian Lay and Christian Niebling

1 Introduction

In its 2021 skills shortage analysis, the Federal Employment Agency, Statistics/Labor Market Reporting, defines a skills shortage as "the state of an economy in which a significant number of jobs cannot be filled by employees with certain skills and abilities because there is not a sufficient number of appropriately qualified professionals available on the labor market."[1]

It thus becomes apparent that the demand for qualified resources is significantly higher than the availability, which massively influences the labor market.

However, if one considers the official number of unemployed people of 2,547,000, which was reported by the Federal Employment Agency in August 2022, and in contrast to this, the number of 886,724 reported open job positions published by Statista, a certain paradox becomes apparent from the figures, since purely mathematically all open positions should be secured by the mere existence of the workforce.

A mere look at the bare numbers would initially not suggest any problems. However, of course, other dimensions, such as the ratio of the required qualification to the actual existing qualification or the ratio of open positions in a certain region to the local labor supply, must be included in the equation.

[1] Federal Employment Agency, Statistics/Labor Market Reporting,
Reports: Focus on the Labor Market—Skills Shortage Analysis 2021, Nuremberg, May 2022.

C. Lay · C. Niebling (✉)
Hanau, Germany

I. Knappertsbusch and G. Wisskirchen (eds.), *The Future of Work*,
https://doi.org/10.1007/978-3-658-45150-9_3

This challenge of the prevailing situation in the labor market had to be faced by the industrial company from the rubber industry, which is used as an example in this article, especially since the fourth quarter of 2021. At all levels of the company, it became apparent that the existing labor market suffers from a lack of qualified resources. While the bottleneck analysis of the Federal Employment Agency has shown that bottlenecks exist particularly in the areas of:

- Nursing professions
- Medical—and non-medical professions
- Crafts professions
- Construction professions
- Sales professions (especially in the food industry)
- Professional drivers in freight transport

the example company had to become aware at all its five German production sites that this shortage also manifests itself in the so-called non-qualified on-the-job training activities.

2 Expected Development

The often described demographic change is already showing its effects on the labor market. The constant growth of the gross domestic product can no longer be covered in the long term by the dwindling workforce. Especially for ergonomically demanding work in multi-shift systems like in the German tire industry, the situation on the labor market will continue to intensify. In addition, for the example company, there is the further challenge of the relatively high average age of the employees. This in turn will lead to large waves of retirement of the baby boomer generations in the coming years.

3 Positive Effects of the Skills Shortage on the Labor Market

The often-quoted saying "The war for talent is over—talent has won!" aptly describes the current situation on the labor market. For the employees, the labor market situation creates the so-called employee market.

Therefore, it is positive to note that companies are more than ever forced to modernize. On the employer side, it is no longer enough to rely solely on the simplest form of employee recruitment. On the one hand, the "brand" of the individual employer, with a few exceptions, is no longer the "selling point" as it once was. On the other hand, creative ways of recruiting must be found again and again. The classic newspaper ad has lost its effectiveness in many cases. In addition, it is positive to note that employers will have to work on the quality of their working conditions across the board, otherwise the newly won personnel will quickly be elsewhere.

4 Challenges of the Skills Shortage for the Labor Market

The positive effects described in the previous point for the applicants bring different challenges for the employers, which the example company also had to face in 2021 and 2022.

In the future, companies will have to openly confront new realities in the labor market, as otherwise they will not have the opportunity to maintain and/or build up the necessary staff in the long term, which will inevitably lead to production targets and thus commitments to customers not being met. This will inevitably lead to an existentially threatening situation for these companies.

Adaptability, speed of adaptation, and flexibility will become new virtues that will decide the success or failure of many companies in the medium term.

5 Solutions and Practical Tips

Assuming that the economy in Germany remains largely stable and planning to continue production operations in the high-wage country of Germany, the company had to take new paths in Germany. Since there is certainly not a universally valid solution here due to the different needs and peculiarities of individual companies, the example company had to adapt and react quickly to situations, as already mentioned in point 4. The company first embarked on a very thorough analysis of the initial situation. It quickly became apparent that the regions of the German production sites were almost fully employed and that many of the surrounding companies were struggling with similar problems. Furthermore, there was a great competition for a few available resources. On the other hand, it also became apparent that the average age of the individual sites would lead to a significant outflow of employees over a medium-term period due to retirement, partial retirement, and early retirement, which needs to be covered in addition to the regular demand.

This made it necessary to develop and implement not only necessary short-term measures, but also medium- and long-term measures.

5.1 Short-term Measures

5.1.1 Modernization of the Recruiting Process

Since the classic recruiting via newspaper ads in the manufacturing sector no longer produced the desired effect, the recruiting marketing mix and recruiting channel mix had to be adjusted accordingly. The adjustments were made in a broad scope, but were tailored to the respective target groups to avoid a "scattergun approach".

Of course, the traditional media for disseminating job advertisements were still pursued, as they also contribute to reaching potential applicants. However, the example company specifically implemented the following measures:

5.1.1.1 A new landing page (via the provider monster.de) was created to specifically address applicants via the Internet, job boards, and social media. In principle, the creation and marketing of landing pages/career pages are nothing new in the recruitment of employees. However, this newly created landing page has the advantage that it focuses very strongly on potential applicants. To ensure this, very catchy and authentic videos about working at the example company's production sites with active employees were shot, among other things. In addition, the application process was simplified in such a way that an SAP input mask, which would be very laborious for applicants to maintain with information, was replaced by simple contact forms with which interested parties can apply in less than a minute of processing time. Within a short time, this career page was able to significantly increase the number of applicants.

5.1.1.2 The described phenomenon of high average ages at the individual production sites suggests that the employees, with an average company affiliation of 18 years, show a high loyalty to the company and the products of the example company.

It was therefore obvious to use the employees as ambassadors for the example company's employer brand. This ambassadorship was implemented as part of an "employees recruit employees" program. Employees who were able to recruit new employees were rewarded with a one-time payment after the new recruits had completed their probationary period.

5.1.1.3 Since, despite all measures taken, the necessary hiring quota could still not be achieved, the process was additionally outsourced as part of outsourcing. In the specific case, the internal recruiting was additionally supported by an external service company. This service was designed to generate further applications and streamline the hiring process through preliminary discussions and screenings.

5.1.2 Modernization of Employee Qualification

The expansion of recruiting measures led to the company having to additionally deal with the fact that the language skills of the new employees often did not meet the requirements to cover safety- and quality-relevant topics of the induction and training process in an adequate framework. However, since occupational safety and the quality of the products are not disposable priorities for the company, it was necessary to work on these processes as well in order to meet these priorities. The focus was on translating the respective documents and process descriptions. Furthermore, as part of the required certification of employees at the individual workplaces, the certification documents also had to be adapted to ensure that processes and regulations are correctly understood and can therefore be implemented.

5.2 Medium-term Measures

The two measures of procurement and employee qualification were able to improve the situation in the short term. In order to enable high retention, the next step was to work on binding the existing and newly acquired workforce to the company. The results of the annual employee surveys and the results of the exit interviews were used as a source for developing medium and long-term measures.

5.2.1 Expansion of Employee Offers

Corporate benefits are a good way to grant employees special discounts for purchasing various goods and services. In connection with the internal health management measures, this offer was expanded in such a way that cooperations were established with local fitness studios, which mean reduced membership fees for the employees.

5.2.2 Investments in Social Areas

Companies often tend to not prioritize social areas in the context of investment planning. This prioritization was adjusted at the respective production sites of the example company mentioned here. In addition, the vending machines were renewed at individual locations and mains-connected water dispensers were installed for the employees.

5.2.3 Expansion of the Training Concept

The dual training concept in Germany offers the opportunity to train in a standardized and sector-specific manner in cooperation with the Chambers of Crafts and the Chambers of Industry and Commerce in the various training professions. The example company has been successfully training in commercial and technical training professions for years. Based on the analysis described in point 5, the numbers of trainees were increased according to the gaps that will open up in the future due to fluctuation.

5.3 Long-term Measures

Where the short and medium-term measures were still perceptible as a sprint, the long-term measures taken are a marathon that has required and will continue to require a high degree of endurance and sustainability. The measures described below are currently still in conceptual phases or in some cases already in initial negotiation rounds with the employee representation.

5.3.1 Adjustment of Shift Systems

The economic situation requires that the production facilities of all sites be occupied with maximum running times in order to enable optimal distribution of fixed costs. The necessary shift work, as the results of the exit interviews clearly show, is a significant influencing factor for the attractiveness of the jobs in the production departments. In order to find new ways that do not necessarily mean the full continuous shift system, working groups consisting of the HR departments, industrial engineering, and works councils are working together very constructively at the individual sites. However, finding a cost-efficient solution proves to be difficult. Finding a combination of cost-optimal working time and optimized work-life balance will be THE big challenge for the future.

5.3.2 Adjustment of Bonus Systems

As already described in point 5.3.1, it is essential to fully utilize machine capacities in order to achieve optimal distribution of fixed costs. In addition, the exit interviews also show that the pressure resulting from this situation often leads to employment relationships being terminated by the employees. To meet these points, it is necessary to look at the variable wage systems and switch from individual piecework wages to solidarity functioning group piecework. However, such a massive intervention in the bonus landscape requires lengthy preparation, coordination, and negotiation with the employee representation. In addition, there is the urgent need to underpin this change process with supportive, targeted communication in order to prevent a drop in productivity and/or a negative engagement effect.

5.3.3 Process Design and Automation

As already described in point 2, it can be expected that the availability of qualified resources will also be limited in the future, which will make it necessary, especially in personnel-intensive production processes, such as those prevalent in the tire industry, to analyze, optimize and in many cases also automate processes within the framework of lean management methods. These automation efforts require significant investments in the industrial location Germany.

6 Summary and Outlook

In summary, it can be said that the shortage of skilled workers actually exists and goes beyond the shortage qualifications determined by the Federal Employment Agency. The measures described were able to help the example company in Germany in the short term, the effectiveness of the medium and long-term measures still has to be proven in practice. The authors agree that the path described in the article can lead to success, but does not guarantee success or provide a standard solution, as the needs of individual companies are sometimes very individual.

When Digital Meets Demographic Change—What Opportunities and Risks Does Digital Transformation Pose in a Shrinking and Aging Workforce?

Oliver Stettes

1 Introduction

Never before have so many people been in employment as in late autumn 2022 (BA, 2022a, 7). The traces of the Covid-19 crisis on the labor market have largely disappeared. Russia's war of aggression in Ukraine has so far not left deep dents in the labor market, even though the access to open positions has weakened at the current edge. However, their non-seasonally adjusted stock remains at a very high level in late autumn 2022, only slightly below the record mark from August 2022 (BA, 2022b). In short, the labor market is in a robust state in autumn 2022.

This is the starting point from which the German economy is expected to slide into recession in the short term. Despite all current uncertainties, the forecasts for the labor market in 2023 remain optimistic. It is expected that companies will want to maintain employment relationships and will resort to short-time work if necessary. Behind this short-term perspective are already the offshoots of demographic and digital change—two of the three mega-trends that will significantly shape the labor market in the medium to long term and have basically always to be considered together.

While it is completely open how decarbonization as the third mega-trend will change the face of the labor market, all the figures are on the table with regard to demographic development. And digitization has been under the microscope of labor market research for some time. The Covid-19 crisis has also triggered a digital push in many companies (e.g. Bertschek, 2020; Bellmann et al., 2021), which

O. Stettes (✉)
Institut der deutschen Wirtschaft, Köln, Germany
e-mail: stettes@iwkoeln.de

I. Knappertsbusch and G. Wisskirchen (eds.), *The Future of Work*,
https://doi.org/10.1007/978-3-658-45150-9_4

has increased interest in the effects of digital transformation on the world of work. However, the term "digitization" hides different facts that are used in different contexts. The contribution follows a broad definition, according to which digitization is understood as the use of digital data and algorithmic systems as a factor of production or as part of new or improved processes and products (e.g. Büchel et al., 2021, 5).

2 Expected Developments

The digital transformation is progressing, particularly in the redesign and digitization of processes (Büchel and Engels, 2022, p. 6 f.), but also with regard to the relevance of AI (Rusche et al., 2022, pp. 15 and 36 ff.). A continuation of this trend can be expected. Firstly, two-thirds of local companies are convinced that digitization will continue to be of great importance to them in the coming years. Secondly, its practical implementation should become easier in the future, as the pandemic-related supply chain problems should at least be resolved in the medium term. Thirdly, during the Covid-19 crisis, digitized processes and products in many companies made a significant contribution to improving organizational resilience. This should therefore serve as an incentive for accelerated implementation for those who have not yet seen the economic added value in the past. In 2020, this still applied to more than half of the companies that found the implementation of data-driven business models challenging (Demary et al., 2021, p. 40).

Digitization can only succeed if employees with the necessary competencies are available to shape the implementation and development of new technologies and to ensure their effective and efficient use. However, according to every second company, this is currently not the case (Demary et al., 2021, p. 40). Employment in professions affiliated to digital technologies and processes is stagnating (Büchel and Engels, 2022, p. 50). This may currently be due to the fact that digitization projects have been postponed or the effects of the Ukraine war are affecting companies' willingness to hire.

In the medium term, however, demographic change will increasingly become a brake on digitization. The curve describing the skills gap in relevant occupations has been rising steeply again since the beginning of 2021 (Burstedde, 2021, p. 16). The prospects are also not better. The annual new supply of MINT professionals will only cover about half of the replacement needs in the next five years alone (Demary et al., 2021, p. 75). Today's skills shortages in certain occupational segments are increasingly turning into a general labor shortage. A glance at the size of the cohort of 15- to 24-year-olds is enough for such a forecast. With 8.4 million people (as of 2020), it is almost 500,000 people smaller than the group of currently 55- to 64-year-old workers who are expected to gradually leave the labor market due to age in the coming decade.

Digital technologies have been and are partly attributed with a great potential for rationalization, because the automation of processes or individual work steps makes the use of human labor superfluous (e.g. Frey/Osborne, 2013). Empirical research does not back this assumption: systematic negative employment effects or even a massive reduction in jobs as a result of digitization are not observable (see e.g. Stettes, 2020). However, it makes sense to understand the substitutability potential of digital technologies as an indicator of the extent to which they can change the tasks or the skill requirements at individual workplaces. This potential has noticeably increased in most occupational fields between 2013 and 2019 due to technological advances (Dengler and Matthes, 2021). Consequently, companies expect that the need for further training will increase (Bellmann et al., 2021, p. 717; Seyda, 2021, p. 81).

3 Positive Impacts of This Factor on the Labor Market

The impending shortage of labor is indeed a major challenge for companies. However, it also leaves room for optimism that advancing digitization, even where it is associated with rationalization effects, will not adversely affect the labor market in the form of (persistently) high unemployment. The chance of finding a new job after losing a job tends to increase, provided that the labor market policy conditions promote labor market mobility instead of preventing it. In addition, shortages of skilled workers may slow down the pace of change, so that most employees will experience digitization not as a disruptive event, but rather as an evolutionary adaptation process.

With the shift from digitizable to non-digitizable activities, the required skills profiles change. Similar to the past, this will lead to a decrease in routine and physically manual activities and a simultaneous increase in the importance of social-interactive activities and cross-functional competencies (multitasking, teamwork, flexibility). Employees will be relieved of physically demanding activities (e.g., Arnold et al., 2016) and can focus on non-digitizable value-adding activities. These also have potential for the (further) development of personal and professional competencies and abilities, given an adequate design of the work environment.

Furthermore, it should be noted that rationalization effects and changes in task composition are associated with higher productivity and thus improved competitiveness of existing jobs. For example, Arntz et al. (2018, 75 ff.) show that the adverse employment effects of digital technologies caused by a change in activities are compensated by a positive employment effect triggered by an increasing demand for products and services.

The Covid-19 crisis has also highlighted the potential for spatial and temporal flexibility of work. Digitized work processes offer companies an opportunity to provide their employees with a better balance between private and professional requirements (e.g., DAK, 2021, 10 f.; Emmler and Kohlrausch, 2021, 16). However, mobile work or home office dissolve the rigid boundaries between private and working life, which can, in turn, trigger conflicts between both areas of life (e.g., Stettes, 2018). Therefore, a lot depends on the personal responsibility and self-organization skills of the employees. Whether working from home increases productivity cannot be predicted in general and depends on the specific conditions of the work environment (Flüter-Hoffmann and Stettes, 2022, 27 ff.)

Finally, mobile work expands the scope to respond to an impending labor shortage. First, part-time employees with family care obligations may extend their weekly working hours by using a home office, as the usual commuting and travel times are at least partially eliminated. Second, companies can expand the pool of applicants to include those individuals whose place of residence is further away from the future workplace.

4 Challenges of This Influencing Factor for the Labor Market

The duration until a position can be filled again is, with an average of more than 160 days (as of November 2022), longer than ever before (BA, 2022c). It is not surprising that the vast majority of companies continue to report problems filling positions (IW personnel panel, 2022) and that securing skilled workers will remain a top issue in companies in the coming years (Demary et al., 2021, 80). The competition among companies for the increasingly scarce labor supply is intensifying. This means that wage and labor costs for companies are likely to increase. This makes it all the more urgent to deploit the productivity potentials of new technologies in order to secure price competitiveness. Labor turnover is likely to accelerate because employees have more options in the labor market and companies have a stronger incentive to poach workers from each other. Therefore, it will be even more important for companies in the future to present themselves as attractive employers in order to attract new employees and retain existing ones.

In doing so, they must take into account that the pool of applicants and workforces are becoming more heterogeneous and that employees can better assert their interests and preferences in negotiations due to the impending shortage of labor. HR managers should also keep in mind that the wishes and preferences of the same person can change over the course of their career and tenure. Human resource management must therefore be aligned flexibly.

The hope of being able to attract new workers with the competencies required for the change in the labor market will be in vain for many companies. Therefore, companies will have to implement the digital transformation with employees who have already completed a larger part of their career and whose proven work routines may be put to the test. This entails two challenges: Although learning ability and willingness to learn are not generally less pronounced in older employees than in younger ones, the heterogeneity within the older cohorts is greater for both characteristics due to the differently progressing careers. Personnel development measures must keep this heterogeneity in mind. Second, change processes can question the status, career paths, and wages of employees with longer tenure. This harbors potential for conflict and can reduce the willingness to change, especially in companies with (age) heterogeneous workforces (Flüter-Hoffmann et al., 2020, 105).

5 Solutions and Practical Tips

Successful management of change depends on how well companies can empower employees for the changes and promote their willingness and acceptance. Dietz et al. (2022) empirically show that employee commitment and corporate adaptability are high when a transformation has a number of characteristics. These include, for example, that the need for change is well explained by management and executives and the derived strategy is transparently presented. But it also includes taking into account existing claims of employees, widening the space for employees to actively shape the transformation, investing in further education, and promoting a culture of error. A flexible design of work organization reduces the probability of a lack of willingness to change, a learning-promoting work environment that of a lack of ability to change (Flüter-Hoffmann et al., 2020, 112).

Demographic change and digitization make the analysis of age structure, current and future competence profiles a permanent task. Where this applies, needs for action can be identified early and appropriate measures can be initiated. A concrete example is the early approach to older employees, whether and under what conditions they can imagine continuing their professional activity beyond their retirement age. This is particularly true for companies that assess the risk of not being able to recruit suitable junior staff as high.

6 Summary and Outlook

The digital transformation takes place against the background of demographic change. Both mega-trends must therefore be considered together; their simultaneity offers special opportunities, but also specific challenges. They are two sides of the same coin. This means that companies can only take advantage of the opportunities if they find adequate corporate solutions for the emerging challenges at the same time. Waiting and hoping that the storm will pass are not options. Because digitization will continue to progress and the effects of demographic change will fully unfold in the coming years. Change will become the permanent state.

References

Arnold, D. et al., 2016, Digitalisierung am Arbeitsplatz, BMAS-Forschungsbericht, Nr. 468, Berlin

Arntz, M./Gregory, T./Zierahn, U., 2018, Digitalisierung und die Zukunft der Arbeit: Makroökonomische Auswirkungen auf Beschäftigung, Arbeitslosigkeit und Löhne von morgen, Mannheim

Bellmann, L. et al., 2021, Digitalisierungsschub in Firmen während der Corona-Pandemie, in: Wirtschaftsdienst, 101. Jg., Nr. 9, pp. 713–718

Bertschek, I., 2020, Digitalisierung – der Corona-Impfstoff für die Wirtschaft, in: Wirtschaftsdienst, 100. Jg., Nr. 9, pp. 653–656

Büchel et al., 2021, Digitalisierung der Wirtschaft in Deutschland. Digitalisierungsindex 2020, Gutachten für das Bundesministerium für Wirtschaft und Energie (BMWi), Köln
Büchel, J./Engels, B., 2022, Digitalisierungsindex 2021. Digitalisierung der Wirtschaft in Deutschland, Gutachten für das Bundesministerium für Wirtschaft und Klimaschutz (BMWK), Köln
BA – Bundesagentur für Arbeit, 2022a, Statistik der Bundesagentur für Arbeit – Monatsbericht zum Arbeits- und Ausbildungsmarkt, Nürnberg, November 2022
BA, 2022b, Statistik der Bundesagentur für Arbeit – Gemeldete Stellen, Nürnberg, November 2022
BA, 2022c, Statistik der Bundesagentur für Arbeit – Arbeitsstellen im Zeitverlauf, Nürnberg, November 2022
Burstedde, A., 2021, Fachkräftesituation in Digitalisierungsberufen – Beschäftigungsaufbau und Fachkräftemangel, Studie für das Bundesministerium für Wirtschaft und Klimaschutz (BMWK), Berlin/Köln
DAK-Gesundheit, 2021, Digitalisierung und Homeoffice in der Coronakrise – Update – Sonderanalyse zur Situation in der Arbeitswelt vor und während der Pandemie, 20.04.2021, Hamburg
Dietz, A./Hammermann, A./Stettes, O., 2022, Hinter den Kulissen des Auf- und Umbruchs: Betriebe im Transformationsprozess. Einblicke in die Transformationserfahrungen von Beschäftigten und Führungskräften und kulturelle Erfolgsfaktoren gelingender Transformationen, IW-Report, Nr. 34, Köln
Demary, V./Matthes, J./Plünnecke, A./Schaefer, T., 2021, Gleichzeitig: Wie vier Disruptionen die deutsche Wirtschaft verändern – Herausforderungen und Lösungen, IW-Studie, Köln
Dengler, K./Matthes, B., 2021, Auch komplexere Tätigkeiten könnten zunehmend automatisiert werden – Folgen des technologischen Wandels für den Arbeitsmarkt, IAB-Kurzbericht Nr. 13/2021, Nürnberg
Emmler, H./Kohlrausch, B., 2021, Homeoffice: Potenziale und Nutzung – Aktuelle Zahlen aus der HBS-Erwerbspersonenbefragung, Welle 1 bis 4, WSI Policy Brief, Nr. 52, 3/2021, Düsseldorf
Flüter-Hoffmann, C./Stettes, O., 2022, Homeoffice nach fast zwei Jahren Pandemie, IW-Report, Nr. 2, Köln
Flüter-Hoffmann, C./Hammermann, A./Stettes, O., 2020, Wandel mit alternden Belegschaften gestalten – Chancen und Barrieren erkennen, in: IW-Trends, 47. Jg., Nr. 1, pp. 99–115
Frey, C./Osborne, M., 2013, The Future of Employment: How Susceptible Are Jobs to Computerisation?, Oxford
IW-Personalpanel, 2022, 30. Welle, Köln
Rusche, C. et al., 2022, KI-Monitor 2022 – Status quo der Künstlichen Intelligenz in Deutschland, Gutachten für den Bundesverband Digitale Wirtschaft, Berlin/Köln
Seyda, S., 2021, Digitale Lernmedien beflügeln die betriebliche Weiterbildung: Ergebnisse der zehnten IW-Weiterbildungserhebung, in: IW-Trends., 48. Jg., Nr. 1, pp. 79–94
Stettes, O., 2018, Mobiles Arbeiten und Vereinbarkeit von Familie und Beruf: Kann das jeder? Will das jeder? IW-Kurzbericht, Nr. 64, Köln
Stettes, O. 2020, (Keine) Angst vor Robotern? Aktualisierte Befunde zu potenziellen Beschäftigungseffekten der Digitalisierung, in: IW-Trends, 47. Jg, Nr. 4, pp. 85–103

Artificial Intelligence as a Key Technology of the 21st Century—Why a Disruption of the Labor Market is Imminent

Inka Knappertsbusch

1 Introduction

Artificial Intelligence (AI) can be considered the key technology of the 21st century, as it influences many aspects of private and professional life. With increasing technological development, the possibilities and advantages of artificial intelligence in companies are also increasing.

In order to gain a uniform understanding of Artificial Intelligence, it is first necessary to clarify what exactly it means. In general terms, artificial intelligence is a branch of computer science that aims to transfer human thinking and cognitive abilities to machines. Among other things, these machines should be able to recognize patterns, make decisions, react appropriately to new situations, and learn from experiences.

The AI Act defines an AI system as follows: An AI system means a machine-based system that is designed to operate with varying levels of autonomy and that can, for explicit or implicit objectives, generate outputs such as predictions, recommendations, or decisions that can influence physical or virtual environments.

Furthermore, a distinction is often made between weak AI, which covers partial aspects of human intelligence and is therefore limited to certain applications, and strong AI, which has equal or better abilities than humans and therefore offers practically unlimited application possibilities. While weak AI is already state of the art today, strong AI is still largely a thing of the future.

I. Knappertsbusch (✉)
CMS Deutschland, Köln, Germany
e-mail: inka.knappertsbusch@cms-hs.com

I. Knappertsbusch and G. Wisskirchen (eds.), *The Future of Work*,
https://doi.org/10.1007/978-3-658-45150-9_5

2 Expected Developments

In a cross-industry survey conducted by Bitkom in 2023, 15% of the 605 participating companies with a minimum size of 20 employees stated that they used artificial intelligence in 2022.[1] 25% planned to use AI in their company during the current year.[2] On the other hand, 52% stated that the use of AI is currently not an issue.[3] Nevertheless, 68% of the participating companies considered AI to be the most important technology of the future.[4,5]

Given the fact that the use of artificial intelligence is still low, no significant effects on the German labor market can be observed at present. Nevertheless, it is expected that artificial intelligence will transform the labor market.

Germany's gross domestic product is expected to grow by €430 billion by 2030 due to AI-based technologies.[6] This is thanks to the many advantages that the use of artificial intelligence offers companies, especially if strong AI is developed, and the expected widespread use that this triggers. Companies from all sectors will use artificial intelligence, including in business, industry, mobility and logistics, medicine and pharmacy, and education.[7] We will experience artificial intelligence as colleagues, as superiors, and as recipients of instructions. AI will replace some jobs and at the same time create new tasks with new qualification requirements.

Artificial intelligence is transforming working world 4.0 into working world 5.0.[8] Working world 4.0 is characterized by networked digitalization and flexibility in connection with work performance.[9] In contrast, working world 5.0 focuses on intelligent assistance systems, learning robots, and user-optimized

---

[1] https://www.bitkom.org/Presse/Presseinformation/Deutsche-Wirtschaft-drueckt-bei-Kuenstlicher-Intelligenz-aufs-Tempo#_.

[2] https://www.bitkom.org/Presse/Presseinformation/Deutsche-Wirtschaft-drueckt-bei-Kuenstlicher-Intelligenz-aufs-Tempo#_

[3] https://www.bitkom.org/Presse/Presseinformation/Deutsche-Wirtschaft-drueckt-bei-Kuenstlicher-Intelligenz-aufs-Tempo#_

[4] https://www.bitkom.org/Presse/Presseinformation/Deutsche-Wirtschaft-drueckt-bei-Kuenstlicher-Intelligenz-aufs-Tempo#_.

[5] https://www.bitkom.org/Presse/Presseinformation/Deutsche-Wirtschaft-drueckt-bei-Kuenstlicher-Intelligenz-aufs-Tempo#_

[6] Miller, HighTech-Startups as Drivers of AI Ecosystems, in: Knappertsbusch/Gondlach (eds.), Working World and AI, p. 31.

[7] See Knappertsbusch/Gondlach (eds.), Working World and AI 2030.

[8] Stowasser, Successful Introduction of AI in the Company—Building Blocks for Change Management, in: Knappertsbusch/Gondlach (eds.), Working World and AI, p. 145.

[9] Stowasser, Successful Introduction of AI in the Company—Building Blocks for Change Management, in: Knappertsbusch/Gondlach (eds.), Working World and AI, p. 145.

provision of information.[10] For employees, the application of artificial intelligence leads to additional flexibility in the context of work performance, a focus on more demanding tasks, the receipt of individually adapted information, and support with monotonous routine mental tasks.[11]

3 Positive Effects of this Factor on the Labor Market

The already foreseeable diverse applications of artificial intelligence will lead to a greater need for specialists and new professions and fields of work, especially with regard to the development, training, and use of artificial intelligence.[12]

3.1 Increasing Demand for Specialists

Given the increasing use of artificial intelligence, it is expected that significantly more IT experts, computer scientists, and data scientists will be needed than today to drive forward the development of artificial intelligence.

Computer scientists and IT experts will be involved in the development and improvement of artificial intelligence in all areas of life, both private and professional. Data scientists generate knowledge and insights from data using scientific methods.[13] The data scientists will be concerned with sifting through high-quality data that can be used to train artificial intelligence. They will also be supported by lawyers, who will ensure that personal data are processed in compliance with data protection regulations.

3.2 Emergence of New Professions and Professional Fields

In addition to the increased demand for experts in the aforementioned areas, there will also be new professions and occupational fields, such as AI experts.[14] These will be needed in particular for the development and further advancement of artificial intelligence, in the field of application of artificial intelligence, and in the field of robotics.[15]

---

[10] Stowasser, Successful Introduction of AI in the Company—Building Blocks for Change Management, in: Knappertsbusch/Gondlach (eds.), Working World and AI, p. 145.

[11] Stowasser, Successful Introduction of AI in the Company—Building Blocks for Change Management, in: Knappertsbusch/Gondlach (eds.), Working World and AI, p. 145.

[12] *Graus/Özgül/Steens,* AI, ROA, 2021, p. 3.

[13] Samek/Squicciarini/Cammeraat, The human capital behind AI, p. 12.

[14] *Graus/Özgül/Steens,* AI, ROA, 2021, p. 3.

[15] Samek/Squicciarini/Cammeraat, The human capital behind AI, p. 11.

Professions that are gaining importance in this context include the following: Artificial Intelligence Specialist, Data Engineer, Big Data Developer, Data Analyst, Analytics Specialist, Data Consultant, Insights Specialist, Insights Analyst, Business Intelligence Developer, and Analytics Consultant.[16] In addition to specialists with an academic background, tradespeople, plant and machine operators, and fitters with AI knowledge are also needed.[17]

The knowledge and skills that are gaining importance in connection with artificial intelligence are primarily technology-related, for example, knowledge of the Python programming language, machine learning, methods for data mining, cluster analysis, natural language processing, and in the field of robotics.[18] In addition, social-emotional knowledge and skills are increasingly in demand.[19] These are used to promote collaboration in interdisciplinary teams, present results, and find creative solutions to difficulties.[20]

3.3 Benefits for Businesses

The use of artificial intelligence is associated with many benefits for businesses. The potential of artificial intelligence is also recognized by the companies participating in the Bitkom survey. Only 5% of the companies surveyed see no benefits in using artificial intelligence.[21]

48%, on the other hand, expect the use of artificial intelligence to accelerate and improve the accuracy of problem analyses.[22] Other benefits recognized by 39% include an acceleration of processes and a 33% reduction in resource consumption.[23] 33% of the companies surveyed believe that the use of artificial intelligence can prevent human errors.[24] 38% believe that artificial intelligence can

---

[16] Future of Jobs Report, p. 32.

[17] Samek/Squicciarini/Cammeraat, The human capital behind AI, p. 12.

[18] Samek/Squicciarini/Cammeraat, The human capital behind AI, p. 11; *Graus/Özgül/Steens,* AI, ROA, 2021, p. 4.

[19] Samek/Squicciarini/Cammeraat, The human capital behind AI, p. 12; *Graus/Özgül/Steens,* AI, ROA, 2021, p. 4.

[20] Samek/Squicciarini/Cammeraat, The human capital behind AI, p. 12; *Graus/Özgül/Steens,* AI, ROA, 2021, p. 4.

[21] https://www.bitkom.org/Presse/Presseinformation/Deutsche-Wirtschaft-drueckt-bei-Kuenstlicher-Intelligenz-aufs-Tempo#_

[22] https://www.bitkom.org/Presse/Presseinformation/Deutsche-Wirtschaft-drueckt-bei-Kuenstlicher-Intelligenz-aufs-Tempo#_

[23] https://www.bitkom.org/Presse/Presseinformation/Deutsche-Wirtschaft-drueckt-bei-Kuenstlicher-Intelligenz-aufs-Tempo#_

[24] https://www.bitkom.org/Presse/Presseinformation/Deutsche-Wirtschaft-drueckt-bei-Kuenstlicher-Intelligenz-aufs-Tempo#_

increase expert knowledge within the company.[25] 29% indicate that the use of artificial intelligence will allow employees to focus on other tasks.[26]

Given these already apparent benefits, it is not surprising that 44% of the companies surveyed expect improved competitiveness due to the use of artificial intelligence and 24% expect an improvement in products and services.[27] 16% even believe that the use of artificial intelligence will lead to completely new products or services.[28]

4 Challenges of This Influencing Factor for the Labor Market

One challenge associated with the increased use of artificial intelligence for companies is the scarcity of AI experts and employees with AI knowledge. In a Bitkom survey from 2022, 55% of the companies surveyed stated that it would help to advance the use of AI if AI experts were available on the labor market.[29] Not only in view of the shortage of skilled workers (see the article "Shortage of skilled workers—myth or reality?"), but also considering the expected rapid development in the AI sector, the demand for AI experts will exceed the supply, at least in the medium term. Many companies will therefore be held back by the fact that they lack the necessary expertise and cannot acquire it externally, for example by hiring new staff.

On the other hand, it cannot be denied that the increased use of artificial intelligence will also lead to job losses. This is because artificial intelligence will replace human labor in certain areas, particularly in professions that can be automated.[30] This is suggested by studies that have found that US companies that make frequent use of AI hire fewer new employees than companies where AI plays a subordinate role.[31]

---

[25] https://www.bitkom.org/Presse/Presseinformation/Deutsche-Wirtschaft-drueckt-bei-Kuenstlicher-Intelligenz-aufs-Tempo#_

[26] https://www.bitkom.org/Presse/Presseinformation/Deutsche-Wirtschaft-drueckt-bei-Kuenstlicher-Intelligenz-aufs-Tempo#_

[27] https://www.bitkom.org/Presse/Presseinformation/Deutsche-Wirtschaft-drueckt-bei-Kuenstlicher-Intelligenz-aufs-Tempo#_

[28] https://www.bitkom.org/Presse/Presseinformation/Deutsche-Wirtschaft-drueckt-bei-Kuenstlicher-Intelligenz-aufs-Tempo#_

[29] https://www.bitkom.org/sites/main/files/2022-09/Charts_Kuenstliche_Intelligenz_130922.pdf

[30] *Graus/Özgül/Steens,* AI, ROA, 2021, p. 3.

[31] Acemoglu/Autor/Hazell/Restrepo, AI and Jobs, p. 3; *Graus/Özgül/Steens,* AI, ROA, 2021, p. 3.

5 Solutions and Practical Tips

Employers would do well to monitor the further development and spread of artificial intelligence and regularly analyze the potential and risks it holds for their own company. In particular, it is worth looking at the United States of America, as technology is generally more advanced there than in Germany and it therefore offers a good indicator of which technological developments could become relevant in Germany at a later date.

Since companies, as outlined above, cannot fully cover the required expertise by employing external experts, it is recommended that interested employees be trained in the field of artificial intelligence now and offered further training, for example on machine learning, data science etc., that they be released from work for further training while continuing to receive their salary, and that the costs for further training be covered.

To increase the likelihood that the promoted employees do not leave the company after the training before they have been able to contribute their newly acquired knowledge, it is advisable to conclude a so-called further training agreement with a repayment clause.

6 Summary and Outlook

With increasing technological development, the possibilities and advantages of artificial intelligence in companies are also increasing. Due to the numerous advantages of using artificial intelligence for companies that are already apparent or foreseeable and the rapid development in this area, it can be assumed that most companies will sooner or later have to use artificial intelligence on a larger scale in order to maintain their competitiveness. Thus, artificial intelligence as a key technology of the 21st century will lead to a disruption in the labor market.

We will experience artificial intelligence as colleagues, as superiors, and as recipients of instructions. AI will replace some jobs and at the same time create new tasks with new qualification requirements. This will not only affect the work of individuals, but the labor market as a whole.

In some cases, the requirements for existing professions will change, in some cases the need for certain professions will disappear because the tasks will be replaced by artificial intelligence, and in other cases new professions will emerge, especially in the field of development and application of artificial intelligence. This creates opportunities for the labor market, because the demand for qualified workers will increase, but on the other hand it also poses considerable challenges, especially with regard to employment opportunities for people whose tasks can be taken over by artificial intelligence and who can therefore be replaced.

The existing shortage of skilled workers will also extend to specialists in the development and use of artificial intelligence. Against this background, it is essential that companies show initiative early on and train employees who are willing to learn about artificial intelligence in order to have the necessary expertise in connection with the development and application of artificial intelligence and thus secure their long-term competitiveness.

References

Acemoglu, Daron/Autor, David/Hazell, Jonathan, and Restrepo, Pascual (2020). AI and Jobs: Evidence from Online Vacancies. NBER Working Paper Series, Working Paper 28257. Retrieved from: https://www.nber.org/papers/w28257 (abgerufen am 07.01.2023).

Graus, Evie/Özgül, Pelin/Steens, Sanne, Künstliche Intelligenz: Die Zukunft der Arbeit anhand von Erkenntnissen aus der Unternehmenspraxis gestalten. ROA, 2021. (ROA External Reports; No. ai:conomics Kurzdossier November 2021), aiconomics_policybrief_german.pdf (maastrichtuniversity.nl) (abgerufen am 07.01.2023).

Knappertsbusch, Inka/Gondlach, Kai, Arbeitswelt und KI 2030 – Herausforderungen und Strategien für die Arbeit von morgen, Wiesbaden 2021.

Samek, Lea, Squicciarini, Mariagrazia, and Cammeraat, Emile (2021). The human capital behind AI: Jobs and skills demand from online job postings. OECD Science, Technology and Industry Policy Papers, No. 120, OECD Publishing, Paris. Retrieved from: https://doi.org/10.1787/2e278150-en (abgerufen am 07.01.2023).

Weltwirtschaftsforum, The Future of Jobs Report 2020, https://www3.weforum.org/docs/WEF_Future_of_Jobs_2020.pdf (abgerufen am 07.01.2023).

Workplace

Working from Home: Perspectives, Challenges, Solutions

Werner Widuckel and Lutz Bellmann

1 Introduction

During the Covid-19 crisis, the use of home office options in Germany and other countries developed very dynamically. However, this tool was particularly heavily used in certain sectors and for certain groups of employees. The main reasons for this lie in the different challenges that employees and companies face when working exclusively from home (home-based telework) and when occasionally working from home (alternating telework). Although the legal obligation to work from home wherever possible has expired, numerous companies are permanently switching to working from home in different regimes. For many employees and managers, based on the experiences already made before or during the pandemic, this is not a completely new situation, but there are still numerous challenges to be overcome in leadership and collaboration, as well as in the areas of technology, health protection, and data security. The focus of our article is on leadership and collaboration.

There are a number of studies on the incidence of working from home in Germany. Comparable data over a longer period can be found in Bonin et al. (2021). According to this, the proportion of employees with at least occasional working from home increased from 24% in June 2019 to 36% in July/August 2020 and 45% in March/April 2021, before falling to 38% in September 2021

W. Widuckel (✉)
Friedrich-Alexander-Universität Erlangen-Nürnberg, Erlangen, Germany
e-mail: werner.widuckel@fau.de

L. Bellmann
Friedrich-Alexander-Universität Erlangen-Nürnberg und Institut für Arbeitsmarkt und Berufsforschung der Bundesagentur für Arbeit, Nürnberg, Erlangen, Germany
e-mail: lutz.bellmann@iab.de

I. Knappertsbusch and G. Wisskirchen (eds.), *The Future of Work*,
https://doi.org/10.1007/978-3-658-45150-9_6

after the expiration of the working from home obligation. However, the large differences become clear when considering the level of qualification. In June 2019, the proportion of employees with a secondary school diploma/intermediate school diploma working from home was 23%, while it was 44% among high school graduates and academics. The proportion of employees with a secondary school diploma has hardly changed during the pandemic. In contrast, it increased significantly among employees with a high school or university degree in March/April 2021 to 58%, where it then fell by 4% in July 2021.

In addition, Frodermann et al. (2021) were able to show with the data from the Linked Personnel Panel that significantly more women (34%) than men (9%) worked from home for the first time during the Covid-19 crisis. There were also many companies that only introduced working from home during the Covid-19 crisis. For example, from the information provided by the companies that participated in the IAB company survey “Establishments in the Covid-19 Crisis” in the first half of August 2020, it is apparent that 23% of all companies newly introduced working from home and 17% expanded it (Bellmann et al. 2020). The sectors “Information and Communication”, “Other Services” as well as “Education, Health, and Social Services” stood out in particular.

2 Advantages of Working from Home

The sharp increase in the use of various working from home options during the Covid-19 crisis has naturally also influenced the evaluation of this form of work. To illustrate this evaluation, we can refer to the data from the employee survey as part of the Linked Personnel Panel 2015 and subsequently to the changes caused by the crisis.

2.1 Advantages for Employees

From the employees’ perspective, the most important argument is the better performance of their duties (56%) (Grunau et al. 2019). This refers to tasks that require a focus on specific work tasks and where too frequent and intense communication with colleagues, employees, and superiors is perceived as a disturbance. Alternating between the workplace in the company and at home is indicated when this focus is not necessary for all tasks that a person performs at a workplace (Bloom et al. 2022). Another argument for working from home from the employees’ perspective, according to the survey within the framework of the Linked Personnel Panel 2015, is the saving of commuting time (55%). A carefully conducted study in China identified greater punctuality at the start of work as a driver for higher productivity in the home office compared to working in the company (Bloom et al. 2015). The compatibility of work and family life was considered the third most important argument with 52% of the mentions. In this context, it should also be mentioned as a finding of this study that employees who worked at home outside their regular working hours, i.e., in their free time, much less frequently mentioned the saved travel time (32%) and the better compatibility of work and private life (30%) as advantages. Considering that many employees could not realize their wishes to work longer before the pandemic, it is understandable that many employees saw longer working hours as an advantage of working from home (38%).

2.2 Advantages for Companies

The company perspective on working from home does not differ in many points or only slightly from the experiences and assessments of the employees. Based on the IAB Establishment Panel Survey 2018, it was shown that the most important advantage of using working from home options for companies lies in the flexibility of the employees: 62% of the surveyed companies mention this advantage. Greater flexibility is understood on the one hand as greater accessibility—also outside of "normal" working hours—and on the other hand as the possibility to interrupt work to take care of private matters. This argument is also the second most frequently mentioned reason for the advantages of reconciling work and family life with 55%. The first mentioned argument was seen as the third most important advantage with 47%. As a fourth advantage, 45% of the companies state that higher productivity is associated with working from home. This could be due to flexibility advantages or productivity gains resulting from punctual compliance with working hours, as demonstrated by Bloom et al. (2015) in the already mentioned Chinese study. In the same direction are also the high proportions of mentions of saving commuting time (36%) and choosing the right workplace (26%). The argument that some tasks can be performed better when working from home was also frequently mentioned by employees. The increase in employer attractiveness was still mentioned as an advantage by 35% of the companies. The optimization of office space use, on the other hand, was only considered an advantage by 10% of the companies.

3 Challenges of Working from Home

As already mentioned, the proportion of employees who have working from home options depends on their job profile. A full 76% of those surveyed in the Linked Personnel Panel 2015 stated that their job did not allow for working from home as a reason against it. Two-thirds of the respondents felt that their superiors considered their presence important. Certainly, the culture of presence plays a significant role. Often, collaboration with colleagues who work from home was also difficult (59%). The separation of work and private life was important to 56% of respondents and posed a particular challenge of working from home, not only when clear rules for availability are lacking. From the employees' perspective, the lack of technical prerequisites also played a significant role, with 54% of mentions.

In the relevant research literature, the negative influence of the mixing of work and private life on job satisfaction and the compatibility of work and private life is particularly emphasized (Bellmann and Hübler 2021). The negative effects of working from home can also include the deterioration of relationships with colleagues (Gajendran and Harrison 2007). The authors even speak of a "home office paradox" because, on the one hand, a better balance between work and private life is associated with less work stress, higher performance, and less stress, but on the other hand, the deterioration of social relationships at work can have the exact opposite effect.

Current evaluations from the DGB Index "Good Work" 2021 survey show that digitally and mobile working employees in the post-pandemic world work more without boundaries, which is reduced by their influence on work time management, but increased by the requirement of constant availability, evening work, unpaid work, shortened rest breaks and rest periods, as well as working under time pressure (DGB 2022).

The difficulty in collaborating with colleagues (22%) and superiors in terms of leadership and control is often not possible while working from home (10%). Thus, the design of personnel management as leading at a distance and work organization pose significant challenges for companies and employees. In personnel management, a trust-based relationship design and a cooperative goal-setting process become central elements of interaction between managers and employees (Breisig, 2020). In terms of work organization, team-related organizational forms are relevant, as they gain importance particularly in the context of transformation processes. The question arises as to how the coherence and a common understanding of team goals, values, and roles can be developed and maintained "at a distance".

4 Practical Solutions

The management of these mentioned challenges and problems is generally associated with the observance of three guiding principles for the organization of work in the home office: voluntariness, participation, and balancing (Widuckel 2021). Thus, it appears in practice and as a result of now extensive research, that voluntariness forms a crucial prerequisite for job satisfaction, commitment, and positive effects on productivity and quality (e.g., Kunze et al. 2021; Ahlers et al. 2021). Participation of employees requires, in addition to voluntariness, the ability to influence flexibility, accessibility, goal setting, and performance expectations in terms of performance fairness. This influence ensures that the potentials of autonomy and scope for action, which home office work can offer, are also realized and show a good fit to the conditions of life conduct such as requirements for health fairness. This requires clear reliable rules and sanctionable participation rights as an expression of a trust-based and appreciative work culture. These participation opportunities seem to be positively related to job satisfaction and commitment of employees in the context of mobile work (Becker et al. 2022). However, we do not regard employees' participation rights detached from collective legal bases (works agreements and collective agreements), but see these as interconnected. The principle of balancing is intended to provide an answer to the aforementioned "home office paradox". Balancing should enable an explicit demarcation between working domain and other life domains and also integrate recovery phases into the time structure of working in the home office. This must be part of the mentioned rules and be lived as a value in the corporate culture and leadership behavior.

The design of "remote leadership" forms a central design content of work in the home office. The research literature offers a whole bouquet of recommendations, some of which are contradictory (e.g., Breisig 2020, Kunze et al. 2021). From our point of view, leadership in the home office intensifies the need for individually differentiated leadership behavior, which is situationally oriented towards the information, communication, and support needs of the respective employees. This is supported by the complex influence of situational factors (e.g., living conditions, experiences in digital work contexts and in the activity, tasks). This differentiation also forms a central basis for the necessary trust basis. This requires a high perception competence of managers and specific knowledge about the required differentiations of interaction, feedback, and intervention, and thus a support need for managers is indicated, which includes suitable further training measures, consulting offers, and time leeway for the design of differentiated leadership.

The design of team-related forms of work organization represents a special field at the interface between operational performance and need-based work. Teams that master agile working methods and have a certain routine in dealing with digitized work processes seem to be able to cope very well with the action requirements in the home office (Krzywdzinski 2022). This speaks strongly for the importance of team-related conditions and maturity levels such as action and decision-making leeway, role clarity, strong common values, and goals. This sets orientations for the design of future team work, which must be based much more on self-organization and requires the appropriate prerequisites for this.

5 Summary and Outlook

Working from home is a form of mobile work, whose spread as a result of the Covid-19 pandemic has received a strong "boost". For the future, according to representative survey data from the Institute for Employment Research, the majority of employees prefer a hybrid form of working from home and in presence, with flexible use of working from home days being very important to employees. The proportion of those who want to work exclusively from home, however, is only 7%. The proportion of those who, despite the possibility, do not want to work from home at all or only as an exception, is 12% (Frodermann et al. 2021). The preferences of companies seem to be more cautious here. Thus, only 21% of companies want to expand their offer for working from home compared to the pre-pandemic period, according to the mentioned survey data, with a spread according to company size being recognizable, ranging from 64% (> 249 employees) to 17% (< 11 employees) (Bellmann et al. 2021). Therefore, one cannot assume a consistent agreement of preferences. This speaks for a high need for discussion and dialogue.

However, the decision for a permanent or expanded offer of working from home also follows demanding design tasks. This form of work can unfold its positive potentials for strengthening job satisfaction, commitment, and health if the three mentioned guiding principles of voluntariness, participation, and balancing are observed. Thus, employees are involved in shaping the flexibility and performance conditions, and situational flexibility as well as reliable rules shape the leadership relationship and the operational framework conditions of working from home. As a result, employees and companies can take advantage of the benefits of working from home.

References

Ahlers, E., Mierich, S. & Zucco, A. (2021.) Homeoffice: Was wir aus der Zeit der Pandemie für die zukünftige Gestaltung von Homeoffice lernen können, WSI-Report, No. 65, Hans-Böckler-Stiftung, Düsseldorf.

Becker, C., Thörel, E., Pauls, N. & Görlitz, A.S. (2022). Homeoffice in Corona-Zeiten – Sind Ausmaß und/oder Flexibilität wichtig für Arbeitszufriedenheit, soziale Unterstützung, Commitment und Arbeitsunterbrechungen? *Gruppe Interaktion, Organisation – Zeitschrift für Organisationspsychologie* 53, 173–187.

Breisig, T. (2020). Führen auf Distanz und gesundes Führen mobiler Arbeit, *Zeitschrift für Arbeitswissenschaft*, 74, 188–194.

Bellmann, L., & Hübler, O. (2021). Working from home, job satisfaction and work-life balance. International Journal of Manpower, 42(3), 424–441.

Bellmann, L., Gleiser, P., Hensgen, S., Kagerl,, C., Kleifgen, E., Leber, U., Moritz, M., Pohlan, L., Roth, D., Schierholz, M., Stegmaier, J., Umkehrer, M., Backhaus, N. & Tisch, A. (2021). Homeoffice in der Corona-Krise: leichter Rückgang auf hohem Niveau, IAB-Forum 11.10.2021.

Bellmann, L., Kagerl, Chr., Koch, T., König, C., Leber, U., Schierholz, M., Stegmaier, J., & Arminian, A. (2020). Kurzarbeit ist nicht alles: was Betriebe tun, um Entlassungen zu vermeiden. IAB-Forum 25.09.2020.

Bloom, N., Han, R., & Liang, J. (2022). *How hybrid working from home works out.* National Bureau of Economic Research Discussion Paper 30292.

Bloom, N., Liang, J., Robert, J., & Zhichun, J.Y. (2015). Does Working from home work? Evidence from a Chinese Experiment. *The Quarterly Journal of Economics* 130(1), 165–218.

Bonin, H. Krause-Pilatus, A., & Rinne, U. (2021). *Arbeitssituation und Belastungsempfinden von abhängig Beschäftigten im von der Corona-Pandemie geprägten Jahr 2021, zentrale Ergebnisse repräsentativer Befragungen vom Februar 2021*, Forschungsbericht Nr. 570, Ministry of Labour and Social Affairs, Berlin.

Deutscher Gewerkschaftsbund (2022). Arbeit der Zukunft im „Neuen Normal". Entgrenzung und Erholung bei digitaler Arbeit. Sonderauswertung des DGB-Index Gute Arbeit. Berlin.

Frodermann, C., Grunau, Ph., Haas, G-Chr., & Müller, D. (2021). Homeoffice in Zeiten von Corona. Nutzung, Hindernisse und Zukunftswünsche. *IAB-Kurzbericht* 05/2021.

Gajendran, R.S. & Harrison, D.A. (2007). The good, the bad and the unknown about telecommuting: meta-analysis of psychological mediators and individual consequences, *Journal of Applied Psychology* 92 (6), 1524–1541.

Grunau, Ph., Ruf, K., Steffes, S., & Wolters, S. (2019). Homeoffice bietet Vorteile, hat aber auch Tücken. *IAB-Kurzbericht* 11/2019.

Kunze, F., Hampel, K. & Zimmermann, S. (2021). Homeoffice und mobiles Arbeiten?, München, UVK-Verlag.

Krzywdzinski, M. (2022). Zusammenarbeit und Produktivität im Team: Erfahrungen agiler, hybrider und traditioneller Teams im Homeoffice während der COVID-19-Pandemie, Weizenbaum Series, No. 27, Berlin.

Widuckel, W. (2021). Diffundieren in das Home Office? Online-Magazin Lateral 7–3.

Work is No Longer a Place to Go—How the Replacement of the Office as a Workplace Creates Opportunities for the Development of Our Society and Cities

Sandra Breuer and Laura Kienbaum

> *"What a wonderful challenge there is! Rarely before has the citizen had such a chance to reshape the city, and to make it the kind of city that he likes and that others will too. (…) Designing a dream city is easy; rebuilding a living one takes imagination."*
>
> *Jane Jacobs (1958)*

1 Introduction

1.1 We No Longer Need Offices Functionally, but Emotionally We Desire Them

Will there soon be a kind of superintelligence that navigates us through the multitude of possible workplaces, meeting settings, informal meetings in cafes, and social media conversations in our everyday life? Will our mobile phone soon automatically book workplaces in the office or in the coworking space (see the article "Coworking Space as a third workplace") around the corner according to our personal habits and preferences—with the way there already planned and potential encounters with interesting people in mind?

Observations over the last few years show that the office, as it used to be, is no longer needed. But a working world completely without offices does not seem to be the measure of all things either. The question of home bases for companies and

S. Breuer (✉) · L. Kienbaum
loop—creating places GmbH, Berlin, Germany
e-mail: sandra.breuer@loop-places.com

L. Kienbaum
e-mail: laura.kienbaum@loop-places.com

I. Knappertsbusch and G. Wisskirchen (eds.), *The Future of Work*,
https://doi.org/10.1007/978-3-658-45150-9_7

teams will also arise in the future—it is about places of gathering and exchange, places for learning and getting to know each other, and about identity. The issue of the office will therefore have to be thought about differently in the future. The task of employers will be to curate an ecosystem of suitable workplaces. Only in this way can the experience of the working world and the company culture be shaped in the interest of the organization.

We dare to take a look into the future. What is currently happening in organizations? What in the real estate industry? What potentials for society, companies, cities and our environment result from this?

1.2 Mobile, Hybrid, Remote, Distributed Working—a Definition of Terms

For generations, work was synonymous with a place to go. Those times are over forever. Knowledge workers can do their work completely digitally, location-independent and multi-local work becomes the norm: At the place where we open the laptop or turn on the mobile phone, we work **mobile**. Office concepts that build on the resulting possibilities promote **activity-based working**—synonymous with the use of a diverse range of different spaces that support various activities. Desk sharing is a promoting element. If individual people work from a location outside the office, we speak of **Remote Work.** If teams or entire organizations fundamentally work from different locations, we speak of **Distributed Work.**

While telephoning was previously the method of choice for communicating synchronously over distance, the use of video conferencing has become established during the pandemic. When physical presence is combined with video conferencing, we speak of **hybrid collaboration**.

In the future, we will have to think of the working world as multi-local, beyond the rigid duality of home office (see the article "Working from Home: Perspectives, Challenges, Solutions") or office. Rather, it will be about integrating the appropriate places in a kind of ***network or ecosystem*** based on activity. Today, many people increasingly use so-called "third places" (see the article "Third places—third workplaces"), places of community between work and private life, some of which are chosen by themselves (café, library, lounge), some of which are defined by the employer, such as coworking spaces (see the article "Coworking Space as a third workplace").

The first companies are beginning to consistently break away from traditional ideas of space usage and to think about new forms of work and corresponding space strategies. These companies are taking very different paths. While some orient themselves toward the idea of the "**flagship store**" and offer high-quality spaces in premium locations that primarily serve the (re-)presentation and experience of the brand identity for employees and customers, others put the emotional component of the employees in the foreground and create urban or rural "**retreats**", where encounters, togetherness and shared experience are prioritized.

Both concepts have in common the departure from the idea of work as a mere completion of tasks. Rather, work is also promoted as a social experience.

As an example of companies that deal innovatively with space for work, the presence concept of the **Sparda-Bank Berlin** is mentioned here, which has given up the previous spatial structures such as headquarters and branch and works in so-called "bases". The "home bases" are specially operated areas that support all activities and tasks of the employees, including former headquarters and branch type of work. The home bases are complemented by "co-bases", either rooms in coworking spaces or premises of partners such as housing cooperatives. Finally, working from home ("home base") is also promoted and accepted as an integral part of the working world. The management level exemplifies the use of the spatial ecosystem in its diversity.

2 Advantages of this Form of Work

2.1 Mobile Work Creates Sociocultural and Economic Added Value

Companies cannot ignore the changes in the world of work. Starting from the basic assumption that there will be no return to an office world as it used to be, mobile work forms offer various advantages for companies and their employees.

Self-determination in terms of the workplace can make a significant contribution to the **increase in efficiency** of knowledge work. A workplace must suit the users and their individual needs and activities. When do I need a contemplative work environment and what does it look like for me? When do I need inspiration and what helps me with that? Which place is the right one to work with my team? Every person reacts differently to external influences, perceives them as enriching or distracting in different situations. If the spatial environment matches the task and the individual condition, work can be done with maximum efficiency.

Companies increase their **employer attractiveness** by flexibilizing work forms. Applicants actively demand the opportunity to work mobile in order to choose their workplace in a self-determined and activity-based manner. Everyday life can be reorganized in this way, the work-life balance can be positively influenced with a corresponding set of rules for mobile work processes agreed upon in the company. Commuting times can be minimized, necessary routes can be consciously planned outside of rush hour. In existing employee relationships, the flexibilization of work forms can increase employee satisfaction and strengthen long-term **employee retention**. In addition, there is enormous **recruiting potential,** as flexible work forms allow employees to be recruited not only at their own location, but also from other places in Germany or beyond. This opens up new opportunities, especially for companies located in less well-connected regions.

After personnel costs, space costs are typically the second largest cost block in knowledge-intensive companies. Since the pandemic, however, we have been experiencing underutilization of areas in most offices. In addition to programmatic changes from classic functional workplace areas to collaborative and emotionally charged areas, **area reduction** can be another sensible way to respond to the current situation in a cost-sensitive and resource-saving manner.

On a societal level, companies can contribute to a transition to positive cities and regions by offering new forms of work. As the office in its traditional form loses importance, mono-functional business districts can develop into **vibrant quarters**—places to live *and* work. New opportunities arise for urban thought models, such as the 15-minute city, in which all important facilities and infrastructures necessary for life can be reached within 15 minutes on foot or by bicycle—a model that promises an improvement in quality of life and climate.[1] This goes hand in hand with a change in mobility—away from the car, towards environmentally friendly alternatives. A **mobility turnaround** could be sparked—with a positive impact on ecology and health. The transformation of urban usage logics would also be a logical consequence. The mono-functionality of buildings and entire quarters would be replaced by a more detailed **mixed use**: during the day and in the evening, during the week and on weekends, above and below in buildings—also an important building block for responsible use of the resource space and rooms.[2]

Finally, rural regions are becoming attractive again: Lower real estate and living costs or proximity to nature lead to an influx or return of a clientele that had increasingly settled in cities in recent decades due to work opportunities. The **strengthening of rural areas** can transform structurally weak areas into vital economic and attractive living spaces and at the same time counteract price increases in the conurbations.

3 Challenges of this Form of Work

Technically, we can work from anywhere today—at least in typical office jobs (see the article "Work from anywhere—The free choice of workplace"). However, cultural techniques of collaboration need to be newly developed and established. As soon as the working world consists of more than a desk and a meeting or conference room, it is necessary to openly and regularly communicate the potentials, expectations, challenges, and "rules of the game" of this form of work in the organization. Until now, we knew which place and spatial setting was suitable and appropriate for a meeting or a specific task. In the future, we will have to include additional locations and possibilities for virtual gatherings in our planning beyond the office work environment provided by the employer. These work possibilities and the associated behaviors need to be recalibrated.

[1] The idea of the "15-minute city" was formulated by C. Moreno in 2016.

[2] The basis are the current possibilities starting from section 6 BauNVO.

If the culture and maturity level of the organization are ready, the spatial change can start immediately and run smoothly—as the experiences of the lockdowns have shown. In our work, we find that **transformation processes** in terms of **collaboration culture** and **leadership styles** are necessary with the introduction or consolidation of flexible work to eliminate existing reservations and fears of contact.

An increasing flexibility of workplaces often goes hand in hand with management's concerns about a dwindling **sense of belonging and collaboration**. In our projects, we experience that the questions of how teams can grow together without regular in person meetings, to what extent casual communication and informal exchange can take place virtually, are not easy to answer and need to be considered individually.

For successful **onboarding processes**, especially of young and inexperienced colleagues, mobile work can pose a difficulty. A 'looking over the shoulder', the immediate possibility to ask questions and discuss partial results in a timely manner, are more difficult to implement when employees work at different locations. Digital tools for organization, communication, and collaboration need to be tested; a corresponding culture transformation needs to be initiated in this regard. Also frequently mentioned is the danger of individualization and self-optimization. The decision about the place of work is often made very individually and less about the question: How does my presence help my colleagues? It is therefore also necessary to create a culture that openly addresses the need to contribute to an organization through presence. Another effect of the current development is that work is becoming less and less clearly separable from leisure time—its former counterpoint. In this context, the issue of **confidentiality** in dealing with sensitive information, e.g. documents, conversations, is also to be mentioned as a challenge of mobile work. Confidentiality requires a lot of trust, clear guidelines and responsibility, as well as education.

On the part of the workforce and works councils, there is an increasing demand in relation to mobile work as to how **health protection** in terms of ergonomics and technical rules for workplaces as well as compliance with legal working and rest periods can be ensured. From the facility management's point of view, there are often concerns about the **difficult predictability** of required space resources due to the constant change in requirements. The real estate market is characterized by little flexibility in terms of lease terms. In addition, built spatial solutions usually require lengthy and complex planning and implementation processes.

While the described implications and challenges apply to knowledge-based companies in general, **manufacturing companies** face the danger of creating a two-class society. Mobile work is not possible for work on the assembly line. After all, efforts had been made for a long time to bridge the gap between "blue" and "white collar", i.e. factory hall and office.

For the implementation of mobile work, companies are currently confronted with the difficulty that an overview of solution spaces, strategies, and concepts is still lacking. Many companies have started to develop their own solution spaces. It will take time until reliable best practice examples and benchmarks are available that provide orientation.

4 Solutions and Practical Tips

To curate a diverse ecosystem of possible, suitable workplaces, an organization must think not only in terms of square meters and euros. In the future, the experience of the working world will be identity-forming and culture-shaping. The rule must be: **Be brave**! Let go and try new things! Embrace digitization! Allow "permanent beta"! We must accept that the current situation is not an exceptional state, but that we must face the changes in the working world and a 'back to office' does not mean a 'back to normal'. So far, no one has the one and only correct solution for the challenges of mobile work. However, it has become clear in recent years that a 'recall to the office', in whatever form, cannot be a solution. Work must be rethought, because mobile work is here to stay.

In practical implementation, this means creating offers, curating an ecosystem of possible workplaces and creating good places as anchor points within it. Key success factors are multimodal **accessibility**, user-friendly **functionality**, and experience-oriented **design**. Especially the spatial anchor points can unfold identity-forming power compared to the logic of a 'flagship store'. As company-specific places with plenty of room for exchange and collaboration as well as small retreat and concentration places, they can become home places for the staff and a representation for the customers. Especially when these places offer a functional, design and emotional added value compared to the home office and third places, the office will again become "the place to be".

The underlying questions must be thought through in several steps. It requires an overall **strategy** for the work of the future—beyond the one specific place. For this, a target image must first be defined and requirements must be clarified, then a concept and a strategy for the network of workplaces must be developed, solution spaces must be determined, established and tested. Then it is necessary to implement this courageously and involve the users. The process towards a future-proof solution for mobile work should always be understood as a **cultural project** and must be accompanied by a change management concept accordingly.

The concrete implementation may mean that new areas need to be found and developed, and that cooperations with operators of office spaces and meeting/event spaces need to be entered into. As a result, the **real estate market** must adapt to the changed requirements in order to offer suitable products. Companies would benefit from starting the search with sufficient lead time and not to let themselves be driven by the market. Rather, they should demand according to their specific requirements, e.g. smaller areas in modular structure, shorter/flexible lease terms, high attractiveness through diversity of use and design quality, and good accessibility.

And our cities must also be active. If fewer people commute to the city centers every day, pressure for change will be put on the corresponding infrastructure. Even the death of city centers is already being talked about. While we do not expect office occupancy beyond 50% to be permanent, we consider this swan song for the city center to be unfounded. **City centers** have always been subject to constant change: After crises (fires, wars, epidemics …) they were always redesigned, they reacted to economic changes such as industrialization, the car, and consumption. Now they are again challenged to change, to adapt to the fundamentally changing living and working conditions.

5 Summary and Outlook

While many knowledge workers greatly appreciate the home office, others understand the entire city as an office, "Work from Anywhere" (see the article "Work from anywhere—The free choice of workplace") is a lived reality for them. For others, the social aspect is in the foreground, they often go to the office to meet colleagues. Hybrid work models are being tested in all shades in between. In this field of tension, the concept of "mobile office" must assert itself in the future. If a work environment concept is to offer relevance and added value for its users, its offer must necessarily go beyond the function 'work' and also integrate the area 'life'. After all, a future-proof work environment concept must be tailored to the respective company purpose and type as well as the corresponding self-image.

The diverse, constantly evolving and company-specific offers of workplaces will in the future be thought of more as hyperlocal platforms and active parts of mixed urban quarters. The resulting potentials for society, economy and ecology have already been formulated in all relevant disciplines. We have it in our hands to actively shape our built environment as a high-quality work and living space for us and future generations. Spaces, buildings and cities can become livable creative places and drivers of innovation if all participants recognize their possibilities and see themselves as co-responsible for shaping the societal transformation process, making the best possible use of opportunities. Companies must open up to the new forms of work, but also the development of (office) real estate and consequently the urban structure must be thought of openly and with constantly change.

To what extent a 'superintelligence' will help us navigate through everyday life in the future, we will see. For now, we need a resilient structure of good places that we consciously and jointly create.

Third Places

Sina Niehues

1 Introduction

Work and work environments are constantly changing driven by the influence of current developments, such as digitalization (see the article "When digital meets demographic change—What opportunities and risks does digital transformation pose in a shrinking and aging working population?"), value change and demographic change (see the article "Historical turning point in the labor market in Germany—How demographic change slows down growth"). The future work environment is characterized by a high degree of flexibility due to the expanded possibilities of designing working hours, workplace, and work organization. With regard to the workplace, there are for example the so-called "Third Places" that enable more flexibility.

The term "Third Place" was originally used by US sociologist Ray Oldenburg to describe places that promote community and communication between people outside of the home (First Place) and work (Second Place). In doing so, he distinguished these living spaces from each other. According to his view, Third Places are informal public meeting points of social interaction that offer community, sociability, and spontaneity. They are characterized by comfort, openness, interactivity, playfulness, and diversity (Oldenburg and Brissett 1982). Third Places, which are perceived by people as "homes away from home" (Oldenburg 1999, p. 1), exist in various forms. Therefore, a Third Place can be a café, a bar, a pub,

S. Niehues (✉)
ifaa – Institut für angewandte Arbeitswissenschaft e. V., Düsseldorf, Germany
e-mail: info@ifaa-mail.de

I. Knappertsbusch and G. Wisskirchen (eds.), *The Future of Work*,
https://doi.org/10.1007/978-3-658-45150-9_8

a restaurant, a community center, a bookstore, or other places (Oldenburg 1999). However, according to Oldenburg, as soon as people who are engaged in gainful or productive work are present at these places, they no longer meet the requirements of a Third Place (Oldenburg and Brissett 1982).

In recent years, however, domestic, productive, and social activities have increasingly merged, making a clear separation of these living spaces difficult (Waters-Lynch et al. 2016). Transfering Oldenburg's considerations to the work context, possible workplaces can be distinguished from each other. Working from home is the First Place. The Second Place is the office (Fels 2022). Third Places are public places that provide a suitable environment for work and where the worker feels comfortable. Thus, these places are characterized not only by promoting communication and social interaction. They also give the possibility to concentrate on work activities (Joo 2020).

Even though Third Places were not originally oriented towards productive activities, they are now also visited for work. Therefore, the significance of Third Places as additional workplaces is increasing for those people who have the opportunity to work flexibly in terms of location. Thus, Third Places are not only attractive workplaces for freelancers, (solo) self-employed, gig workers, and students. Also, employees who are allowed to work mobile are increasingly taking advantage (Matiaske and Seifert 2022; Mimoun and Gruen 2021). As a result of both the actual customers and workers visiting Third Places, changed requirements for the services (e.g., WLAN, power outlets, long stay duration) and new strategies have emerged (Mimoun and Gruen 2021). According to Mimoun and Gruen (2021), there are four types of Third Places (see Fig. 1). Depending on the form, workers are thus given different opportunities to pursue the social or productive activities of their work. In particular, the productive Third Places, such as Working-Cafés, are oriented towards workers in their strategy and with their services.

Coworking Spaces (see the article "Coworking Space as a third workplace") or Hubs are not considered to be Third Places by Mimoun and Gruen (2021) as they are usually not public places. However, since they can be seen as an alternative to working from home and the company's office and also support social activities and networking, some authors still define these concepts as Third Places (Bonin et al. 2022; Fels 2022; Matiaske and Seifert 2022; Brown 2017). Firdaus and Fuad (2021) find that Coworking Spaces can be both Second Place and Third Place at the same time. The assignment of the various workplaces is often dependent on the underlying concept and the associated characteristics (Joo 2020).

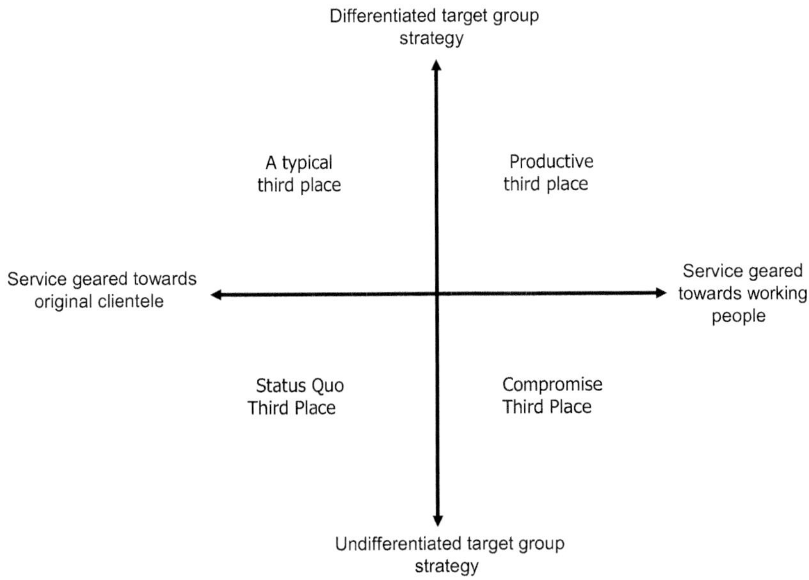

Fig. 1 Own representation based on Mimoun and Gruen (2021)

2 Benefits of Using Third Places

Third Places, especially for dependent employees, complement the workplace and home office. Therefore, Third Places are attractive to employees when they offer individual added value compared to the alternatives (Bonin et al. 2022). Enabling work at Third Places is also in the employer's interest, as it can ensure the satisfaction of its employees and be perceived as an attractive employer in the job market (Bonin et al. 2022).

Since Third Places can be various locations, workers have the opportunity to visit a workplace where their physical, social, and emotional needs are best met (Joo 2020). Thus, the flexible, personal choice of the physical location can improve the match between the work mode (e.g., focus, collaboration, social exchange, learning) and the spatial environment, thereby promoting productivity (Firdaus and Fuad 2021; Mimoun and Gruen 2021). Third Places also bring people together, counteracting the social isolation and loneliness often attributed to working at home (Bonin et al. 2022; Mimoun and Gruen 2021). Workers meet other "like-minded" individuals who can support and motivate each other (Mimoun and Gruen 2021; Brown 2017). The opportunity for social interaction that Third Places offer, therefore, promotes the satisfaction of social needs. The harmony between a workplace and one's self-understanding can potentially deviate more at the company workplace than at a self-determined location. Thus, a unity between the characteristics of a place and personal identity is more likely at Third Places and can have a positive effect on the fulfillment of emotional needs (Joo 2020).

Third Places overall promote flexibility at work, offering opportunities for both employees and companies. Workers, especially those who cannot or can only work with difficulty at home due to personal circumstances (e.g., no space, noisy environment), are provided with alternative workplaces besides the company location. They can benefit from advantages of workplace flexibility, such as shorter commuting times or improved work-life balance (Bonin et al. 2022; Fels 2022; Mimoun and Gruen 2021). Compared to the home office, Third Places enable physical and psychological separation between work and home (Matiaske and Seifert 2022; Brown 2017). This allows for a more structured workday and prevents work from encroaching on personal life. Household activities and potential distractions at home can also be avoided (Bonin et al. 2022; Brown 2017). In addition, workers at some Third Places, specifically coworking spaces, can benefit from higher quality and more professional office infrastructure with on-site technical support (Bonin et al. 2022). At Third Places, "auras of unexpected" can occur according to Oldenburg and Brissett 1982, p. 274), leading to serendipities. This means that new ideas can develop or new customer relationships can emerge through social exchange. The fact that Thrid Places can be used on demand results in a variety of usage scenarios (Bonin et al. 2022; Brown 2017). For example, Third Places can be visited on the go (e.g., on a business trip) to use free time productively. Meetings with colleagues or customers can also take place at a Third Place that is easily accessible to everyone, thereby reducing travel times and facilitating the establishment of close business relationships (Mimoun and Gruen 2021). In addition to workplace flexibility, Third Places also promote flexibility in terms of working hours (Matiaske and Seifert 2022; Brown 2017), as some Third Places offer, for example, longer opening hours compared to the company location (Bonin et al. 2022).

If companies allow the use of Third Places, they give their employees the opportunity to combine the advantages of working from home with the advantages of working at the company location and can ideally benefit from their improved productivity and well-being. From a human resources perspective, the commitment of employees can also be strengthened and the recruitment of new employees facilitated (Bonin et al. 2022). Among other things, the recruitment of skilled workers can be promoted by companies' openness regarding the decentralized distribution of workplaces, as relocation is no longer necessarily required for future employees. If Third Places and the home office are regularly used as alternative workplaces by employees, economic benefits can also be achieved through space savings in the company (Fels 2022; Matiaske and Seifert 2022).

3 Challenges in Using Third Places

Third Places offer employees alternatives to the company location and home office. However, not everyone can benefit from the associated advantages. Third Places can only be used by employees with tasks suitable for mobile work. Thus, employers must ensure that the expanded possibilities regarding workplace flexibility do not lead to dissatisfaction among employees who cannot work at Third Places (Bonin et al. 2022; Mimoun and Gruen 2021).

Mobile work challenges companies in terms of occupational safety and health protection. The employer is responsible for the safety and health of employees at work. If work takes place mobile at another T location, the employer can only partially influence the working conditions. Therefore, it can be difficult to ensure compliance with the requirements for human-friendly work design (Stowasser et al. 2019). For example, the technical and ergonomic equipment at Third Places may be poorly designed (Matiaske and Seifert 2022). Data protection and data security also pose a challenge for companies at Third Places in the context of mobile work (Bonin et al. 2022; Mimoun and Gruen 2021). The possibilities for influence and misuse by third parties are significantly increased in public places, while the company's control options are limited (Stowasser et al. 2019). Companies must therefore consider data protection, data security, and safety and health protection when they support work at Third Places. However, it is necessary to differentiate according to the form of the Third Places. For example, coworking spaces can offer advantages, especially when it comes to legal issues such as data protection or workplace regulations (Matiaske and Seifert 2022).

With the increase in alternative workplaces, companies are also faced with the challenge that the company location can lose its importance. If employees see no reason to perform their work tasks at the company location, they will likely work on-site less frequently. This can then affect internal collaboration, creativity and innovation, and identification with the company (Rief 2021).

Depending on the extent to which the employees can work mobile and whether they live in the city or in the country, they have various opportunities to visit Third Places (Bonin et al. 2022). This not only creates an imbalance in terms of the different opportunities for employees in the context of workplace flexibility, but also poses challenges for the employees itself. For example, depending on the form and design of the Third Place, there may be tensions between conversation and concentration or distractions. Employees who want to work concentrated and undisturbed at a Third Place may feel disturbed by the conversation of other guests (Joo 2020). It is also possible that the social contacts on site and the associated joint conversations represent a distraction from the actual tasks (Bonin et al. 2022). Overall, employees are thus faced with the challenge of choosing the most suitable workplace from the available Third Places depending on the work task.

4 Solutions and Practical Tips

When companies implement workplace flexibility in the form of mobile work, they must deal with the various possible workplaces and define at which of these places outside the company location work may be carried out. Regulations that relate, for example, to the topics of safety and health protection, data protection, data security, ergonomics, technical equipment, and the permissible working time at these places should be appropriately determined in this context.

A differentiated view of the various workplaces is necessary for Third Places. It is important to inform employees and applicants who are allowed to work mobile about the options available to them and to point out the associated regulations. To promote appropriate use of Third Places, the provision of further information is also useful. For example, the advantages and disadvantages of the various workplaces should be explained and possible usage scenarios for Third Places should be highlighted. Employees should know which aspects to consider when choosing a Third Place and when working at the selected location. They need to be sensitized to the match between workplace and work task. Companies can make or collect recommendations on which Third Places in the area are suitable for which work tasks and promote the exchange of experiences at various specific Third Places among employees.

To prevent the company location from losing its importance due to the increase in alternative workplaces, companies must provide their employees with reasons and motivation to continue performing their work at the company location. Therefore, they should design their own location in such a way that not only concentrated work, but also various forms of collaboration are supported by the premises. In particular, the opportunities for encounter, collaboration, exchange, learning, and innovation become increasingly important for the company location (see the article "Work is no longer a place to go—How the detachment from the office as a workplace creates opportunities for the development of our society and cities"), as individual work can usually be done just as well at home or at certain Third Places. A focus on promoting these aspects in office design is therefore crucial for the attractiveness of the location. Since Third Places put social interaction at the center, companies can learn from their design. Companies should work with their employees to design areas at the company location that reflect the characteristics of Third Places. This then also offers employees who actually have no opportunity to work mobile the chance to benefit from spaces that strengthen community and communication.

5 Summary and Outlook

In the work context, public places that offer workers the space to pursue their work activities, particularly social but also productive ones, can be referred to as Third Places. There are different forms of these Third Places, which can specifically meet the physical, social, and emotional needs of the employees.

Third Places make it possible to combine the advantages of working from home with the advantages of working at the company location. This increases the need for companies to deal with rules for the use of Third Places and to make their own location attractive so that it does not lose its importance. Because with the increasing possibilities of workplace flexibility, employees will in the future weigh up the effort and benefit in choosing their workplace every day. Thus, these Third Places will increasingly play a larger role in these decisions and represent a sensible addition to the home office and company location.

References

Bonin H, Eichhorst W, Krause-Pilatus A (2022) Bedeutung von Coworking Spaces als Dritter Arbeitsort in Deutschland. Forschungsbericht 595

Brown J (2017) Curating the 'Third Place'? Coworking and the mediation of creativity. Geoforum 82:112–126

Fels B (2022) Büroflächen auf dem Prüfstand. Dezentralisierung der Wissensarbeit als Wegbereiter für Dritte Arbeitsorte. In: Pfnür A, Eberhardt M, Herr T (Eds.) Transformation der Immobilienwirtschaft, Springer Gabler, Wiesbaden, S 649–660

Firdaus S, Fuad AH (2021) Coworking space: second place, third place, or both? IOP Conf. Series: Earth and Environmental Science 673

Joo J (2020) Customers' psychological ownership toward the third place. Service Business 14:333–360

Matiaske W, Seifert H (2022) Coworking Spaces als dritter Arbeitsort – eine Alternative zur Arbeit von zu Hause. In: Rump J, Eilers S (Eds.) Arbeiten in der neuen Normalität, Springer Gabler, Berlin, S 179–187

Mimoun L, Gruen A (2021) Customer Work Practices and the Productive Third Place. Journal of Service Research 24(4):563–581

Oldenburg R (1999) The Great Good Place: Cafes, Coffee Shops, Bookstores, Bars, Hair Salons, and other Hangouts at the Heart of a Community, Da Capo Press, Cambridge

Oldenburg R, Brissett D (1982) The Third Place. Human Sciences Press: 265–284

Rief S (2021) Auf dem Weg in eine hybride Arbeitswelt – Büros und Büroarbeit in der Post-Corona-Epoche. DGUV Forum 3:19–25

Stowasser S, Altun U, Hartmann V et al (2019) Institut für angewandte Arbeitswissenschaft (Eds.) Gutachten zur Mobilen Arbeit. Erstellt im Auftrag der Bundestagsfraktion der Freien Demokratischen Partei (FDP)

Waters-Lynch J, Potts J, Butcher T et al (2016) Coworking: A Transdisciplinary Overview. SSRN Electronic Journal

Coworking Space as a Third Workplace

Ann-Sophie Amler

"Coworking Spaces are decentralized professional workplaces with innovative power"

– Ann-Sophie Amler

1 Introduction

As early as 2005, the first coworking space opened in San Francisco, and in 2009, the first coworking space in Germany was established with betahaus in Berlin.[1] Since then, the exponential growth of coworking spaces has continued. Between 2018 and 2020, the number of coworking spaces in Germany quadrupled.[2]

The demand for location-independent and flexible working opportunities arises, among other things, from the increasing digitalization of the economy and the world of work.[3] The term "New Work" not only encompasses the trend towards location-independent and flexible working, but also refers to a more agile and project-based way of working. Both aspects allow for a more specific response

[1] BMAS (2022, p. 18).

[2] Dell (2020).

[3] BMAS (2022, p. 9); Dohrmann (2022, p. 664).

A.-S. Amler (✉)
WERFT 4.0, Coworking Space und Business Center, Langenfeld/Rhld., Germany
e-mail: a.amler@werft4-0.com

I. Knappertsbusch and G. Wisskirchen (eds.), *The Future of Work*,
https://doi.org/10.1007/978-3-658-45150-9_9

to individual requirements and skills of employees in personnel deployment.[4] In addition, during the 2020/21 pandemic, employers' willingness to offer mobile working opportunities increased, partly due to office space reductions at the company's location.[5] This was akin to a natural field experiment to enable and evaluate decentralized, agile working.

The Federal Ministry of Labour and Social Affairs (BMAS) distinguishes in its current research report between traditional and commercial coworking spaces. While traditional coworking spaces focus on the values of coworking and their community,[6] purely commercial coworking spaces focus on offering professional workplaces and meeting rooms.[7] For the sake of completeness, coworking spaces in hotels should also be mentioned here as so-called "Workation" models (see the article "Working where others vacation - 'Workation', a model with a future?").[8]

At their core, coworking spaces are a manifestation of the "Shared Economy". On the one hand, they offer a material benefit by sharing equipped office workstations with corresponding office infrastructure and office spaces at one location. On the other hand, they also offer an immaterial benefit by sharing information and ideas. [9]

The essential difference to other forms of mobile working, such as in a café, hotel or in a shared office, is the sharing of immaterial goods. Coworking spaces are places of sharing and encounter with employees of other entrepreneurs, freelancers, start-ups, self-employed etc.[10] They have a connected network (so-called community). They live values such as collaboration (support), community, sustainability, openness and accessibility.[11] In this respect, they represent a special feature among the Third Places (see the article "Third places - Third workplaces").

It is necessary to differentiate between various forms of coworking spaces. There are coworking spaces that openly design their accessibility to social or knowledge networks, or are selectively shaped for certain professional groups.[12] They can offer typical office equipment or cater to special requirements.[13]

---

[4] BMAS (2022, p. 11).

[5] Roscher (2021).

[6] BMAS (2022, p. 20).

[7] BMAS (2022, p. 22).

[8] BMAS (2022, p. 23).

[9] BMAS (2022, p. 16).

[10] Besgen (2022, pp. 383, 384); BMAS (2022, p. 18).

[11] DGUV (2022, pp.10–11); BMAS (2022, p. 16).

[12] DGUV (2022, p.11).

[13] For example, laboratories at the BioCampus Cologne, https://www.biocampuscologne.de/bcc/de/home Accessed: 28.11.2022.

2 Advantages of this Form of Work

The advantages of coworking spaces are obvious: Users of a workplace in a coworking space usually enjoy a professionally furnished workplace including a corresponding office infrastructure, stable internet connection, sanitary facilities, kitchen, usually including attractive beverage offers and social areas (lounge, outdoor area etc.).[14] Cleaning is usually included. Some coworking spaces also offer additional office services, such as secretarial tasks.[15]

Also for meetings and discussions, this "outsourcing model" provides, by offering flexibly bookable meeting and discussion rooms. In some places, there are also childcare offers[16] and networking events of an affiliated community.

2.1 Benefits for Employees

Coworking spaces are characterized by flexibility and accessibility. They can combine the advantages of home offices with those of the workplace by offering the employee a workplace close to home, which can be used flexibly, with the associated shorter commuting times, but also offers social interaction opportunities, potentially better workplace equipment, and office infrastructure.[17]

Commutes are not completely eliminated, but they can be reduced. The shorter commuting times can promote an improvement in work-life balance.[18] In addition, the time saved leads to higher job satisfaction, which can have a long-term positive effect on health.[19] Furthermore, a spatial separation of living and working place is possible.[20]

With a professional office infrastructure in place, an employee can be supported promptly in the event of technical disruptions, in addition to the daily provision of beverages, cleaning, etc.[21]

The community culture of a coworking space is another advantage. By bringing together target groups from various professional sectors, coworking spaces promote synergies, whether in the project area or for personal networking. The availability of social contacts thus represents an advantage over isolated work in the home office (see the article "Working from Home: Perspectives, Challenges, Solutions")[22]

---

[14] DGUV (2022, p.9).

[15] DGUV (2022, p.9).

[16] BMAS (2022, p. 16).

[17] BMAS (2022, p. 8).

[18] BMAS (2022, p. 13).

[19] BMAS (2022, pp. 32, 33).

[20] BMAS (2022, p. 14).

[21] BMAS (2022, p. 13).

[22] BMAS (2022, p. 14).

and also offers a creative environment, which can provide impulses for innovation through accompanying events.

Sharing office infrastructure and space represents a sustainable offer for employees and employers. Reducing commuting also makes a concrete contribution to the environment, like the home office.[23]

2.2 Benefits for Employers

Coworking spaces can represent an entrepreneurial advantage due to their flexibility and accessibility. Flexibility includes particularly short contract terms[24] as well as the partial 24/7 provision of workplaces with office infrastructure. Companies can react flexibly to short-term business changes as well as crises using coworking spaces. Long-term use offers the possibility of reducing company office spaces and decreasing fixed costs.[25] This is also followed by monetary benefits for employers, as a fixed monthly workplace in a coworking space averages around EUR 324.[26] The flexibility also extends, if available, to connected project and meeting rooms.

The incentives of coworking spaces for employees listed above can also be a significant competitive advantage for employers in the “War of Talents”. The possibility of relocating work to locations throughout Germany, possibly even Europe-wide or worldwide, expands the circle of people from whom staff can be recruited.[27] The associated promotion of the compatibility of family and career can also be a means of employee recruitment. [28]

Compliance with occupational safety regulations, including the Occupational Safety Act (ASiG), the Working Time Act (ArbZG), and the Occupational Safety Act (ArbSchG), must also occur in coworking spaces. Workplaces in coworking spaces fall under the Workplace Ordinance (ArbStättV).[29] Therefore, the responsibility for the safety and health of an employee remains with the employer.[30] However, by renting a workplace in a coworking space, the employer gains the significant advantage of a simpler review of required standards compared to the

[23] BMAS (2022, pp. 14, 15).

[24] Roscher (2021).

[25] BMAS (2022, p. 22).

[26] BMAS (2022, p. 16).

[27] BMAS (2022, p. 14).

[28] BMAS (2022, p. 8).

[29] DGUV (2022, p.19).

[30] DGUV (2022, p.19).

home office.[31] In addition, he could contractually regulate further compliance with occupational safety with the coworking space.[32]

Similarly, compared to the home office, the risk of productivity loss due to an unprofessional workplace can be specifically addressed.[33] Potential distractions from possible domestic work can be reduced. The office infrastructure provides direct help in case of technical disruptions and can thus reduce the risk of work stoppages.[34]

3 Challenges of this Form of Work

The active use of decentralized work is not only a cultural change for employers, but also for employees. Various criteria of cooperation must be considered and clarified or defined in advance between the employer and employee, including technical, personnel, organizational and cultural aspects.[35]

In terms of IT infrastructure and the external use of a workplace, the known risks in the area of data protection exist. These include not only the use of an external internet connection and possibly interface problems with the employer's own IT infrastructure, but especially the possible inspection of internal company documents by third parties. [36] Nevertheless, some coworking spaces offer lockable units per workstation or other precautions to minimize risks. The employer could counter this risk with a binding guideline with labor law, organizational and technical requirements for the employee.[37]

Regarding occupational health and safety at the workplace, it should be noted that an independent control of the legally standardized or additional quality standards has not yet taken place. Expressions of professional workplaces are very heterogeneous. In particular, compliance with standards regarding a sufficient square meter area per workstation, ergonomically and qualitatively functional furniture etc. have not yet been determined.[38] Comparison portals on the internet provide potential users with clues.[39] The German Coworking Federation offers a workshop

[31] BMAS (2022, p. 32).

[32] Grimm/Singraven, ArbRB 2019, pp. 178, 179.

[33] BMAS (2022, p. 15).

[34] BMAS (2022, p. 13).

[35] BMAS (2022, p. 11).

[36] *Grimm* in: Tschöpe, Arbeitsrecht Handbuch, 2021, Kapitel 6, Teil F, Rn. 389; Grimm/Singraven, ArbRB 2019, pp. 178, 179.

[37] *Grimm* in: Tschöpe, Arbeitsrecht Handbuch, 2021, Kapitel 6, Teil F, Rn. 390a.

[38] DGUV (2022, p. 18).

[39] Examples of various comparison portals: https://disq.de/2021/20211201-Co-Working-Spaces.html Accessed: 03.10.2022; https://www.ridestore.de/mag/coworking-spaces-europa/ Accessed: 03.10.2022.

with a certificate on coworking standards for providers.[40] In addition, certificates can also be issued for certain properties, such as for Corona protection measures.[41]

Compared to the home office, a higher noise level can be a disturbing factor in a coworking space.[42] To counteract this, some coworking spaces offer different usable areas (loud or quiet areas) to meet the needs of the users.

4 Solutions and Practical Tips

The challenge of a lack of uniform quality standards in coworking spaces is first to be put into perspective. The BMAS assumes that in particular standards of occupational health and safety are also observed in coworking spaces.[43] This consideration is based in particular on the consideration of the economic self-interest of coworking spaces.[44] However, since the possibility of control in coworking spaces is easier compared to the home office, the actual compliance with these standards can be better ensured.[45] In this context, it may be advisable to resort to coworking chains, as these as operators of several locations, possibly also worldwide, usually adhere to their own standards.[46]

Until a corresponding quality control has developed in the market, primarily the own control of standards is necessary. A definition of concrete standards for workplaces in coworking spaces and a control of the same is recommended in the future.[47]

5 Summary and Outlook

In the course of digital transformation and the digitization of the economy, mobile work has established itself as an attractive and modern solution in the labor market.

Coworking spaces, as providers of a professional environment for mobile work, represent an important alternative workplace and can be sustainably operated for employees and employers as a target group.[48]

40 https://www.coworking-germany.org/get-certified/ Accessed: 03.10.2022.

41 WeWork (2021).

42 BMAS (2022, p. 33).

43 BMAS (2022, p. 32).

44 BMAS (2022, p. 32).

45 BMAS (2022, p. 32).

46 BMAS (2022, p. 47).

47 BMAS (2022, p. 33).

48 BMAS (2022, p. 51).

By combining the advantages of home office and office workplaces, coworking spaces can gain importance in the future. By offering local work with professional office equipment, office infrastructure, and social exchange with a local or national community, they combine the benefits of home office with those of an office workplace and offer additional advantages for innovation development. At the same time, they can represent a significant competitive advantage for employers in the "War of Talents".

References

Bundesministerium für Arbeit und Soziales, BMAS (2022) Bedeutung von Coworking Spaces als Dritter Arbeitsort in Deutschland. Forschungsinstitut zur Zukunft der Arbeit GmbH (IZA), März 2022. https://www.bmas.de/SharedDocs/Downloads/DE/Publikationen/Forschungsberichte/fb-595-expertise-bedeutung-von-coworking-spaces.pdf;jsessionid=8E277A86296B096D18D0E295B8833566.delivery2-master?__blob=publicationFile&v=1 (abgerufen am 03.10.2022).

Besgen, Nicolai, Agiles und flexibles Arbeiten – ein Überblick über die Problemfelder, B+P, 2022, pp. 379–386.

Dell, Julian (18.06.2020) Zahl der Coworking Spaces hat sich in 2 Jahren vervierfacht. https://polis-magazin.com/2020/06/zahl-der-coworking-spaces-hat-sich-in-2-jahren-vervierfacht/ (abgerufen am 03.10.2022).

Deutsche Gesetzliche Unfallversicherung e.V., DGUV (2022) Sicherheit und Gesundheit in Coworking Spaces. https://publikationen.dguv.de/widgets/pdf/download/article/4427 (abgerufen am 03.10.2022).

Dohrmann, Vanessa Dorothea, New Work nach der Corona Pandemie, DB 2022, pp. 664–668.

Grimm in: Tschöpe, Arbeitsrecht Handbuch, 12. Aufl. 2021, Kapitel 6, F. Beschäftigtendatenschutz und Social Media, Rn. 389.

Grimm, Detlef/Singraven, Jonas, Desk-Sharing und Co-Working als neue Arbeitsplatz-Modelle, ArbRB, 2019, pp. 175–179.

Roscher, Susanne, Coworking Spaces – ein alternativer mobile Arbeitsort? DGUV-Forum, 06/2021, https://forum.dguv.de/ausgabe/6-2021/artikel/coworking-spaces-ein-alternativer-mobiler-arbeitsort (abgerufen am 03.10.2022).

WeWork (14.01.2021) WeWork's COVID-19 Health and Safety Efforts receive global Certificate of Conformity. https://www.wework.com/newsroom/weworks-covid-19-health-and-safety-efforts-receive-global-certificate-of-conformity (abgerufen am 03.10.2022).

Working Where Others Vacation—“Workation” a Model with a Future?

Friedrun Domke

“If you love what you do, you’ll never work a day in your life.”

Confucius

1 Introduction

The term “Workation” is not a fixed legal term, but a so-called portmanteau. It is composed of the two English words “Work” and “Vacation”. The basic idea is: vacation away from the workplace, but not from work itself.

This form of workplace design must be distinguished in particular from telework, mobile work, and home office.

According to section 2 para. 7 of the Workplace Ordinance (ArbStättV), teleworkplaces are screen workplaces in the private sector set up by the employer.

Mobile work is characterized precisely by the fact that it is not agreed between employer and employee in terms of spatial requirements or regular working time contingents. The ArbStättV does not apply to it.

Working from home is a form of mobile work that allows temporary work in the private sector, usually at the registered address, depending on the agreement with the employer.

A workation can be compared to the home office. The employees are just at the beach or in the mountains, instead of in their own study. It is thus a subcase of mobile work, which is usually planned for a limited time around the annual vacation.

The trend among employees in recent months has been moving away from the rigid back office and revealing a desire for more flexibility not only in terms of

F. Domke (✉)
Pusch Wahlig Workplace Law, Köln, Germany
e-mail: Domke@pwwl.de

I. Knappertsbusch and G. Wisskirchen (eds.), *The Future of Work*,
https://doi.org/10.1007/978-3-658-45150-9_10

working hours (keywords: 4-day week, lifetime working time accounts, sabbaticals etc.), but especially also in terms of the workplace. A recent survey by EY[1] shows the trend. 50% of younger employees would consider quitting if they are not allowed a flexible workplace. 68% would rather take a workation than stay in the home office.

Extending the stay at the personal desired location by cleverly combining the two aspects of life, work and vacation; this dream of many employees is becoming increasingly tangible. The Covid pandemic was certainly a major driver for this.

However, even according to recent case law, there is no right to mobile work or workation[2] without a corresponding provision in the employment contract.[3] Despite the lack of legal entitlement, it is necessary and possible to grant a contractual claim or reservation for the use of workation. The co-determination of the works council must be observed.

2 Advantages of this Form of Work

2.1 General Advantages

Offering workation can certainly serve as a drive for recruiting. In the current labor markets, companies must pay more attention to how they can convince the available workforce. With regard to the mentality of Generation Z and probably the following generations, it will be essential that companies are open to modern designs of working conditions.

It is obvious that offering a workation can increase the satisfaction of employees and the attractiveness of the company. At the same time, as an employer, you show trust in the employees by giving them more freedom. This ultimately has a positive effect on the entire working atmosphere. In addition, it can lead to savings in infrastructure costs in the office, especially when combining workation with other workplace models.

2.2 Keeping up with the Times

Companies should also keep up with the times in this development. Looking at the processes of the last few months, the trend seems unstoppable. The young generation of well-qualified employees is no longer attracted by company cars and salary

---

[1] https://www.ey.com/de_de/news/2021/05/ey-zukunft-der-arbeitswelt-2021, Accessed: September 13, 2022.

[2] LArbG Cologne, BeckRS 2022, 10911 or LArbG Cologne, judgment 12.01.2022–3 Sa 540/21; LArbG Munich, COVuR 2021, 620 or LArbG Munich, judgment 26.08.2021–3 SaGa 13/21.

[3] LArbG Berlin-Brandenburg, ArbRAktuell 2019, 47 or LArbG Berlin-Brandenburg, judgment 14.11.2018–17 Sa 562/18; ErfK/*Preis*, 611a BGB Rn.85b.

increases. Workation is part of the desire for the so-called "Work-Life-Balance". Employees gain flexibility in their private lives when a workation is introduced.

A study by the TU Chemnitz[4] found that about 60% of respondents who work from home believe that the boundary between work and private life is missing in the home office. More than one in four find this stressful.

3 Challenges of this Form of Work

3.1 General Hurdles

The employer is deprived of a control option for this time. He must give the employees a vote of confidence and, in addition, set up or convert company-wide tools that enable digital work. But not only the hardware and software need to be adjusted accordingly. The mindset in the company also needs to be adjusted. Overall, the employer should create transparency and develop clear procedural instructions that are implemented in quality management and communicated unambiguously to the employees. An outcome-oriented approach can be one way to do this.

3.2 Applicable Legal System

When working abroad, it must first be checked which legal system applies during this time. Temporary mobile work abroad, such as during a workation, does not fundamentally change the application of German law. According to Art. 8 para. 1 s. 1 Rome I Regulation, the applicable law is determined by the one chosen by the parties, Art. 3 Rome I Regulation. The usual place of work (Art. 9 para. 2 Rome I Regulation) does not change due to the workation. This does not change if the work is only temporarily carried out in another state (Art. 8 para. 2 Rome I Regulation). The term "temporary" is understood to mean that it is expected that the employee will resume his work in the original contract state.[5] However, the local law of the place from which the workation is carried out applies as an exception. For Germany, this only applies within narrow limits, namely whenever a so-called intervention norm (Art. 9 Rome I Regulation) makes the fulfillment of the employment contract abroad ineffective (Art. 9 para. 3 Rome I Regulation for the place of performance). This applies in particular in the areas of working time rules, statutory holidays and such norms that serve to protect the employee (maternity protection, prohibitions, health).[6]

---

[4] https://www.tu-chemnitz.de/tu/pressestelle/aktuell/10445, Accessed: September 13, 2022.

[5] MüKo BGB/*Martiny*, Art. 8 Rom I-VO Rn. 65; BeckOK ArbR/*Schönbohm*, VO (EG) 593/2008 Art. 8 Rn. 23.

[6] EuArbRK/*Krebber*, VO (EG) 593/2008 Art. 9 Rn.16.

3.3 Reporting and Registration Obligations, Aspects of Posting

Two other aspects are particularly relevant in this context: firstly, a possible reporting and registration obligation abroad, and secondly, the question of the applicability of the posting directives. Regardless of whether it is assumed that the Enforcement Directive 14/67/EU, which is relevant for the reporting and registration obligation, applies, it must be checked for each country what obligations exist on site. These can vary under certain circumstances.[7]

Whether and how the concept of posting applies to the constellation of workation is not yet clearly clarified. However, the answer to this question can have decisive effects on the area of working conditions (minimum wage, overtime, etc.) as well as social security.

The term posting, however, already includes an element of instruction from its literal meaning,[8] which is not compatible with the basic idea that the workation is desired and demanded by the employee. The employee is also not sent away on instruction, but actively decides to temporarily relocate his place of work. The European Commission also takes this approach. In addition, in the case of workation, the employee does not integrate into the foreign labor market, but only uses the conditions to temporarily relocate his place of work due to external circumstances. He therefore does not participate in the competition that is to be regulated by the directives.[9]

3.4 Social Security

With regard to social security, the question of posting becomes relevant again. If the period of the workation in a calendar year comprises less than 5% of the regular working time or less than 5% of the total remuneration, the question of the applicable social security law can be neglected. If the de minimis limit is exceeded, however, a closer look is needed. In principle, the obligation to pay social security contributions is based on the so-called principle of the place of activity (Regulation (EC) No. 883/2004). According to this, a person who carries out an activity in one state is generally subject to the legal provisions of this

[7] See registration deadline Belgium https://www.brussels.be/registration-foreigner, Accessed: September 13, 2022, with Spain https://administracion.gob.es/pag_Home/en/Tu-espacio-europeo/derechos-obligaciones/ciudadanos/residencia/obtencion-residencia/inscribirte-residente.html#-f3b5b9e009bb, Accessed: June 13, 2022.

[8] EN—Practical Guide December 2013 (17–02–2014) (1).pdf, page 7/53.

[9] https://ec.europa.eu/social/main.jsp?catId=471&langId=de#:~:text=Was%20versteht%20man%20unter%20Entsendung,Zeitraums%20eine%20Dienstleistung%20zu%20erbringen, Accessed: September 8, 2022.

state. This would mean that in the case of workation, several social security systems would apply to the employment relationship. This result can be prevented firstly via a hardly practical exception agreement (Art. 16 Regulation [EC] No. 883/2004) and secondly if a posting within the meaning of Regulation (EC) No. 883/2004 were assumed. In this case, according to Art. 12 of the Regulation, German social security law remains applicable for 24 months.

3.5 Practical Tip

Even if the Posting of Workers Directive is presumably not applicable to workation, due to the unclear legal situation and the ongoing discussion in academia and practice, a solution-oriented approach is recommended. The German Contact Point for Health Insurance Abroad (DVKA) follows the approach that German social security law remains applicable during the temporary activity of employees abroad, if the employer accepts and remunerates the work performance in knowledge of the foreign activity and then applies for an EU posting (A1 certificate). It is advised to apply for a certificate in time, even if the 5% limit is not reached.

3.6 Tax Law

Tax law also plays a role in the implementation of a workation in certain circumstances. With regard to the permanent establishment analysis, the question arises whether the employee establishes a permanent establishment for the employer abroad. This also involves a complex examination that requires careful scrutiny. However, the foreign activity should be limited in time and ideally not always carried out at the same location. Coordination with local tax law experts seems helpful.

3.7 Compliance with Other Legal Regulations

The digitization of work through the workation model, as well as remote work, also raises the question of data protection and IT security for the employer. Employers should particularly train employees in these areas and take the necessary security measures.

Employees must ensure their availability during their absence and bear the costs for this, such as internet and mobile phone connection. As in the home office, the challenge may also be to comply with working hours and especially break times to the extent required by law (or contractually agreed). However, if the home office is to be relocated to a location outside the EU, the employee needs a visa and a corresponding permit to work and stay. This also applies to non-EU citizens within the EU.

3.8 Co-Determination

The works council will certainly want to have a strong influence on the design of the workation and other flexible workplace models. The focus here is on the protection of employees, especially the compliance with legally permitted working hours. If there is no specific regulation for time recording or it is not clear how the employer ensures occupational safety in other respects, this could prompt the works council to make the workation option more difficult.

4 Solutions and Practical Tips

4.1 General Guidelines

Employers should first create clear, internal guidelines around the topic of workation. These can initially be temporary or introduced as a so-called pilot project, taking into account the involvement of the works council. Ideally, a clear procedure for applying for workation as well as the personal and factual scope of application should be covered. In addition, the conditions that the company sets for the workation period should be specifically outlined.

4.2 Individual Agreements

In the second step, a written supplementary agreement with the employee is recommended. In addition to general information, it should contain an obligation for the employees to inform themselves in advance about local registration requirements, documents to be carried, and insurance.

From a strategic and practical point of view, it is advisable to involve the works council in the process as early as possible. Here, attention should be paid to a uniform, clear, and non-discriminatory approach. It is also recommended to create short guidelines for the different models (telework, home office, mobile work, workation) that provide an overview for the employees. Open communication with employees about the models, the prerequisites, differences, and similarities in advance prevents risks and uncertainties afterwards.

4.3 Building Expertise

The implementation of a workation model requires expertise in the areas of IT, data protection, as well as labor, social security, and tax law. It is important to start the journey early, initially with training for managers, but also for all other employees, in order to be able to develop attractive and legally secure models in the company. This is primarily to prevent misuse by employees from the outset.

For employers who have not established a good basis for workation through transparent regulations, it poses a risk when employees enforce their supposed right themselves and work in unauthorized places. For example, social security contributions may be levied at the place of work or fines may be imposed if the employee does not carry the appropriate certificate.

4.4 Observance of Co-Determination Rights

The works council does not have the right to initiate the introduction of workation. It only has co-determination rights regarding the design of the conditions according to the Works Constitution Act (section 87 para. 1 no. 14),[10] so regarding the "how". Even an occasion-related or even one-time workation for the employees of the company is generally covered by the co-determination fact of mobile work. In addition, the other facts of co-determination continue to apply. For the case of "workation", section 87 para. 1 no. 2, no. 6, no. 10 and no. 7 Works Constitution Act are particularly worth mentioning. Both the works council and employees should be open to workation. In the end, it offers greater autonomy and satisfaction for employees. As always, the tariff reservation according to section 77 para. 3 S. 1, 87 para. 1 Works Constitution Act must be observed if the place of work and/or deployment outside the company premises is regulated by collective agreement or is usually regulated.

5 Summary and Outlook

The topic of workation will have a lasting impact on the world of work. Especially for Generation Z and subsequent generations who are soon to enter the job market, a strict office obligation is a deal breaker. The keyword is flexible workplace design.

The spread and importance of this form of work will not only continue to evolve in the coming years. It will undoubtedly quickly gain more importance and forms an important development trend in the area of "New Work". This has also arrived in politics. The last coalition agreement has already covered flexible work.[11] It now remains to be seen whether the legislator will take a—urgently needed—step on the legislative level and address the question to be clarified, how in the future, ideally already in the next holiday season, workation can be made possible for employers and employees in a legally secure and easy-to-handle manner.

Everyone might then have come a little closer to the vision of Confucius.

---

[10] Richardi Works Constitution Act/*Maschmann*, § 87 Works Constitution Act Rn.989 f.; ErfK/*Kania*, § 87 Works Constitution Act Rn. 137.

[11] Coalition Agreement 2021 p. 54, https://www.spd.de/fileadmin/Dokumente/Koalitionsvertrag/Koalitionsvertrag_2021-2025.pdf, Accessed: September 7, 2022.

References

Richardi, Reinhard, Betriebsverfassungsgesetz Kommentar, 17. Auflage, München 2022 [zit.: Richardi BetrVG/Bearbeiter, Rn.].

Erfurter Kommentar zum Arbeitsrecht, 22. Auflage, München 2022 [zit.: ErfK/Bearbeiter, Rn.].

Münchener Kommentar zum Bürgerlichen Gesetzbuch, Band 12: IPR, 8. Auflage, München 2020 [zit.: MüKo BGB/Bearbeiter, Art. Rn.].

Beck'scher Online Kommentar Arbeitsrecht, Hrsg. Rolfs/Giesen/Meßling/Udsching, 65. Edition [zit.: BeckOK ArbR/Bearbeiter, Art. Rn.].

Beck'scher Online Kommentar GewO, Hrsg. Pielow, 57. Edition [zit.: BeckOK GewO/ Bearbeiter, Art. Rn.].

Kommentar zum europäischen Arbeitsrecht, Hrsg. Franzen/Gallner/Oetker, 4. Auflage, München 2022[zit.: EuArbRK/Bearbeiter, Art. Rn.].

Internet Sources

https://www.spd.de/fileadmin/Dokumente/Koalitionsvertrag/Koalitionsvertrag_2021-2025.pdf, Accessed: 07. September 2022.

https://www.brussels.be/registration-foreigner, Accessed: 13. September 2022.

https://administracion.gob.es/pag_Home/en/Tu-espacio-europeo/derechos-obligaciones/ciudadanos/residencia/obtencion-residencia/inscribirte-residente.html#-f3b5b9e009bb, Accessed: 13.06.2022.

https://ec.europa.eu/social/main.jsp?catId=471&langId=de#:~:text=Was%20versteht%20man%20unter%20Entsendung,Zeitraums%20eine%20Dienstleistung%20zu%20erbringen, Accessed: 08. September 2022.

https://www.tu-chemnitz.de/tu/pressestelle/aktuell/10445, Accessed: 13. September 2022.

https://www.ey.com/de_de/news/2021/05/ey-zukunft-der-arbeitswelt-2021, Accessed: 13. September 2022.

Work from Anywhere—The Free Choice of Workplace

Inka Knappertsbusch and Hannah Stute

1 Introduction

"Work from Anywhere" means working from any location. Work from Anywhere is also known as "location-independent working". As the wording suggests, this model offers employees the greatest possible choice of work locations, as it includes the employer's business premises, private offices at employees' places of residence (see the article "Working from home: Perspectives, Challenges, Solutions"), coworking spaces (see the article "Coworking Space as a third workplace"), third places (see the article "Third places—Third workplaces"), working while traveling (during flights or on train journeys), and working abroad. Essentially, the Work from Anywhere model allows employees to decide each day where they want to work.

Since the Work from Anywhere model can include any location at home or abroad, it has to take not just labor law into account if it is implemented, but tax, social security and data protection aspects as well.

I. Knappertsbusch (✉) · H. Stute
CMS Deutschland, Köln, Germany
e-mail: inka.knappertsbusch@cms-hs.com

I. Knappertsbusch and G. Wisskirchen (eds.), *The Future of Work*,
https://doi.org/10.1007/978-3-658-45150-9_11

2 Advantages of this Form of Work

2.1 Increased Productivity

A consumer survey conducted by McKinsey in May 2020 found that 41% of respondents reported being more productive when working remotely than in the office.[1] In addition, a company survey as part of a study by the Capgemini Research Institute revealed that 63% of the companies surveyed recorded productivity gains as a result of remote work in the third quarter of 2020.[2]

2.2 Cost Savings

Even if, as is often the case, the employer wants to continue to provide its employees with a workstation on its premises after implementing Work from Anywhere, there is little doubt that this will be used less and the employer can therefore downsize its premises (e.g. through desk sharing). In turn, Work from Anywhere enables employees to work in places where they do not need to travel (long distances) and therefore to save on travel costs.

2.3 Employer Attractiveness and Expansion of the Applicant Pool

Employees want more flexibility and freedom of choice in the future world of work. According to a survey conducted by FlexJobs in 2020, 65% of respondents wanted to work "fully remotely" and 31% wanted a hybrid model in the future.[3] Employers who meet these wishes by offering Work from Anywhere will become more attractive on the job market. This is also likely to lead to an increase in the selection of applicants.

With the offer of Work from Anywhere, the geographical location of the company is no longer a decisive factor for applicants. Once working on company premises becomes voluntary, the area eligible applicants can be pulled from expands significantly, almost infinitely. Employees can live and work far away from the employer's immediate location (often in metropolitan areas) and save on living costs.

Residence and work permits are no longer necessary, for example, if international employees can work for an employer in Germany from their home country,

---

[1] https://www.mckinsey.com/featured-insights/future-of-work/whats-next-for-remote-work-an-analysis-of-2000-tasks-800-jobs-and-nine-countries

[2] https://www.capgemini.com/wp-content/uploads/2022/04/The-Future-of-Work_Final.pdf

[3] https://www.flexjobs.com/blog/post/survey-productivity-balance-improve-during-pandemic-remote-work/

as German residence law does not apply in these cases.[4] This way, provided that the relevant legal restrictions are observed, in particular that the social security contributions of the respective country are paid, a company can recruit skilled workers from abroad without having to overcome the hurdles of residence and immigration law. This is relevant for HR in times of a shortage of skilled workers in order to keep expanding the pool of applicants in the future, especially internationally.

2.4 Improved Work-Life Balance

By allowing employees to choose their own place of work, Work from Anywhere makes it possible for them to improve their work-life balance. Specifically, this may involve cases where somebody's partner's job requires frequent changes of location (e.g. in the context of military service, hotel management, etc.) and Work From Anywhere prevents partners from being physically separated from one another or their family. In general, living near extended family is made easier without having to compromise on your choice of job. Employees who have Work from Anywhere as an option can pursue activities that are only possible in certain regions and would otherwise be incompatible with the employer's location. Finally, Work From Anywhere allows employees to live in areas with better healthcare or a more pleasant climate.

3 Challenges of this Form of Work

Challenges in establishing Work from Anywhere arise in particular with models involving work from abroad. Framework conditions under labor, tax and social security law must be strictly adhered to in order to contain possible cost and liability risks.

3.1 Applicable Employment Law

If the employment relationship is subject to German labor law according to the content of the employment contract, this is not affected by temporary (remote) work abroad. This is because individual employment contracts are generally subject to the law chosen by the parties in accordance with Art. 8 para. 1 sentence 1 Rome I Regulation. Regardless of the choice of law, mandatory provisions of employee protection law at the usual place of work must be applied in accordance with Art. 8 para. 1 sentence 2 Rome I Regulation. Mandatory norms of the foreign country, which, if violated, result in the illegality of a contract, must also be taken

[4] See Bergmann/Dienelt/Dienelt AufenthG § 1 Rn. 13.

into account. These primarily include prohibitions on work, maximum working hours and minimum rest periods, health and safety law, maternity protection law, and public holiday law. The country in which the work is usually performed does not change if the employee temporarily performs their work in another country. "Temporary" within the meaning of recital 36 of the Rome I Regulation presupposes that the employee is expected to resume their work in their home country after the assignment abroad. The term "temporary" is not defined in terms of length of time in Art. 8 para. 2 sentence 2 Rome I Regulation. However, in a case where an employee worked abroad for two years without interruption for a posting, Hamburg Regional Labor Court ruled that this did not contradict the classification as "temporary".[5] For employees who only work abroad intermittently, there are likely to be far higher hurdles to overcome to bring about a change of statute.

3.2 Social Security Law

Social security law for work in Germany and in other EU countries is governed by Regulation (EC) No 883/2004. Under this regulation, the legal provisions of the Member State in which the employee carries out their work generally apply (so-called principle of the place of work). If the work is carried out in Germany and from another European country at the same time, the situation described as "pursuit activities in two or more Member States" exists (Art. 13 Regulation (EC) No 883/2004). According to the German Liaison Office for Health Insurance—International (*DVKA*), this is assumed if it is expected that work will be carried out in different Member States on at least one day per month or at least five days per quarter within the next 12 calendar months.[6] As a result, the applicable social security law is determined according to where the significant part of the work is carried out. If employees have their country of residence in the country where they carry out a significant part of their work (generally a share of 25% or more,[7] measured in terms of working hours and remuneration), the statutory provisions of that country apply.

In line with the pragmatic view of the *DVKA*, a posting (Art. 12 Regulation (EC) No 883/2004) can also be accepted as an arrangement for working abroad within the framework of Work from Anywhere. Contrary to the wording—which requires an employer's instruction—German social security law remains applicable if the employer is aware of the work abroad, agrees to it, and accepts and remunerates the work performed. However, social security law is not uniformly regulated for work in non-European countries and the posting requirements do not help either, meaning that there is a risk that the employee may lack insurance coverage or pay double for coverage.

---

[5] LAG Hamburg, judgment of 21.12.2021 – 4 Sa 10/21, BeckRS 2021, 44046, para. 72.

[6] https://www.dvka.de/de/arbeitgeber_arbeitnehmer/faq_1/faq_1.html

[7] BeckOK SozialR/*Utz* VO (EC) 883/2004 Art. 13 para. 5.

3.3 Tax Law and Permanent Establishment Risk

Employees are generally liable to pay tax in their country of residence. If an employee regularly works in a country other than their country of residence, so-called double taxation agreements (DTAs) may be considered for assessing tax liability. Under these agreements, an employee can generally work in another country (besides their country of residence) for up to six months without the tax assessment changing. The tax consequences of Work from Anywhere in countries without DTAs are far less predictable and can only be determined on an individual basis. In addition, there is a risk in individual cases that the employee will create a permanent establishment abroad, especially if they represent the company externally.

3.4 Further Challenges

Outside the countries in Europe where freedom of movement applies, it may be necessary to obtain a residence and work permit. Failure to obtain such a permit may constitute illegal employment, depending on the regulations of the respective country, with consequences under administrative or criminal law. What can also lead to difficulties in implementing Work from Anywhere for the employer is compliance with labor and data protection law. On the one hand, protective orders under public law (e.g. the German Occupational Safety and Health Act (*ArbSchG*)) must be complied with to avoid fines. On the other hand, internal company compliance requirements must be continued and company data must be protected.

In addition, important work components such as onboarding, coaching and mentoring, joint problem-solving, performance evaluation, knowledge sharing and socializing are made more difficult within the framework of Work from Anywhere. This is because, in principle, the employee can also choose not to work in the employer's offices at all under this model, with the result that personal contact is either completely absent or very limited.

4 Solutions and Practical Tips

Firstly, employers should analyze whether Work from Anywhere is suitable for the entire company or only for individual business units or certain employees. The opportunities and risks should be carefully weighed up and concepts for implementing a Work from Anywhere model should be developed on this basis. Once these concepts have proven themselves in theory in terms of feasibility and legal consequences, the Work from Anywhere model can be set out in detail and tested in collaboration with individual employees.

In any case, it is recommended to formulate internal company and corporate framework conditions for the introduction of Work From Anywhere in order to overcome the aforementioned challenges and prevent possible risks. Since the works council has a right of co-determination with regard to the form of remote work that is performed by means of information and communication technology (section 87 para. 1 no. 14 German Works Constitution Act (*BetrVG*)), works agreements must be concluded for the implementation of Work from Anywhere in companies with works councils. In a written supplementary agreement to the employment contract, details on the timing, scope and form of Work from Anywhere are then regulated. For all other companies, the corresponding provisions of the works agreement should generally be stipulated in individual contracts with the employees. The following conditions are appropriate for the content of the Work from Anywhere contracts:

By definition, the time, place and subject constraints of the Work from Anywhere model are determined and the scope of application is regulated. For example, work abroad can be limited to EU, EEA and DTA countries as well as to countries with which a social security agreement (*SVA*) exists in order to simplify social security and tax bracket classification. The social security agreements are listed and can be viewed on the website of the German Federal Ministry of Labor and Social Affairs.[8]

A choice of law clause, according to which German labor law is applicable (Art. 8 para. 1 in conjunction with Art. 3 Rome I Regulation), is also practical in order to prevent foreign labor law, with whose regulations the employer will usually not be familiar, from being applicable.

Cross-border Work from Anywhere should only be allowed for a maximum of half the year abroad and no more than six weeks at a time in one place. To avoid risking a change in social security law, it should also be stipulated that at least 25% of the work must carried out in the employee's country of residence.

To reduce the risk of creating a permanent establishment, the employee should not represent the company externally. Representatives should therefore not be granted power of attorney for foreign activities. In addition, the employee should only work with their own hardware resources or obtain full ownership of the employer's work equipment. In this way, the employer no longer has any power of disposal over the "facility" within the meaning of section 12 German Tax Code (*AO*).

To be doubly certain, the work can be classified as a "posting" in accordance with Art. 12 Regulation (EC) 883/2004. For this, it should be noted that before each implementation of cross-border Work from Anywhere, the employer must contact the German Liaison Agency for Health Insurance—International (*DVKA*), coordinate the procedure with it, and apply for an A1 certificate (e.g. from the statutory health insurance provider).[9] In this case, the period for work abroad must be determined in advance. As a rule, a lead time of one week is sufficient for the application process. In addition, the employee must be made aware of their notification requirement in accordance with section 18 German Act on Mandatory Working Conditions for Workers Posted Across Borders and for Workers Regularly Employed in Germany (*AEntG*).

[8] https://www.bmas.de/SharedDocs/Downloads/DE/zweiseitige-abkommen.pdf;jsessionid=0B221C08575FE420EC6B15C16F7687DE?__blob=publicationFile&v=9

[9] https://www.dvka.de/de/arbeitgeber_arbeitnehmer/faq_1/faq_1.html

Since accident and health insurance abroad generally only cover accidents at work and emergencies, it is advisable for the employee to take out foreign health insurance for all other health risks in their own interest.

In addition, the employee should be required to prove that they have a residence and work permit for the respective country, or that they do not need one. This reduces the effort and minimizes corresponding risks for the employer.

It is advisable to stipulate that the employee must inform the employer of the overriding mandatory provisions and the existence and content of any DTAs for the respective country. However, the employer must first inform the employee of which provisions can generally be overriding provisions (see sec. 3.1.). Even if this procedure cannot rule out the possibility that the employee will overlook essential provisions, appropriate preparation by the employee, on which the employer can then build a further examination, should represent a considerable relief for the employer.

It must be ensured that work outside the office can also comply with occupational health and safety and the company's data protection standards. Occupational health and safety provisions must be implemented through regular information seminars, as it is generally not possible to carry out a risk assessment of the workplace. Furthermore, the employee should be required to work with specified software and VPN access, in order to make access by third parties largely possible, and to inform the employer in good time if they suspect the computer is suffering from a virus or software malfunction.

Like for a posting, there should be a recall clause granting the employer the right to recall the employee with reasonable notice for operational reasons and to terminate Work from Anywhere prematurely.[10]

In order to prevent the employee from losing all personal contact, their presence can be required for team events and project days or weeks, though limited to a certain total duration.

If the employee intends to Work from Anywhere in a country without a contract, authorization should only be given on the condition that the employee has settled any double insurance obligations with the statutory health insurance provider and consulted foreign officials to ensure that they will not be subject to double taxation.

5 Summary and Outlook

A study of 20 countries by Indeed and OECD shows that the proportion of job advertisements mentioning mobile work has almost tripled since the time before the pandemic—from an average of only 2.5% in January 2020 to almost 7.5% in September 2021.[11] Companies that want to maintain or increase their attractiveness on the job market should be aware that there is an increasing desire for

---

[10] See MSG Contract Design ArbR/Göpfert 180 Foreign Assignment Rn. 21 f.

[11] https://www.hiringlab.org/2021/12/16/will-remote-work-persist-after-the-pandemic/

flexible work models like Work From Anywhere. The demands for work that suits people's lifestyles are growing louder. If a business accommodates employees in this respect with Work from Anywhere and respects or even encourages their individual lifestyle, it expands the pool of applicants available to them immensely and establishes itself as a modern, forward-looking employer.

References

Bergmann, Jan/Dienelt, Klaus (Hrsg.), Ausländerrecht, 14. Auflage, München 2022.

Bmas.de „Zweiseitige Sozialversicherungsabkommen" (https://www.bmas.de/SharedDocs/Downloads/DE/zweiseitige-abkommen.pdf;jsessionid=0B221C08575FE420EC6B15C16F7687DE?__blob=publicationFile&v=9) (abgerufen am 13.12.2022).

Capgemini Research Institute (2022) „The Future Of Work – From remote to hybrid" (https://www.capgemini.com/wp-content/uploads/2022/04/The-Future-of-Work_Final.pdf) (abgerufen am 13.12.2022).

DVKA.de „FAQ" https://www.dvka.de/de/arbeitgeber_arbeitnehmer/faq_1/faq_1.html (abgerufen am 06.12.2022).

FlexJobs.com (2020) „FlexJobs Survey: Productivity, Work-Life Balance Improves During Pandemic" (https://www.flexjobs.com/blog/post/survey-productivity-balance-improve-during-pandemic-remote-work/) (abgerufen am 13.12.2022).

Hiring Lab Economic Research by Indeed "Will Remote Work Persist after the Pandemic?" (https://www.hiringlab.org/2021/12/16/will-remote-work-persist-after-the-pandemic/) (abgerufen am 13.12.2022).

Maschmann, Frank/Sieg, Rainer/Göpfert, Burkard (Hrsg.) Vertragsgestaltung im Arbeitsrecht, 3. Auflage, München 2020.

McKinsey Global Institute (2020) „What´s next for remote work: An analysis of 2,000 tasks, 800 jobs, and nine countries" (https://www.mckinsey.com/featured-insights/future-of-work/whats-next-for-remote-work-an-analysis-of-2000-tasks-800-jobs-and-nine-countries) (abgerufen am 13.12.2022).

Rolfs, Christian/Giesen, Richard/Meßling, Miriam/Udsching, Peter, BeckOK Sozialrecht, 66. Edition, München 2022.

Working Time

Fields of Action for Current and Future Working Time Design

Ufuk Altun and Veit Hartmann

1 Introduction

Both companies and employees have an increasing need for flexible and demand-oriented working hours. The main reasons for flexible and demand-oriented working time arrangements include:

- Capacity adjustments to economic and seasonal workload fluctuations
- Consideration of employee interests in certain life situations, e.g., child rearing, care of relatives, and further education
- Increasing employer attractiveness to attract new staff and retain existing staff
- Securing jobs by accumulating time credits in "boom phases" for "bad times"

These flexibility requirements increasingly lead to traditional working time models with rigid working hours reaching their limits. The normal working day with an eight-hour day and a five-day week is losing its significance. A Bitkom study from 2019 shows that rigid weekly working hours are also not desired by employees. According to the study, German professionals strive for more self-realization in their job. 96% of respondents wish to be able to freely arrange their working hours and 82% prefer a better balance between work and private life. In addition, 58% of respondents want to switch from a daily to a weekly maximum working time (bitkom 2019).

U. Altun (✉) · V. Hartmann
ifaa—Institut für angewandte Arbeitswissenschaft e. V., Düsseldorf, Germany
e-mail: u.altun@ifaa-mail.de

V. Hartmann
e-mail: v.hartmann@ifaa-mail.de

I. Knappertsbusch and G. Wisskirchen (eds.), *The Future of Work*,
https://doi.org/10.1007/978-3-658-45150-9_12

However, these needs and expectations pose a number of challenges and areas of action for flexible and demand-oriented working time design and the distribution of working time volume, which will be discussed in the following sections.

2 Advantages of Flexible and Demand-Oriented Working Time Models

Flexible and demand-oriented working time design brings benefits for both companies and employees. Instead of a largely rigid working time model, various working time models can be used that are adapted to operational and individual circumstances. This allows companies to "breathe" in order to respond to fluctuating economic and seasonal order situations. Employees can adapt their working hours to individual wishes and concerns. Experience shows that a single working time model for the entire working biography with different life phases and changing tasks, such as raising children, caring for parents, and professional development, is no longer sufficient. A survey by AOK, for example, shows that 40% of the mothers and fathers surveyed believe that they lack time (AOK Federal Association 2018). The consequences of this time shortage can be the neglect of social relationships within the family and circle of friends.

Overall, flexible and demand-oriented working time design increases the motivation and performance of employees, from which companies also benefit. The difficulty or complexity, however, lies in answering the question of how to reconcile the different interests mentioned above. Compromise and willingness to compromise are required from all parties involved in order to best harmonize the competitiveness of companies and the compatibility of work and private life, especially with regard to the family.

3 Challenges of Flexible and Demand-Oriented Working Time Models

The challenge at the operational level is to align the respective operational requirements with the wishes and needs of the employees and to optimally coordinate them. The flexibilization of working hours, which is desired by both companies and employees, can be seen differently in the company and in the daily "doing" of employees and companies.

While employees expect advantages from flexible working time arrangements in terms of compatibility of work and private life, quality of life, health, social activities, companies associate advantages in terms of quick response to customer requirements, improved response to rapidly changing markets and optimized personnel and resource deployment, as well as higher recruitment successes through improved employer attractiveness.

Consequently, flexible and demand-oriented working time design should allow for operational solutions. To achieve this, two perspectives should be equally considered:

- On the one hand, operational flexibility for always reliable and economical fulfillment of customer needs and
- on the other hand, the individual flexibility of employees in terms of a life situation-specific working time, such as when caring for children, nursing sick relatives or further education.

3.1 Operational Flexibility

Operational flexibility continues to be an important key factor for Germany as a business location. Globalization, demographic change, and digitalization pose new challenges to companies. Operational flexibility is characterized by short reaction times to fluctuating seasonal and economic order situations and extended operating and service times and will gain even more importance in the future. Companies and their employees are jointly called upon to fulfill the wishes of customers promptly and qualitatively. The primary goal of a flexible working time design in the company is therefore to reliably cover the capacity requirements needed. Because in the course of globalization, customer wishes are becoming increasingly unpredictable.

The consequences of the Corona pandemic and the current discussions about supply chains and energy supply have made it clear that companies are subject to constant pressure to change, which requires that production systems and service concepts must be quickly adapted to the changed conditions without high financial expenditure.

In this respect, operational flexibility is to be organized in a targeted, strategic, and systematic way. "Blanket" solutions cannot be successful. Here, for example, working time corridors for an even or uneven distribution of working time depending on employee groups and life phases can be a solution. As experience shows, it is not sensible in every area to work the same length every week. Also, rigid working hours are not desirable for every employee. Through flexible and demand-oriented working time design, it is possible to work longer on individual days, weeks, or months and to compensate by working shorter in another period.

3.2 Individual Flexibility

By expanding the scope for design, greater account can also be taken of the different concerns of employees. They can reduce, increase, and flexibly design their working hours as needed and according to their life phase.

Employees' expectations of working time design have become more complex. They want to organize and design their working hours, their tasks, and their workplace increasingly independently. The predictability of working hours is also one of the most important factors of successful working time design. This allows employees to better manage the different stress phases of working life up to reaching retirement age, achieve a better balance between work and private life, and ensure personal well-being.

4 Solutions and Practical Tips

From the described aspects of flexibility, different working time models with versatile flexibilization options can be derived. To achieve flexibility desired by both employees and companies, flexible control instruments are required in addition to formal and organizational regulations.

4.1 Working Time Accounts

A crucial tool for implementing flexible working time structures in companies are working time accounts in different variants (see figure below). On the one hand, working time accounts secure employment, on the other hand, they offer employees the opportunity to reconcile professional and personal needs at different stages of life. Thus, companies can respond more flexibly to seasonal and economic fluctuations in orders and the resulting changing personnel requirements using working time accounts. Employees can also organize their working hours and tasks independently and better reconcile their professional and private lives. Especially in the context of the Corona pandemic, it has become apparent what advantages can be derived from the use of working time accounts. Hours could be built up or reduced to meet the changed circumstances without additional costs.
Variants of working time accounts (Jaeger et al. 2017)

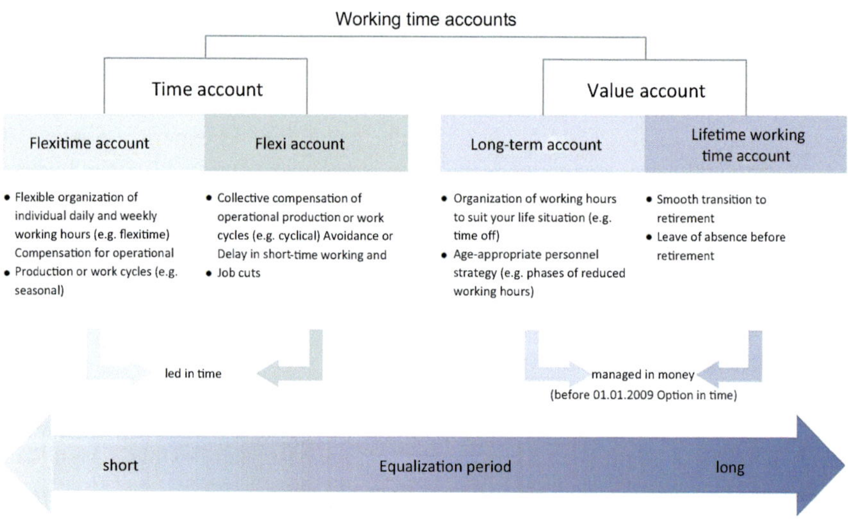

However, when introducing and designing working time accounts, it should be taken into account that working time accounts are divided into time accounts and value accounts. With the time accounts, the daily or weekly working time is flexibly designed or operational production or work cycles are balanced. Value accounts finance a longer-term social security protected exemption of employees, for example for parental leave, care time, further education, early retirement or temporary part-time work. Employment security accounts (flex accounts) are also an important component of flexible and needs-based working time design and are of central importance for the preservation of jobs and the competitiveness of companies (ifaa 2020).

However, the "formal" existence of a working time account is not yet a guarantee for flexibility. Working time accounts that serve as a "collecting pool" for accumulated hours and are only slightly or not at all built up and reduced, not only contradict the actual purpose of working time accounts, they even prevent the desired flexibility and can even lead to rejection by the employees. In the worst case, they even restrict a desired operational flexibility if certain employees or groups of employees are only available to a limited extent due to high hour contingents (credits).

4.2 More Employee Responsibility

The flexibilization of action and design scopes as well as an improvement in the compatibility of work and private life are valuable resources for employees. They can contribute to an increase in the performance of employees and to a favorable ratio of mental stress and strain. An increasing autonomy of employees in the design of working hours, as also desired by employees, should therefore also be accompanied by a "more" of responsibility for their own health and occupational safety.

When flexibilizing working hours (and the workplace), the personal responsibility of employees should be strengthened. This is especially true when employees themselves decide when, how long and possibly where they work. In any case, employees have a higher personal responsibility to realistically assess their own stress factors in order to organize time- and location-flexible work. Thus, strains that favor unfavorable stress consequences can be avoided as far as possible. This duty to cooperate can be derived from Section 15 para. 1 Occupational Safety and Health Act (ArbSchG), which states: "Employees are obliged to take care of their safety and health at work according to their possibilities and in accordance with the instruction and directive of the employer." However, appropriate instruction is required here, which the employer must carry out for the safe and health-conscious handling of work equipment according to Section 12 ArbSchG.

However, in order for the expanded and self-controlled and desired design options or the phenomenon of so-called "interested self-endangerment" not to lead to impairing consequences, company-related and pragmatic agreements and regulations (e.g., reading, editing, answering emails after work) are needed (see the article "Organizational Recovery—How Organizations Promote the Recovery of Their Employees"), which are based on a culture of trust and above all on a high degree of personal responsibility of employees for their health and the maintenance of performance. In particular, the health and social aspects such as regeneration and recovery times, i.e., switching off and relaxing after work, are indispensable for every person in order to remain healthy and motivated in the long term, to participate in social and cultural activities and to have time for family, friends and oneself. Resilient people are aware of these personal resources and have the mental resilience (the so-called resilience) to deal with difficult situations and (everyday) challenges as calmly as possible (ifaa et al. 2018).

4.3 Integration of Ergonomic Findings in Service and Shift Schedule Design

The economic importance of shift and night work has been increasing for years. According to Eurostat, in 2019, around 15.6% of the 15- to 64-year-old workers in Germany were engaged in shift work (Statista 2022). The drivers of this increase are both macroeconomic and business economic reasons, as well as the provision of services to the population. Shift work is indispensable for the provision of services to the population. This includes hospitals, police, fire departments, as well as power plants, data centers, restaurant and hotel businesses, and the media industry. The expansion of services with extended service and shopping hours and the increasing care effort in the health and nursing sector due to demographic change also contribute to the growth of shift work.

For an ergonomic shift schedule design, the consideration of ergonomic findings is still essential. The Working Time Act stipulates that the working time of persons employed in night and shift work must be determined according to established ergonomic findings on the human-friendly design of work (Section 6 para. 1 ArbZG). Ergonomic findings are considered to be the results of extensive research on night and shift work, which are summarized in various recommendations (see Beermann 2005).

Previous studies show that shift and night work can have different health effects depending on age, chronotype, shift model, etc. The research findings of the Institute for Prevention and Occupational Medicine of the German Social Accident Insurance (IPA) show that chronobiology in particular plays an important role in shift work research. Chronobiology classifies people into different chronotypes, whose preferred sleeping times can differ by up to twelve hours (Griefahn 2011). According to the findings of chronobiologists, every human being has an internal biological clock that also controls general performance and concentration ability over the course of a 24-hour day ("circadian rhythm": circa—approximately, dian—one day long). This internal clock is genetically determined and does not need external signals.

Even in shift operations, the future will increasingly be about making shift work more individual, flexible, and health-friendly. It is of central importance to convince both managers and employees of the importance of occupational science and occupational medical findings and to integrate the ergonomic recommendations even more strongly than before into flexible and needs-based working time design.

5 Summary and Outlook

Flexible working time design, taking into account employee wishes, allows more leeway for operational solutions and thus requires a holistic overall concept. However, there is no patent recipe for a flexible and needs-based working time design. Numerous combinations of criteria and aspects, such as short reaction and delivery times, response to seasonal and economic capacity fluctuations, chronobiology, age, gender, and personal risk profile are crucial for the success of a flexible, needs-based, and health-friendly working time design.

Here, companies and their employees should jointly find out which working time model suits their own company and the operational conditions and needs of the employees. The direct involvement of employees and—if available—the works council not only promotes their constructive cooperation, but also the acceptance of the new working time model in the company. The goal must be to reconcile the different interests of the company and the employees and to implement the new working time model permanently and successfully. Consequently, the primary concern is not to adopt supposedly successful working time models from other companies one-to-one, but to develop own and company-specific and—if necessary—several working time models for different areas and groups of employees.

References

AOK Bundesverband (Hrsg) (2018) AOK-Familienstudie 2018. KomPart Verlagsgesellschaft, Berlin

Beermann B (2005) Leitfaden zur Einführung und Gestaltung von Nacht- und Schichtarbeit, 9., unveränderte Auflage. Bundesanstalt für Arbeitsschutz und Arbeitsmedizin – BAuA, Dortmund

bitkom (2019) (Hrsg) New Work: Wie arbeitet Deutschland? www.bitkom.org/sites/default/files/2019-09/bitkom-charts-new-work-i-11-09-2019_final_0.pdf (abgerufen am 23.08.2022)

Griefahn B (2011) Schichtarbeit. Morgen- und Abendtypen. In: DGUV Forum – Fachzeitschrift für Prävention, Rehabilitation und Entschädigung. Thema: Schichtarbeit und Gesundheit – eine Bestandsaufnahme (Ausgabe 4/2011) DGUV (Hrsg.)

ifaa – Institut für angewandte Arbeitswissenschaft e. V. (Hrsg.) (2020) Gestaltung und Steuerung von Arbeitszeitkonten. Für mehr Flexibilität und Individualität. ifaa, Düsseldorf

ifaa – Institut für angewandte Arbeitswissenschaft e. V., Institut für Arbeitswissenschaft, Technische Universität Darmstadt (IAD), Institut der deutschen Wirtschaft Köln e. V. (IW), Hochschule Fresenius Düsseldorf (Hrsg.) (2018) Resilienzkompass zur Stärkung der individuellen und organisationalen Resilienz in Unternehmen. Düsseldorf

Jaeger C, Altun U, Glaser S, Lawonn C, Matthes A, Gesamtmetall, ifaa – Institut für angewandte Arbeitswissenschaft (Hrsg) (2017) Arbeitszeit im Wandel. IW Medien, Berlin

Statista (2022) Anteil der Erwerbstätigen in Deutschland, die Schichtarbeit leisten, bis 2021. https://de.statista.com/statistik/daten/studie/360921/umfrage/anteil-der-erwerbstaetigen-in-deutschland-die-schichtarbeit-leisten/ (abgerufen am 23.08.2022)

The Four-Day Week

Jan Bühren, Nina Meier-Hahasvili, Carsten Meier and Gregor Kalchthaler

> *"My favorite things in life don't cost any money. It's really clear that the most precious resource we all have is time."*
>
> *Steve Jobs*

1 Introduction

With the COVID pandemic, one of the largest involuntary experiments in work history began. And the result: It works. It took a shock to the system to try out new modes. The waves are smoothing out somewhat after the pandemic, and for many, it is back to the office or hybrid working. Many benefit from an increase in flexibility in terms of the workplace. But should the flexibility not go a bit further?

More and more countries and companies are coming to this conclusion and are changing the classic work cycles of five days and 40 hours for full-time. Iceland, New Zealand, Japan, Sweden, Spain, the United Kingdom, the United Arab Emirates, and Belgium are actively testing these models or have already partially introduced them (Worldpopulationreview 2022). The example of Belgium makes it clear that very different forms of the four-day week (hereinafter referred to as 4DW) exist: there, the government has decided on a 4DW with the same total working time. In a 40-hour week, this means working 10 hours a day for four days. Iceland reduced the working hours to 35 hours in four days with the same pay (Worldpopulationreview 2022).

J. Bühren (✉) · N. Meier-Hahasvili · C. Meier · G. Kalchthaler
Intraprenör GmbH, Berlin, Germany
e-mail: team@intraprenoer.de

I. Knappertsbusch and G. Wisskirchen (eds.), *The Future of Work*,
https://doi.org/10.1007/978-3-658-45150-9_13

A "real" 4DW reduces the working time by one day, so in a classic 40-hour week to 32 hours, with full salary compensation. The largest experiment in this form is currently being conducted in the UK, with more than 3300 employees from 70 different companies participating. The researchers call their model "100-80-100": 100% of the salary for 80% of the time for 100% performance (4 Day Week Global 2022a). This distinguishes this new form of work from the broader term "flexible work", which in the literature encompasses everything from weekend work to shift work, overtime, annual work contracts, part-time work, job sharing, flexitime, temporary work, fixed-term contracts, home office, telework, and compressed work weeks. Apart from the discussed attempts of the 4DW, there are only a few examples of companies that have reduced working hours while maintaining full-time pay (e.g., Perpetual Guardian, a financial service provider in New Zealand).

The advancement of technology and society makes this reduction in working hours possible in the first place. According to Moore's Law, we can continue to expect that the speed and performance of our systems will increase and that they will become cheaper (Gilligan et al., 2019; Theis & Wong, 2017). In HR, artificial intelligence is taking over increasingly complex tasks, such as Thurfir, which manages role and competence profiles of employees and helps with networking.

So, a trend reversal seems to be emerging. A key to getting this on the right track is the reorganization of work and established work procedures.

2 Advantages of this Form of Work

Since the 4DW in this form (100-80-100) is still quite young, there are so far only a few scientific data. However, the first results from the pilots are promising. The experiment by the company Perpetual Guardian from New Zealand in 2018 was monitored by scientists. They concluded that the values for engagement improved by 30 to 40%, the work-life balance indicators by 44%, empowerment by 26%, leadership qualities by 28%, work incentives by 27%, and organizational commitment by 29% (Haar, J. 2018). The long series of experiments with a shortened work week in Iceland is also considered a great success. Participants reported feeling less stressed and less at risk of burnout, and that their health had improved. Despite the shortened working hours, productivity remained the same or even increased (Haraldsson, G.D., Kellam, J. 2021). The 4DW test by Microsoft Japan in 2019 resulted in a 40% increase in productivity, and higher operational efficiency was also reported as electricity and printing costs were reduced. The large-scale experiment in the United Kingdom also looks back on positive results halfway through the planned time: 88% of the people surveyed said that the 4DW is working "well" for their company at this stage of the trial; 46% of respondents said that their company's productivity has "remained about the same", while 34% said it has "slightly improved" and 15% said it has "significantly improved" (4 Day Week Global 2022b).

A British study of nearly 2000 full-time office workers in 2017 found that the actual working time averages only two hours and 53 minutes per day (Vouchercloud 2017). The rest of the time, employees spent using social media and reading news websites, making personal calls and texts, talking to colleagues about non-work-related matters, looking for new jobs, taking smoking breaks, or preparing food and drinks.

Upon closer inspection, the 4DW is already a reality for most and is only hidden under unnecessary processes. The trials in various countries have shown that productivity may even increase in four days, thus demonstrating that a rethink in the way of working is needed rather than a strict focus on time.

Every company has inefficiencies, many of which are repeated so often that they become habit or even ritual. It takes a system shock to change these hard-learned behaviors. The 4DW can play a transformative role in the company because it forces these inefficiencies to be recognized and eliminated. Many of the participating companies report that the introduction of the topic almost immediately initiated team discussions about productivity and the teams consciously reflected on their ways of working (4 Day Week Global 2022b).

The 4DW not only has an internal effect, it is a clear competitive advantage. For smaller companies like our HR transformation consultancy *Intraprenör*, it is not possible to compete with the top 1% in terms of salaries, but we have the chance to keep up with the top 1% in terms of working hours. In addition to the clear advantages for our work, applications also show that the 4DW exerts a real pull effect. Companies like *Atom Bank* in the United Kingdom have seen a 500% increase in applications for open positions since switching to a 4DW (Atombank 2022). The battle for the best talent is no longer decided solely by salary, but by the ability to remain individual and lead a good life outside of work.

Unlike many companies where the boundaries between work and private life are unclear or deliberately crossed, the 4DW promotes a demarcation. Research on flexible working models shows that the mental strain is lower in these models because conflicts between work and family decrease. People have more energy available for their relationships, which tend to improve as a result, leading to happier employees (Obrenovic et al., 2020).

The *World Health Organization* issued a warning as early as 2021 and calculated that overwork costs more than 745,000 people their lives each year (Pega et al., 2021). In addition to all the economic advantages, we should therefore work to bring the workload for society back into line with health.

3 Challenges of this Form of Work

It is rightly often referred to as an "experiment" when the 4DW is introduced. It is not a panacea, but requires a coordinated implementation process to lead to long-term improvements. If this new form of work is "rushed", it creates more stress than before. If the structures and working methods do not change along with it, we only have a system shock that cannot be absorbed and positively channeled. The work of five days simply cannot be done in four days using the same working method, which increases the perceived burden.

It is also important in the implementation that all participants are brought to the table and exchange takes place about the planned project. Otherwise, there can quickly be a separation of areas, those who now feel preferred and those who still work traditionally and have to carry the workload of the others.

Classic concerns are initially directed at the fear of a loss of productivity or a restriction in customer satisfaction. Both points have so far been refuted by the trials. Also in our practical experience, it shows that through clear communication with customers, any concerns can be quickly alleviated and rather a curiosity about this new way of working arises.

For the traditional office jobs, there is a presumption that it is easier for the more creatively working departments to bundle their workflows and adjust to the shorter time, whereas administrative departments traditionally tend to work through things and achieve more with more time. Here the leap is somewhat larger and must be accompanied by more guidance.

4 Solutions and Practical Tips

As with most change initiatives, communication and exchange are also among the most important factors here. The company management must clearly define and communicate the direction, which includes the purpose and the goals of the initiative, but also the metrics for the process. The announcement of a test phase has proven successful for the participating companies of the British pilot (4 Day Week Global 2022b). After the intention and the goal were communicated, it is up to the managers to empower the employees as best as possible to jointly define the details for the process. The largest and most sustainable productivity increases were achieved by companies that chose a bottom-up approach in implementation, allowing employees to work out the changes in workflows necessary for the redesign of their work themselves. Employees should be encouraged to independently consider how they can organize the time within the team and meet customer and business requirements. Seasonal differences in workflows must be taken into account and the new policy must be flexible enough to be adjusted accordingly.

With the cut in working hours, the focus must initially be on reducing disruptions and distractions in everyday work. Microsoft found that the number of meetings increased by 250% during the pandemic (Microsoft 2021). Identifying unnecessary meetings should be high on the list for every company, as it is essential for the successful reduction of working hours to 32 hours.

One of the biggest distractions in everyday work is emails—it can take up to 20 minutes to get back to productive work after receiving an email (Mark et al., 2016). A gradual reduction should be tried in any case. Project management tools like Asana or Microsoft Teams offer the opportunity to bundle communication project-related and minimize unnecessary coordination.

In the spirit of a joint experiment, a forum for exchange between employees should be created in the company, in which all participants can share their experiences and suggestions. Each attempt will run individually and should, depending on feedback, always offer the possibility for adjustments. Whether you opt for a 4DW, reduced working hours or flexible working hours, be prepared to adapt to the needs of your employees as the company grows or changes.

For the transition, a standby on one of the free days can help and give customers the appearance of the status quo. At Intraprenör, we have chosen a fixed day when the company closes: we are never there on Fridays. This has the advantage of easy communication and regulated expectations. Of course, there is also the option to distribute the free day differently, so that continuous staffing over five days is guaranteed. Since the creative exchange between employees is most profitable for our consulting, we have chosen the fixed day so that as many contact points as possible between employees can arise on the remaining days.

5 Summary and Outlook

The initial successes of the 4DW experiments give reason for hope: employees are empowered, collective and structural solutions are produced, efficient feedback systems are created, gender-specific prejudices are reduced, and they help to make work more meaningful.

The times in the job market are currently anything but calm. A further development of the relationship between employers and employees is overdue, especially now, where the demographic change (see the article "Historical Turn in the German Job Market—How Demographic Change Slows Down Growth") is so clearly noticeable in the shortage of skilled workers (see the article "Shortage of Skilled Workers—Myth or Reality?"): Trust must go in both directions. The 4DW meets a need that more and more people are feeling and thus becomes an absolute competitive advantage.

Where the 4DW has been tried out, it usually stays. Since the experiments, 86% of Icelandic workers have a contract that either already enables them to work shorter hours or gives them the right to do so in the future. In the United Kingdom, 70 companies are testing the 4DW, and Panasonic is also testing the benefits in Japan. Since January, the United Arab Emirates have also been in a 4.5-day week. This was introduced nationwide for government employees—but by now most private companies have also followed suit (Worldpopulationreview 2022).

COVID created the impression that New Work had already arrived in society—it was largely simply equated with home office (see the article "Working from Home: Perspectives, Challenges, Solutions") (Schermuly, Geissler, 2021). But New Work is much more than just home office. The co-founder of Intraprenör, Gregor Kalchthaler, sums it up: "New Work must be understood as a leap innovation, it is also a different management paradigm than the previous one. Management by

Objectives and pure number orientation is replaced by a new understanding in which the person is put at the center. He is no longer seen just as a resource that has to maximize its productivity, but also the non-working time becomes a relevant and promotable factor. A decision for real New Work is therefore not just a numbers decision, but also a conviction." To take the discussion on this topic a step further in Germany, such an experiment is now also starting in Germany. In partnership with 4 Day Week Global, initiators of the world's largest pilot studies in the UK, South Africa, Australia and Ireland, Intraprenör is organizing the first large-scale pilot study on the 4-day week for Germany (www.4tagewoche.org). The official start is in September 2023 and the first data collection phase runs for 6 months—so the first results can be expected in April 2024.

References

4 Day Week Global (2022a) Why Trial a 4 Day Week? https://www.4dayweek.com/why-pilot (abgerufen am 29.09.2022)

4 Day Week Global (2022b) UK Companies in 4 Day week Pilot Reach Landmark Halfway Point https://www.4dayweek.com/news-posts/uk-four-day-week-pilot-mid-results (abgerufen am 29.09.2022)

Atombank (2022) Will 2022 be the year of the Four Day Week? https://www.atombank.co.uk/newsroom/2022-year-of-four-day-week/ (abgerufen am 29.09.2022)

Gilligan, C., Leontaris, J., & Lopez, A. L. (2019). The timing of work: Re-thinking the US convention on the full-time hourly workweek. Graziadio Business Review, 22(3). https://gbr.pepperdine.edu/2019/12/the-timing-of-work/ (abgerufen am 29.09.2022)

Haar, J. (2018) Overview of the Perpetual Guardian 4-day (paid 5) Work Trial. Auckland University of Technology

Haraldsson, G.D., Kellam, J. (2021) Going public: Iceland's journey to a shorter working week. Alda, Association for Democracy and Sustainability

Mark, G., Iqbal, S. T., Czerwinski, M., Johns, P., Sano, A., & Lutchyn, Y. (2016). Email Duration, Batching and Self-interruption. In Proceedings of the 2016 CHI Conference on Human Factors in Computing Systems. CHI'16: CHI Conference on Human Factors in Computing Systems. ACM. https://doi.org/10.1145/2858036.2858262 (abgerufen am 29.09.2022)

Microsoft (2021) The Rise of the Triple Peak Day. https://www.microsoft.com/en-us/worklab/triple-peak-day (abgerufen am 29.09.2022)

Obrenovic, B., Jianguo, D., Khudaykulov, A., & Khan, M. A. S. (2020). Work-Family Conflict Impact on Psychological Safety and Psychological Well-Being: A Job Performance Model. Erschienen in Frontiers in Psychology (Vol. 11). Frontiers Media SA. https://doi.org/10.3389/fpsyg.2020.00475 (abgerufen am 29.09.2022)

Pega, F., Náfrádi, B., Momen, N. C., Ujita, Y., Streicher, K. N., Prüss-Üstün, A. M., Descatha, A., Driscoll, T., Fischer, F. M., Godderis, L., Kiiver, H. M., Li, J., Magnusson Hanson, L. L., Rugulies, R., Sørensen, K., & Woodruff, T. J. (2021). Global, regional, and national burdens of ischemic heart disease and stroke attributable to exposure to long working hours for 194 countries, 2000–2016: A systematic analysis from the WHO/ILO Joint Estimates of the Work-related Burden of Disease and Injury. Erschienen in Environment International (Vol. 154, p. 106595). Elsevier BV. https://doi.org/10.1016/j.envint.2021.106595

Schermuly, C.C, Geissler, C. (2021) Ergebnisbericht zum New Work-Barometer 2021. Institute for new work and coaching & personal magazin

Theis, T. N., & Wong, H. P. (2017). The end of Moore's law: A new beginning for information technology. Computing in Science & Engineering, 19(2), 41–50. https://doi.org/10.1109/mcse.2017.29

Vouchercloud (2017). How Many Productive Hours in a Work Day? Just 2 Hours, 23 Minutes. https://www.vouchercloud.com/resources/office-worker-productivity (abgerufen am 29.09.2022)

Wirtschaftswoche (2022) Wie den Deutschen der Spaß an der Arbeit vergeht. https://www.wiwo.de/my/erfolg/beruf/teilzeit-4-tage-woche-kuendigung-diese-5-grafiken-zeigen-wie-den-deutschen-der-spass-an-der-arbeit-vergeht/28705074.html (abgerufen am 29.09.2022)

Worldpopulationreview (2022) What Countries Have Four-Day Work Weeks. https://worldpopulationreview.com/country-rankings/what-countries-have-4-day-work-weeks (abgerufen am 25.10.2022)

Elective Working Time: The Basis for an Employee-Oriented Working Hours Design

Andreas Hoff

1 Introduction

Current surveys show a great interest among German workers in reducing contractual working hours compared to the full-time standard. A representative survey conducted in the summer of 2022 revealed that 48% of full-time employees in Germany would switch to part-time if they were given the opportunity by their employer; among professionals under 40, this figure was even 51%. However, the responses "Yes, definitely" and "Rather yes" are combined, which somewhat relativizes the reported result (see HDI 2022).

Against this background, the concept of "elective working time" developed as early as the late 1980s is of great importance. It gives employees the right to repeatedly redefine the duration of their contractual working hours within a certain range, without having to change jobs, and is therefore also open to managers. The distribution of working hours remains unchanged within the respective company's working time system; the employee, for example, remains in his or her shift team, is scheduled according to the previous rules within the monthly or weekly service plan, or continues to work self-dependent within a flexitime system or in trust-based working hours.

Elective working time largely goes beyond the legal regulations with which German employees can currently pursue a part-time request:

- The *Part-Time and Fixed-Term Employment Act (TzBfG)* basically gives them the right to reduce their contractual working hours indefinitely or (in the case of "bridge part-time") temporarily. However, (a) it does not apply to all

A. Hoff (✉)
Dr. Hoff Arbeitszeitsysteme, Potsdam, Germany
e-mail: hoff@arbeitszeitsysteme.com

I. Knappertsbusch and G. Wisskirchen (eds.), *The Future of Work*,
https://doi.org/10.1007/978-3-658-45150-9_14

employees—especially not to those in smaller companies -, (b) the employer can object to the part-time request (if necessary, legal clarification), (c) employees have no claim to an increase in contractual working hours in the case of indefinite part-time work or must commit to a period between one year and five years without the right to change within this period in the case of temporary part-time work, and (d) a further indefinite or temporary reduction of contractual working hours can only be requested after a period of 2 years or 1 year, respectively.
- The *Federal Parental Allowance and Parental Leave Act (BEEG)*, the *Care Time Act (PflegeZG)* and the *Family Care Time Act (FPfZG)* only apply to the respective affected employees—just as the *Social Code Ninth Book (SGB IX)* only applies to severely disabled people and the *Partial Retirement Act (AltTZG)* only from the age of 55.

Elective working time in the extensive form promoted here currently only exists in very few companies (see Hoff 2017). However, precursors to this have spread significantly in recent years—such as "money or time" options in collective agreements of the Railway and Transport Union (EVG) and IG Metall (see Hoff/Gruschka 2019), in which employees have predominantly chosen time as expected, and the individual flexible working hours according to the "Potsdam Model" in the Eastern Chemical Industry, which can be introduced since 2019 by voluntary company agreement.

2 Advantages of Flexible Working Hours

While the advantages of elective working time for employees are immediately apparent, it makes sense to take a closer look at the potential associated with it for the employer:

- With elective working time, the employer signals that he or she highly values the personal concerns of his or her employees ("appreciation") and is interested in their long-term employment. This gives employees a relatively high level of planning security—and they should repay this with comparatively low turnover and good motivation.
- Elective working time is also attractive on the external labor market—and thus fit very well into the current era of widespread "worker shortage".
- Within the framework of elective working time, time/money options can be offered to employees in a very simple form and can also be reclaimed.
- Elective working time usually result in shorter average contractual working hours—which can also contribute to ecological relief (see Schumacher et al. 2019)—and can thus lead to lower sickness-related absences and possibly also to higher hourly productivity.

- Elective working time in the form promoted here, close to full-time, can lead to those interested in part-time work working *longer* than actually desired and planned, thereby gaining additional capacity for the employer.
- Last but not least, operational resilience is promoted by the fact that organization and personnel capacity (both quantitatively and qualitatively) have to be put to the test again and again as a result of adjustments to contractual working hours.

All the factors mentioned contribute to a reduction in labor costs, the extent of which, however, cannot be reliably estimated in general terms, as it depends on the respective starting point.

3 Challenges of Elective Working Time

In most German companies, culture, organization, and working time systems are still predominantly based on (over-)full-time work, which is why the introduction of elective working time entails profound changes—such as the transition from a presence-oriented to a results-oriented work culture. In this context, I will only discuss the possibly necessary adjustments of the company's working time systems, which basically fall into the two categories (a) self-regulated by the employees or (b) scheduled (see Hoff 2021).

Let's first look at the working time systems in which the working hours are primarily *self-regulated* by the employees. Here, work is usually done in day shifts and on a 5-day week, so that the respective working time system must not only unproblematically allow daily contractual working hours within the chosen range—for example, from 6 to 8 hours with a standard working time of 40 hours per week—but should also support their productive use. This requires, in particular, the abolition of traditional core times with individual attendance obligations, which, where there is a need for immediate services for internal and/or external customers, are replaced by team-related service times (e.g., "Monday to Friday from 08:00-17:00"). All team members, regardless of the duration of their contractual working hours, contribute to covering such service times—although it is certainly open to discussion and probably even legally required to oblige employees with reduced contractual working hours to work proportionately during socially unfavorable times.

All of this applies in "normal" flexible working time systems with a working time account as well as in trust-based working hours, where, by definition—because the employer waives the control of compliance with the contractual working hours—no working time account is kept. Thus, the introduction of elective working time also supports a potentially (because it depends on the working time behavior of the employees) more customer-oriented and economical (avoidance of wasting working time) use of working time.

Now to the *scheduled working time systems*, which are usually much more stressful for the employees—also because of the fewer individual working time design options. Since these burdens are often materially compensated today—for example, through surcharges for night, Sunday, and holiday work—elective working time is particularly suitable here for one (reduction of stress) and, on the other hand, due to the generally higher wages under otherwise equal conditions, they meet relatively good implementation conditions.

In *shift work*—which has a lot to catch up on in terms of part-time work—reduced contractual working hours lead to (more) individual free shifts when the shift plan reaches the standard working hours, under otherwise equal conditions. If, on the other hand, the shift plan does not reach the standard working hours and therefore additional shifts have to be performed, they lead to a reduction in the number of additional shifts to be performed under otherwise equal conditions. Since, in my experience, employees are particularly interested in the latter, shift systems with additional shifts provide a particularly good basis for optionally reduced contractual working hours.

If the respective shift system is accompanied by a working time account—which is unfortunately not yet standard—the implementation of differentiated contractual working time durations is very simple. I would like to illustrate this using the example of a conventional 5-day shift operation, where I assume 8 hours of work per shift, a standard working time of 37.5 hours per week, and elective working hours in 1.25-hour steps down to 30 hours per week (employment rates thus 100/96.67/93.33/90/86.67/83.33/80%). This results in the following standard movements on the working time account from the deviations between scheduled working time (8 hours) and daily contractual working time (1/5 of the weekly contractual working time):

Contractual working time	37.5 h/w	35 h/w	32.5 h/w	30 h/w
Scheduled work	+0.5 h	+1 h	+1.5 h	+2 h
Scheduled free time	−7.5 h	−7 h	−6.5 h	−6.00 h

This shows that employees working regular hours must work 15 scheduled days to enjoy a scheduled day off, while those working 35 hours per week only need 7 scheduled workdays for this, those with a 32.5 hours per week contract just over 4, and those with a 30 hours per week contract only 3 such workdays. And since the employer must anyway take care of the needs-based distribution of days off in shift systems to avoid both over- and under-staffing, their increase usually associated with elective working time is not a problem, but rather part of the solution.

Conversely, this works analogously. Here I assume that in a fully continuous 5-shift plan, under otherwise equal conditions, only an average of 4.2 shifts per week are worked and accordingly only 33.6 hours per week of work is achieved. In this case, the following standard movements from the deviations between shift-scheduled working time (still 8 hours) and daily contract working time (weekly contract working time: 4.2) occur on the working time account:

Contract working time	37.5 h/w	35 h/w	32.5 h/w	30 h/w
Scheduled work	−56 min	−20 min	+16 min	+51 min

Thus, employees working regular hours must perform an additional scheduled shift for approximately every 8.5 scheduled workdays. For the 35 hours per week employees, this is reduced to one scheduled additional shift per 24 scheduled workdays, while employees with 32.5 and 30 hours per week contracts even receive days off—namely one day off per 29 or approximately 8.5 scheduled workdays. Here too, the decreasing number of additional shifts and possibly the days off are not a problem, because the employer must anyway ensure their needs-based control.

Finally, if employees are deployed within the framework of *monthly service plans or other deployment plans*, they must, under otherwise equal conditions, perform fewer services and have correspondingly more free days when they do not wish for shorter average services with reduced contract working time.

4 Solutions and Practical Tips

The legal entitlement of employees within the elective working time is usually—strategically—limited, while the statutory entitlements naturally remain unaffected:

- The entitlement to vary the contractual working hours only exists in the area close to full-time; my recommendation in this regard is towards approximately 75–80% to 100% of the company's regular working hours (depending on their duration), i.e., for example, from 30–40 h/w or from 28–35 h/w. This limitation is made on the one hand because this entitlement, due to the relatively small changes in capacity, can then actually be almost unlimited and, which is of particular importance to the employees, can always take place at the same workplace. On the other hand, it includes an incentive for employees to "stretch themselves to the ceiling" in terms of working hours—i.e., for example, to work 30 h/w instead of traditionally part-time in consultation with their life partner—so that the employer can even gain working time capacity. Contractual working hours below the range of elective working time are of course still possible, but in particular do not include the entitlement to their (re-)increase.
- The range is simplistically only available in steps that make sense within the respective company's working time system, but which—to keep the entry threshold low and to give employees, for example, the opportunity to consume a pay increase in the form of reduced working hours—should not differ by more than about 3%. If elective working time is used, for example, in flexible day service with a 5-day week, the following intermediate steps within a range of 30–40 h/w could make sense, where the daily contractual working hours are each 15 minutes (just over 3%) apart: 38.75 h/w—37.5 h/w—36.25

h/w—35 h/w—33.75 h/w—32.5 h/w—31.25 h/w. Models with additional scheduled days off—e.g., 5, 10, 15 or 20 such days per year, which corresponds to an employment rate of 97.5%, 95%, 92.5% or 90% respectively (see Hoff/Gruschka 2019)—are also fundamentally conceivable, but they are particularly associated with a higher need for coordination and representation and should therefore only be considered as a secondary option.

- The variation of the contractual working hours is only implemented with a certain time delay, to give the employer the opportunity to make any necessary organizational and/or capacity adjustments. I recommend a notice period of 6 months to the first of the month for employees, although this period can of course be mutually reduced to zero. In addition, the employer should have the right to postpone desired increases in contractual working hours by up to 6 months once if there is no operational need.

  Alternatively, employees could also, for example, only have the opportunity to vary their contractual working hours annually (with notification, for example, by 30.09.), which includes the chance that capacity effects partially cancel each other out. On the other hand, this loses flexibility for both sides and the operational requirements and conditions are constantly changing anyway, which is why I prefer the initially mentioned procedure.
- The most important point, however, is that the entitlement of employees—unlike the statutory entitlements—does *not* also apply to a specific distribution of contractual working hours. This is intended to prevent particularly attractive working time distributions such as “4-day week with Friday off” or “only in the morning” from being enforced within the framework of elective working time: because this would be at the expense of the other employees, who, for example, would also like to have Friday off more often or who would then be left with the staffing of an afternoon service time, but also because it can endanger the workplace occupations required by customers and/or for economic reasons.

  With elective working time, the respective contractual working hours are instead basically performed under otherwise identical conditions, which requires a correspondingly flexible working time system (see above under Sect. 3.). This does not exclude individual agreements on the distribution of working hours, which must always be measured against the standard of equal treatment of employees. Such agreements can in particular include a different basic distribution of contractual working hours over fewer working days—up to sabbaticals according to the principle “9 months work, 3 months off, employment rate 75%”, which can also lie within the range of elective working time.

So anyone who uses the offer of elective working time as an employee instead of the possibly legally given options, has greater rights and securities on the one hand, but on the other hand may have to make compromises with regard to a (higher than actually desired) duration of contractual working hours and/or their distribution—both of which are in line with company interests.

5 Summary and Outlook

Elective working time, in the sense of the free choice of the duration of contractual working hours by the individual employee within certain limits, can easily be implemented in any self-regulated working time system that dispenses with unnecessary attendance obligations (e.g., the classic "core time"), and just as easily in any scheduled working time system accompanied by a working time account. Not only do employees benefit from this, as it allows them a contract working time duration that suits their current life situation or is as desired within the set limits. Rather, employers can also expect reduced labor costs despite the likely increase in staffing needs: particularly due to reduced turnover, better labor market position, lower sickness rate, and higher hourly productivity. Therefore, in my view, there can be no doubt that this concept will spread significantly further.

References

HDI (2022), Teilzeit und 4-Tage-Woche stehen hoch im Kurs, https://www.berufe-studie.de/2022_01-kernergebnisse.html (abgerufen am 27.09.2022)

Hoff, Andreas (2017), Von der Vollzeitarbeit zur Wahlarbeitszeit, in: Hans Diefenbacher/Benjamin Held/Dorothee Rodenhäuser (Hg.), Ende des Wachstums – Arbeit ohne Ende? Arbeiten in einer Postwachstumsgesellschaft, Marburg 2017, S. 101–116

Hoff, Andreas (2021), Gestaltung betrieblicher Arbeitszeitsysteme. Ein Überblick für die Praxis, 2. überarbeitete Auflage, Wiesbaden 2021

Hoff, Andreas/Gruschka, Christian (2019), Zeit statt Geld. Auf die richtige Ausgestaltung der Wahloptionen kommt es an, in: Personalführung 9/2019, S. 20–26

Schumacher, Katja et al. (2019), Arbeitszeitverkürzung – gut fürs Klima? Texte 105/2019 des Bundesumweltamts

Free Space for Employees—Planning Security for Employers

How Companies Can Successfully Flexibilize Working Time with Additional Vacation Days and Promote Work-Life Balance

Georg Pepping and Tanja Werner

> *"We shape our tools, and the tools shape us." (Marshall McLuhan, The Medium is the Message, 1967). "We have invented smartphones. But what we read on them does not change us. Rather, the fact that we read on them. We offer spaces of freedom. And the spaces of freedom affect us in return. I am curious to see how they will change us."*
>
> *(Georg Pepping)*

1 Introduction

FreiRaum embeds itself in a working world that has already changed in many ways and will continue to change rapidly.

In a Randstad study, almost three-quarters of respondents believe that location independence will shape the working world of tomorrow.[1] 63% assume that this world will also be more flexible in terms of time. Digitization (see the article "When digital meets demographic change—What opportunities and risks does digital transformation pose in a shrinking and aging working population?") makes tomorrow possible already today. In the IT industry, hybrid work as a switch between office and home office was already standard before the pandemic. Now,

[1] Randstad.

G. Pepping
T-Systems Internat. GmbH (until 31th of Dec 2023), Bonn, Germany
e-mail: georg@pepping.me

T. Werner (✉)
Deutsche Telekom AG, Bonn, Germany
e-mail: Tanja-Werner@telekom.de

I. Knappertsbusch and G. Wisskirchen (eds.), *The Future of Work*,
https://doi.org/10.1007/978-3-658-45150-9_15

mobile work has also arrived in other sectors to stay. And while it contributes to work-life balance on the one hand, it hinders it on the other due to a lack of separation between work and life.[2]

Recent studies, such as those by Bertelsmann, Hays or Randstad, have investigated how important work-life balance is to employees.[3] Accordingly, 54% of those capable of working value a balanced work-life balance when choosing an employer. 51% of employees would even change employers for this. In a generational comparison, only 27% of the Boomers, i.e. the generation 1955-1964, consider it important to have a lot of free time. For Generation Z, those born from 1995 onwards, it is already about twice as many with 53%.

Especially in the competition for talent in an increasingly dynamic and limited labor market, it is clear for every HR manager: working time models must match the expectations of those being courted. Relying solely on part-time models is no longer sufficient. Especially in knowledge work and an "always on" working world, traditional part-time models sometimes lead to a situation where the task volume is remaining the same, but less working time is being available. This often leads to dissatisfaction, increased stress and runs counter to work-life balance. Therefore, these models are no longer an option for many. This was the reason for us to develop a new model with FreiRaum ("FreeSpace").

2 Advantages of this Form of Work

The requirements for a work-life balance are individual. Whether the sense and purpose ("Purpose") is sought in work or perhaps in volunteering. Whether you bring the team onto the screen or the Netflix series. Whether children need to be supervised in homeschooling or elderly parents need to be cared for. Whether you want more time for sports, hobbies or a long-cherished travel dream or a long overdue renovation of your own four walls. And: Models for work-life balance are not a contradiction to productivity—especially in knowledge work. Both questions—individual needs on the one hand and productivity on the other—were guiding principles for the model.

In practice, FreiRaum works like this: Participation is based on double voluntariness of employee and manager. With participation, working time decreases by 5%. The weekly working time remains the same. In return, employees have free days available. For each month of participation, employees working a five-day

[2] Whether the obligation derived from § 3 para. 2 no. 1 ArbSchG according to the BAG for employers to introduce a system with which the working time performed by the employees can be recorded (decision of 13.9.2022 – 1 ABR 22/21, PM. On the net at https://www.bundesarbeitsgericht.de/presse/einfuehrung-elektronischer-zeiterfassung-initiativrecht-des-betriebsrats/ (accessed on: 17.9.2022)), can and will counteract such a blurring of boundaries, remains to be seen.

[3] Thiede, R., Buckler, A.; Hays.

week receive an additional day off—proportionally for employees with less than five working days per week. Accordingly, employees with a five-day week receive twelve additional days off per calendar year. Although the salary also decreases, T-Systems subsidizes it with a partial wage compensation of 10%. Thus, the actual reduction of the annual target salary is only 4.5% instead of 5%.

The FreiRaum working time model at a glance

- **Participants** (double voluntariness): All employees who fall under the scope of the collective agreements of T-Systems as well as AT forces (means: Employees who don´t fall under the scope of a collective agreement, but are still governed by the Works Consitution Act).
- **Working hours**: Reduction of working hours by 5% while maintaining the individual weekly working hours.
- **Salary**: Reduction by 5%. Partial wage compensation of 10%. This corresponds to a real wage reduction of 4.5%.
- **Gain of additional free days**: For each month in the 5-day week, participants receive an additional day off (proportionally for employees with less than five working days per week).
- **Application**: Via workflow, smart form.

The free days are granted from participation in the model. They do not have to be worked in advance—as with working time account models. A certain company affiliation is not required. Even newly hired employees can take advantage of FreiRaum.

A clear advantage for employees is that the free days are treated like vacation days, i.e., they must generally be granted and taken within the calendar year. Neither sick days nor flexitime or public holidays reduce the number of FreiRaum days. A carryover to the next calendar year—as with vacation—only occurs in exceptional cases.

The fact that FreiRaum is as planable as annual leave is also an advantage from a company perspective. The conscious design as a mutually voluntary model ensures the acceptance of the managers, as there may be individual situations—be it that other success-critical employees have dropped out, be it that a certain project takes significantly longer—in which a reduction of working time cannot currently be enabled.

3 Challenges of this Form of Work

The business of T-Systems is essentially a so-called people business, i.e., skills, commitment, and collaboration across departments and national borders are crucial success factors for the provision of our IT services. With more than 4500 IT customer projects per year, it is important that top-qualified personnel are predictably available for the projects. In the IT business, employees are needed with 100% of their available working time during high project times—for example, during the introduction of a new IT solution. However, if work-life balance is neglected, commitment and health will suffer sooner or later. The result is increasing sickness rates up to burnouts and high turnover.

3.1 Balance between Autonomy and Corporate Interests

With FreiRaum, this balance between autonomy and corporate interests is achieved: The FreiRaum days are to be planned for managers and employees—as explained—similar to vacation.

The double voluntariness was not a hindrance: Managers have very rarely rejected FreiRaum for their employees, namely in less than five percent of the cases. An agreed escalation process did not have to be applied even once.

Overview of the Escalation Process
Principle of double voluntariness: Model participation working time requires the approval of the manager. If the manager rejects, the following escalation process applies:

1. At the request of the employee, the rejection or revocation must be justified in writing.
2. If the employee disagrees with the rejection, an escalation discussion with the works council and the manager is arranged at his request with the aim of reaching a mutual agreement.
3. If no agreement is possible in this discussion, a further escalation takes place at the level of the works council chairman and the next higher manager (last instance: labor director of the TSI). Here, an agreement should be reached.

The handling of the FreiRaum days within the calendar year worked successfully in the pilot year 2021. Only a few employees asked for a carryover into the next year. The fear that employees would withdraw the FreiRaum application in December because they could not accommodate the additional free days in time, did not come true. The model was well received by everyone and was therefore transferred into a regular model after the pilot phase.

4 Solutions and Practical Tips

The success of the pilot project was clearly promoted by its simplicity. The application of the model and the handling of the FreiRaum days is uncomplicated and possible at the push of a button in the HR system. And even after the push of a button, the participants remain open for new decisions: They only commit for one year. At the end of the year, they assess their life situation and make the decision whether they want to continue participating in the working time model. Extensive IT adjustments, as usually necessary with new working time models, could be avoided by treating the additional working days like vacation.

Starting Point Project manager Erika Muster, 41 years old, works in a 5-day week

- She receives information about the FreiRaum model
- She informs herself in detail about FreiRaum in the company intranet. The working time model can be well combined with her project activity.
- She fills out the smart application, which is automatically sent to her managers at the push of a button.
- The manager receives the application via workflow and approves it. The model allows for good planning, so that Erika Muster can complete her project in the usual time. In general, rejections must be justified appropriately.
- The Shared Service Team processes the application. At the start of the FreiRaum model, the changes in salary are implemented and the FreiRaum days are deposited in a working time account.
- Erika Muster now has additional FreiRaum. For a salary reduction of 4.5%, she receives 12 FreiRaum days per calendar year.

4.1 Success and Simplicity—No Contradiction!

FreiRaum is a result of collective bargaining. A small cross-functional team from various corporate units developed the basic features in close cooperation with the social partner in 2021. Works agreements on the distribution of working hours did not have to be changed, and complex IT programming was not necessary. To allow non-tariff employees ("AT-employees") to also use FreiRaum, a so-called transfer agreement was concluded with the general works council of T-Systems after the collective agreement was concluded. The main contents of the agreements are as follows:

- Pilot phase: Temporary collective agreement (duration 1st June 2021 to 31st December 2022).
- Personal scope: All employees. The only exceptions are employees in partial retirement.
- Reduction of working hours at the request of the employees and with the consent of the employer temporarily by 5% (principle of mutual voluntariness). Two periods: 1st July to 31st December 2021 and 1st January 2022 to 31st December 2022.
- For the period of the temporary reduction of working hours, the individual regular weekly working hours remain unaffected. Neither does this change the distribution of working hours, nor the status as part-time or full-time employees.
- In addition to their annual leave entitlement, employees receive twelve additional days off per calendar year for the period of the temporary reduction in working hours (six additional days off for six months of use in 2021). The remuneration for the additional days off is calculated according to the holiday pay for the annual leave.

- The individual annual salary of the employees is reduced by 4.5% at the start of the temporary reduction in working hours.
- The reduction must be requested at least six weeks before the start of the planned reduction period. If the manager does not agree, a multi-level escalation process involving the works council is initiated. The final decision lies with the employer.
- The additional days off are generally to be taken and granted in longer consecutive periods. The wishes of the employees are to be taken into account, as long as they do not conflict with urgent operational requirements or reduction requests from other employees.
- The additional days off must be granted and taken in the current calendar year. A transfer to the next calendar year is only permissible in accordance with section 7 para. 3 BUrlG (Federal Paid Leave Act) if urgent operational reasons or reasons related to the person of the employees justify this.
- If employees fall ill during the additional days off, the days of incapacity for work proven by a medical certificate are not counted towards the additional days off. The same applies to periods of medical prevention and rehabilitation measures.
- For employees on maternity leave and parental leave, the statutory regulations on annual leave are applied accordingly to the additional days off (section 24 MuSchG—Maternity Protection Act, sections 16, 17 BEEG—Parental Allowance and Leave Act).
- If the additional days off cannot be granted in whole or in part due to early termination of the term of the employment contract for urgent operational reasons or reasons related to the person of the employees, they must be compensated.

FreiRaum was deliberately concluded as a pilot agreement, as we did not know on both sides whether and how the model would be accepted and whether operational problems might arise that would prevent a permanent application of the model. The model was therefore initially limited until the end of 2022. Due to the success of the model, it was clear for both sides even before the end of the pilot phase that the model would be extended and continue to be a permanent part of T-Systems' HR offering.

5 Summary and Outlook

The high resonance and number of participants confirm: FreiRaum meets a need. About 10% of T-Systems' employees voluntarily chose to participate during the pilot phase. An initial evaluation shows: Not only young employees use the model. 42% of the participants are over 50 years old. Slightly more women opted for FreiRaum. And it is not only of interest to employees in the higher salary classes: Just under a third of the applicants are non-tariff employees.

The pandemic was only the trigger for the application for FreiRaum in exceptional cases. The desire for self-determined freedom is a perennial issue that does not require a specific trigger. FreiRaum is a contribution to employee and customer satisfaction. And a plus for employee recruitment and retention as well as mental and physical well-being, from well-being to resilience.

And: FreiRaum is not alone. The program is another manifestation of the "We. Work.New." approach pursued by T-Systems. In addition to a flexibilization of working hours through FreiRaum, this includes the flexibilization of the workplace ("activity based working") and soon also the possibility to work a certain number of days from abroad in Europe ("Workation") (see the article "Working where others go on holiday—"Workation", a model with a future?"). Always in the sense of the greatest possible flexibility for all involved and the conviction that employee satisfaction ("Employee-X") leads to customer satisfaction ("Customer-X"). Or as it is called at T-Systems: #Peoplemakeithappen.

References

1 ABR 22/21, 2022, https://www.bundesarbeitsgericht.de/presse/einfuehrung-elektronischer-zeiterfassung-initiativrecht-des-betriebsrats/ (abgerufen am 17.09.2022).

Hays, 2021, HR Report 2021: https://www.hays.de/documents/10192/118775/hays-hr-report-2021-new-work-de.pdf/5ed9a4bf-2cd6-beea-ed16-6662389005c6?t=1610717468553 (abgerufen am 22.09.2022).

Randstad, 2021, New Work Trendreport: https://www.randstad.de/s3fs-media/de/public/2021-10/randstad-new-work-trendreport-1.pdf (abgerufen am: 22.09.2022).

Thiede, R.; Buckler, A., 2020: Work-Life-Balance Meilenstein: https://www.bertelsmann-stiftung.de/fileadmin/files/BSt/Publikationen/GrauePublikationen/GP_Work-Life-Balance_Meilenstein.pdf (abgerufen am 22.09.2022).

Trust Vacation—"Unlimited" Vacation as Part of an Innovative Working World

Daniela Rindone

1 Introduction

There is no legal definition of trust-based vacation. Therefore, it is understood to mean that employees can independently and responsibly determine the number of their annual vacation days, as long as the completion of work and achievement of goals is ensured. In this construct, they are not bound by the company's specifications, if one understands the concept broadly. Instead, the vacation is granted on a trust basis. The experiences with this concept in the start-up scene and in technology companies are quite positive. However, the topic of trust-based vacation is also viewed critically. Especially in industries where skilled workers are desperately sought and there is immense time and cost pressure, the flexible vacation model could be disadvantageous and particularly lead to recovery times being used only to a limited extent. Living trust-based vacation "correctly" is not only in the sphere of responsibility of the employees. Employers are also asked to contribute—through clear framework conditions, an open corporate culture, and active control and remediation of grievances.

The Federal Vacation Act (*BUrlG*) regulates the legal minimum entitlement to recreational leave and does not contain any provisions on trust-based vacation. According to section 3 BUrlG, employees who work five days a week are entitled to at least 20 vacation days per year. So-called additional vacation, which is granted beyond the legal minimum entitlement, can be freely regulated by the

D. Rindone (✉)
CMS Deutschland, Köln, Germany
e-mail: daniela.rindone@cms-hs.com

I. Knappertsbusch and G. Wisskirchen (eds.), *The Future of Work*,
https://doi.org/10.1007/978-3-658-45150-9_16

parties to the employment contract.[1] Against this background, from a labor law perspective, the term "trust-based vacation" refers to the legal minimum vacation entitlement plus an (unlimited) additional vacation over the course of the year. The (theoretical) maximum limit of trust-based vacation is then determined by the working days of a calendar year.

2 Advantages of Trust-Based Vacation

Trust-based vacation can be a decisive marketing tool, especially for companies competing for skilled workers. It is seen as a new status symbol that is supposed to take into account the changed interests of employees, whose ideals are focused on autonomy and freedom. Companies thus present themselves as future-oriented and open to change employers. In addition, the administrative effort involved in applying for and recording vacation days is significantly reduced. Employees can also avoid additional work, as they do not have to make arrangements with the HR department and superiors if they decide when to take their vacation. The workforce freed up as a result can be used elsewhere in a meaningful way.

For employees, trust-based vacation means an increase in flexibility, freedom, personal responsibility, and above all: appreciation. At the same time, predominantly self-determined leisure time can contribute to a "more" of relaxation, as stress perception, need for rest, and regeneration are very individual. At the same time, a motivating work environment regularly leads to higher productivity and fewer sick leaves. In addition, the trust advance can strengthen the work relationship and lead to a higher identification with the company, and thus have a positive effect on the willingness to work and employee retention.

3 Challenges of this Form of Work

However, trust-based vacation also carries risks that the company must be aware of and for which it should take precautions.

3.1 Overload/Neglect of Contractual Work Obligations

Aside from legal concerns, it is particularly important to note that not every employee is capable of organizing themselves in such a way that the free allocation of their own vacation days, while simultaneously coordinating with the team and achieving agreed goals, works well. This can lead to conflicts within the workforce and thus have negative effects on the working atmosphere or group cohesion.

[1] Cf. BAG v. 4.5.2010 – 9 AZR 183/09, NZA 2010, 1011.

There is also concern about excessive, abusive use of trust-based vacation, for example when employees continuously fail to properly fulfill their contractual work obligations due to vacation.

3.2 Create and Promote Space for Self-Organization

On the other end of the spectrum is the fear that the trust advance builds additional pressure among employees and promotes comparative thinking. Especially in the context of high work(time)loads, employees adapt to the overload situation in companies by foregoing vacation. A recent survey by Glassdoor, a provider of information about jobs and companies, also shows that almost one in three German employees has already let vacation entitlements expire.[2] In extreme cases, this can lead to employees not taking any vacation at all, becoming ill, and being absent for a long time. For the success of the concept, it is crucial that managers lead by example and create a work atmosphere that encourages the use of vacation without inhibitions or even feelings of guilt.

3.3 Formulate Clear Framework Conditions

Employers must also keep an eye on the legal framework conditions. Without clear guidelines and transparent company handling, trust-based vacation cannot function successfully. With questions such as "How are work accidents handled when vacation and work time flow into each other and are possibly not sufficiently documented?", "How does the company prevent abuse?", "Does a trust-based vacation claim have to be compensated for upon termination?", "Can vacation claims be accumulated?" employers should deal with these issues early on and especially before introducing this vacation concept.

3.4 Collective Agreement Reservation/Operational Co-Determination

Legal concerns can also arise in the area of collective labor law, for example due to the necessity of carrying out a favorability comparison (see section 4 para. 3 Collective Agreement Act (*TVG*)) or in connection with the collective agreement reservation regulated in section 77 para. 3 Works Constitution Act (*BetrVG*). If there is a workers' representation in the company, the introduction and design of trust-based vacation must also take into account the participation rights of the works council.

---

[2] Glassdoor survey as of July 2022, n. v., hints available for example under Study: Vacation does not always lead to recovery—Personnel Economy (accessed on 24.10.2022).

4 Solutions and Practical Tips for Implementation

The "trust-based vacation" model is a construct that is not equally suitable for every company. It is also clear that there are industries (such as the care sector) or initial situations (such as low-threshold jobs) that—at least at first glance—appear less suitable for the introduction of trust-based vacation. Nevertheless, the benefit associated with trust-based vacation and the positive feedback in the workforce should not be underestimated. If the introduction of trust-based vacation is therefore considered, an explicit regulation should be made, which in particular regulates the following aspects. If an already implemented model is to be subjected to a critical review, the following hints are equally important:

4.1 Compatibility with Collective Labor Law

When agreeing on discretionary leave in individual contracts, any collective bargaining regulations must be taken into account.[3] According to section 4 para. 3 TVG, agreements that deviate from the legal norms of a collective agreement are only permissible if they are permitted by the collective agreement or contain a change in favor of the employees. If a comparison of favorability is necessary, the following should be noted:

- The comparison of favorability is only necessary if there is a statutory collective bargaining obligation. This presupposes that general applicability or mutual collective bargaining obligation exists according to section 3 para. 1 TVG and the employment relationship is covered by the scope of the collective agreement.
- If the collective bargaining obligation is established by contractual reference in the employment contract, no comparison of favorability is made.
- Whether the contractual regulation of discretionary leave is more favorable must be determined based on a comparison of subject groups.
- If it is not objectively and unequivocally ascertainable that the regulation deviating from the collective agreement is more favorable for the employees, which is the case with an ambivalent or neutral regulation, the mandatory validity of the collective agreement remains.

As a rule, one can assume the favorability of the individual contractual regulation for discretionary leave. This is certainly the case if the other regulations of the collective agreement, which concern the additional leave, its creation and transfer, as well as the payment of holiday pay and holiday money, are not changed, but are adopted without restriction. However, it is likely to be important that holiday

[3] See also Gaul/Kaule, BB 2022, 757., 757 f.

money, if this is paid in addition to holiday pay, is fully paid out as soon as the conditions specified for this are met with reference to the holiday provided for in the collective agreement. The fact that the granting of discretionary leave can in individual cases also lead to less leave being taken than would be the case with the agreement of a specific amount does not contradict the favorability, since abstract regulations are decisive, not the result of their application in individual cases.[4] If and insofar as this does not violate binding provisions of a collective agreement (section 4 para. 3 TVG), discretionary leave should be depicted in the individual contract in case of doubt. This also avoids a further discussion about the collective agreement reservation in section 77 para. 3 BetrVG.

If discretionary leave is to be regulated by a works agreement, the following must be observed: In the case of a collective introduction, the "whether" of discretionary leave, i.e. the basic decision on the granting of discretionary leave, is not subject to co-determination at company level. This is a voluntary service by the employer that cannot be enforced. However, when determining the "how", i.e. the detailed content design of this leave construct, the works council must be involved. In this respect, it is at least a matter of establishing general holiday principles according to section 87 para. 1 no. 5 BetrVG, which requires the co-determination of the employee representatives. As soon as regulations for the use of discretionary leave are to be made, this requires a prior (!) agreement with the works council.

4.2 Contractual Differentiation of Minimum and Additional Leave/Documentation

To avoid the Federal Holiday Act and the directive-compliant interpretation of Directive 2003/88/EC[5] being applied to additional leave, it should differentiate between minimum leave and additional leave in the employment contract or in an additional employment contract agreement and clarify that the entitlement to statutory minimum leave remains unaffected by the possibility of discretionary leave. To ensure the fulfillment of the statutory holiday entitlement, it should also be regulated that taken leave is first credited to the statutory holiday and only after its fulfillment to the additional leave.

In addition, documentation of the use of minimum leave should ensure that this is adhered to, also to avoid overloading employees. The documentation obligation can also be transferred to the employees, although the employer should regularly check this.[6]

---

[4] BAG v. 5.4.2015 – 4 AZR 587/13, NZA 2015, 1247 Rz. 29.

[5] Directive 2003/88/EC of the European Parliament and of the Council of 4.11.2003 on certain aspects of the organization of working time.

[6] So also Niklas, ArbRB 2022, 211, 213.

4.3 Providing for Differentiated Expiry Clauses

Under no circumstances should a provision be waived that stipulates the additional vacation expires at the end of the year. Otherwise, there is the not to be underestimated risk that unused vacation days will accumulate to a considerable extent and can lead to a significant compensation claim when the employment relationship is terminated. A corresponding clause should therefore provide that

- regulations deviating from the minimum vacation regulations apply with regard to the expiry of additional vacation;
- the additional vacation generally expires at the end of the calendar year;
- this applies even if the employer has not given the employee any corresponding notice and has not requested the vacation to be taken.[7]

4.4 No Compensation for Trust Vacation

Employees with trust vacation could assert that they are entitled to a vacation claim for each working day on which the employment relationship existed and that this—if it has not expired through fulfillment—is to be compensated. Then, especially in the case of longer company affiliation, considerable payments are at stake. To avoid this, it should be clarified to what extent a compensation of the vacation claim theoretically due to the employee is possible. Outside of a statutory collective agreement, the trust vacation can be completely excluded from compensation.[8] If there is a statutory collective agreement, from which deviations can only be made in favor of the employees due to section 4 para. 3 TVG, the compensation should be limited to the collective agreement's additional vacation claim.[9]

A regulation on compensation becomes particularly important against the background of the decision of the European Court of Justice (*ECJ*) issued on 22.09.2022.[10] In it, the ECJ ruled that compensation for vacation days only fails due to the expiration of vacation claims if the employer has ensured that the employee could actually take his vacation claim.

4.5 Providing Framework Guidelines for Determining Vacation

Even if one wants to understand the construct of trust vacation broadly and maximally flexibly, it is advisable to regulate possibilities of influence by the employer.

[7] Cf. in this regard BAG v. 26.5.2020 – 9 AZR 259/19, NZA 2020, 1416 para. 22.

[8] BAG v. 4.5.2010 – 9 AZR 183/09, NZA 2010, 1011 para. 23.

[9] Cf. also Gaul/Kaule, BB 2022, 757, 759.

[10] ECJ v. 22.9.2022 – C-120/21 (LB/TO), NZA 2022, 1326.

For example, it could be provided that the company reserves the right to set different guidelines under certain conditions to be determined in more detail in order to ensure proper operational processes. In addition, it could be agreed that maximum limits per vacation period or minimum staffing levels of the employees remaining in the company during the vacation are necessary.

4.6 Exclusion of Trust Vacation in Certain Case Constellations

In the interest of the company, it is also sensible to set at least some limits to vacation freedom. An exclusion during the probationary period therefore seems appropriate in order to ensure the necessary trial period. It is also advisable to exclude trust vacation after notice has been given. Otherwise, a proper handover cannot be guaranteed. In addition, such a clarification can prevent employees from unilaterally taking leave for the duration of the notice period, and at the same time ensure that such an agreement remains the subject of termination negotiations.

The taking of trust vacation should also be excluded in connection with illness. The background to this is that section 3 para. 1 EFZG only provides for a claim to continued payment of wages for a period of six weeks in the event of illness. Sick employees could therefore be tempted without a corresponding regulation to take vacation instead of further sick leave, even though they are still unfit for work. This could achieve unlimited wage continuation, although only a claim to sick pay actually exists during this time. The same applies following statutory maternity protection or for the duration of parental leave.

4.7 Prevention of Abuse/Right of Revocation

In court proceedings, it is likely to be difficult for the company to prove when the threshold for excessive use of trust vacation has been exceeded. Therefore, it seems sensible to subject the use of it to at least certain rules, e.g. by limiting the contiguous vacation period, specifying a period that must lie between two vacations and/or the maximum duration of a vacation. In addition to this, it could be agreed that trust vacation that goes beyond a certain period is dependent on the explicit consent of the supervisor. Then the existence of a contract-violating use of trust vacation would be concretized and thus the implementation or enforcement of employer sanctions facilitated. It would also be advisable to regulate a right of revocation. However, such a right of revocation is only effective if the reasons for revocation are expressly regulated in the agreement itself.

5 Summary and Outlook

Trust-based vacation will continue to gain importance, especially in the battle for qualified and motivated professionals. Instead of material wealth, freedom and autonomy are becoming the focus of employee interests. Additional, freely selectable vacation days as an alternative model to salary increases or special payments are becoming increasingly important. And companies can also benefit from higher productivity and motivation of employees. To prevent or limit abuse, there are a multitude of contractual design options. Above all, clear, careful agreements are important to avoid ambiguities, disputes, and the associated burdens.

References

Gaul, Björn/Kaule, Victoria, Unbegrenzter Urlaub statt Geld – Vertrauensurlaub als Zeichen kultureller Veränderungen, BB (BetriebsBerater) 2022, 757–761.

Niklas, Lisa-Marie, Vertrauensurlaub als Urlaubsmodell für die Zukunft? Chancen, Risiken und sinnvoller Gestaltungsrahmen, ArbRB (Arbeits-Rechtsberater) 2022, 211–214.

Free Time Management with the workSPACE Concept—A Model for More Personal Freedom and Efficiency in the Home Office, Remote and In-Person

Julia Schmidbauer, Karsten Lohmeyer and Stephan Goldmann

1 Introduction

"Nine to five"—this idea of working hours has dictated the actions of employers and employees for decades. Agencies, too, have lived this idea of fixed working hours between 9 a.m. and 5 p.m. Perhaps often more "nine to five plus plus", as it was not uncommon to work well into the night when an important project was pending.

The "nine to five" model has its merits. After all, it's easier to work during the day. Everyone is present at roughly the same time, can coordinate directly, and participate in conferences. The fixed working hours are reliable and support work-life balance.

So, what should replace this model, and why?

Well, nothing SHOULD replace the model. It is more about not imposing the "nine-to-five" model without a choice and adapting it to the requirements (and the technical possibilities) of today's times. That is why sayang.gmbh has decided to offer the model of flexitime with free work time allocation. In short: employees choose when they work.

J. Schmidbauer · K. Lohmeyer (✉) · S. Goldmann
München, Germany
e-mail: karsten.lohmeyer@sayang.gmbh

J. Schmidbauer
e-mail: julia.schmidbauer@sayang.gmbh

S. Goldmann
e-mail: stephan.goldmann@sayang.gmbh

I. Knappertsbusch and G. Wisskirchen (eds.), *The Future of Work*,
https://doi.org/10.1007/978-3-658-45150-9_17

Closely linked to the model of free work time allocation is the free choice of workplace. Although sayang.gmbh has its headquarters in Munich, the employees work in Hamburg, Cologne and Landsberg and sometimes abroad (see the article "Work from anywhere—The free choice of workplace"). This last international component also only works if workers can sensibly adjust their times themselves, since there is often a time difference. It is a form of empowerment with high personal responsibility.

This freedom has its charms, but requires clear rules to establish fairness among employees and not to endanger the company's effectiveness. In addition, these freedoms are accompanied by the loss of an identity that the workplace easily provides, such as a gate with a company logo through which workers stream in the morning. There is no longer a coffee counter with cups bearing the company motto and no office.

Giving up a common working time at a common workplace must therefore be accompanied by a new definition of company values. Sayang.gmbh has developed its own answer to this. The workSPACE concept.

2 Advantages of this Form of Work

Employers are currently finding it difficult to hire suitable employees. Even though many older employees are keen to return to the central workplace after the pandemic, the disruption caused by COVID-19 has made the younger generations even more self-confident—they demand new working time models that are adapted to their digital lifestyle and desire for personal freedom.

In the USA, this is noticeable through a high departure of important employees which burdens the local labor landscape. "Great Attrition"(1) is what McKinsey calls this phenomenon, or also "Big Quit".

Many employees, according to McKinsey, have taken the pandemic as an opportunity to reorient themselves. They are now paying more attention to their mental health and personal desires and want to feel valued.

The answer lies in high flexibility and autonomy: working when and where you want. This flexibility, along with fair pay and a belief in the purpose of one's actions drives the younger generations. Generations Z and Y, in particular, have made it very clear in recent years how important flexibility and purpose in working life are to them, writes the British HR consultancy UKG in their blog. Even within the same organization, different expectations of the employer can be identified at the generational boundaries. In a study by the University of Bucharest, about 26% of the respondents belonging to Generation Z stated that flexible working hours and the possibility of working from home were among the top criteria when choosing a job.

According to Brad Stulberg, there are three desires among employees: autonomy or at least some control over how one uses one's time and energy. Mastery of specific skills combined with the feeling of concrete progress. Belonging to a community or community.

So if companies want to recruit qualified specialists in the future, flexible working hours should be included in the offer to avoid a disadvantage in the job market.

However, there is another reason why employers could use this model profitably. Especially in the service sector and creative field, there are peak loads in working hours, for example when a project is nearing completion. The company can react to this and easily reduce the resulting overtime. In addition, the remote work concept—especially in COVID-19 times—continues to protect against employees infecting each other.

At the same time, the difference between "part-time" and "full-time" contracts is eliminated when hiring. At least in perception, because of course there is a legal difference between (flexibly designed) working hours and hourly pay. Nevertheless: The opinion spread by the Bild newspaper in its campaign against the new Munich IT consultant Laura Dornheim, that only full-time employees "count fully" and 40-hour employees are more valuable and experienced than those with fewer hours, is at least refuted by sayang.gmbh.

Flexitime with free work scheduling is just one manifestation of the new desire of many employees for more flexibility in the job. The other, especially fueled by the experience of the COVID-19 pandemic, is the desire for the free choice of workplace.

An international survey by PWC from 2022 found that three out of ten employees worldwide would like to work completely remote (Germany: 42%), 19% predominantly remote (Germany: 22%) and 19% at least half remote. Only 13% would prefer to work exclusively in -person (Germany: 5%) according to the study.

It is now increasingly common for parents to show themselves in video conferences with a sleeping toddler in their arms.

After the years in which burnout played a major role, awareness for mental health and fitness has now moved to the forefront, as the aforementioned study by McKinsey shows. The free choice of location and time also addresses this important aspect. Employees can go to the gym asynchronously or jog or walk the dog at any time. Something that the employees of sayang.gmbh often use. Even visiting the doctor becomes easier with the free work schedule.

Sayang.gmbh has implemented this and goes one step further: If it turns out that employees are working too much and accumulating overtime, we actively approach the affected employees and develop a strategy together on how to prevent excessive workloads and quickly reduce overtime.

The company thus ensures that the team maintains the necessary recovery phases and supports this without prescribing service times or core working hours.

3 Challenges of this Form of Work

Naturally, the combination of choosing any location and flexible time management demands a lot from companies. These are new forms of work. The legal situation is inadequately adapted—and particularly difficult to understand for smaller companies without their own HR and legal departments.

For example, what happens if employees break their foot on the way from the study to the children's room is not as clearly regulated as if employees move from the company office to the company toilet.

In addition, companies are obliged to check working hours and workplaces for compliance with legal rules. After all, time recording on the computer is not really a problem; there is plenty of software. However, employers must ensure that the main workplace is ergonomic when working from home. This means someone has to visit employees and check a possible telework place for compliance with ergonomic guidelines. Although this does not apply if mobile work is agreed upon, responsible employers should pay attention to this as far as possible.

There is another disadvantage of remote work: If many employees work at a different place and at a different time, the coordination of meetings and agreements becomes much more complex. The effort for the team and managers increases; communication and processes require an agile approach. Not every company offers the necessary framework that takes into account the needs of the company and its stakeholders on the one hand, and the flexible and location-independent working methods of the employees on the other.

Surprisingly, this does not have to be formulated in detail and managed "top-down". It is enough to define certain guidelines within the framework. The experience of sayang.gmbh shows that self-managed teams, in cooperation with a supportive leadership, solve many of these problems among themselves, often with more finesse and fairness than a supervisor can manage. However, this requires that the company management supports, trains and trusts the team members—or in modern terms, "enables" them.

Companies solve all the technical challenges through careful planning and the use of appropriate software. But when many workers work at different times and in different places, another problem emerges: How do you create and live company culture? What gives people a sense of belonging? Do employees still feel part of a common company and identify with it?

Even worse: If some go to the office and others stay at home, do separate bubbles form? Do those in the office then belong to the "inner circle"? The danger exists.

Another major challenge is the employers themselves. Because as a company, you have to be ready for work detached from space and time. Some larger international companies are marching in exactly the opposite direction, wanting to return completely to the model before the pandemic.

Elon Musk, for example, wrote to his employees at Tesla that everyone must spend at least 40 hours a week in the company's offices. Anyone who does not appear at the workplaces specified by Tesla will be treated as if they had resigned.

Amazon and Apple initially saw it similarly harshly. But here the workforce has prevailed. After Amazon wanted to order a complete return of employees to the offices after the end of the COVID-19 restrictions, Amazon CEO Andy Jassy backpedaled in September 2022. At the Code Conference in Los Angeles, he explained that Amazon would not force anyone to return to the office. Instead, they wanted to adopt an adaptive approach and leave it to individual managers to regulate the attendance requirement in the areas they are responsible for.

Amazon and Apple are now running hybrid models. On some days attendance is mandatory; on others work can be done outside the office.

4 Solutions and Practical Tips

The sayang.gmbh has found a solution for the challenges of complete remote work with free time management. The workSPACE concept lays a set of values as a basis for the company, essentially a constitution that—if formulated and lived correctly—creates the necessary identification with the operation. workSPACE is an acronym for "work Support, Purpose, Appreciation, Culture, Environment".

4.1 The workSPACE Concept of sayang.gmbh

Support

The sayang.workspace is the platform on which the teams pursue their goals quickly and with minimal obstacles.

For this we build:

- *a knowledge space that we use together*
- *reliable and lean processes*
- *empathy between team members*
- *"We've got your back and you've got ours"*
- *a common space for questions and solutions*
- *a center for education and learning*

Purpose (Goals)

We clearly communicate our goals and share them. These goals are in line with personal beliefs and a shared sense of responsibility for our world.

Therefore, we ensure:

- *transparent leadership*
- *a common code of conduct*
- *the pursuit of meaningful work*
- *best intentions towards our customers*
- *the pursuit of the best outcome*
- *a healthy balance between performance and recovery*
- *a pursuit of excellence*

Appreciation (Valuation)

Different types of people mean different ways of working and communicating.

Therefore, we support:

- *the transparency of different workflows*
- *fair and helpful feedback to learn from*
- *the celebration of failures and successes*
- *rewarding work through financial participation in success*
- *patience on the way to results*

Culture

The interaction between all members contributes to the functionality of the team. Our culture ensures the opportunity for personal development.

Therefore, we acknowledge:

- *showing weakness is not a weakness*
- *empathetic communication should be non-violent*
- *the need for undisturbed concentration times*
- *communication should be as precise as possible*
- *balanced times for meeting participants*
- *an attitude of creativity and inspiration*
- *patience towards others and results*
- *resilience through the acceptance of best intentions*

Environment

Even if there is no brick and mortar office holding the company together, there is still a common working environment.

Therefore, we offer:

- *funding for mobile work*
- *creating a shielded, secure space*
- *high-performance hardware*
- *the best software in the industry*
- *support for physical and mental health*

However, adopting the concept is not enough. At sayang.gmbh, there are therefore several roles that create and monitor the foundations and processes for the workSPACE.

The Chief Happiness Officer is a point of contact for personal and communicative matters. They are specifically not part of the operational leadership, but of the human resources department. Supportive Leaders flank the teams and promote the initiative for self-management. Together, they create the “spaces” in which employees work, chat informally (so-called Fikas—remote coffee rounds according to the Swedish model), or make arrangements in the form of meetings.

In addition, at sayang.gmbh, there is the opportunity to meet during work via video conferencing system and work as if sharing an office. So it does not even have to be the same project, but you keep each other company, can make some small talk, or clarify short-term questions. We call this co-working.

5 Summary and Outlook

At sayang.gmbh, we believe: If companies couple flexible working hours with the freedom to choose the workplace, they not only meet the job needs of many people, but they also expand their catchment area beyond their location.

The prerequisite for this is a set of rules and tools that go hand in hand with focused leadership.

In this approach, we are not alone. Petra Justenhoven, spokesperson for the management of PwC Germany, also says that managers need to find answers to questions about personnel management and customer communication that arise from hybrid working.

Especially for the younger generations, flextime with free work schedule and free choice of workplace will not only gain in importance—we believe it will even become a basic requirement.

References

McKinsey & Company: 'Great Attrition' or 'Great Attraction'? The choice is yours, https://www.mckinsey.com/capabilities/people-and-organizational-performance/our-insights/great-attrition-or-great-attraction-the-choice-is-yours

UKG: The Antidote to the Great Resignation. https://www.ukg.co.uk/blog/what-works-uk/antidote-great-resignation

Laut Brad Stulberg, Autor des Buchs "The Practice of Groundedness: A Transformative Path to Success That Feeds – Not Crushes – Your Soul", https://bstulberg.medium.com/the-truth-about-quiet-quitting-b4f90d5d1b94

Work Organization

Flexible Workforce: The Role of Freelancers in the Workforce of the Future

Daniel Barke

1 Introduction

1.1 Why it's Worth Rethinking Talent

Almost 75% of all C-level managers are convinced that the use of freelancers will continue to increase slightly or significantly by 2023. This is suggested by a study conducted at Harvard Business School in 2020. Only two out of ten executives believe that the use will decrease partially or significantly (see Fuller et al., 2020). A future without freelancers seems hardly conceivable. But what role will they play?

Our time is characterized by challenges: On the one hand, the rapid technological revolution is driving the demand for skilled workers. In addition, demographic transformation and the accompanying value change of younger generations make it increasingly difficult for companies to find and retain employees. The chronically difficult search for the right workforce was already one of the hotly debated topics in pre-Covid times, for which solutions had to be found with new work tools.

Approaches such as deregulation and more agile working models (see the article "Agile Working") experienced a real boom due to the coronavirus pandemic. Suddenly, companies were forced to find answers and new ways within weeks or even days. After initial difficulties of many companies to lead their employees remotely, the crisis turned out to be a driver for digitization in medium-sized businesses. The integration of freelancers was also made easier by the improved

D. Barke (✉)
WorkGenius GmbH, New York, USA
e-mail: db@workgenius.com

I. Knappertsbusch and G. Wisskirchen (eds.), *The Future of Work*,
https://doi.org/10.1007/978-3-658-45150-9_18

infrastructure, which further promoted the disruption of traditional working models. The concept of permanent full-time employment has apparently run its course; it's time for dynamic, hybrid models. Building a smart on-demand workforce could, for example, be the key to competitiveness and the answer to new work questions. So, what could the workforce of the future look like?

1.2 A new form of work—On-Demand

Freelancers: These are independent workers who perform tasks for clients without being employees of the client. When a company integrates several freelancers into internal processes and projects as needed, this is understood as an on-demand workforce. The staff is expanded by the use of freelancers. And scalable and individually deployable; depending on the time and professional needs.

Freelancing is and remains a trend worth investing in. And this is not only underlined by the steadily increasing numbers of freelancers worldwide. A look at the upward trend in market development of talent platforms (see Fuller et al., 2020) also reveals that the demand for flexible workers is growing. In recent years, several large companies have already recognized the advantages of hybrid working models and laid the foundation for cooperation with freelancers. Already now, 60% of CEOs consider it very likely to work with a significantly smaller core workforce in the future. Instead, they prefer to supplement their fixed teams with flexible talents that they "borrow" or "share" with other companies (see Fuller et al., 2020). To find suitable freelancers for project-related or task-oriented work, companies use digital talent platforms like Upwork, WorkGenius, Freelance DE or InnoCentive. These connect the client directly with qualified freelancers and thus greatly simplify the search.

2 Advantages of this Form of Work

2.1 Agility and Cost Efficiency

Faster, further, higher? More agile, flexible, scalable—especially the scalable integration of flexible workers increases cost efficiency and competitiveness on the company side. And not only because items such as the provision of an additional workplace, equipment, training, and social benefits for a permanent employee are eliminated.

An on-demand workforce also enlarges the pool of highly qualified, immediately available labor. Temporarily expanding the existing team with a talent, instead of permanently filling a position, promotes agility. Managing a larger workload—in the same time, with constant fixed costs—is no problem for the company. Especially in times when the economic situation is uncertain, the scalable use of freelancers can counteract fluctuations in sales. It also facilitates the management of resources depending on seasonality or economic cycles. The use of freelancers represents an opportunity for entrepreneurial freedom—and at clearly calculable costs.

2.2 At the Pulse of Time

Through their work in various companies and fields of activity, freelancers bring a wealth of experience, individual skill sets, and new approaches to solutions. Their range of cross-industry knowledge enhances a company's ability to innovate. Permanent employees also benefit from the expertise of freelancers: If specialist knowledge is not represented within the team, an expert from the global network can provide a solution. This ensures a smooth project process and increases the productivity of the entire team.

With new perspectives and impulses, freelancers also bring a breath of fresh air to the corporate culture and counteract operational blindness. The cooperation closes qualification gaps and creates fertile ground for innovative business models.

2.3 Value Change and the Desire for New Work

More life than work, mental health, and autonomy: The priorities of Generation Y and Generation Z are changing (see Anonymous, 2022). Digital Natives no longer define satisfaction solely in terms of monetary values, their motivation is increasingly intrinsic. They desire meaningful activities as well as individuality and expect diversity, sustainability, and inclusion in their work environment (see Perna, 2022). Covid-19 has also influenced the desires of the labor market's newcomers: Fears for the future as well as the dominant concern about climate change and their own mental health shape the young generations. Thus, their greatest wish as early as the beginning of 2022 was for shorter working hours—closely followed by more flexibility and remote work (see Anonymous, 2022). It will foreseeably become more difficult to make full-time standard employment attractive to bind Millennials and "Zoomers". Freelancing can be a good alternative here.

Layoffs during the coronavirus pandemic also fuel the rising numbers of freelancers. More than half of these "new" freelancers see a long-term career opportunity in their new occupation and do not want to return to their original profession. Because for many, freelancing means: freedom. It allows them to fulfill their desire for individual life designs, variety, and self-realization.

3 Challenges of this Form of Work

3.1 Lack of Technical Infrastructure

Incorporating external talents into personnel strategies takes time. It is not surprising that early adopters mainly include established corporations such as Amazon,

Royal Dutch Shell, and Unilever (see Fuller et al., 2020). For fundamentally progressive medium-sized companies, the threshold is higher, as missing processes make collaboration with freelancers inefficient for them. Acquisition, verification of respective qualifications, onboarding, and compliance: selection, management, and handling of flexible workers lead to a significant additional effort on the part of the company. Also, the risk of pseudo self-employment and the associated legal regulations are aspects that both employers and employees must keep in mind.

3.2 Foreign Corporate Culture

On-demand economy also means: Little room for training and integration of the freelancer into the corporate culture (see the article "Corporate Culture—How the Culture of a Company Determines Success or Failure"). Flexible workers bring a wealth of experience, but they have little to no knowledge about the specific product or the company's goals. Especially in traditionally managed companies, a freelancer may therefore take longer to understand the customer's needs.

There are complex workflows that require industry knowledge or knowledge of internal programs or tools. Getting used to these takes a lot of time. Also, especially in industries like banking and FinTech, NDAs and confidentiality can prove to be a difficulty when it comes to handling company-internal confidential information such as salaries or customer data. A permanent employee is subject to the confidentiality obligation of a single company. However, if freelancers work for various companies, they repeatedly come into contact with new confidential information. This makes NDA management a time-consuming and bureaucratic additional burden for the client.

3.3 Security and Downsides

The talent also incurs a significant additional effort through the search for suitable assignments, applications, and acquisition. Generating a predictable income is laborious—as is building a network to get assignments. Self-marketing and social selling take time and may have more weight in job allocation than the talent's skills.

Especially the younger generations have fears of the future due to the fear of rising living costs and further crises. They are looking for flexibility and meaningfulness, but at the same time long for economic security and consistency in the job (see Anonymous, 2022). Pure freelancing is a risky profession—especially when it comes to social security. There is still a lack of sustainable regulations regarding social benefits and social protection for freelancers. Also, on the rocky road to "employee sharing" and hybrid, fluid earning situations, there is still much to do: Currently, it is not legally possible to work "permanently" for more than two employers at the same time. Employees are generally allowed to perform several activities at the same time, but the Working Time Act complicates implementation in practice. Because apart from the fact that the prescribed total working time of eight hours per day must not be exceeded, eleven hours of rest must be maintained between working days.

4 Solutions and Practical Tips

4.1 Gig Economy through Technology

Gig economy (see the article "Crowdworking/Platform Work—Revolution of the Labor Market?") is more than a New Work buzzword—it also determines everyday life. Whether it's food delivery, transportation, choosing a pet sitter, or assembling the kitchen cabinet: For consumers, on-demand gig work is a given. Orders are organized intuitively and clearly via the respective platforms. With the help of technology, time and resources can also be saved in building an on-demand workforce. The steadily growing number of digital job matching platforms offers companies and contractors an interface for collaboration.

And it promises success: Almost 90% of the managers surveyed in a Harvard study are confident that the platform economy will continue to bring significant competitive advantages to their company (see Fuller et al., 2020). Being able to access highly qualified freelancers increased the go-to-market speed, productivity, and innovation capability of their operation, according to 40% of executives. IT expert, copywriter, lawyer, or art director: Specialists for individual needs can be found on online platforms.

Such marketplaces greatly facilitate the selection process and handling. Especially for orders that require specific industry knowledge, it is important to find the optimal workforce—and that is based on skills. Whether the matching is done manually or via rating systems and customer satisfaction or AI-based technology (see WorkGenius, 2022), collaboration is booming.

4.2 Holistic Integration

Efficient collaboration between permanent employees and flexible talents is essential for building an on-demand workforce. Only when all participants see cooperation as an opportunity and meet on an equal footing can they achieve common goals as a team. Therefore, a change in corporate culture towards a comprehensive integration of freelancers is needed. In addition, internal processes, guidelines, and policies must be adapted. Removing possible technical and legal hurdles, such as the protection of intellectual property, paves the way for quick onboarding and familiarization of the freelancer with the corporate culture.

In many companies, it has been commonplace since Covid-19 to lead teams remotely or in a hybrid manner (see the article "The Role of Executives in Hybrid Work—All New or Old Hat?"). Nevertheless, it may be worthwhile to retrain HR managers at the management level in recruiting and leadership. It is important that they are able to bring geographically separated teams together in a good working atmosphere. Once freelancers are accepted as support for the core team, success and synergy in this constellation can be redefined.

4.3 Hidden Potential through Datafication

To find suitable talents as quickly as possible, it helps to break down projects into smaller tasks. Also, setting clear main and intermediate goals provides an overview: What skills are needed to complete a project and which are perhaps already represented in the permanent team? Assuming that management knows its employees and their skills well, the clear structure helps in the next step to determine the need for freelancers as well as time expenditure and workload. This makes the order well planned for both the client and the talent.

Another advantage of this "datafication" of work: By segmenting into small project areas, freelance technology can be transferred to the management of internal employees. Employees can work on specific subtasks with unimagined or unused skills, even if their main focus lies elsewhere. The potential of permanent employees and freelancers is managed via a platform—and hidden capacities of companies are thus optimally used.

4.4 Pilot Projects—With Courage to Experiment

Building an on-demand workforce doesn't have to be a leap into the unknown. Conducting pilot projects helps to experiment and weigh up opportunities and risks. The foundation for successful collaboration with flexible workers is to draw from one's own potentials. For example, those who invested in adapting the company's internal technical infrastructure during Covid-19 can now use it for collaboration with freelancers. Which processes already work well and where is there a need for action? The example of Covid-19 also made clear how dynamic and capable of action the working world can be. When companies were forced to rethink, the breeding ground for new processes was created. Integrating innovative forms of employment and making them the norm is therefore just a question of willingness to experiment.

4.5 Framework Conditions and Social Benefits

New, hybrid forms of work are on the rise. If in the future job and employee sharing or crowdworking (see the article "Crowdworking/Platform Work—Revolution of the Labor Market?") replace the traditional concept of full-time employment, a reform of labor and social law is also needed. Because in times of platform economy, gig economy, and mixed teams, the boundaries between permanent employees and freelancers are blurring. New terminologies and rule sets need to be created to improve the framework conditions for freelancers in the labor market.

5 Summary and Outlook

5.1 Exchange Means Growth

A future without freelancers is unthinkable and the shift towards more diversity and flexibility in the world of work is unstoppable. Larger numbers of qualified freelancers on the market meet companies that have a high demand for specialists to cover. The work form of the future is called: On-Demand Workforces. Matching platforms provide a blueprint for networking, from which both clients and contractors benefit equally.

It is clear that with the interest in collaborating with flexible workers, the demand for online talent marketplaces is also increasing and that these will play a significant role in filling the current skills gap. The market development speaks volumes: in 2009 there were only 80 job matching platforms, in 2014 already 190 and by 2019 the number rose to about 330 worldwide. Investment also increased from 180 million US dollars in 2009 to 1.9 billion in 2019 (see Fuller et al., 2020).

To remain future-proof, building an On-Demand Workforce is essential. The digital infrastructure of the working world 4.0 (see the article "When digital meets demographic change—What opportunities and risks does digital transformation pose in a shrinking and aging working population?") makes the realization of non-precarious employment models simply possible. Why do HR departments still often have reservations about this type of recruitment? Whether the integration of freelancers also makes the leap to HR topics in traditional industries largely depends on whether obsolete ways of thinking are adapted.

Hybrid forms of employment increase competitiveness. In addition to new ways of working and legal frameworks, acceptance is becoming the keyword. Because if company management and management recognize the opportunities of working with freelancers and integrate them holistically into their teams, companies can tap into entirely new potentials. Need-oriented On-Demand culture and global networking determine the societal present. Transferring these ideas into the world of work paves the way for a fluid, flexible future. A future in which cooperation, meaningfulness, networking and agility are paramount. Because exchange means growth.

References

Fuller, Joseph B. et al. (November 2020). *Building the on-demand workforce*. Harvard Business School und BCG.

Anonymous (2022), *Deloitte Global 2022 Gen Z and Millennial Survey, Country Profile: Germany,* Deloitte Global DTTL.

WorkGenius (2022). Homepage: https://www.workgenius.com/de/ (abgerufen am 21.09.2022).

Perna, Mark C. (Mai 2022), 5 *Ways That Satisfying The Gen Z Workforce Can Help Every Other Working Generation*. Forbes. https://www.forbes.com/sites/markcperna/2022/05/12/5-ways-that-satisfying-the-gen-z-workforce-can-help-every-other-working-generation/?sh=6fa73bce6110 (abgerufen am 25.10.2022).

Platform Work: Revolution of the Labor Market?

Kira Falter and Arne Schmieke

1 Introduction

Platform work (also known as crowdworking or crowdsourcing) refers to a type of work assignment via (mostly digital) platforms. Companies outsource small-scale work packages or even entire projects by offering tasks on a platform which platform workers then perform against payment. The allocation of these tasks (or "gigs") to crowdworkers via the platform is regularly facilitated by algorithmic systems which seek to find the most efficient and convenient solution for (end-) customers. The tasks offered vary considerably in terms of the achievable hourly wage, depending on their scope and level of difficulty. Crowdworking is used for simple, small-scale tasks (e.g., categorizing photos), but also for highly specialized activities, especially in the IT sector. Sometimes tasks have to be performed at a certain location (e.g., food deliveries), but many can also be carried out at any location (e.g., programming).

This chapter will delve deeper into specific labor law implications of the new EU directive on platform work, its current status in Germany, and the potential consequences for both workers and platform operators.

K. Falter (✉) · A. Schmieke
CMS Deutschland, Köln, Germany
e-mail: kira.falter@cms-hs.com

A. Schmieke
e-mail: arne.schmieke@cms-hs.de

I. Knappertsbusch and G. Wisskirchen (eds.), *The Future of Work*,
https://doi.org/10.1007/978-3-658-45150-9_19

1.1 Platform Work in Numbers

In the EU, more than 28 million people work via one (or more) digital labor platforms. This figure is expected to rise to 43 million by 2025.[1] Around 500 digital labor platforms are active in the EU throughout all Member States.[2] The growth of this sector is demonstrated by the fact that revenues from the platform economy in the EU increased almost fivefold between 2016 and 2020, from an estimated €3 billion to around €14 billion.[3]

It is estimated that the greatest revenue streams will be generated in the areas of delivery and cab services.

According to a study commissioned by the German Federal Ministry of Labor and Social Affairs (*Bundesministerium für Arbeit und Soziales*) there are 3 million crowdworkers in Germany.[4]

1.2 EU Directive on Platform Work

The EU is currently working on a directive concerning platform work to address various labor rights issues associated with the gig economy.[5] This directive seeks to establish clearer definitions and protections for workers engaged in platform-based jobs, ensuring fair treatment, adequate working conditions, and information as well as access to social security benefits. In Germany, the anticipated impact of this directive includes enhanced job security for crowdworkers, improved transparency regarding their rights and the use of their personal data, and a more equitable labor market. As the country navigates the complexities of integrating these new regulations into national law, the resulting changes are likely to shape the future landscape of platform work, balancing innovation with the protection of workers' rights.

In Germany, the implementation of this directive is particularly significant given the country's robust labor laws and the growing prevalence of platform work. The German government is currently in the process of aligning national regulations with the EU framework, focusing on key areas such as the classification

---

[1] EU rules on platform work, available at: https://www.consilium.europa.eu/en/policies/platform-work-eu/ (accessed 27 August 2024).

[2] EU rules on platform work, available at: https://www.consilium.europa.eu/en/policies/platform-work-eu/ (accessed 27 August 2024).

[3] EU rules on platform work, available at: https://www.consilium.europa.eu/en/policies/platform-work-eu/ (accessed 27 August 2024).

[4] BMAS, Faire Arbeit in der Plattformökonomie, available at: https://www.denkfabrik-bmas.de/fileadmin/Downloads/eckpunkte-faire-plattformarbeit_1_.pdf (accessed 27 August 2024).

[5] The interim version published on 8 March 2024, available at: https://data.consilium.europa.eu/doc/document/ST-7212-2024-ADD-1/en/pdf (accessed 27 August 2024).

of workers, the right to collective bargaining, and the provision of essential benefits.

It is currently expected that the directive on platform work will go through the "corrigendum procedure".[6] This means that errors have been identified in the version of the text that was adopted by Parliament, which are still being corrected. The Parliament will vote on the corrected version first (after it has been reformed), and then the Council will adopt it at first reading. Once this legislative process is concluded, the German legislator will have to transpose the directive into German law.

2 Benefits of This Form of Work

Crowdworking offers great opportunities for both companies, and crowdworkers. Companies benefit from the enormous flexibility. In times of skilled labor shortages, platform work provides an efficient way to manage fluctuating order volumes.[7] It also speeds up processes and relieves the burden on the company's own workforce, for example by outsourcing small-scale tasks. The high number of potential contractors, who can cover different specializations, creates an enormous pool of knowledge. This is why many well-known companies use this form of work.

For crowdworkers, the work is extremely flexible and self-determined.[8] They are free to decide whether, when and for whom they fulfill orders. Moreover, crowdworking operates on an egalitarian basis. Since most tasks no longer require presence at a specific location or adherence to fixed working hours, numerous new opportunities have emerged for many interested parties to participate in the workforce.

This relatively new form of work also poses risks for crowdworkers. The remuneration for tasks is often lower than in the context of an employment relationship.[9] Due to the frequent classification of external crowdworkers as self-employed, there is a lack of corresponding social security.

Not only for the companies, but also for the crowdworkers, it is often unclear which law they are subject to and thus whether any minimum wages are applicable or how the work is to be taxed.[10]

[6] Council Recommendation ST 10078 2024 INIT, available at: https://data.consilium.europa.eu/doc/document/ST-10078-2024-INIT/en/pdf (accessed 27 August 2024).

[7] *Meyer-Michaelis/Falter/Schäfer*, DB 2016, 2543 (2543).

[8] *Wisskirchen/Schwindling*, ZESAR 2017, 318 (319).

[9] *Taeger*, NJW 2016, 3764 (3769).

[10] *Wisskirchen/Schwindling*, ZESAR 2017, 318 (326).

3 Challenges of This Form of Work

From a legal perspective, crowdworking raises various questions that can lead to uncertainties among companies and crowdworkers.

3.1 Employment Law

In Germany, whenever companies work with external staff, it is crucial that these individuals work as genuine freelancers to avoid being accused of employing bogus self-employed people. This is because bogus self-employment has considerable legal and financial consequences in Germany (up to and including criminal offenses).

The distinction between employment and freelance work is often extremely difficult and unfortunately there are often vague cases, so that companies sometimes have to take unintentional risks if they can only hire certain skills externally. Ultimately, it depends on whether the person commissioned is bound by the client's instructions and is integrated into the client's organization. It is also relevant whether the external person bears an entrepreneurial risk with entrepreneurial opportunities. In Germany, whenever companies work with external staff, it is crucial that these individuals work as genuine freelancers to avoid being accused of employing bogus self-employed people. Contract design is important, but the decisive factor is how the collaboration is practiced.

Decision of the German Federal Labor Court

In its first judgment on platform work in 2020, the German Federal Labor Court (*Bundesarbeitsgericht*) ruled that the crowdworker involved as an employee.[11] In this case specifically, the company used an app to distribute tasks to the crowdworkers. The app was based on a "level system", which led to an "incentive effect" when accepting orders. With a large number of completed orders, higher levels in the rating system could be reached, which only then opened up the possibility of accepting several orders in parallel. Working for the platform was therefore only economically worthwhile if the crowdworkers continuously took on more tasks and reached higher levels. According to the German Federal Labor Court, the app's incentive system enabled the company to control the crowdworker's behavior. Due to the "actual constraints" created by the organizational structure, the individual user's work was determined by a third party in a way that is typical of employees.[12] Furthermore, the court argued that personal dependence is generally more likely in the case of simple tasks than in the case of complex activities, as the crowdworker's ability to make individual decisions and organize

[11] BAG, Urt. v. 1.12.2020–9 AZR 102/20-, BAGE 173, 111–137.

[12] BAG, Urt. v. 1.12.2020–9 AZR 102/20-, BAGE 173, 111–137.

himself is severely limited in the case of simple tasks. However, the court did not give a clear statement on when a crowdworker is to be classified as an employee.[13] The judgment has therefore not eliminated the existing uncertainties of many companies, and, in some cases, has even "fueled" them.

No Clarification by the EU Directive

After a lengthy process, the European Parliament agreed on the directive on improving working conditions in platform work on April 24, 2024. The core of the directive is a legal presumption in Art. 5, which is intended to make it easier to determine the correct employment status of individuals working via platforms. It states that the contractual relationship between a digital work platform and a person performing platform work through that platform is legally presumed to be an employment relationship if there are facts indicating control and direction in accordance with national law, collective agreements or practice in the Member States, taking into account the case law of the European Court of Justice. The Member States are required to define the criteria for the rebuttable legal presumption of dependent employment within the framework of national regulations. If these criteria are met, the digital work platform must prove that the contractual relationship in question does not constitute an employment relationship within the meaning of national law to rebut the legal presumption.

It must be emphasized that the regulation significantly deviates from the Commission's original proposal regarding the structure of the presumption rule. The Commission's original proposal suggested that the presumption would apply if two out of five criteria set out in the draft of the directive were met. The Council increased this requirement to three out of seven criteria. The Parliament, however, rejected any differentiation based on fixed criteria and instead advocated focusing on actual working conditions. As it was not possible to reach agreement on harmonising the criteria, specific criteria were ultimately omitted, giving Member States considerable flexibility in implementation. On the one hand, this may result in a patchwork of diverse regulations regarding platform work within the EU. On the other hand, the vague guidelines lead to uncertainties regarding the extent of discretion national legislators actually have and whether their implementation will comply with the directive's provisions. Member States have two years to transpose the directive into national law.

It remains to be seen how Germany will implement the directive and whether the legal uncertainties will actually be resolved or whether they will ultimately reappear due to the directive's vague wording, once the "corrigendum procedure" is completed and the final version of the directive is adopted. It can be assumed that Germany will largely base its implementation on the decision of the Federal Labor Court, the case law of the social and labor courts, and the demarcation criteria developed in this respect.

[13] *Wisskirchen/Haupt*, RdA 2021, 355 (359).

What Do Companies Need to Do?

Companies must ensure that freelancers (regardless of whether they are engaged through a platform or not) operate in such a way that there are no indications that they are to be classified as employees. This relates to the terms of the contract, but even more to the question of how the contractual relationship is "lived". According to the German Federal Labor Court, incentive systems for the continuous acceptance of orders must be avoided. Especially with simpler tasks, any instructions should be avoided by clearly describing the task to be performed in advance.[14] Nonetheless, the order has to leave enough leeway for the freelancer to decide, how, when and where the tasks are to be carried out.[15] In addition, all regulations for the cooperation with external personnel must be complied with.

Co-Determination Rights of the Works Council?

Finally, (co-determination) rights of the works council may also apply.[16] Whether such rights exist depends on whether the crowdworker is to be classified as an employee or not. Works councils have a number of co-determination rights in internal crowdworking. In the case of freelancers, however, the German Works Constitution Act (*BetrVG*) generally does not apply due to the lack of employee status, so the works council rights are limited e.g., to information rights pursuant to Sect. 80 para. 2 Sentence 1 German Works Constitution Act (*BetrVG*). It is recommended to cooperate with the works council when introducing platform work in order to prevent potential issues.

3.2 General Terms and Conditions

Another aspect to consider when integrating crowdworkers into the workforce is the applicable General Terms and Conditions (GTC). The configuration of the underlying contractual relationship between the digital labor platform, the company and the crowdworker largely depends on the GTC of the respective platform.[17] Typically, platforms only act as intermediaries between the company and the crowdworker. This means that platforms have (intermediation/usage) contracts with both parties and are used to digitally intermediate or facilitate the conclusion of contracts between the company and the crowdworker. The contracts concluded with the platform are typically subject to (platform) GTC.

If crowdworkers were to be considered "consumers" within the meaning of Sect. 13 of the German Civil Code (BGB), the very strict German consumer law (on GTC) would have to be respected. However, even if crowdworkers only work

---

[14] *Grimm/Singraven*, Digitalisierung und Arbeitsrecht, Rn. 10.35.

[15] *Temming*, JA 2021. 687 (690).

[16] *Meyer-Michaelis/Falter/Schäfer*, DB 2016, 2543 (2546).

[17] *Meyer-Michaelis/Falter/Schäfer*, DB 2016, 2543 (2544).

occasionally, they will regularly not be considered "consumers" but "traders" (Sect. 14 BGB). They will often exceed the relatively low threshold for "traders" when they somehow act "in exercise of their trade, business or profession".[18]

However, even GTC for traders are strictly regulated under German law. While the strict consumer protection rules do not directly apply in B2C scenarios, courts are still reluctant to apply significantly less restrictive rules. Furthermore, since crowdworking is commonly aimed at an international crowd, the applicability of German law and the jurisdiction of German courts may need to be specifically addressed in the GTC. And drafting legally valid choice of law and forum clauses is very tricky, especially when consumers are involved.[19]

3.3 Algorithmic Management

One of the characteristics of digital labor platforms is that they are working with algorithmic decision making. Sophisticated artificial intelligence is used to reach the most efficient outcome when allocating gigs to crowdworkers.

To reflect the growing importance of algorithms in this sector, Chapter III of the new Platform Work Directive is dedicated to algorithmic management. Key elements of this chapter are promoting transparency for crowdworkers towards the algorithmic systems and establishing a system of human oversight and supervision. The idea is that crowdworkers should have a basic understanding of what factors influence the allocation of gigs via the platform and should be able to approach a human supervisor for queries.

3.4 Data Protection

The use of algorithms for allocating gigs necessarily requires the processing of personal data from crowdworkers. In addition to applicable GDPR rules, Chapter III of the directive also includes specific provisions related to personal data.

For instance, certain limitations are imposed on processing, particularly for personal data from "special categories" within the meaning of Art. 9 GDPR. This includes a prohibition on processing personal (health) data regarding the emotional or psychological state of persons performing platform work, their ethnic origin, political opinions, disabilities or religious beliefs.

It is further clarified that a data protection impact assessment according to Art. 35(1) GDPR must be made for personal data used in the algorithmic decision-making. For this assessment, the views of crowdworkers and their representatives must be taken into consideration.

---

[18] *Däubler/Klebe*, NZA 2015, 1032 (1037).

[19] *Pelzer/Grimm/Singraven*, Digitalisierung und Arbeitsrecht, Rn. 10.10; *Däubler/Klebe*, NZA 2015, 1032 (1039).

3.5 Knowledge Management

Knowledge contributed by the crowd is no longer pooled and retained within the company. Furthermore, company knowledge, which may needs to be passed on to crowdworkers for them to be able to perform the tasks, is less protected. Therefore, platform work might not be suitable for tasks that involve sensitive information. Appropriate contractual arrangements must be made to ensure that know-how remains within the company.

3.6 Acquisition of Copyrights

Companies may also encounter copyright issues, as existing intellectual property regulations apply only to employees.[20] Since crowdworkers are generally not considered employees, contractual provisions are necessary in order for them to acquire intellectual property rights.[21] Rights to project results must be secured. If a third-party platform is used, it should be checked whether usage and intellectual property rights are effectively transferred based on the platform's general terms and conditions.[22] If there are only contracts with the platform and the crowdworker, the author's consent to sublicensing is required.[23] An additional individual contractual agreement may also be concluded.[24]

4 Solutions and Practical Tips

Crowdworking is a new, rapidly growing form of work that offers both companies and crowdworkers greater flexibility than traditional employment relationships. However, as with almost all new forms of work, there are numerous legal uncertainties. In particular, the question of when a crowdworker is to be classified as an employee or as self-employed is unclear and thus carries risks, which can be addressed with a compliance-oriented structure and individual orders. Where algorithms are used, a balance must be struck between fulfilling the legitimate transparency interests of platform workers and protecting the trade secrets of platforms.

[20] *Werner/Arnold/Günther*, Arbeitsrecht 4.0, § 5, Rn. 146 ff.

[21] *Hötte*, MMR 2014, 795 (796).

[22] *Meyer-Michaelis/Falter/Schäfer*, DB 2016, 2543, (2545); *Hötte*, MMR 2014, 795 (798).

[23] *Hötte*, MMR 2014, 795 (798).

[24] *Hötte*, MMR 2014, 795 (798).

5 Conclusion and Outlook

It is widely assumed that crowdworking will have a significant impact on the future of work and will become part of everyday working life for more and more workers.[25] The massive growth of some crowdworking platforms in 36 recent years shows a clear trend towards platform work. As part of this growth, crowdworking is becoming increasingly professional[26] and will be subject to even more regulation in the future. However, some of the platforms have already voluntarily adopted a "Code of Conduct" that includes various principles of cooperation.

Despite the growth of crowdworking, it is not expected to replace traditional employment.[27] An employee offers a company more than just the pure value of the work they perform. Especially in the service sector, companies have a great interest in promoting and retaining knowledge internally. Furthermore, there is a need to retain employees within the company especially in times of skilled labor shortages.

The decisive factor will be how Member States transpose the regulations of the EU directive into their respective national law. Given the significant weaknesses of the legal presumption, it is feared that legal uncertainties may not be eliminated. Platform operators should closely monitor legislative developments to be able to react promptly. This is especially important for companies operating across borders.[28]

References

Arnold, Christian/Günther, Jens (Hrsg.), NZA, Arbeitsrecht 4.0, 2. Auflage, München 2022.

Budras, Corinna, "Crowdworking" – Tschüss Büro, https://www.faz.net/aktuell/wirtschaft/crowdworking-als-neue-arbeitsform-14993621-p3.html (accessed 27 September 2022).

Bundesministerium für Arbeit und Soziales, Eckpunkte des BMAS – Faire Arbeit in der Plattformökonomie, https://www.denkfabrik-bmas.de/fileadmin/Downloads/Eckpunkte_des_BMAS_Faire_Arbeit_in_der_Plattformoekonomie.pdf (accessed 27 September 2022).

Däubler, Wolfgang/Klebe, Thomas, Crowdwork: Die neue Form der Arbeit – Arbeitgeber auf der Flucht?, NZA 2015, pp. 1032–1041.

Dierks, Benjamin, Berufsbild „Crowdworker" – Die digitalen Tagelöhner, https://www.deutschlandfunk.de/berufsbild-crowdworker-die-digitalen-tageloehner-100.html (accessed 27 September 2022).

Grimm, Detlef/Singraven, Jonas (Hrsg.), Digitalisierung und Arbeitsrecht – Personalarbeit 4.0 – Gestaltung – Best Practices, 1. Auflage, Köln 2022.

Hanau, Hans, Schöne digitale Arbeitswelt? NJW 2016, pp. 2613–2616.

---

[25] *Budras*, FAZ, 3.

[26] *Kothe*, Wirtschaft Nordhessen 2016, 8, 20.

[27] *Hanau*, NJW 2016. 2613 (2614).

[28] *BMAS*, Faire Arbeit in der Plattformökonomie; *SPD, BÜNDNIS 90/DIE GRÜNEN, FDP*: Mehr Fortschritt wagen – Bündnis für Freiheit, Gerechtigkeit und Nachhaltigkeit, 57; *Waas*, ZRP 2022, 105.

Hötte, Daniel Antonius, Crowdsourcing – Rechtliche Risiken eines neuen Phänomens, MMR 2014, pp. 795–798.
Kothe, Helga Kristina, Crowdsourcing und Crowdworking: Wie wichtig ist der neue Trend? Klickarbeit ist ein Wachstumsmarkt, Wirtschaft Nordhessen 8, 2016, p. 20.
Meyer-Michaelis, Isabel/Falter, Kira/Schäfer, Amelie, DB 2016, pp. 2543–2546.
SPD, BÜNDNIS 90/DIE GRÜNEN, FDP, Mehr Fortschritt wagen – Bündnis für Freiheit, Gerechtigkeit und Nachhaltigkeit, https://www.spd.de/fileadmin/Dokumente/Koalitionsvertrag/Koalitionsvertrag_2021-2025.pdf (accessed 15 November 2022).
Taeger, Jürgen, Die Entwicklung des IT-Rechts im Jahr 2016, NJW 2016, pp. 3764–3770.
Temming, Felipe, Zur Arbeitnehmereigenschaft eines Crowdworkers, JA 2021, pp. 687–690.
Waas, Bernd, Verbesserung der Arbeitsbedingungen von Plattformbeschäftigten, ZRP 2022, pp. 105–108.
Wisskirchen, Gerlind/Haupt, Jan, Crowdworker: Arbeitnehmer oder Selbstständiger?, RdA 2021, pp. 355–360.
Wisskirchen, Gerlind/Schwindling, Jan, Crowdworking im Lichte des Arbeitsrechts, ZESAR 2017, pp. 318–327.

Disruptive Change in Organizational Design—Introduction of Flexible Organizational Structures at T-Systems International GmbH

Jan Krellner and Raihan Kleinmann

1 Introduction

"The effort of the company management to structure the complex process of operational performance creation and utilization in such a way that efficiency losses at the execution level are minimized."[1] This is the definition of a company's organization. Conceptually, a distinction is made between a process organization, which includes regulations for spatial, temporal, and personnel work processes, and the structural organization, which includes the hierarchical structure for the permanent regulation of rights and duties of individuals and business areas. Over the past century, depending on economic goals and the value creation mandate, various organizational structures with their respective advantages and disadvantages have been established in companies.[2] These include the classic hierarchical structure or the matrix organization, to name two examples.

The subject of this article is the further development of the organizational structure of T-Systems International GmbH from a mixed variant of the product-oriented/project-oriented matrix structure towards a flexibilization of the structural elements with a strong competence-based and value stream-oriented (e.g., limitation to certain markets) focus.

[1] Wöhe (2005), p. 131

[2] Wöhe (2005, pp. 133 ff.); Häusling (2018, pp. 64 ff.).

J. Krellner
T-Systems International GmbH, Stuttgart, Germany

R. Kleinmann (✉)
T-Systems International GmbH, Frankfurt, Germany
e-mail: raihan.kleinmann@t-systems.com

I. Knappertsbusch and G. Wisskirchen (eds.), *The Future of Work*,
https://doi.org/10.1007/978-3-658-45150-9_20

With approximately 29,000 employees worldwide in 18 countries and a turnover of 4.2 billion euros (2020), T-Systems is one of the leading providers of digital services. T-Systems operates in a very dynamic environment, characterized by changes in technology, market, and customer requirements in ever shorter cycles and a resulting and necessary need for adaptation. A more flexible organization provides the suitable organizational framework to meet these ever faster changing priorities and development cycles.

The basis for T-Systems' flexible organizational model is the basic framework of the so-called Spotify model. The company Spotify has grown rapidly as a start-up since 2006 and faced the challenge of coordinating 30 teams in three cities simultaneously and efficiently. To master this challenge, Spotify introduced a model characterized by flexible structures, which has since served as a prototype for many technology-driven companies.[3]

The introduction of the flexible organization at T-Systems is to be seen in the context of a global culture change initiative[4] and the introduction of agile working methods, which are actively accompanied by change measures.

The overall works agreement for the introduction of the flexible organization, which was concluded with the works council of T-Systems at the beginning of 2019 and revised and adapted in 2022 based on the agreed joint evaluation, forms the basis for this.

The implementation of the flexible organizational model was carried out iteratively in retrospect, with each step transforming larger sections of the organization. Approximately 30% of T-Systems employees are based in the German organization. By the end of 2019, 70% of them had been transferred to the flexible organization in several waves. By the beginning of 2022, the proportion was almost 100%. Internationally, the flexible organizational model was tested in individual countries or smaller units. In 2023, the flexible model will be introduced for about 45% of employees outside of Germany. This will make professional collaboration in T-Systems much more flexible and efficient across national and departmental boundaries.

1.1 Main Goals of the Transformation

Considering the market challenges, the following main goals were in focus of the T-Systems transformation:

- Focus on strategic and systematic competence development through separation of professional and disciplinary leadership
- End-to-end responsibility along the value chains and cross-departmental collaboration through flexible composition of professional teams

[3] Haufe (2022); Agile Pocket Guide T-Systems (2019, pp. 15 ff.).

[4] The focus of the T-Systems culture initiative is on living the Outward Mindset, Agile Mindset, and Growth Mindsets more strongly in the daily work of all employees.

- Building the organization not around people and their positions, but for the purpose of creating maximum customer benefit
- Quick, needs-based possibility of adapting the organization with flexible structural elements (Squads and Tribes)

1.2 Structural Elements

The heart of T-Systems' flexible organizational model is formed by the so-called Chapters, Tribes, and Squads. Each of these organizational structural elements is occupied by a leadership role—the Chapter, Tribe, and Squad Leads. The units of T-Systems differ in the structure of the next higher disciplinary level in order to meet their individual needs, which will not be discussed further here (Fig. 1).

1.2.1 Chapters

A Chapter groups employees based on similar competencies (guideline size 10-35 employees, Ø 25). Other criteria can be, for example, technology knowledge or industry expertise. Chapters are the disciplinary home of the employees and thus constant. At the same time, they represent the organization as an element of an organizational unit in the T-Systems org chart. Within a Chapter, members exchange their experiences and challenges and jointly develop improvements regarding the tools and methods used.

Chapter Leads primarily lead the members of a Chapter in their working time, while they can also take on the role of a Squad member (up to 40% of their working time). They are responsible as so-called "gardeners" of the organization for:

- Disciplinary leadership of the employees in the Chapter with a focus on coaching & competence development
- Alignment of the Chapter according to uniform guidelines and clear objectives

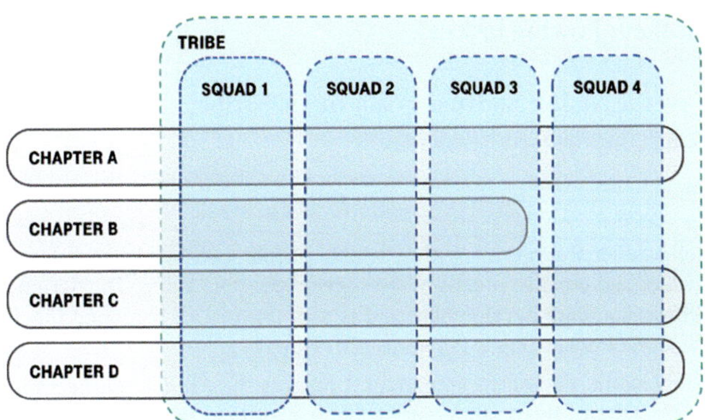

Fig. 1 Overview of the flexible organizational model and the individual structural elements. Flexible (virtual and temporary) structural elements are marked with a dashed line

- Balanced assignment of employees to Squads and prioritization of requests from the Tribes
- Execution of employee-oriented processes (performance and competence assessment, feedback discussions)

1.2.2 Squads

In Squads, employees come together for a certain period of time to work end-to-end on a common professional goal (e.g., product, process, customer) (guideline size eight to eleven employees). They organize themselves largely independently and work on the overall goal of their Tribe. Depending on the task and customer context, classic or agile methods such as Scrum[5] are used. Squads are flexible, virtual, and temporary structural elements of the T-Systems organization.

Squad Leads are the closest leaders of the employees and are responsible for the following tasks:

- Professional leadership and development of the employees in the Squad
- Development, communication, compliance, and prioritization of clear professional Squad goals and tasks
- Coordination with Chapter Leads regarding competencies and further development of the employees
- Exchange & prioritization on professional topics with the Tribe Lead
- If the Squad works according to Scrum methodology, the Squad Lead can, for example, take on the role of the Product Owner[6]

1.2.3 Tribes

Tribes bundle thematically similar Squads for the duration of their existence (guideline size 20-150 employees, Ø 100). They can also be aligned according to different purposes, such as the development of a product. Like Squads, Tribes are characterized by their flexible, virtual, and temporary structure. Tribes and Squads can operate across legal, regional, or organizational boundaries.

Tribe Leads are the direct professional leaders of the Squad Leads and are responsible for the following tasks:

- Definition of the vision and the goals of the Tribe, taking into account overarching goals

---

[5] *Scrum* is a well-known framework within which people can tackle complex tasks, thereby delivering productive and creative results of the highest possible value. The Scrum method originated in the 1990s in software development and is now used in all corporate functions. (Source: Atlassian (2022); Agile Pocket Guide T-Sytems (2019), p. 19)

[6] In the Scrum framework, one of the important 3 roles is the *Product Owner* role. This is seen as the professional leader of the development team, who acts as the client, sets requirements for the team, and assesses the later implementation of, for example, a product in terms of functionality, usability, performance, and quality together with the customers. (Source: West (2022); Agile Pocket Guide T-Sytems (2019), p. 23)

- Compliance with Tribe metrics and the Tribe budget
- Business development, stakeholder management, and exchange at the Tribe Lead level
- Professional leadership and coordination of the further development of the Squad Leads with the respective Chapter Leads

2 Advantages of Flexible Organization

The advantages of making organizational structures more flexible are multifaceted and depend on various transformative factors.

The flexible organizational model of T-Systems has shown the following advantages at different maturity levels based on experiences since 2019:

- Reduction of hierarchy levels from 9 to 5 in larger delivery units or to 3 in cross-sectional areas, resulting in a general simplification and reduction of reporting paths and structures
- Optimization of the disciplinary leadership span to an average of 1:25
- Greater breaking up of silo structures and promotion of cross-departmental collaboration
- Strong focus on skill development of employees on a professional and personal level through a responsible duo consisting of the chapter lead in conjunction with the employees. For example, the number of employees with at least one agile skill has increased by over 30% since 2019. Agile certificates have increased by over 400%
- Flexible and quick possibilities for changing the deployment of employees in similar work contexts (squad changes) as needed, without the involvement of the works council
- Better organizational framework for switching between traditional and agile working methods, although this was also possible in T-Systems without the flexible organization
- Formal separation of disciplinary and technical leadership responsibility leads to an improvement in the leadership quality of the organization

3 Challenges of Flexible Organization

A transformation project of T-Systems' magnitude is confronted with various challenges before, during, and after implementation, despite good planning. The following are these challenges:

The reality of a highly complex and globally operating company cannot be represented by a standardized organizational model.

Flexible organizational structures are not necessarily suitable for teams with highly repetitive tasks. This is particularly true for teams with little need for skill change or development in the medium term.

Upper management levels and transformation managers are still heavily influenced by their history and develop organizational structures that are organized around key leaders/players and do not follow customer needs or end-to-end completed value chains.

The urge to accurately depict the current situation leads to the development of new and additional roles and/or designations, with the aim of adapting the flexible organizational model to individual needs, which inevitably leads to a higher complexity of the organizational model.

Suitable "people leaders" for the role of chapter leads are hard to find, as a primarily disciplinary leadership role appears unattractive to many traditionally influenced executives and coaching skills for the role need to be strongly developed.

Without an accompanying change in corporate culture and the development into agile working methods, the advantage of changing the organizational model is not fully exploited. However, these changes require a high degree of perseverance and persistence over a long period of time.

4 Practical Tips and Recommendations for Implementing Flexible Organizational Structures

As a basic principle, the introduction of flexible organizational structures requires a coordinated and sustainable change management approach, which can draw on approaches such as the eight steps by John Kotter[7]. In general, the authors suggest considering the following recommendations:

The introduction of flexible organizational structures, like any major transformation project, should be carried out in the context of a business challenge, otherwise there is a risk that the necessity and benefit of the change will not be understood by the employees.

The top management should communicate and endorse the project at the beginning of the transformation to clarify its importance for all employees. The entire executive board should strongly support the transformation teams. Examples of this are:

- A clearly defined framework and guidelines help those responsible for transformation within the business units to implement the flexible organization and its objectives consistently.
- Hidden hierarchy levels should be avoided by introducing sub-chapter or super-chapter designations.

[7] Kotter (2014, pp. 28 ff.).

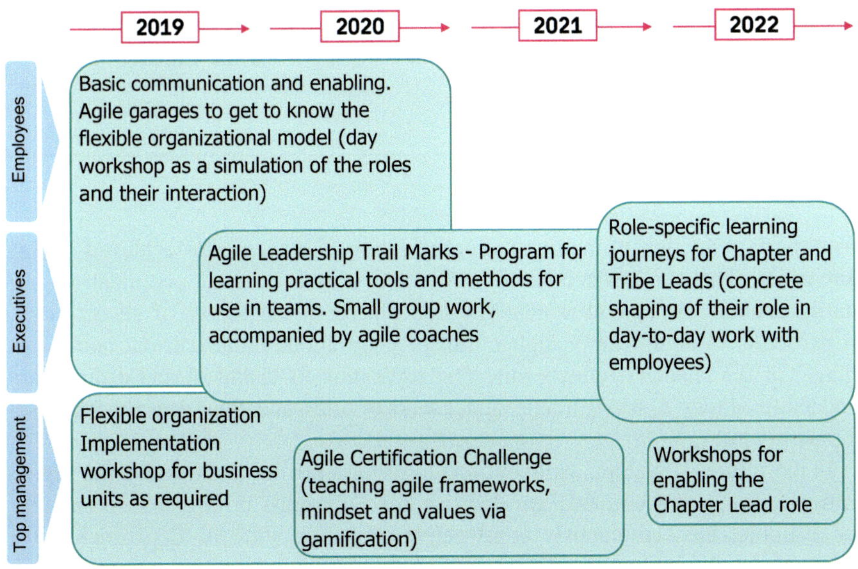

Fig. 2 Example of target group- and need-based change and enabling measures for collaboration and role requirements in the flexible organization over time

The transformation is usually painful for the participants at four points, which is why appropriate countermeasures should be planned in the transformation project:

- Top management's handling of middle management following traditional reporting and control paths
- Works councils' handling of information and approval rights in individual personnel measures (sections 80, 99 BetrVG); purely technical changes of assignment between squads and tribes do not constitute a transfer, as only the technical, not the disciplinary superior changes[8]
- In the middle management levels due to a visual loss of status in the organization chart due to the separation of technical and disciplinary leadership
- In the relationship between employees and their direct supervisor, because communication paths, contacts, and responsibilities have to be established anew

The adjustment of collaboration approaches, reporting and meeting structures of leadership roles is of considerable importance, as otherwise the advantages of the flexible organization do not lead to the expected faster responsiveness, more transparency and empowerment.

Role-specific enablings for the entire organization and especially for the leaders (Chapter-, Tribe-, Squad-Lead) in the flexible organization, are essential for

[8] For more details, see Steffan ArbRB 2022, 80 ff.

successful implementation. The needs of the areas are to be recorded over time and planned measures are to be adapted accordingly. See the illustration for the approach at T-Systems (Fig. 2).

5 Summary and Outlook

With the introduction of the flexible organization, T-Systems has achieved important goals. The competence-based and value stream-oriented organization primarily enables the customer benefit to be placed at the center of all activities. In particular, a significantly higher transparency about skills (current and target image) in the chapters reflects this. The separation of technical and disciplinary leadership allows a strong focus of leadership roles and thus directly increases competitiveness.

In the future, T-Systems will continue to professionalize and develop the organizational design. Factors that are decisive for T-Systems in this context include, for example, the continuously constructive exchange with the departments, the employees and social partners. The continuous concretization of the collaboration model of the various leadership roles, global standards for structural elements and roles, and thus greater transparency in the process organization ensure this.

Employees and especially leaders in the flexible organization are also increasingly offered need-based information platforms, role-specific leadership programs, and a broad range of qualification offers. Future implementations will be accompanied by the introduction of a workshop format to check the implementation of the flexible organizational design and continuous optimization. In addition, an IT-side representation of the flexible organizational elements (squads and tribes) is currently being piloted.

Based on the previous experience with the flexible organization at T-Systems, it can be assumed that further flexibilizations can be expected in the future. Decisive factors in this context are labor law conditions.

References

Agile Pocket Guide T-Systems (2019),https://issuhub.com/view/index?id=213392 (abgerufen am 01.11.2022).

Atlassian (2022), https://www.atlassian.com/de/agile/scrum (abgerufen am 25.10.2022).

Häusling, Andre (2018), Agile Organisationen – Transformationen erfolgreich gestalten – Beispiele agiler Pioniere; 1. Auflage, Haufe-Lexware, Freiburg.

Haufe (2022), https://teampact.haufe.com/blog/agile-spotify-modell-einfuehren-erfolgreich-machen?akttyp=organische%20suche&med=google&aktnr=84834&wnr=04393672 (abgerufen am 01.11.2022).

Kotter, John (2014), XLR8 – Accelerate: Building strategic agility for a faster-moving world, Harvard Business Review Press, USA.

West, Dave (2022), https://www.atlassian.com/de/agile/scrum/roles (abgerufen am 25.10.2022).

Wöhe, Günter (2005), Einführung in die allgemeine Betriebswirtschaftslehre, 22. Auflage, Vahlen Verlag, München.

Agile Working

Jonas Kannen

1 Introduction

Agile work has been one of the major trends in the modern working world for years. According to a study by the personnel service provider HAYS from 2018[1] the flexibilisation of work structures is even one of the three most important HR topics. In the context of labour law, agility in working life is understood to mean various types of flexible cooperation. In the broadest sense, agility means the flexibilisation of working methods.[2] The discussion particularly covers the flexibilisation of working hours, the place of work and organisational forms with as flat hierarchies as possible.[3] The introduction of agile work is intended to transfer a high degree of personal responsibility to employees, as decisions are no longer made "from the top down", but democratically within the respective team.[4]

The reason for rethinking is that traditional, i.e. hierarchical and directive, work in a fixed organisational structure is increasingly proving to be inefficient. Agile organisational structures and work processes are increasingly being proposed as a solution.[5] Employees should be flexibly deployable according to their abilities and experiences, without being tied to a fixed department in the company. The classic

[1] *Eilers et al.*, in: HAYS HR-Report 2018 Focus Agile Organisation on the Test Bench.

[2] cf. *Kania*, in: Küttner, Personnel Book 2023, Agile Working Rn. 1.

[3] cf. *Günther/Böglmüller*, in: NZA 2019, 273, 273.

[4] *Eufinger/Burbach*, in: DB 2019, 1147, 1148; *Hoffmann-Remy*, in: DB 2018, 2757, 2758.

[5] cf. *Günther/Böglmüller*, in: NZA 2019, 273, 273.

J. Kannen (✉)
Trade Republic Bank GmbH, Berlin, Germany
e-mail: jonas.kannen@traderepublic.com

I. Knappertsbusch and G. Wisskirchen (eds.), *The Future of Work*,
https://doi.org/10.1007/978-3-658-45150-9_21

departments led by a department head are replaced by self-organising teams that are put together according to the needs of the specific project (see the article "Cross-functional expert teams—How mixed ad-hoc teams master projects and product development in the digital working environment").[6]

2 Advantages of Agile Work

The advantages of agile work are obvious. Increased self-determination and self-realisation at work due to actually transferred responsibility lead to employees identifying more strongly with their work. Higher employee satisfaction can increase productivity and quality of work performance and thus ultimately the competitiveness and profitability of the company. In addition, an eight-hour day at a fixed workplace in the employer's office, clear company hierarchies and a rigid remuneration system are increasingly often considered outdated.[7] Companies must adapt to the new ideas and wishes of employees. Only in this way can they remain competitive in the face of a continuing shortage of skilled workers.

3 Challenges in Relation to Agile Work

The introduction of agile work needs to be well thought out, as numerous individual and collective labour law questions arise.

3.1 Individual Employment Law

3.1.1 Working Hours

The rigid requirements of the Working Hours Act (ArbZG) also apply to agile workers. Deviating regulations are only permissible within the limits of section 7 ArbZG. As a rule, even working time accounts and trust-based work cannot guarantee further flexibility.[8] Especially in the final phases of a project, e.g. during a "Scrum Sprint", however, the daily maximum working time of ten hours (section 3 ArbZG) and the eleven-hour rest periods (section 5 ArbZG) can hardly be adhered to.[9] In addition, there is the comprehensive obligation to record working time according to the case law of the ECJ.[10] So far, the prevailing opinion[11] has

[6] *Hoffmann-Remy*, in: DB 2018, 2757, 2757.

[7] *Eufinger/Burbach*, in: DB 2019, 1147, 1147.

[8] *Kania*, in: Küttner, Personnel Book 2023, Agile Working Rn. 8.

[9] *Günther/Böglmüller*, in: NZA 2019, 273, 278.

[10] ECJ, judgment of 14.5.2019 – C-55/18, NZA 2019, 683.

[11] cf. *Roloff*, in: ErfK, 23rd ed. 2023, ArbZG § 16 Rn. 4 m. w. N.; contrary opinion ArbG Emden, judgment of 24.09.2020 – 2 Ca 144/20.

been that the obligation to record overtime remains until a decision by the ECJ on the German regulations or until the ECJ's requirements are implemented into German law. However, the BAG decided on 13.9.2022 that employers are already obliged to introduce a system for recording working time according to section 3 para. 2 no. 1 ArbSchG.[12] The mere obligation to document working hours does not have to stand in the way of the self-determination of agile workers, as this does not impose any restrictions on when, where and how they complete their tasks.[13]

3.1.2 Place of Work

During the course of the COVID-19 pandemic, a large number of employees have become accustomed to being able to switch flexibly between home office and the company workplace. However, after the expiry of section 28b para. 4 IfSG (old version), there is no general entitlement to the establishment of a home office workplace. Such a claim does not even exist if the employees have not (yet) been expressly instructed to return to the office.[14] Conversely, the employer is also not entitled to assign telework to the employee solely on the basis of his contractual right of direction.[15] Furthermore, according to the prevailing opinion, there is also no claim by the employee to a specific workplace, so that in particular the introduction of desk sharing and an open-space concept is permissible by way of the right of direction, subject to compliance with occupational safety and co-determination regulations.[16]

3.1.3 Termination of Employment Contracts for Operational Reasons

Finally, the agile transformation can also affect the feasibility of terminations for operational reasons. Firstly, due to the constantly changing areas of application, it will be more difficult to prove the lack of further employment opportunities.[17] In addition, the often accompanying reduction of hierarchy levels in an agile transformation also affects the social selection required according to section 1 para. 3 KSchG, as all employees who are comparable in terms of their work activities at the same hierarchy level must be included.[18]

[12] BAG, decision of 13.9.2022 – 1 ABR 22/21, NZA 2022, 1616.

[13] *Heintke*, in: DB 2021, M20, M20.

[14] cf. *Jordan/Schwinn/Löw*, in: ArbRAktuell 2022, 306, 307.

[15] LAG Berlin-Brandenburg, judgment of 10.10.2018 – 17 Sa 562/18, BeckRS 2018, 34001.

[16] *Günther/Böglmüller*, in NZA 2019, 273, 278; *Kania*, in: Küttner, Personnel Book 2023, Agile Working Rn. 7.

[17] PSSTK, Flex. Work, 2nd ed. 2022, B. Rn. 999o.

[18] *Eufinger/Burbach*, in: DB 2019, 1147, 1150; *Kiel*, in: Ascheid/Preis/Schmidt, 6th ed. 2021, KSchG § 1 Rn. 612.

3.2 Collective Employment Law

3.2.1 Information, Instruction, and Consultation Rights

Due to the general right to information according to section 80 para. 2 BetrVG, the works council must be informed in a timely and comprehensive manner before the introduction of an agile work organization.[19] With regard to the planning of work procedures and workflows, an obligation to inform may arise from section 90 para. 1 No. 3, 4 BetrVG.[20] The works council must be informed already in the planning phase and not only when the plan is fully formulated.[21]

3.2.2 Codetermination in Personnel Matters

The assignment of an agile task can be a transfer in the sense of section 95 para. 3 sentence 1 BetrVG, so that according to section 99 para. 1 sentence 1 BetrVG the consent of the works council is required. A transfer is, according to the legal definition of section 95 para. 3 sentence 1 BetrVG, the assignment to another work area, which is expected to exceed a duration of one month or is associated with a significant change in the circumstances under which the work is to be performed. A transfer is likely to be assumed when employees are assigned to a hierarchy-free work unit, as this can represent a significant change in working conditions due to changing tasks and responsibilities.[22] However, if the activity constantly switches between classic work organization and agile work, this can be characteristic for the employment relationship. These changes would be evaluated as a characteristic of the activity, so that a transfer due to the exception of section 95 para. 3 sentence 2 BetrVG is excluded.[23] This is likely to apply also to a later switch to another Scrum team.[24]

3.2.3 Co-determination in Social Matters

According to section 87 para. 1 no. 2 BetrVG, the works council has a co-determination right regarding the distribution and according to section 87 para. 1 no. 3 BetrVG regarding temporary changes in working hours. The co-determination rights cover all changes to existing working time systems, e.g. the initial introduction of trust-based working hours.[25] The co-determination right according to section 87

---

[19] *Kania*, in: Küttner, Personnel Book 2023, Agile Working No. 14.

[20] *Günther/Böglmüller*, in: NZA 2019, 417, 420, 421; *Schulze/Volk*, in: ArbRAktuell 2019, 404, 405.

[21] *Annuß*, in: Richardi, 17th ed. 2022, BetrVG § 90 No. 18.

[22] *Eufinger/Burbach*, in: DB 2019, 1147, 1152; *Kania*, in: Küttner, Personnel Book 2023, Agile Working No. 18.

[23] *Günther/Böglmüller*, in: NZA 2019, 273, 277; PSSTK, Flex. Work, 2nd ed. 2022, B. No. 999u.

[24] *Kania*, in: Küttner, Personnel Book 2023, Agile Working No. 18; contra *Schulze/Volk*, in: ArbRAktuell 2022, 553, 555.

[25] PSSTK, Flex. Work, 2nd ed. 2022, B. no. 999s; *Richardi/Maschmann*, in: Richardi, BetrVG, 17th ed. 2022, BetrVG § 87 no. 297.

para. 1 no. 3 BetrVG plays a particularly important role when there are peaks in work during project high phases and thus a temporary extension of working hours.[26]

In addition, the works council may have a co-determination right according to section 87 para. 1 no. 6 BetrVG with regard to the use of software in the context of project work, e.g. if the project progress is recorded in an electronic database, filing systems for knowledge management or other collaboration tools are used.[27]

Furthermore, the introduction of agile work can be group work within the meaning of section 87 para. 1 no. 13 BetrVG. The co-determination only refers to principles on the implementation of group work, not its introduction and termination.[28] Group work, according to the legal definition of the 2nd sentence, exists when a group of employees essentially independently completes a total task assigned to them within the operational work process. It is necessary that a total task has been assigned to the employees grouped together in the organizational community of the work group for a certain duration.[29] The employees must be authorized to independently regulate the daily work processes, i.e. the group must be able to determine largely free of instructions from the employer how the work steps necessary to fulfill the overall task are distributed, coordinated and controlled within the operational guidelines.[30] For the qualification as group work, it is therefore crucial whether the group can decide at least partially autonomously about the work performance and what role it plays in the overall organization of the operational work processes.[31]

3.2.4 Co-determination in Economic Matters

The agile transformation can represent a change in operations in the sense of section 111 BetrVG.[32] Particularly when reducing hierarchy levels,[33] introducing an agile project organization or desk-sharing[34] a fundamental change in the operational organization in the sense of section 111 S. 3 No. 4 BetrVG may exist.[35] Also conceivable is the introduction of fundamentally new working methods in the sense of section 111 S. 3 No. 5 BetrVG. A change is only fundamental if it

---

[26] *Schulze/Volk*, in: ArbRAktuell 2022, 553, 554.

[27] *Günther/Böglmüller*, in: NZA 2019, 417, 421; *Hoffmann-Remy*, in: DB 2018, 2757, 2758 f.

[28] *Gutzeit*, in: GK-BetrVG, 12th edition 2022, § 87 BetrVG, no. 1097.

[29] *Werner*, in: BeckOK ArbR, 68th ed. 1.6.2023, BetrVG § 87 no. 203.

[30] *Günther/Böglmüller*, in: NZA 2019, 417, 422; *Richardi/Maschmann*, in: Richardi, BetrVG, 17th ed. 2022, BetrVG § 87 no. 979.

[31] *Eufinger/Burbach*, in: DB 2019, 1147, 1151; *Richardi/Maschmann*, in: Richardi, BetrVG, 17th ed. 2022, BetrVG § 87 no. 979a.

[32] *Eufinger/Burbach*, in: DB 2019, 1147, 1152; *Günther/Böglmüller*, in: NZA 2019, 417, 423.

[33] BAG, judgment of 26.10.2004 – 1 AZR 493/03, NZA 2005, 237.

[34] LAG Düsseldorf, decision of 9.1.2018 – 3 TaBVGa 6/17, NZA-RR 2018, 368.

[35] *Annuß*, in: Richardi, BetrVG, 17th ed. 2022, BetrVG § 111 Rn. 109.

significantly affects the operational process.[36] If a change in operations exists, the works council has a right to consultation and information according to section 111 S. 1 BetrVG, furthermore, section 112 BetrVG results in a right of the works council to negotiate for the conclusion of a reconciliation of interests.[37]

3.2.5 Other Participation Rights

Finally, other general participation rights must also be observed, such as the co-determination right in connection with qualification and further training according to sections 96 ff. BetrVG or the participation right before issuing a (change) termination according to sections 99, 102, 103 BetrVG.

4 Solutions and Practical Tips

Although there are no original legal requirements for agile work and the general labor law provisions apply, there are some peculiarities that need to be observed for a successful agile transformation to ensure the necessary legal certainty.

Even if decisions are to be made in the team, the right of instruction should not be contractually waived. It is sufficient if (temporarily) the exercise of the power of instruction is factually waived. This makes it possible to use the disciplinary right of instruction in case of breaches of duty.[38] Even if, according to the case law of the BAG, the non-exercise of the right of direction over a longer period of time regularly does not create a trust situation to the effect that the employer does not want to make use of the right of direction in the future,[39] a contractual clarification is nevertheless recommended that the right of instruction is not limited by this.[40]

In co-determined companies, it is advisable to involve the works council as transparently and early as possible, i.e. already in the planning phase, and to fully observe its participation rights. In this way, the transformation to an agile work organization can be legally secured.[41] To avoid later disputes, the conclusion of a framework works agreement can also be recommended, in which regulations on relevant topics such as the question of a transfer, group work or qualification topics are agreed.[42] In addition, regulations on working hours are advisable in order to be able to react to work peaks at short notice in a legally secure manner.[43]

---

[36] BAG, decision of 22.3.2016 – 1 ABR 12/14, NZA 2016, 894; *Annuß*, in: Richardi, BetrVG, 17th ed. 2022, BetrVG § 111 Rn. 118.

[37] *Schulze/Volk*, in: ArbRAktuell 2022, 404, 406 f.

[38] *Günther/Böglmüller*, in: NZA 2019, 273, 275 f.

[39] BAG, judgment of 17.8.2011 – 10 AZR 202/10, NZA 2012, 265.

[40] *Heise*, in: Maschmann/Sieg/Göpfert, Contract Design ArbR, 3rd ed. 2020, 15 Agile Work and Scrum Rn. 40.

[41] *Hoffmann-Remy*, DB 2018, 2757, 2761; *Schulze/Volk*, in: ArbRAktuell 2019, 404, 405.

[42] *Günther/Böglmüller*, in: NZA 2019, 417, 420 f.

[43] *Rossa*, in: Oberthür/Seitz, Works Agreements, 3rd ed. 2021, B. III. Rn. 33.

5 Summary and Outlook

Agile work presents companies with a multitude of labor law challenges. Nevertheless, the advantages associated with it outweigh the disadvantages for both employers and employees, as the transformation to an agile organization can increase employers' attractiveness in the "War for Talents" and simultaneously improve their products or services, as collaboration in agile teams is considered particularly innovative.[44] Therefore, more and more companies have decided not only to have individual projects handled agilely, but to replace traditional structures with agile organizations of entire business areas.[45] The study by the personnel service provider HAYS from 2018[46] shows that this trend is likely to continue.

Even though—as shown—there are some peculiarities to consider with agile work, these can be solved with traditional labor law.[47] Legal certainty can be achieved in particular through early and transparent involvement of the works council and the conclusion of (framework) works agreements. However, the rigid boundaries of the ArbZG and the restrictive case law of both the BAG and the ECJ, which continue to set tight limits on the desired flexibility, remain problematic.

References

Eilers, Silke et. al. (eds.), HAYS HR-Report 2018 Schwerpunkt Agile Organisation auf dem Prüfstand, Weinheim 2018.

Eufinger, Alexander/Burbach, Nils, DB 2019, pp. 1147–1153.

Günther, Jens/Böglmüller, Matthias, NZA 2019, pp. 273–278.

Günther, Jens/Böglmüller, Matthias, NZA 2019, pp. 417–424.

Heintke, Thorsten, DB 2021, pp. M20–M21.

Hoffmann-Remy, Till, DB 2018, pp. 2757–2761.

Jordan, Christopher/Schwinn, Christina/Löw, Christine, ArbRAktuell 2022, pp. 306–309.

Maschmann, Frank/Sieg, Rainer/Göpfert, Burkard (eds.), Vertragsgestaltung im Arbeitsrecht, 3. Auflage, München 2020.

Oberthür, Nathalie/Seitz, Stefan (eds.), Betriebsvereinbarungen, 3. Auflage, München 2021.

Richardi, Reinhard (eds.) Betriebsverfassungsgesetz, 17. Auflage, München 2022.

Rolfs, Christian/Giesen, Richard/Meßling, Miriam/Udsching, Peter, BeckOK Arbeitsrecht, 68. Edition Stand: 01.06.2023, München 2023.

Röller, Jürgen (eds.), Küttner Personalbuch, Arbeitsrecht, Sozialversicherungsrecht, Steuerrecht, 30. Auflage, München 2023.

Schulze, Marc-Oliver/Volk, Tatjana, ArbRAktuell 2019, pp. 404–407.

Schulze, Marc-Oliver/Volk, Tatjana, ArbRAktuell 2019, pp. 553–556.

[44] *Eufinger/Burbach,* in: DB 2019, 1147, 1153.

[45] *Heise*, in: Maschmann/Sieg/Göpfert, Contract Design ArbR, 3rd ed. 2020, 15 Agile Work and Scrum Rn. 3.

[46] *Eilers et al.*, in: HAYS HR-Report 2018 Focus Agile Organization on the Test Bench.

[47] *Eufinger/Burbach,* in: DB 2019, 1147, 1153.

Digital Connectivity in the Context of New Work

Sarah Genner

1 Introduction

With smartphones and tablets, we can be online almost anytime and anywhere. At least in Western countries, the options have increased exponentially in a short time to access digitized information and communication at any time and to be digitally reachable both privately and professionally regardless of location. Mobile internet has become indispensable for many in technologized countries—historically speaking, in record time. The mediatization of private and professional everyday life is accompanied by blurred boundaries between working hours and leisure time, as well as a significantly increased screen time. The new world of work benefits in many ways from the convenience of being able to work from home if desired (see the article "Working from Home: Perspectives, Challenges, Solutions"), using a coworking space near the place of residence (see the article "Coworking Space as a third workplace") or integrating childcare and workdays flexibly. Not spending every day from 8 to 6 at an office location, but being able to better reconcile sports, napping, and family (see the article "New Work and Family - How companies in the new world of work benefit from a new family friendliness") with professional obligations, is for many the epitome of New Work, which promises them more meaningfulness and motivation personally.

With the pandemic, debates about who should appear how often on site in the office have intensified massively, because even companies and organizations that had not allowed mobile work before Corona were forced to send their employees to the home office (Bitkom, 2020). While some have found an improved

S. Genner (✉)
Hochschule für Wirtschaft Zürich, Zürich, Schweiz
e-mail: sarah@genner.cc

I. Knappertsbusch and G. Wisskirchen (eds.), *The Future of Work*,
https://doi.org/10.1007/978-3-658-45150-9_22

work rhythm for themselves, others complain that they have trouble switching off from work with constant digital availability and blurred working hours and feel increasingly exhausted. Already ten years before the pandemic, a broad debate about increased burnout numbers reached the European public, in which even the German federal government named constant digital availability as a central factor (Genner, 2017; Lehmann & Quadbeck, 2014). In addition to health issues, aspects of digital availability are also coming into focus with the increase in remote work, which are related to cybersecurity and digital surveillance (Levy, 2022; Romy, 2020).

There is still little understanding for different personality types in relation to "boundary management": individual preferences around the demarcation between working hours and leisure time. At one end of the spectrum are the "integrators" (who like a mix of work and leisure), at the other end are the "separators" (who like to clearly separate private and professional life). While integrators are able to exploit the advantages of digital availability more, there is a risk for separators that the availability preferences of integrators in their professional environment undermine their desire for clearly separable leisure time (Genner, 2017).

This article is dedicated to the question of how a healthy, safe, and professional handling of the possibilities and risks of constant online access can succeed in the context of New Work. The employer's perspective is brought into focus.

2 Advantages of constant online access in the work context

It turns out that for organizations, the satisfaction of employees was a central driver in pre-pandemic times to introduce remote work in order to retain motivated employees on the one hand and to remain attractive as an employer in the job market on the other (Work Smart Initiative, 2019). From the perspective of many employees, remote work and—at least for integrators—digital availability are a blessing. Those who depend on the compatibility of work and private life usually appreciate the opportunity to be reachable regardless of time and location and not to be tied to marking presence in an office for eight to nine hours at a stretch. This can involve family care duties, such as children or care-dependent relatives, club activities, a political side office, or a hobby that is weather-dependent.

With the shortage of skilled workers, this aspect has gained even more importance: If the best talents can choose where they want to work under what conditions, this also means that they may choose an employer who offers them maximum flexibility in terms of work location and time, which in turn is directly related to digital availability. Those who find it more important to be able to work flexibly than to have structured office hours and regulated availability, are more likely to choose an employer with a flexible model.

From the perspective of organizations, it can also be attractive not to expose employees to the pressure of presenteeism in the office, but to have them available when they are needed and need to be reached. This holds the promise of increased productivity and more motivated employees if they do not have to commute or can work in their holiday home, and therefore put even more effort into their job. In the context of New Work, autonomy, freedom, and personal development are central values that can ideally be upheld thanks to digital hyper-connectivity.

Especially in international companies that operate in different time zones, availability during classic office hours has long been of little use. The same applies to job profiles such as press spokesperson or communications manager, for whom different availability rules apply in case of urgent inquiries than for employees in accounting. In exceptional cases, organizations allow their employees to continue doing their usual job in a workation (mixture of travel, vacation, and work, see the article "Working where others vacation—'Workation', a model with a future?") or as digital nomads (employees without a fixed residence and workplace, see the article "Work from anywhere - The free choice of workplace"). Some even deliberately use digital nomads, for example, to cover a night shift in Europe by someone in a different time zone (e.g., online news portals).

3 Challenges of Constant Digital Accessibility

The greatest challenge of constant online access is the risk of exhaustion leading to burnout, because personal boundary management fails in a persistent stress situation, because recovery is lacking due to personal boundary skills, which often goes hand in hand with an untrained "no muscle". The ability to say "no" is statistically related to whether someone feels stressed by constant digital accessibility: The better the individual ability to deal with social pressure, the less accessibility becomes a stress factor (Genner, 2017, p. 105 f.).

How important regular recovery and distance from work are is shown by numerous work and organizational psychological research results (Sonnentag et al., 2008, 2022; Sonnentag & Bayer, 2005). In addition to helpful measures within organizations, individual self-care and recovery skills of employees are also necessary to counteract overload. Organizations are well advised to regulate digital accessibility so that integrator personality types do not interfere with those employees who can be counted as separators in their sacred leisure time and thus demotivate them. The danger that integrators infer from themselves to others exists insofar as, unlike separators, they are generally not bothered by being contacted in their free time or even on vacation.

In addition to health risks, there are also labor law risks in the context of constant digital accessibility, which fall into the area of lack of due diligence by employers. Operational health management and a clear regulation of accessibility is in the interest of companies in several respects: prevention against exhaustion, but also to avoid productivity losses due to long-term illnesses. Employers have a statutory duty of care towards their employees. In addition, labor law provides protection against round-the-clock work, which, however, also prevents a certain (actually welcome) flexibility. Labor law varies from country to country, which is why companies and organizations are well advised to clarify whether and how they can let their employees work elsewhere under what labor law conditions.

Risks of constant online access also need to be considered in the context of cybersecurity. Those who work remotely often use devices such as laptops, tablets and smartphones in the home office or as part of a BYOD strategy ("Bring Your Own Device") that do not meet the security standards of professionally maintained devices that would be available on site at the company or organization. In the home office and on the go, insecure networks are also much more likely to be used, which may provide an entry point for cybercriminals. Constant professional accessibility thus also carries an increased risk of being more vulnerable in terms of data as an organization, at least outside the company (Romy, 2020).

In addition to health and data technical risks, the increase in remote work has exacerbated another challenge: Digital surveillance of employees has experienced a real boom. What had initially established itself more in the transport and logistics industry (Levy, 2022) has also increasingly spread to other activities in the course of the pandemic (Kantor et al., 2022). In 2020, the demand for tools to monitor employees increased significantly (Ibrahim, 2021). Measuring people with data points is popular and a big business field. There are numerous risks in the work context: incorrect measurements, legal gray areas and the danger of demotivating productive and loyal employees with wrong incentives. The danger is great that "Productivity Scores" (Kantor et al., 2022) measure the wrong thing just because it can be measured. Many data points say nothing about the quality and effectiveness of work at the end of the day. Perhaps central things were worked out beyond the screens or using other digital tools. Being constantly digitally accessible for work does not necessarily mean working more efficiently.

4 Solutions and Practical Tips

Digital accessibility and some rules of thumb are not taboo in a healthy organizational culture. Expectations vary depending on the industry or professional function. Ideally, the team should discuss how to manage accessibility. Some organizations, for example, stipulate that digital contact is acceptable from Monday to Friday from 7 a.m. to 7 p.m., outside of these times a valid reason is needed to contact someone. Some also use the option to send messages with a delay. It should be clarified with the closest employees who is best reachable on which channel in an emergency (and what is understood by an emergency). Otherwise, both professionally and privately, there is increased pressure to regularly check all channels to see if and what new has arrived. When superiors send digital messages from their vacations, many employees interpret this as an implicit request to also have to be available in their free time. Many superiors do not intend this. Therefore, it makes sense to explicitly clarify mutual expectations on the subject of digital accessibility. Superiors often shape the organizational culture in their role model function—also with regard to digital accessibility. Therefore, the training of managers is also important in this respect.

In terms of cybersecurity and data sensitivity, internal training is useful, especially when organizations adopt a BYOD strategy that outsources a relevant part of cybersecurity to employees. The following practical tips for improving individually controllable data security are helpful, which can be summarized under the acronym "SUPER" (NCSC—National Center for Cybersecurity, 2022):

- **S**ave your data regularly on at least one second medium.
- **U**pdate your system, your programs and apps regularly with the latest version.
- **P**rovide your device with an installed antivirus program and an activated firewall.
- **E**ntry: only with strong passwords.
- **R**educe fraud risks by staying alert and always using your common sense.

The use of productivity scores and surveillance technologies by organizations undermines the trust relationship with employees. Before such tools are used for productivity enhancement or to counter mistrust of the workforce, all measures should be taken and exhausted that contribute to mutual trust and motivation of employees.

5 Summary and Outlook

Remote work is an improvement in quality of life for many. However, this also requires better self-regulation skills and dealing with "Always On", the ability to be online both professionally and privately anywhere and anytime. Constant digital accessibility can lead to a harmful cycle of stress and exhaustion. Leaders model their handling of digital accessibility and contacts from their vacations, thereby shaping an organizational culture that either allows for boundaries and recovery or not. Superiors are obliged to ensure a kind of operational health protection in terms of accessibility and to regulate rules of thumb for digital accessibility. Ideally, this also somewhat protects separators from integrators and their uncomplicated contact at all times. Clear regulation of representation in case of illness, vacation and other absences can noticeably reduce the pressure to be always on. Employers do well to explicitly tackle the issue of "dealing with constant digital connectivity".

The following checklist for companies and organizations can help:

- Can our employees work remotely in terms of time and space so that they can deliver their best performance?
- Are our employees sufficiently trained in data security for remote work?
- Do we have enough internal exchange opportunities so that professional relationships can be maintained offline and face-to-face in addition to digital communication?
- Do we have the organizational culture we desire in terms of digital contacts outside office hours?

- Has it been explicitly communicated to all our employees when we expect them to be digitally connected and when not?
- Are our employees informed that they are not expected to be digitally accessible during sick leave?
- Have our managers been sensitized that digital contacts outside working hours implicitly increase the pressure of hyper-connectivity on employees?
- Is there a clear attitude of the organization towards replacements during vacation?
- Do our employees consistently refrain from email responses when they have activated an absence message?
- Have we reduced the digital communication channels as much as possible? And have we defined on which channel official information is communicated and who can be reached where in an emergency?

References

Bitkom. (2020). Corona-Pandemie: Arbeit im Homeoffice nimmt deutlich zu. https://www.bitkom.org/Presse/Presseinformation/Corona-Pandemie-Arbeit-im-Homeoffice-nimmt-deutlich-zu

Genner, S. (2017). On/Off. Risks and rewards of the anytime-anywhere internet. vdf Hochschulverlag AG an der ETH Zürich. https://vdf.ch/on-off-e-book.html

Ibrahim, S. (2021, January 23). Überwachung im Homeoffice: Wenn die Vorgesetzten zu Spionen werden. SWI swissinfo.ch. https://www.swissinfo.ch/ger/wirtschaft/ueberwachung-im-homeoffice%2D%2Dwenn-die-vorgesetzten-zu-spionen-werden/46298546 (abgerufen am 02.10.2022)

Kantor, J., Sundaram, A., Aufrichtig, A., & Taylor, R. (2022, August 15). The Rise of the Worker Productivity Score. The New York Times. https://www.nytimes.com/interactive/2022/08/14/business/worker-productivity-tracking.html (abgerufen am 02.10.2022)

Lehmann, R., & Quadbeck, E. (2014, August 26). Andrea Nahles: „Mein Ziel ist Anti-Stress-Verordnung". Rheinische Post. https://rp-online.de/politik/deutschland/andrea-nahles-mein-ziel-ist-anti-stress-verordnung_aid-16580349 (abgerufen am 02.10.2022)

Levy, K. (2022). Data Driven. Princeton University Press. https://press.princeton.edu/books/hardcover/9780691175300/data-driven

NCSC – Nationales Zentrum für Cybersicherheit. (2022). Cybersicherheit | S-U-P-E-R.ch. https://www.s-u-p-e-r.ch/de/startseite/

Romy, K. (2020, November 17). Homeoffice – Einfallstor für Cyberkriminelle. SWI swissinfo.ch. https://www.swissinfo.ch/ger/gesellschaft/homeoffice%2D%2D-einfallstor-fuer-cyber-kriminelle/46155880 (abgerufen am 02.10.2022)

Sonnentag, S., & Bayer, U.-V. (2005). Switching off mentally: Predictors and consequences of psychological detachment from work during off-job time. Journal of Occupational Health Psychology, 10(4), 393–414. https://doi.org/10.1037/1076-8998.10.4.393 (abgerufen am 02.10.2022)

Sonnentag, S., Binnewies, C., & Mojza, E. J. (2008). „Did you have a nice evening?" A day-level study on recovery experiences, sleep, and affect. Journal of Applied Psychology, 93, 674–684. https://doi.org/10.1037/0021-9010.93.3.674

Sonnentag, S., Cheng, B. H., & Parker, S. L. (2022). Recovery from Work: Advancing the Field Toward the Future. Annual Review of Organizational Psychology and Organizational Behavior, 9(1), 33–60. https://doi.org/10.1146/annurev-orgpsych-012420-091355

Work Smart Initiative. (2019). Auf dem Weg zu Work Smart. Wo stehen Organisationen, die die Work Smart Charta unterzeichnet haben, in der Umsetzung von flexiblen Arbeitsformen? https://work-smart-initiative.ch/wp-content/uploads/2022/07/Resultate.pdf (abgerufen am 02.10.2022)

The Future of Corporate Co-Determination

Nele Urban and Benjamin Münnich

1 Introduction

The previous contributions of this work have shown that the world of work is undergoing a transformation. Some of the developments described, especially decentralized and mobile work (see the contribution "Work from anywhere - The free choice of workplace"), home office (see the contribution "Working from Home: Perspectives, Challenges, Solutions"), Workation (see the contribution "Working where others vacation—'Workation', a model with a future?"), Open Offices and collaboration in "Remote Teams", were suddenly implemented or at least significantly accelerated by the Corona pandemic. These developments pose challenges for the application of labor law. This particularly affects co-determination in the company, which is the subject of this contribution.

The purpose of co-determination in the workplace is to protect employees by involving elected employee representatives in decisions relevant to the company and in shaping the work environment. The individual employee has a committee at his disposal through the works council to enforce employee interests collectively and thus achieve a position on an equal footing with the employer. But do the basic terms of labor law—especially the concept of the operation ("Betrieb")—still reflect the realities of New Work? Does traditional co-determination in the workplace ensure effective representation of employees in the future of work?

N. Urban
Urban Rechtsanwaltskanzlei, Köln, Germany
e-mail: Nele.Urban@urbanrechtsanwaltskanzlei.de

B. Münnich (✉)
CMS Deutschland, Köln, Germany
e-mail: benjamin.muennich@cms-hs.com

I. Knappertsbusch and G. Wisskirchen (eds.), *The Future of Work*,
https://doi.org/10.1007/978-3-658-45150-9_23

2 Challenges of Co-determination in the Workplace in the Light of Modern Forms of Work

It is of fundamental importance whether or not the classic concept of the company encompasses the digitized world of work, especially mobile work, and whether there is still an organizational unit in which co-determination in the company can be exercised. This can be doubted, as the Works Constitution Act (Betriebsverfassungsgesetz—BetrVG) originates from a time when the world of work was shaped by industry and manufacturing trades and the operation was therefore usually clearly demarcated spatially.

The operation is defined according to prevailing opinion as a union of personal, material and material resources for the continued pursuit of the work-technical purpose set by one or more legal entities.[1] For this purpose, the material and immaterial resources available in an operation must be combined, ordered, specifically used and the human labor force controlled by a unified management apparatus.[2] For the demarcation of the operation, it is therefore decisive whether or not the employees form a community through the work assignment given to them and the spatial cooperation, which presents itself as a uniform workforce.[3]

2.1 Significance of Spatial Connectedness

As a rule—one only has to think of classic production sites—spatial connectedness is necessary for the cooperation of employees to achieve a common work result. However, it is not a constituting criterion for an operation within the meaning of works constitution law.[4] The uniform employee community within an operation and thus the sense of community of the employees is not decisive for the determination of the operation. The spatial unity of workplaces can speak for an operation but it does not have to.[5] The lack of spatial unity does not necessarily speak against an operationas Sec. 4 BetrVG shows.[6]

Since the spatial connectedness of the workforce is not a constitutive characteristic for the existence of an operation, mobile work does not per se exclude an operation in the sense of the BetrVG.

Decisive for the operation as a co-determination unit is the unified management apparatus in matters subject to co-determination.[7] This means that regardless of

[1] BAG, decision of 13.08.2008 – 7 ABR 21/07, NZA-RR 2009, 255, 256.

[2] BAG, decision of 15.10.2014 – 7 ABR 53/12, NZA 2015, 1014, 1016.

[3] *Maschmann*, in: Richardi, BetrVG, § 1 BetrVG Rn. 20; *Gamillscheg*, AuR 2001, 411, 415.

[4] *Maschmann*, in: Richardi, BetrVG, § 1 BetrVG Rn. 32; *Besgen*, in: BeckOK ArbR, § 1 BetrVG Rn. 21; *Urban*, ArbRAktuell 2022, 221, 222.

[5] BAG, decision of 23.09.1982 – 6 ABR 42/81, AP BetrVG 1972 § 4 No. 3.

[6] *Koch*, in: ErfK, § 1 BetrVG Rn. 11.

[7] BAG, decision of 17.01.2007 – 7 ABR 63/05, NZA 2007, 703, 705.

the spatial conditions, the operation and the assignement to this operation can be delimited and defined by the unified management apparatus.

2.2 Home Office

This understanding of the term also allows for an assessment of the implications under works constitution law for employees working from home. Employees working from home can be assigned to a specific operational site, even though the legislator, by using the term "operation" in Sec. 1 para. 1 BetrVG, generally refers to the physical operational site, which typically forms the place of work; this area generally ends at the boundary of the operational property or the operational premises.[8] However, this does not mean that employees who perform their work outside the premises of the operation are not considered to be part of the operation. Rather, they remain part of the operation if they are integrated into the operational organization, as is the case, for example, with field staff.[9]

Even if employees are working from home, they can, based on this, be assigned to specific operational sites.[10] These premises can be visited, if face-to-face meetings are necessary and desired. Therefore, there is still a physical point of contact where the works council may have its own office. Even in these cases, the extent of the management powers of the management apparatus tied to the respective operational site will determine the spatial boundaries of the operation. It is irrelevant whether employees regularly work from home, as a management apparatus assignable to an operational site exists. Since the concept of operation in the BetrVG is not spatial, but functional, the home office is a workplace that is considered part of the operation.[11] The assignement of such an employee to the operation is already established by the fact that he is integrated into the operational organization due to the communication technology connection usually required and pursues the operational purposes in the home office.[12] The operational character of the home office is further supported by the provision of IT technology by the employer and its content, organizational and temporal specifications.[13]

The same applies to co-determination rights. They are not limited to activities within the operational site owned or used by the employer, as they do not only concern the organization of the resources available to the employer. Rather, they also cover the activities of employees outside the operational site, because the employer regulates the operational behavior of the employees there as well. The

[8] *Maschmann*, in: Richardi, BetrVG, § 1 BetrVG no. 112b.

[9] BAG, decision of 29.01.1992 – 7 ABR 27/91, NZA 1992, 894, 896 f.

[10] *Urban*, ArbRAktuell 2022, 221, 222.

[11] *Maschmann*, in: Richardi, BetrVG, § 1 BetrVG no. 112c.

[12] *Maschmann*, in: Richardi BetrVG, § 1 BetrVG no. 112c.

[13] *Müller*, Home Office no. 533.

location where an operational activity is carried out is irrelevant. Therefore, the works council also has a say when it comes to the behavior of employees outside the operational site.[14] Proper work in the home office requires numerous instructions that are subject to co-determination according to Sec. 87 BetrVG. In addition, the electronic devices used in the home office generate personal data, which typically allow the behavior and performance of the employees to be monitored; however, the works council has a say in this according to Sec. 87 para. 1 no. 6 BetrVG. If necessary, these devices can be used to record or control working hours; this is also subject to co-determination Sec. 87 para. 1 no. 2 BetrVG. Furthermore, questions of health and safety at work, which are subject to co-determination according to Sec. 87 para. 1 no. 7 BetrVG, arise, e.g. with regard to the temporal extent of accessibility and the guarantee of occupational safety outside the operational site. Since integration into an operational work organization does not require a minimum amount of work performed for an operation, the home office workplace of a part-time employee also represents an operational workplace.[15]

2.3 Purely Mobile Work

The mobilization and digitalization of work is culminating in a state where collaboration is exclusively digital, meetings also only take place digitally, and there are no longer any common spatial points of reference. This development extends to companies that no longer have any company-owned premises to use and where teams are agile, especially in terms of space. Can an exclusively digitally mediated management apparatus establish an operation in this case? This is not a scenario for the future: Especially in some IT companies, there is already no spatial binding of employees. In such companies, employees are sometimes completely free to choose where they perform their work. These employees are also referred to as digital nomads. In these companies, there is no longer any management apparatus at the registered company headquarters, but often only a mailbox and a scanner for the incoming paper mail. The company is managed and controlled exclusively remotely via mobile devices.

In our opinion, an operation also exists in these cases if the case law of the Federal Labor Court is used as a basis. The decisive factor for the operation as a co-determination unit is the uniform management apparatus in matters subject to co-determination.[16] If a company is managed exclusively digitally, the co-determination-relevant management apparatus is also digitally mediated.[17] Even if the

[14] *Maschmann*, in: Richardi, BetrVG, § 1 BetrVG no. 112b.

[15] *Maschmann*, in: Richardi, BetrVG, § 1 BetrVG no. 112c.

[16] BAG, decision of 17.01.2007 – 7 ABR 63/05, NZA 2007, 703, 705.

[17] *Urban*, ArbRAktuell 2022, 221, 223.

concept of a purely digitally acting management apparatus is unusual, this instrument is a direct consequence of digital change and its manifestation in terms of co-determination law.

This means that the operation in terms of co-determination law for purely digitally managed companies is where the co-determination-relevant management apparatus takes place. This also means that all employees who are uniformly controlled in terms of personnel management form a business. Their actual place of work and residence is not decisive.

2.4 Employees Abroad

Another special feature arises when individual or several employees are permanently resident abroad but are uniformly digitally controlled from Germany. Here too, existing case law can be referred to: The question is less whether or not an operation can be identified at all, but whether or not the foreign activity of the employee can be attributed to the domestic operation, thus whether the co-determination law "radiates" to this employee and he thus belongs to the domestic business in terms of co-determination law or not.[18] This is to be determined in each case taking into account all the circumstances of the individual case.

What is ultimately required is that the respective person is integrated into the domestic business.[19] The domestic employer must have actually assumed a co-determination-relevant (even if partial) employer position vis-à-vis the employee working abroad. A domestic connection can therefore result from the fact that the right of direction vis-à-vis the employee working abroad is exercised by the domestic business.[20] Based on this case law, employees who are digitally managed from Germany but are permanently resident abroad are also to be assigned to a German operation.

2.5 Concept of Operation in Terms of Protection Against Dismissal in Mobile Work

The Protection Against Dismissal Act (Kündigungsschutzgesetz—KSchG) does not contain a definition of the concept of operation, just like the BetrVG. For the concept of operation in dismissal protection law, the concept shaped by Sec. 1 para. 1 BetrVG is primarily to be used. Also required here is a management

[18] *Urban*, ArbRAktuell 2022, 221, 223.

[19] See BAG, judgment of 24.05.2018 – 2 AZR 54/18, NZA 2018, 1396 f.; decision of 20.02.2001 – 1 ABR 30/00, AP BetrVG 1972 § 101 No. 23.

[20] BAG, judgment of 24.05.2018 – 2 AZR 54/18, NZA 2018, 1396.

apparatus that independently makes essential decisions in personnel and social matters.[21] However, a distinguishing feature is that – in accordance with the purpose of the Protection Against Dismissal Act – for the assessment of sufficient personnel management competence for the determination of the business in terms of protection against dismissal, the competence to conclude, terminate and amend employment contracts is particularly important.

Based on the explanations on the concept of operation in terms of co-determination law, employees in home office or exclusively mobile working employees are also part of a business in the sense of Sec. 23 KSchG, provided they are subject to the management apparatus there. This fact is particularly important when determining the threshold value according to Sec. 23 para. 1 KSchG for the applicability of the Protection Against Dismissal Act, but also in the context of social selection according to Sec. 1 para. 3 sentence 1 KSchG.

3 Solutions and Practical Tips

As shown, the operation in the sense of the KSchG and the BetrVG can be identified even with completely mobile work. However, assigning (partially or completely) mobile working employees to an operation can still be difficult in practice. Therefore, employers should—especially in the case of individual personnel measures—check whether a works council is responsible for the respective affected employee or not. This is to be assessed for integration into a specific operation, ultimately primarily based on the lines of instruction. If an employee working from home receives employment law instructions from an operation in which a works council has been formed, this may need to be involved.

It also follows that the operational affiliation of exclusively mobile working employees can be changed simply by altering the reporting lines. This alone assigns the employee a new digital workplace organizationally—naturally, without this having to manifest spatially. The decisive factor for assigning employees to a specific operation in these cases is whether or not the employees are integrated into the digital work organization of this unit qualifying as an operation and receive professional instructions from this unit.[22] The criteria mentioned above can be used as a basis, so that the content, organizational and temporal specifications from the respective manager are particularly important.

To prevent cases of doubt and to limit and thus keep track of the "digital operation", it is recommended to record the functional assignement of employees and the respective reporting lines in the form of organizational charts.

---

[21] *Kiel*, in: ErfK, § 23 KSchG para. 3.

[22] *Maschmann*, in: Richardi BetrVG, § 1 BetrVG Rn. 112c; BAG, Beschl. v. 26.05.2021 – 7 ABR 17/20, NZA 2021, 1494, 1498.

4 Summary and Outlook

Even though the realities in the world of work have dramatically changed as a result of digital transformation and the Corona pandemic, they are still captured and depicted by the basic terms of labor law. Employees who work from home form operations with the existing establishments. Even in companies that work exclusively mobile and no longer have traditional offices, the digitally mediated management apparatus constitutes an operation in terms of works constitution law.

However, the establishment of a body intended for the representation of employee interests, the works council, encounters significant new challenges in such digital organizational units:

The establishment and work of a works council requires a certain degree of employee organization and collective will formation. After all, the establishment of a works council begins with the conduct of a works council election. This is usually initiated by the company's employees, which rarely happens in practice by a single employee alone.

The works council election must then also be conducted properly. According to the provisions of the BetrVG and the election regulations based on it, the works council election, in short, is to be conducted in the operation. These provisions include, for example, the execution of the election, which is generally provided as an election in person (Sec. 11 para. 1 Regulations for the Works Councils Elections—WahlOBetrVG), as well as the obligation to display the voters' list (as well as other election documents) in the operation for inspection (Sec. 2 para. 4 s. 1 WahlOBetrVG). This seems difficult to implement for purely remote working employees, although the essential election documents can at least additionally be "made known using the information and communication technology available in the operation" (see, for example, Sec. 2 para. 4 s. 2 WahlOBetrVG regarding the voters' list).

Irrespective of this, meaningful works council work requires a certain degree of "employee proximity" and "decision proximity". Both are not easily guaranteed in pure remote teams when both colleagues and superiors are only digitally accessible. This certainly does not exclude the trust-based cooperation between employer and works council required in Sec. 2 para. 1 BetrVG—but the distance alone is likely to at least make it more difficult to build a trust-based relationship between employer and works council (and between works council and employees). As employers also have an interest in well-functioning works councils work, for example to be able to implement (personnel, social or economic) decisions quickly and with the support of the workforce, this development in the world of work should be approached from both sides.

References

Müller, Stefan, Homeoffice in der arbeitsrechtlichen Praxis, 3. Auflage, Baden-Baden 2022.
Müller-Glöge, Rudi/Preis, Ulrich/Schmidt, Ingrid (Hrsg.), Erfurter Kommentar zum Arbeitsrecht, 22. Auflage, München 2022.

Richardi, Reinhard (Hrsg.), Betriebsverfassungsgesetz, 17. Auflage, München 2022.
Richardi, Reinhard (Hrsg.), Kommentar zum Betriebsverfassungsgesetz, 17. Auflage, München 2022.
Rolfs, Christian/Giesen, Richard/Meßling, Miriam/Udsching, Peter (eds.), Beck'scher Online-Kommentar Arbeitsrecht, 65. Edition, München 2022.
Urban, Nele, Der Betriebsbegriff in Zeiten von mobilem Arbeiten, ArbRAktuell 2022, 221.

Digital Access Right of the Trade Union to the Company

Volker Stück

1 Introduction

The Covid pandemic has turned labor law and work models upside down.[1] Telework and mobile work have spread rapidly, albeit involuntarily, and have proven their worth.[2] The legislator has followed suit and with the Works Council Modernization Act, in force since June 18, 2021,[3] made the "how" of mobile work subject to co-determination in section 87 para. 1 no. 14 BetrVG[4] and enabled virtual works council work in section 30 para. 2 BetrVG, after section 129 BetrVG a. F. expired on June 30, 2021.[5]

Of the home office-capable functions, a foreseeable 30–60% will work outside the company, so the question of digital accessibility of employees for internal works councils[6] and also external trade unions arises. The latter will be presented here with a design proposal, which is necessary because the legislator has refrained from regulations of the right of coalition and has pushed the

[1] *Stück/Wein*, AuA 2020, 200; *this.*, AuA 05/2022, 14.

[2] *Maiß/Hützen*, AuA 2020, 696; *Stück/Salo*, AuA 04/2021, 22: Sample BV as well as AuA 12/2021, 14.

[3] BGBl. I 2021, 1762.

[4] *Bayreuther*, NZA 2021, 839; *Fitting*, § 87 BetrVG Rz. 580 ff.

[5] *Boemke/Roloff/Haase*, NZA 2021, 827; Fitting, § 30 BetrVG Rz. 24 ff.

[6] *Klebe*, NZA 2020, 996, 999.

V. Stück (✉)
BWI GmbH, Bonn, Germany
e-mail: volker.stueck@bwi.de

I. Knappertsbusch and G. Wisskirchen (eds.), *The Future of Work*,
https://doi.org/10.1007/978-3-658-45150-9_24

clarification—as often—to the practice and the courts in the way of legal development: Legislative Low/Zero Performance par excellence.[7]

2 Advantages

So far, classic works council and trade union work regularly took place analogously via notices on the blackboard, manual distribution of flyers, personal address/actions at info/advertising stands in or in front of the companies or on the company premises including company parking lot[8] or speeches at works (part) meetings, which from 01.03.2020 to 30.06.2021 according to section 129 BetrVG; section 39 SprAuG a. F. could be conducted virtually/online, but no longer since then,[9] although they had proven themselves in practice in times of epidemics.

Since employees are increasingly working remotely or at home outside the classic operation, a digital access right to employees for works councils and trade unions is being discussed in view of the "de-operationalization"[10] for the performance of their tasks and rights. E-mail access or virtual communication and collaboration via the company's internal intranet is the blackboard of today and tomorrow.[11] It is certainly sustainable and economical in times of climate crisis and energy shortage/cost increase and maintains contact/exchange despite "empty/deserted" operations.

3 Challenges

The challenges in relation to the digital access right of the trade union to the operation are based on the balancing of the basic rights of the trade union with those of the employer.

3.1 Based on Art. 9 Para. 3 GG

Art. 9 Para. 3 GG guarantees for everyone and for all professions the right to form coalitions for the protection and promotion of working and economic conditions. This basic right protects the individual's right to establish such an association, to join it or to abstain from it (negative freedom of association). It also protects the

[7] On labor law low performance: *Stück*, AuA 2012, 632; *Wetzling/Habel*, Dealing with Low Performers, 2021.

[8] *BVerfG*, decision of 9.7.2020 –1 BvR 719/19, NZA 2020, 1118; *BAG*, judgment of 20.11.2018 –1 AZR 189/17, NZA 2019, 402: Amazon/Verdi—labor dispute on parking lot.

[9] Fitting, § 42 BetrVG Rz. 1a.

[10] *Hanau*, NJW 2016, 2613, 2614.

[11] *Klebe*, NZA 2020, 996, 999.

coalitions in their existence and their organizational structure, as well as activities aimed at preserving and promoting working and economic conditions.[12] Among the protected activities that serve to maintain and secure a coalition is the recruitment of members. Through this, the coalitions create the foundation for fulfilling their tasks and securing their continued existence. Furthermore, their negotiating strength and social power depend on the number of members.[13] Without advertising for new members, there is a risk that the membership of a trade union will decline over time to such an extent that it can no longer properly fulfill its task of preserving and promoting working and economic conditions. Therefore, the freedom of a trade union includes the right to strengthen its power with the aim of maintaining and recruiting members.[14] For trade unions, member recruitment in the companies is of particular importance. Effective advertising requires the attention and openness of the employees being courted. This can be assumed especially in the company.

In principle, there is a right for trade unionists who are not part of the company to have—actual—access to a company, whereby a notice period of one week must be observed.[15] It is up to the trade union to determine which and how many people it entrusts with an advertising measure it has designed. Therefore, not only the location for trade union advertising, but also the personal selection of the advertisers falls within the scope of protection of Art. 9 Para. 3 GG. A trade union does not need to be referred to entrust only employees belonging to the company with the implementation of member recruitment. Rather, it is generally entitled to use agents who are not part of the company for this purpose.[16] Art. 9 Para. 3 GG generally leaves it to a coalition to choose the means it considers suitable and necessary for its coalition-specific activity. Accordingly, a trade union can decide for itself where, by whom and in what way it wants to advertise for members.[17]

3.2 Basic Rights of the Employer and Practical Concordance

However, it should be taken into account that the trade union, in order to carry out advertising measures in the company, depends on the cooperation of the company owner. It can only operate in the company through external representatives if the employer allows them access and tolerates their activity. Thus, such member recruitment/information collides with the constitutionally protected rights of the

---

[12] *BVerfG*, decision of 10.9.2004 – 1 BvR 1191/03, NZA 2004, 1338; *BAG*, judgement of 28.2.2006 – 1 AZR 460/04, NZA 2006, 798.

[13] *BVerfG*, decision of 14.11.1995 – 1 BvR 601/92, NZA 1996, 381.

[14] *BAG*, judgement of 31.5.2005 – 1 AZR 141/04, NZA 2005, 1182.

[15] *BAG*, judgement of 28.2.2006 – 1 AZR 460/04, NZA 2006, 798.

[16] *BAG*, judgement of 22.6.2010 – 1 AZR 179/09, NZA 2010, 1365; *LAG Köln*, judgement of 16.9.2016 – 10 Sa 328/16, BeckRS 2016, 111602.

[17] *BAG*, judgement of 28.2.2006 – 1 AZR 460/04, NZA 2006, 798.

employer and company owner, including his right to property and ownership protected by Art. 13, 14 GG, as well as his economic freedom of activity protected by Art. 2 para. 1 GG, which is particularly affected in case of a disruption of the work process and company peace.[18] The different interests have to be balanced in the sense of practical concordance.[19] If a responsible trade union carries out trade union advertising measures once in a calendar half-year during break times, this is not objectionable. Recognized security and confidentiality interests are sufficiently taken into account by restricting the right of access for member recruitment to those areas of the company that do not concern the production area and the offices.[20]

Practical Tip If the trade union's chosen method of member recruitment and third-party information collides with the employer's legal positions from Art. 14 para. 1, Art. 12 para. 1 and Art. 2 para. 1 GG, it is – in the absence of legislative action – the task of the courts to capture these conflicting basic rights positions and – possibly by way of legal development – to balance them in individual cases according to the principle of practical concordance, so that they become as effective as possible for all parties involved.[21]

3.3 No Regulatory Authority of the Works Parties

The right of trade union members working in the company, protected by Art 9 para. 3 GG, to actively participate in the coalition-like activity of their trade union by distributing trade union information or advertising material in the company and thus to support it in pursuing its coalition-specific goals, whether analog or digital, is not subject to the regulatory power of the works parties, so that a regulation by works agreement is excluded. There is no room for co-determination by the works council according to section 87 para. 1 no. 1 BetrVG, which is also shown by section 2 para. 3 BetrVG.[22]

Practical Tip The works parties cannot make provisions for trade unions and their members within the framework of section 87 para. 1 no. 1 BetrVG as to whether and under what conditions a coalition-specific activity in the company is permissible. This must be regulated by the employer himself with the coalition if

[18] *BAG*, Judgement of 28.2.2006 – 1 AZR 460/04, NZA 2006, 798; *BAG*, Judgement of 22.6.2010 – 1 AZR 179/09, NZA 2010, 1365.

[19] *LAG Hamm*, Judgement of 16.12.2014 – 12 Sa 1020/14, NZA-RR 2015, 249.

[20] *LAG Cologne*, Judgement of 16.9.2016 – 10 Sa 328/16, BeckRS 2016, 111602.

[21] *Schwarze*, RdA 2010, p. 116

[22] *BAG*, Decision of 28.7.2020 – 1 ABR 41/18, NZA 2020, 1413.

the tariff partners do not do so. If the employer's basic rights are violated, he must seek legal protection from the labor courts.

3.4 Data Protection Aspects

The transfer of employee data such as emails (max.mustermann@X-gmbh.de) to third parties – including trade unions[23] – is only permissible if there are no statutory obligations of confidentiality (section 79 BetrVG, section 82 para. 2 s. 3, section 83 para. 1 s. 3; section 99 para. 1 s. 3, section 102 para. 2 s. 5 BetrVG) and this is necessary according to the BetrVG for the performance of statutory tasks of the works council. Data collection/use beyond the statutory tasks of the works council would only be possible with the prior consent of the data subject (Art. 7 DSGVO, section 26 para. 2 BDSG n.F.) and could otherwise justify exclusion under section 23 para. 1 BetrVG.[24] Since there are no control-free areas, the data protection officer is entitled and obliged under Art. 38 para. 2 DSGVO to advise and control works councils, but also professional secret holders such as company doctors and in-house lawyers (cf. section 203 StGB).[25]

4 Solutions and Practical Tips

Since the employer is not obliged under Art. 9 para. 3 GG to actively distribute trade union information to its employees using its own resources or to maintain or operate a page of the trade union in its intranet using its own resources,[26] the practical solution is for the employer to provide a page in the intranet for the trade unions represented in the company to "operate responsibly" in order to inform or communicate with the workforce. An agreement between the employer and the trade union could be based on the following model.[27]

Model
Agreement on coalition-specific activity @ A GmbH

[23] *Stamer/Kuhnke*, in: Plath, DSGVO/BDSG, § 26 BDSG Rz. 158; *Seifert*, in: Simitis/Hornung/Spiecker, Data Protection Law, Art. 88 DSGVO Rz. 213.

[24] *Seifert*, in: Simitis/Hornung/Spiecker, Data Protection Law, Art. 88 DSGVO Rz. 214; *Stück*, ZD 2019, 256, 259 f.; *BAG*, decision of 22.5.1959 – 1 ABR 2/59, AP BetrVG § 23 No. 3: Salary data to trade union due to contribution honesty.

[25] *Drewes*, in: Simitis/Hornung/Spiecker, Data Protection Law, Art. 39 DSGVO Rz. 27; *Stück*, ZD 2019, 256, 259; *LAG Baden-Württemberg*, decision of 20.5.2022 – 12 TaBV 4/21, ArbRAktuell 2022, 360.

[26] *ArbG Bonn*, judgement of 11.5.2022 – 2 Ca 93/22, NZA-RR 2022, 351.

[27] See Stück, ArbRAktuell 2021,.518; Stück/Wein, AUA 10-2021, 11.

Between the
A GmbH
and
the G Trade Union (G)
The following is agreed:

I. Preamble & Background

As a trade union represented in the company, G has a right to coalition-specific activity from Art. 9 para. 3 GG, which according to case law includes in particular the addressing of employees, trade union advertising and actions, information on trade union topics within the framework of applicable laws.

A operates .... nationwide, but increasingly also abroad, with a decentralized setup at many different locations of different sizes. Both the own A or customer locations as well as the ICT are subject to special protection and disruptions in/for the operational process of A as well as its customers/clients are to be avoided at all times.

The employees of A work – even before the Corona pandemic, but especially afterwards – to a large extent mobile or remote in various forms, e.g. telework at home or onsite at the customer, as well as in largely self-determined working hours or also – according to the order – 24/7 or shifts 365 days/year. They are deployed domestically and abroad. From these circumstances, continuous, comprehensive and secure accessibility & communication can only be achieved with modern and protected ICT.

II. Contents & Regulations

In order to best and legally account for mutual interests, particularly in terms of easy and good accessibility/access on the one hand and protection/disturbance prevention on the other, the parties agree as follows:

(1) A will technically set up and maintain a separate page for G in A's own intranet/ICON for the duration of this agreement. This page will be clearly marked as the G-page. It is generally securely accessible at all times throughout the entire federal territory as well as from abroad.
(2) A will immediately inform G in writing or in text form about the functionality of the page.
(3) This G-page will be operated by A for G under the content responsibility of G. G is responsible for the content posted there and the operation in accordance with the GDPR, press/media law, and other legal provisions.
(4) G will designate to A, in writing or in text form, no later than 2 weeks after notification of the operational setup of this page, up to a maximum of 5 union trust members/members who are employees of A, who will independently fill and maintain this page on behalf of G and are solely authorized to do so. These authors will be appropriately trained by the responsible department of A.

Due to the principle of separation of mandates/functions (e.g., supervisory board, works council, union official/member), G will ensure that the content posted

on the G-page and the authors/editors responsible for it appear in their union-specific function and this is clearly evident in their external appearance.
(5) In the event of obviously illegal, defamatory, insulting, racist, religious, sexual, discriminatory, secrecy-relevant, data protection-violating or comparable content/disturbances that are detected on the page, A will immediately point this out to G and is entitled to temporarily deactivate the page until the disturbance is eliminated. This does not affect the right to terminate without notice for good cause.
(6) Since A has no influence on the content design of this page towards G, A assumes no liability for it. Should A be held liable for legal violations caused by or from this page or the responsible persons according to clause (4), G will indemnify A from damages that have demonstrably occurred to A.
(7) This agreement comes into effect upon signing and is initially limited to a trial period until 31.12.202X.
(8) If the page proves successful in the opinion of both parties, this agreement will continue indefinitely from 01.01.202X and can be terminated at any time from this date with a notice period of 3 months to the end of the quarter without any after-effects. The right to terminate without notice for good cause (e.g., according to clause (5)) remains reserved for both parties.
(9) Should a provision of this agreement be or become invalid, the parties commit to replace it within 2 months with a regulation that comes closest to the intended content and purposes (clause A).
(10) Should content changes to this agreement arise due to a future legal regulation or a supreme court ruling (i.e., BAG, BVerwG, BVerfG, ECJ) on a digital access right of the unions or similar, the parties will enter into negotiations on the adjustment of this agreement no later than 2 months after the legal regulation comes into effect or the court decision is publicly announced.
(11) Should other unions, demonstrably represented at A, demand a corresponding page, A will set it up analogously and under the same conditions/regulations.

5 Summary and Outlook

The digital access right of the trade union to the company is at the beginning of its development and has arrived in jurisprudence[28] and literature[29]. In the 2021 traffic light coalition agreement, there are indeed corresponding regulatory announcements, but these are not concrete and one should not have too much

[28] *ArbG Bonn*, Judg. of 11.5.2022 – 2 Ca 93/22, NZA-RR 2022, 351; *ArbG Hamburg*, Judg. of 31.3.2022 – 4 Ca 248/21, AuA 07/2022, 59.

[29] *Göpfert/Stöckert*, NZA 2021, 1209; *Stück*, ArbRAktuell 2021, 516; Stück/Wein, AuA 10/2021, p. 8; Meyer, NZA 2022, 1567.

hope considering the previous non-codification of the right to form coalitions: A "contemporary right for digital access" to companies is to be created, which corresponds to the existing analog rights. Presumably, the employers' associations-trade unions or the company practice will also develop more practical solutions here faster, better and more targeted than a often sluggish general legislator.

The need seems to be there, as even after Corona many employees no longer work regularly in the company and work in the home office or remote/off-site has become a constant, which also serves work-life balance and sustainability/environmental protection goals by eliminating unnecessary commuting.

References

Bayreuther, Frank: Mitbestimmung bei mobiler Arbeit nach § 87 I Nr. 14 BetrVG, NZA 2021, pp. 839–841.

Fitting, Karl (Begr.)/Schmidt, Ingrid/Trebinger, Yvonne/Linsenmaier, Wolfgang/Schelz, Hanna: Betriebsverfassungsgesetz, Kommentar, 31. Aufl., München 2022.

Göpfert, Burkard/Stöckert, Susanna: Digitaler Zugang der Gewerkschaft zum Betrieb?, NZA 2021, pp. 1209–1214.

Hanau, Hans: Schöne digitale Arbeitswelt?, NJW 2016, pp. 2613–2617.

Klebe, Thomas: Betriebsverfassung digital?, NZA 2020, pp. 996–999.

Maiß, Sebastian/Hützen, Peter: Echte Flexibilität nur mit neuen Gesetzen – Interview zur neuen Normalität im Homeoffice, AuA 2020, S. 696–701.

Plath, Kai-Uwe (Hrsg.): DSGVO/BDSG, Kommentar, 3. Aufl., Köln 2018.

Simitis, Spiros/Hornung, Gerrit/Spiecker gen. Döhmann, Indra (Hrsg.): Datenschutzrecht – Kommentar, Baden-Baden 2019.

Stück, Volker: Richtiger Umgang mit Low Performern, AuA 2012, pp. 632–635.

Stück, Volker: Digitales Zugangsrecht der Gewerkschaften zum Betrieb – Rechtlicher Rahmen und Mustervereinbarung, ArbRAktuell 2021, pp. 516–519.

Stück, Volker: Betriebsrat oder Geheimrat?, ZD 2019, pp. 256–261.

Stück, Volker/Salo, Christina: My Homeoffice is my Castle – Muster Betriebsvereinbarung zu Telearbeit, Homeoffice, Mobile Work, AuA 04/2021, S. 22–28.

Stück, Volker/Salo, Christina: Out of Office oder back to Office – Aktuelle rechtliche Aspekte von Tele-, mobiler, remoter Arbeit und New-Work-Konzepten, AuA 12/2021, pp. 14–19.

Stück, Volker/Wein, Boris: New Trade Union Work – Digitales Zugangsrecht der Gewerkschaften zum Betrieb, AuA 10/2021, S. 8–12.

Stück, Volker/Wein, Boris: Pandemie und Arbeitsrecht, AuA 2020, pp. 200–206.

Stück, Volker/Wein, Boris: Zwei Jahre Pandemie: Update Corona-Rechtsprechung, AuA 05/2022, pp. 14–20.

Wetzling, Frank/Habel, Maren: Umgang mit Low Performern, München 2021.

Teamwork and Leadership

From Functional Excellence to Transactional Excellence—The Organization as a Network of High-Performance Teams

Verena Schaad and Marco Böhmer

"If everything is to remain as it is, everything must change."

(loosely based on Giuseppe Tomasi Prince of Lampedusa)

1 Introduction

1.1 Why Are New Forms of Work Organization Necessary?

The frequency, impulse, and scope of changes on organizations are constantly increasing. This challenges and questions established paradigms and logics of classical work organization. The way solutions for business challenges are collaborated on within organizations does not match the requirements of the markets and the perceived realities of the employees. The question arises whether the currently still valid architecture of organizations is still capable of dealing with emerging uncertainties in a targeted, swift, and solution-oriented manner. Where do you start when you want to adapt something as complex and finely tuned as an organization and how work is done within it to current realities? The paradox of transformation usually goes like this: What seems feasible is not transformative, and what is transformative seems unfeasible. As a result, this leads to an endless series of optimizations that rarely manage to adapt the work organization to current requirements. Organizations should focus more on the business challenge rather than squeezing the challenges into a functional organization. What is missing is clarity about what an alternative work organization could look like.

V. Schaad (✉)
Bayer AG, Berlin, Germany

M. Böhmer
Bayer AG, Leverkusen, Germany

I. Knappertsbusch and G. Wisskirchen (eds.), *The Future of Work*,
https://doi.org/10.1007/978-3-658-45150-9_25

1.2 Definition: What Do New Forms of Work Organization Mean?

We use aspects of classical and newer organization theory to introduce a new organization model based on the design of new ways of working ("New Ways of Working").

1. **Challenge: The task of the organization.** The new form of work organization should be thought of exclusively from the challenges to be solved. In the conventional pattern, the organization and its structure determine the quality of the solution; in modern forms of organization, the typology of the task determines the type of organization. In this process, the employees organize themselves around the described tasks or challenges, instead of fitting the tasks into a functionally pre-structured organization. An organization set up in this way is adaptive and thus capable of flexibly providing a suitable solution team with the right skills for each business challenge, which tackles the next challenge in a new composition after developing the solution.
2. **Principle: The basic principle of the organization.** Economically considered based on transaction cost theory, the existence and amount of costs for internal transactions compared to transactions on the market is the reason for the existence and determinant of the size of companies.[1] An organization can assert itself in the market if the quality of decisions—understood as a transaction towards solving a challenge—can be processed more efficiently, cost-effectively, and less prone to errors internally than externally. The aim is to avoid defensive[2] and too lengthy decisions and instead bring about fast, high-quality decisions. The importance of coordinating internal interfaces as a supposed management achievement is significantly lower today, the primacy of excellent transactions and the associated new ways of working must come back into focus.[3]
3. **DNA: The smallest cell of the organization** are teams that build on collective intelligence and psychological safety and are maximally enabled to solve problems and perform excellent transactions through a clever interplay of skills, fueled by new ways of working.[4] For this, decision-making must become more inclusive, expert knowledge loses its importance and above all, the basic requirements of successful interpersonal communication must be taken into account in order to increase the probability of success of team work. The most important building block for inclusive decision-making is establishing a

[1] Coase, R. H., (1937), The Nature of the Firm.

[2] Artinger, F.M., (2019), C. Y. A.: frequency and causes of defensive decisions in public administration.

[3] Barnard, C., (1948), Organization and Management.

[4] Pioneering factors determining high-performing teams and the relationship with collective intelligence: Duhig, C. (2016), What Google Learned From Its Quest to Build the Perfect Team.

safe emotional environment ("psychological safety") in the team.[5] This safety stimulates the introduction of as many different perspectives as possible and thus constructive collaboration for the rapid development of a solution. Since the quality and speed of the decision largely depend on how close the teams work to the challenge, clearly defined decision-making competencies and capable, authorized teams are essential. It is important that teams have a clear view of their relationships, priorities and roles, have built a healthy level of psychological safety and are able to make better decisions together than any individual could. With the application of the new ways of working, trust is gradually built, the speed as well as organizational learning is increased and the practices are incorporated into the work culture as a permanent component due to their proven effectiveness in business.

4. **Brain: The intelligence and memory of the organization**. The programmers' striving to automate new processes again and again and thus to give them a stringent logic of 0 and 1 or beyond in 0 and 1 at the same time—only the quantum computer, which is before a technically feasible scaling, can do this[6]—is unprecedented. Something is happening to us humans, the effects and potentials of which are not yet sufficiently determined, also on the currently transforming work organization of today. However, it is clear that in addition to the above-mentioned strengthening of human-to-human communication through new ways of working, the interaction of humans and machines will reach a new dimension. The computing operations will dramatically shorten per unit of time, so we speak of a real fourth disruption of communication media (after language, writing and printing) that significantly influences all interactions and offers enormous positive possibilities for the further development of our society and organizations. The use of AI opens up a wide range of potentials for safe, self-responsible and self-determined work as well as attractive and competitive workplaces.

1.3 Classification and Delimitation: How Can New Forms of Work Organization Be Introduced Into the Organization?

We summarize the previous considerations in the following model (see Fig. 1)[7].

The special focus is on describing the respective challenge and the required skills as precisely as possible. The introduction of Micro Practices as new working methods is the special trick that contributes to the excellence of transactions. By applying the new working methods within the framework of the New Ways

---

[5] Edmondson, A., (1991). Psychological safety and learning behavior in work teams.

[6] Ruane, J. et al., Before the Quantum Leap, Harvard Business manager, 05/2022.

[7] Zak, P. (2017), The Neuroscience of Trust

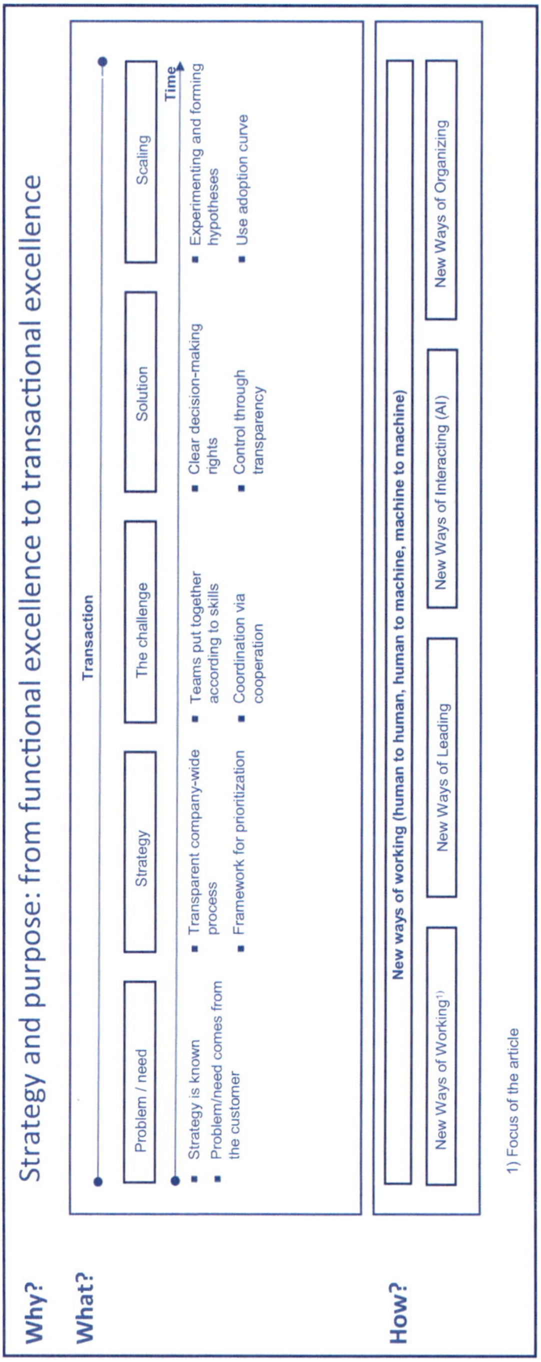

Fig. 1 The cornerstones of a transformation in relation to the establishment of new working methods

of Working, communication and cooperation within the team and externally are explicitly negotiated and agreed upon and used throughout the entire duration of the execution of a transaction or handling of a challenge. Psychological safety and trust are basic prerequisites for high-performing teams.[8] However, these must be consciously worked out and continuously renewed. The inclusive method "Rounds" (each team member speaks individually and undisturbed one after the other, social or position-related hierarchies are actively faded out) is suitable for giving each team member a voice and inclusively hearing, evaluating and incorporating all perspectives into the solution finding. When a team comes together to solve a new challenge, a "Team Chartering" (team inclusively agrees on vision, mission and deliverables) is initiated, in which vision and purpose—and thus the concrete task—as well as "Decision Rights", "Team Tactics" and "Cadence", i.e. the framework in which the solution is worked out, are negotiated and clarified in a multi-stage process. Once this has been achieved, there is the greatest possible transparency within the team and externally about expected work results and responsibilities. Progress (or the lack thereof) becomes visible and automatic monitoring and self-control are established. To ensure that the team remains on the right track, a "retrospective" is recommended at regular intervals. The new working methods used along the transaction chain thus ensure that the team-based organization is simultaneously stable (in its constructive, learning-oriented culture), clear (correct prioritization in the strategic framework and weighing of polarities), adaptive (cadence as weekly prioritization vs. mere following of a plan, coordination with stakeholders and decision-makers in a meeting), always collectively intelligent (psychologically safe, joy and energy) and technologically supported (quantity frameworks, simulations, insights from the past etc.). We can already say today from our experiences in practice that new working methods have made a positive contribution to business results. For example, we were able to achieve, through the introduction of these practices coupled with the handling of very clearly defined challenges, that speed and innovation in a team were switched to a dynamic rhythm (bi-weekly meetings with clear results) leading to further work without time loss. Within eight weeks, four new innovative product ideas were tested with a thousand customers - with a fivefold increased speed of innovation. It was quickly possible to start testing the most important key features of the products together with the customers. With the new decision-making method "Safe-to-try", the team analyzed and implemented a redistribution of several hundred customers in just seven days. Such an undertaking would have taken much longer in the past due to the necessary coordination with numerous participants. The risks in order processing were reduced by almost 50%, while the high percentage of complete and timely deliveries could be maintained. New working methods can also help to order and clearly formulate strategic prioritization according to the "cake-before-ice

[8] Zak, P. (2017), The Neuroscience of Trust.

principle". "Cake before ice"—this is an easy way to remember how to express a strategic preference when faced with two good options. These "Even Over Statements" help teams to prioritize important topics in everyday business life that guide action in dynamic situations.

2 Advantages of this Form of Work

The advantages for the employer lie in the significantly faster problem-solving as well as the higher quality of the decision—Time to Market is shortened and the use of resources is more flexible and efficient. The working method is effective against silo thinking and through transparent communication and democratic handling of information, short-term, self-centered, political and thus uncooperative behavior of individual actors is not rewarded, but punished. The main incentive for the acting individuals is to constantly qualify themselves technically and personally for the next interesting business task and the next team and to always have the next step towards solving the business question in mind. The assessment "would I work with this person again?" thus guides action. Cooperation does not have to be demanded, but is the only way to successful action and added value.

Advantages for employees lie in the learning and development potential that the regular assumption of new tasks brings with it. There is an intrinsic incentive for qualification and further development—networking in the organization is a natural by-product of the organizational form. Employees are continually given the opportunity to contribute their knowledge and experience in the best possible way. This leads to high appreciation and job satisfaction and to increased employability. Qualification and further development for the internal as well as the external labor market occur automatically and are in the interest of employees and employers. Transparency in dealing with information and project progress leads to social control and mutual support in order to achieve company goals together.

3 Challenges of this Form of Work

The challenge for companies lies mainly in the loss of power for many executives who are successful in today's system. Leadership is mostly understood as precise instructions to employees and teams on what to do and how to do it. It is scientifically proven and theoretically arrived in the minds of many (top) executives that trust-based leadership, i.e., a leader who sees himself as a coach and acts from the background ("leading from behind"), is significantly more effective, but this requires different leadership personalities. Until now, assertiveness, clear own strategies, and "executive presence", i.e., visibility in the room, were considered necessary success criteria for executives. This favors narcissistic personalities over self-questioning and reflective leaders who lead by setting the framework, trusting, enabling, and communicating clear expectations. Team-based leadership requires moderating, solution- and result-oriented characters. It is not uncommon to hear "facilitation is the new leadership". Many currently successful superiors have no interest in introducing the new work forms due to their personality; they would have to move outside their comfort zone. In addition, well-maintained networks and built-up "fiefdoms" would neither be sustainable nor successful in the new way of working. Leveraging collective intelligence and setting clear expectations weighs much more than the charisma and expert knowledge of individual executives.

The challenge for employees lies in the transparent culture, which also makes individual performance transparent and comprehensible. It becomes difficult to rest on acquired expert knowledge, and the guarantee of a consistently defined role with precisely described and constant requirements and routines is a thing of the past. This also requires much more flexibility and above all curiosity about new challenges and ever new problems from the individual. Creativity and a willingness to experiment are just as necessary as a good error culture that incentivizes learning and further development. Employee representatives fear that transparency will increase stress and performance pressure. New ways of working often require more frequent role changes for individual employees and require mental agility, which is often a hindrance in today's systems. Similar to the executives, it is also a question of personality among employees. Creative and curious characters are generally more successful than people who need the security of always the same routines. The adaptive human and creative abilities along with the striving for clarity and progress in dynamic decision-making situations will be more important in the future than striving for perfection and leadership that is oriented towards political and not scientific standards.

4 Solutions and Practical Tips

For companies in reorganization, the New Ways of Working are a real alternative without having to change the organization immediately. New ways of working can also unfold their effect in an existing structure. For companies already successful in the market, who see a chance in the New Ways of Working to become even more successful, it is recommended to focus the introduction initially on sub-areas and to follow the "pull principle". In case of success, it can then be scaled quickly, a good first benchmark would be to have a maximum of 20% of the company's employees organize their work through new ways of working. In addition, there are still areas that function well with the classic organizational form and can also remain. A "one size fits all" approach, which compulsively transforms all areas at once, would provoke unnecessary friction losses through resistance and is not recommended.

5 Summary and Outlook

For companies that want to remain sustainable in the market, it is therefore important to find new forms of value-creating cooperation, how they can flexibly face new challenges with as little friction loss and low transaction costs as possible. The organizational form in high-performing teams while ensuring effective communication through the New Ways of Working is one way to achieve this flexibility. They eliminate the current reality of many companies, which is to struggle from one energy-draining reorganization to the next, thus unnecessarily tying up many resources for internal projects and initiatives. The new form of work allows resources to be focused on the market and customers, increases or improves the skills of employees, and thus sustainably secures the chances of the company's successful continuation as a constant response to the numerous challenges, the solution of which is the core task of organizations.

References

Artinger, F.M., (2019), C. Y. A.: frequency and causes of defensive decisions in public administration.
Barnard, C., (1948), Organization and Management.
Coase, R. H., (1937), The Nature of the Firm.
Duhig, C., (2016). What Google Learned From Its Quest to Build the Perfect Team, in: New York Times Magazine 01/2020.
Edmondson, A., (1991). Psychological safety and learning behavior in work teams. Administrative Science Quarterly 44 (2), pp. 350–383.
Ruane, J., McAfee, A., Olivier, W., (2022), Vor dem Quantensprung, Harvard Business manager.
Zak, P. (2017). The Neuroscience of Trust. Harvard Business Review, 83, pp. 100–109.

Cross-Functional Expert Teams—How Mixed Ad-Hoc Teams Master Projects and Product Development in the Digital Work Environment

Daniel Halft

> *"The strategies that made you successful in the past will, at somepoint, reach their limit. Don't let your previous choices set yourfuture ceiling. The willingness to try new ideas allows you to keepadvancing."*
>
> *(James Clear, Writer)*

1 Introduction

The structure upon which most companies and organizations are still built today developed under the bureaucratic and industrial production conditions of past centuries. This structure reflected the need at that time for formalized processes, knowledge accumulation, specialized expertise, and the greatest possible avoidance of errors.

Today, however, this structure fails to meet the needs of organizations in an increasingly digitized working world and stands in the way of their success. Because in this new world of work, participation, trial & error, testing, quick releases with the fastest possible failure, creativity in further development, and dealing with complex tasks play the primary role. Companies that are prepared for this are leading in economic competition and displacing those competitors who have not or only insufficiently evolved organizationally.

D. Halft (✉)
idealo internet GmbH, Berlin, Germany
e-mail: me@danielhalft.com

I. Knappertsbusch and G. Wisskirchen (eds.), *The Future of Work*,
https://doi.org/10.1007/978-3-658-45150-9_26

1.1 The Establishment of Cross-Functional Teams

How do these successful companies achieve the necessary flexibility and speed in competition? Leading digital companies have set up cross-functional ad-hoc teams for this purpose. When a challenge or product development arises, a business unit takes the lead in forming an ad-hoc team. The leading department appoints a project manager who, however, has a purely organizational function and ensures communication with the leading department. After preliminary discussions with all relevant departments, the project scope and the timeframe in which the project should be completed are defined. Subsequently, depending on the task and project, the appropriate experts from the various departments of the company are appointed to the respective project team. During the project period (usually four to eight weeks), these experts work as a permanent part of the ad-hoc project team exclusively for the project and are released from other tasks by their departments.

1.2 Goals and Functioning of Cross-Functional Teams

Through the limited period and the establishment of a fixed team without other tasks, the following functions are supported, which are important for achieving the project goal:

- The entire team has a common goal and result orientation ("Focus").
- The team continuously works towards project success according to agile principles ("Flow").

For this reason, work in cross-functional ad-hoc teams is often referred to as "Focus & Flow projects".

Important for the success of the teams is the creation of a common workplace. This can be done physically by setting up a team space or digitally by means of a common digital whiteboard for project control and representation of project progress. Usually, the project starts with a kick-off event where the team members get to know each other and the project goals are presented. The further procedure of the project team then depends on the project requirements and the team's decisions for achieving the goals.

However, regular exchange within the team and coordination of the next steps are always in the foreground. All relevant processes that are part of or result from the project are documented and visualized.

This simultaneously creates a documentation of the project and its results, which serve both the project team during and after the project for orientation, as well as other teams and company units later on, if they want to learn from it or build upon it.

1.3 Project Completion

After the completion of the project, the entire team participates in a meeting called a "retrospective". The retrospective is about reflecting on the project and the "lessons learned" from the joint project work for the team and its individual members and preserving them as much as possible for the future. In this context, concrete steps are also named with which, for example, mistakes can be avoided in similar situations. This allows the company as a learning organization to benefit from the experiences of each project team in order to approach future projects more effectively.

Furthermore, it is common to celebrate the project success together as a team. This should also be done if the original project goal was not achieved and the project was changed or aborted. Then one has found a way how not to do it, which is also a success. Whoever celebrates leaves the Focus & Flow project with a good feeling and will be ready next time to contribute with passion and full commitment to the team's success. It also strengthens the bonds between team members, who sometimes come from very different departments, but may need to form a powerful team again in the next project.

2 Advantages of Cross-Functional Expert Teams

The cross-functional ad-hoc team enables companies to respond quickly and flexibly to challenges and projects in a complex environment. It thus meets the requirements of the Digital Economy, which has long since grown beyond the core area of IT companies. Today, more and more companies are becoming part of this Digital Economy, as there are connections in Industry 4.0 that link the entire ecosystem to the needs of the fastest subsystem. Those who cannot keep up and slow down the common processes will be removed from the ecosystem in the medium term.

Compared to traditional projects across several departments, this way of working has the advantage that the departments no longer have to wait for each other if the resources and work results are not synchronized, which often happens. All team members—and thus all areas of expertise—can devote their full attention and work power to the upcoming project.

Cross-functional teams strengthen the exchange between different company departments. This enables a significant knowledge transfer as well as quick decisions, as all relevant departments are represented in the team. Through regular collaboration with other specialist departments, team members learn new competencies in the areas of communication, project organization, and knowledge that was previously exclusive to these specialist departments. This allows employees to approach the solution of department-specific challenges more holistically in the future and to take into account their perspectives and needs, even if these departments are not directly involved.

The cross-functional team thus makes an important contribution to a good corporate culture in which all departments can communicate and work quickly and productively with each other.

3 Challenges in Relation to Cross-Functional Expert Teams

The overall organization has the task of creating a working environment in which cross-functional teamwork can function. This includes premises (on-site) and software (hybrid or location-independent), which meets the needs of changing teams and the requirements of different specialist areas. These can be very different, as some areas work creatively, while other areas require hardware resources. To best support the teams, a larger number of options with low access barriers must therefore be offered. This makes a certain standardization of the support offers inevitable in order to realize this with economically justifiable effort.

Not all project sizes can be solved in an acceptable time by a single cross-functional team alone. Thus, a team cannot be enlarged indefinitely, as it no longer works beyond a certain size. If a project is too large, it must therefore be transferred into several sub-projects. These can be processed by one or changing teams one after the other or by several teams at the same time. However, it is important to avoid interdependencies, as otherwise delays in one part of the project can significantly hinder the overall project. And then exactly the situation arises in which traditional organizations regularly get stuck and which is to be avoided with the cross-functional ad-hoc team: a project backlog arises.

The establishment of cross-functional teams requires a high degree of flexibility from the individual departments and specialist areas in terms of resource planning and resource use. Colleagues from the involved departments who are not active in the cross-functional team also provide advice as needed and cover the team member's back.

Last but not least, employees must be willing to adapt to changing work situations and team members. This is not easy for everyone, and especially when introducing Focus & Flow projects, many employees still have inhibitions about temporarily leaving their familiar work areas.

4 Solutions and Practical Tips

The introduction of cross-functional ad-hoc teams working on Focus & Flow projects should be well prepared and accompanied by coaches. The project management should also have experience with this type of project work or get the opportunity to practice with "smaller projects". Ideally, the organization has already gained experience with agile working methods, as Focus & Flow projects in mixed teams require a high degree of self-organization and self-discipline. But when the projects are running and the team is functioning, team members in Focus

& Flow projects often develop more passion and take on more responsibility for achieving the project goal, as it is about the goal of their team and not the goal of a foreign department to them.

The personnel deployment for the overall organization can be minimized if the company works with Core and Support teams. While members of the Core team work fully for the project, the Support team includes employees who cannot or do not need to contribute to the project success on a daily basis. This usually includes the legal department, for example. This can explain the legal framework conditions at the project kick-off and is then regularly and, if necessary, involved at short notice. The members of the Support team are also fixed for the duration of the entire project and commit a part of their working time to supporting the project's success. If this does not happen, bottlenecks and bottlenecks arise again, which are to be avoided by the cross-functional team in the Focus & Flow project.

5 Summary and Outlook

Cross-functional ad-hoc teams in Focus & Flow projects enable digitally-affine companies in a highly competitive innovation environment to achieve competitive advantages, as projects and products can be implemented and adapted quickly. For this, these companies have made some organizational and personnel changes to support, practice, and perfect this type of project work.

With the increasing spread of a networked Industry 4.0, more and more economic sectors are being included in the digital world of work, which also increases the need for fast and flexible project work and development. Companies and organizations that learn the necessary processes today and adapt them for their organization will achieve significant competitive advantages in the future.

The Role of Leaders in Hybrid Work—All New or Old Hat?

Oliver Herrmann

1 Introduction

Today's leaders are not to be envied, they are supposed to be more of a coach than a manager, more of a servant leader than a top-down manager always empathetic, naturally achieving their goals, conveying visions, motivating, becoming more digital and—newly in focus—being able to lead teams in a hybrid context. The leaders among the readers do not have to run away screaming now, because actually this "hybrid leadership" is not really "new leadership", instead, it offers a great opportunity: if implemented correctly, it can lead to significantly more well-being and productivity, in the team and for the leaders themselves.

Much remains unchanged: "Leadership is about people." It's about people and people have feelings, emotions, needs and personal goals. And that's what leadership is all about—building a real emotional connection with people. Everything begins and ends with people and the basics of human behavior. These basics of human needs and behavior patterns have not changed just because we are now increasingly working from home.

Let's first take a look at what we want to understand by hybrid work (Fig. 1).

Hybrid work not only has a spatial dimension (people are in the same/different rooms), but also a temporal one: collaboration can take place simultaneously—synchronously, such as in an (online or presence) meeting—or at different times—asynchronously, e.g. via documentation in a shared notebook by different team members in different time zones. The choice of the appropriate dimension for the respective tasks to be completed is something that teams should determine

O. Herrmann (✉)
Deutsche Telekom AG, Bonn, Germany
e-mail: oliver.herrmann@mcoh.de

I. Knappertsbusch and G. Wisskirchen (eds.), *The Future of Work*,
https://doi.org/10.1007/978-3-658-45150-9_27

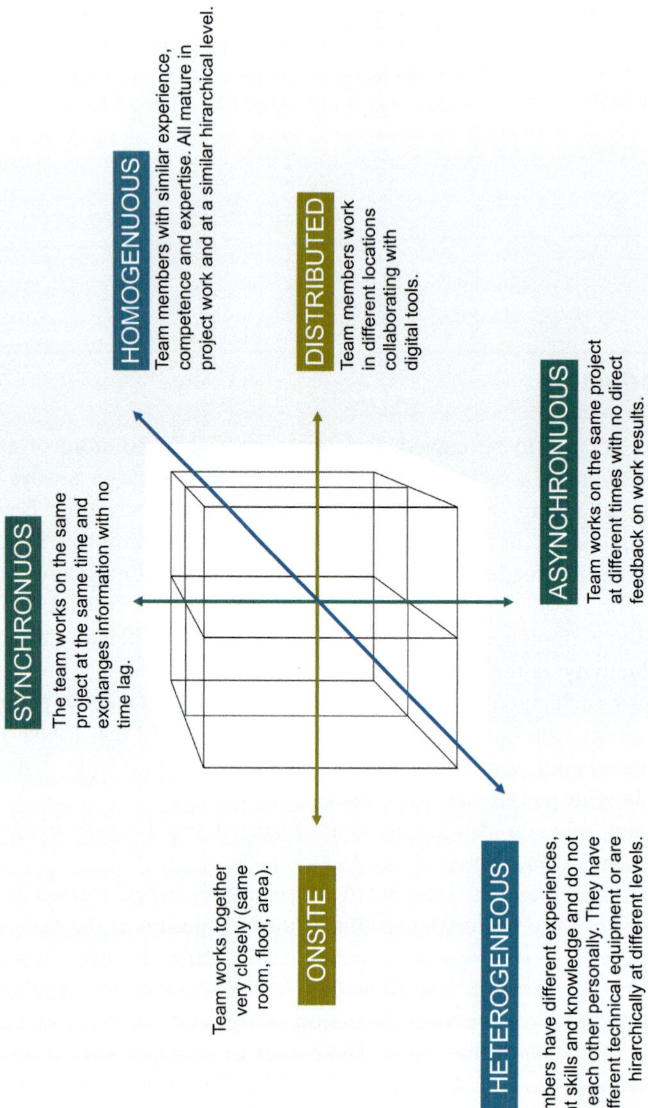

Fig. 1 –The dimensions of hybrid work

for themselves at the beginning and regularly check for suitability. Another often underestimated dimension results from the more or less homogeneous team composition. This refers to the different levels of experience or the typical dimensions of diversity in a team. While diverse team compositions are generally associated with higher creative performance, they are not a given: getting diverse teams with different levels of experience to settle in requires relationship work. And this is primarily to be done synchronously with all people in one room.

Why do leaders need to deal with these issues? "Hybrid is here to stay"—most experts agree on this. The focus is mainly on remote work and means that the high proportion of distributed work during the mandatory home office phase in the pandemic—even if somewhat lower today, will remain significantly higher than before the pandemic. And: the office has lost its monopoly on work. This means that there will be more and more situations where people are not working together at the same time in the same place. And the demand for increasing diversity and more inclusive working methods will also not decrease until certain target values are reached—and thus there will certainly be more heterogeneity in the teams than today.

No leader will be able to avoid dealing with hybrid collaboration and its further development!

2 Advantages of this Form of Work

However, it is worthwhile to tackle this challenge!

There are impressive studies showing that hybrid collaboration increases productivity and other relevant motivational factors.[1] Several drivers work together here. The possibility of distributed and asynchronous work gives employees greater autonomy over the "when" and "where" they do their work. This demonstrably drives engagement. It also enables them to achieve a better work/life integration.

In practical terms, they save time that they previously used for commuting and now often convert—at least partially—into productive work. In team agreements, the teams determine which work they perform in which of the above dimensions. By choosing the optimal (a)synchronous format and the suitable (physical or virtual) space, the teams achieve higher effectiveness. Hybrid work is superior to pure synchronous remote work, as the increase in video conferences has demonstrably negative effects on the health of employees.

New hirings can be done location-independent (provided the work can also be performed location-independent), thus enlarging the potential recruiting

[1] Bloom, Nicholas and Han, Ruobing and Liang, James, How Hybrid Working from Home Works Out (July 2022). NBER Working Paper No. w30292, Available at SSRN: https://ssrn.com/abstract=4173636.

market—a not to be underestimated advantage in the current shortage of experts (see the article “Shortage of skilled workers—myth or reality?”).

And the investment in relationship work is also worthwhile, especially for diverse teams. The accompanying psychological safety that is built up is the basis for high-performing teams.[2] During the pandemic time with its almost exclusive remote work for many employees, a high degree of equality was created—everyone was equally affected by the consequences of the pandemic, such as home-schooling or isolation, regardless of status or hierarchy. This has made inclusion much easier. With more people returning to offices and real hybrid collaboration attention must be paid that this equality and inclusion are not lost. People have, among other things, an in-group bias and perceive people and their opinions more if they encounter them more frequently in presence.

3 Challenges of this Form of Work

The last point in the previous paragraph already gives a first hint that, despite all the advantages, this form of work is not without risks, which—if not actively managed—certainly have the potential to neutralize the advantages.

There is basically the danger that “physical distancing” becomes “social distancing” if those affected do not develop rituals and practices with which they can also meet for no other reason than building relationships in the virtual space: in order to enable social exchange, which can easily be left behind in a purely task-oriented appointment. Furthermore, we know that a sense of belonging[3] and innovative power[4] decrease when people meet less physically and do not create an appropriate replacement for it. What these can be, more on that in the next section.

While, as already mentioned, inclusion seems easy in purely virtual collaboration, the hybrid work form carries the risk that two subcultures develop, an on-site culture and a remote culture, from which an “us against them” phenomenon can easily arise, which rather emphasizes the differences (on site vs. distributed) instead of the commonalities (same goals, same purpose). A possible consequence of this can be poorer career opportunities for employees who spend less time in an office. The risk is higher the more managers are in the office.

A prerequisite for successful hybrid work is that a certain culture of trust exists. If this is not given and hybrid work is still carried out, it can be assumed that the

[2] SZ Magazin, 11.09.2028: https://sz-magazin.sueddeutsche.de/die-loesung-fuer-alles/was-macht-ein-gutes-team-aus-86087 and https://www.nytimes.com/2016/02/28/magazine/what-google-learned-from-its-quest-to-build-the-perfect-team.html?_r=1.

[3] “The effects of remote work on collaboration among information workers”, Yang L., Holtz D. et al, Nature Human Behaviour 6, 43–54 (2022), https://www.nature.com/articles/s41562-021-01196-4.

[4] “The returns to face-to-face interactions: knowledge spillovers in Silicon Valley”, Atkin D., Keith Chen M., Popuv A., June 2022, https://www.nber.org/papers/w30147.

risks just mentioned will more likely occur: poorer career opportunities, exclusion, subcultures, lower innovative power and weaker identity.

So is it not perhaps better to organize all work in the office again?

4 Solutions and Practical Tips

As described in the introduction, hybrid is here to stay and work no longer takes place exclusively in the office. It is now the task of managers to shape the way forward so that the advantages and not the possible risks will manifest.

4.1 Human-centeredness, Empathy, and Psychological Safety

The success factors in a hybrid setup are essentially no different than usual: the pivot of all efforts is the human being, the employees—some also speak of human-centeredness. Richard Branson hits the nail on the head when he says, "Take care of your employees, and they will take care of your business."[5] Other successful company leaders see it similarly.[6] The pandemic has acted like a magnifying glass here, as the needs and formerly purely private life situations of people suddenly found obvious entry into the professional context: be it through video conferences that have given insights into living rooms, be it scheduling restrictions due to homeschooling or illness in the family.

This has always been the case: the human being was never just a workforce, he was always involved in work with all his needs and emotions. This played no major role in factories for a long time and was also often and easily ignored when going to the office. However, with increasing empowerment, increasing proportions of knowledge work, higher demands on innovation, etc., the whole person is of course required, with all his creativity. However, this means that all influencing factors and all emotions start playing a role, regardless of whether they are of private or professional origin. Emotions and (unfulfilled) needs can no longer be ignored if I want to achieve peak performance.

A crucial basis for how we deal with emotions in professional team situations is how safe I feel. Amy Edmondson coined the concept of psychological safety for this[7] and Google, with Project Aristotle, demonstrated its crucial influence on high-performing teams[2].

But how does this work in concrete terms? The key factors are empathy and a basic understanding of how we humans "tick". Daniel Goleman describes in

[5] https://twitter.com/richardbranson/status/651735024472064000

[6] For example, John Ledger: https://www.linkedin.com/pulse/listen-your-customers-employees-shut-up-do-what-tell-you-stephenson/ or Bodo Janssen: https://www.der-upstalsboom-weg.de/.

[7] https://fearlessorganization.com/the-fearless-organization

"Emotional Intelligence" how leaders can strengthen team relationships with empathy, self-love, and conflict management as well as open and constructive communication.[8] And Kim Scott expands in "Radical Candor"[9] the aspect of "caring" to include "demanding". A good working relationship is always a very personal one. Without personal relationships, serious "caring" cannot be represented, and building these relationships requires relationship work and the creation of corresponding—temporal and physical—spaces. There are some peculiarities for working in a hybrid setup that leaders should pay attention to.

4.2 Activity-based Work and Team Agreements

Every job is different, so we often talk about "activity-based work" to distinguish them and name their specific requirements. Focused work, for example, needs different environments (mainly quiet) than creative work (e.g., open creative space to be able to take different perspectives). If everyone plans their appointments independently of each other, this can lead to team members only rarely and randomly meeting each other. However, personal encounters are very helpful in strengthening the aforementioned personal relationships. It is therefore advisable to agree on so-called "team agreements" with the entire team, which describe, among other things, when and where the team meets physically and virtually for which occasions. The frequency of these physical meetings depends on the factors described in the introduction: how well does the team already know each other, how complex is the task to be processed, how diverse is the team? The team agreement can also describe the tools and apps with which work is done and documented.

4.3 Role-based Work

Teams that work role-based also describe the roles in the team and who takes them on in the agreements. Examples of roles can be: who moderates which meetings (moderator role), who documents them (Transparency Master), who has disciplinary leadership, who has technical leadership, who takes care of strategic future topics (scouting role), who does the communication (foreign minister role). Ideally the roles are assigned or chosen by the team members based on their strengths. Leaders can also be elected. The open exchange about which role and associated tasks suit me (and which do not) brings a team closer together. The transparency gained about strengths and preferences and also dislikes—in general: about needs—is a cornerstone on the way to more openness and psychological safety in every team.

---

[8] For example, ISBN 978-1-5266-3362-0.

[9] For example, ISBN 978-1250235374.

4.4 Planning and Check-Ins

The team agreements are not static, but are reviewed from time to time for their meaningfulness and validity. The team agreements are a strong and visible expression of what matters more than ever in hybrid work: the intention. Since chance encounters are becoming rather unlikely, more planning and intention are needed to enable these formerly spontaneous and unplanned encounters. If I am in the office on a certain day, then everyone in the team should know. To ensure that I, as a leader, regularly have personal contact with everyone in the team, phone lists (or planned personal encounters) are recommended. In any case, deliberate planning is needed.

Another simple way to engage in a more personal exchange is to hold regular "check-ins", which can be initiated with short, varying check-in questions that have no business or content-related reference. For example, "How was your weekend?" or "What is your favorite animal?". They start each meeting more relaxed and present and gain a variety of impressions from your team members in a relatively short period of time.

4.5 Interim Result

The examples show that every leader who wants to enable a good hybrid collaboration environment has to develop a basic competence in certain methods and tools.

This includes the choice of the appropriate space for different forms of collaboration. Not every space is equally suitable for every activity. A simple rule of thumb can help: the more emotions are involved, the more synchronous the communication should be. However, this becomes even more complex when diversity and different experiences come into play. As a leader, you do not have to train yourself to be a facilitator, but you should be aware of the importance of these decisions and designate or train members in your team who can help you and the team navigate through the hybrid jungle.

The same applies to dealing with the increasingly numerous and powerful communication tools. Whether it is Zoom, Webex, MS Teams or other video conferencing or collaboration applications, as a leader, you should develop an ease in using these tools that are used in your team for collaboration, so that it is not you decreasing productivity in the team.

5 Summary and Outlook

Hybrid will remain and leaders play an important role in its productive design. In order to take on this role, leaders must develop a basic competence in dealing with the available communication tools and the methods that lead to excellent collaboration. This includes the physical space as well as the possibilities that the virtual spaces offer with their increasingly powerful tools. And each space needs different methods and is better suited for different activities. This is the new thing about hybrid work. However, the most important success factors for leaders have not changed due to this form of work: they are still empathy and a fundamental interest in people and building personal relationships.

Agile Leadership Models as the Basis for the Work Organization of the Future

Heiko Schröder and Juliane Pilster

1 Introduction

In his book "Sapiens: A Brief History of Humankind," historian Yuval Noah Harari writes that humans are characterized by their ability to completely overthrow their social structures, interpersonal relationships, and all sorts of other behaviors within one or two decades (Harari & Neubauer, 2015). This seems almost a bit too slow and at the same time ambitious in a VUCA world, where volatility, uncertainty, complexity, and ambiguity constantly change the framework conditions, especially for large, traditional, and hierarchically structured organizations.

The ability to change—or adaptability—must therefore be practiced and trained so that later routine processes lead to teams gaining speed and being agile. Self-organization and autonomy are the goals of a new form of collaboration, in which adaptation to the environment is no longer driven by individual people (aka managers), but by teams and entire organizations. In this way, the mandate noted in the German Works Constitution Act to protect and promote the free development of the personality of the employees in the company and to promote the independence and initiative of the employees and work groups can also be fulfilled.[1]

[1] Section 75 para. 2 BetrVG

H. Schröder (✉)
TRUMPF Werkzeugmaschinen SE + Co. KG, Ditzingen, Germany
e-mail: heiko.schroeder@trumpf.com

J. Pilster
pierzwo UG (haftungsbeschränkt), Herzogenrath, Germany
e-mail: juliane.pilster@pierzwo.de

I. Knappertsbusch and G. Wisskirchen (eds.), *The Future of Work*,
https://doi.org/10.1007/978-3-658-45150-9_28

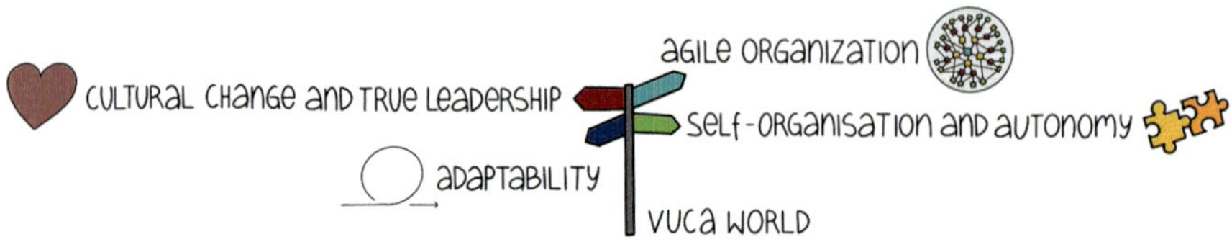

Fig. 1 Adaptation of the organizational structure to new behaviors. (based on Schröder & Pilster, 2020)

Leadership is broadening, the focus is shifting to the design of framework conditions, culture is changing. The result is an agile organization that is also structurally capable of adapting to requirements and needs that are addressed to it. The change in the organizational structure therefore follows a changed way of working and consequently a new culture. This in turn requires a new understanding of leadership, which we want to describe in the following. An overview of the described adaptation steps is shown in Fig. 1.

One aspect plays a special role in shaping the framework conditions for tomorrow's cooperation and in going through the evolution model: eye level. Only when employees feel respected, taken seriously, and psychologically safe in professional discussions will they contribute, so that adaptability, self-organization, cultural change, and real agility become possible. Therefore, the proposed leadership model is characterized by a separation of professional and disciplinary leadership, so that employees do not face their disciplinary superior in professional discussions. Especially in the transformation phase, such a setup supports the openness of employees to bring in both ideas and points of criticism.

2 Advantages of this Form of Work

In traditional organizations, technical and disciplinary leadership usually lies with the same person and the employees adopt their behavior to these structures in which they find themselves. In the past, this has led to the development of silo thinking in hierarchically shaped organizations. Responsibility regularly remains at the upper levels of the hierarchy. Numerous transformations regularly fall victim to these circumstances when it is not possible to break out of such behavior patterns.

To change behavior, the leaders of an organization come into play at this point, who obviously have a high influence on the design of cooperation in a hierarchy due to their position. Accordingly, they also play a crucial role in organizational change. They have it in their hands to create a new culture by starting to behave differently. The following thought experiment shows how this can work (see Fig. 2): First, we imagine the hierarchical organization as a cone. Now we grab the cone at its tip and pull it towards us. As soon as the tip points horizontally to us

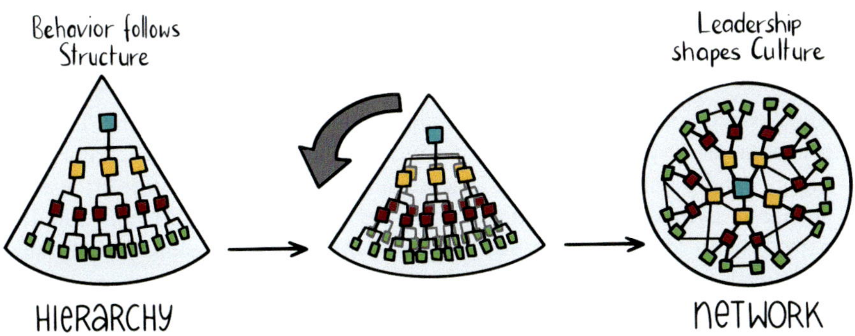

Fig. 2 Thought experiment on culture change. (Own representation based on Kruse, 2010)

and we have reached a complete top view, we see that even a hierarchical organization ultimately presents itself as a network. If leaders now start to follow the network idea in this hierarchy, even without changing the organizational structure, and act accordingly across departments and levels, employees are likely to follow this behavior. Regardless of the actual structure, the organization can still function as a network in this way. This small thought experiment only makes it clear with one example how leaders can shape conditions.

Nevertheless, the recommendation is to manifest eye-level relations by separating technical and disciplinary leadership in the organizational structures. This ensures that responsibilities remain clearly distributed and hidden hierarchies are avoided.

Independent thinkers who actively shape their organization are the guarantors of success for an agile transformation. The division of responsibilities in the agile leadership model therefore leads to another advantage: The focus of a disciplinary leader is on empowering the employees. They act as a development partner and can respond to employees individually—without having their own specialist agenda. In the leadership model presented here, the focus is on people in order to strengthen them and enable them to self-organize in teams. The process of empowerment can vary greatly. Based on existing knowledge, skills and experiences, the leader and the employees jointly design the development path—again on an equal footing.

3 Challenges of this Form of Work

The consistent introduction of an agile leadership model with technically and disciplinarily separated leadership roles usually involves a comprehensive change in the structural organization of the affected organizational unit. On this path, there are typically several stumbling blocks:[2]

[2] For concrete examples, see e.g. (Schröder & Pfeiffer, 2022).

- **Overload in Transition:** What distinguishes an "agile" reorganization including the introduction of a new leadership model from a "classic" one, which sometimes also deeply interferes with the existing hierarchical structure? The former not only reorganizes disciplinary relationships, but also involves a change in understanding what disciplinary leadership actually entails and means (and what it does not). The organization is thus confronted with a change in two dimensions and must face the inertia of change in both simultaneously. This leads to a multitude of stimuli that all participants are confronted with, such as maintaining operations, understanding and accepting a new leadership model, comprehending changed team structures and anticipating their significance for the process organization, or applying new decision-making and escalation paths. The human brain is quickly overwhelmed with so much input, we fall into a state of cognitive overload. If this is not resolved in time, the entire project is at risk of failure. Finding an appropriate pace of transformation is therefore one of the central challenges in transition.
- **Clinging to the Proven:** Due to the lack of established procedures in the new role model, it is often indispensable and necessary to rely on the still pronounced "nervous system" of the previous organizational structure in order to meet the challenges of everyday operations. As important as the stability gained in transition may be, the participants risk missing to practice themselves in the new role model. Because with increasing duration, the old nervous system slowly fades as the structures have been adapted and the tasks, competences and responsibilities have been re-sorted. With too many people clinging to the proven, the performance promise of the new organization does not materialize. The advance of trust dwindles and the change runs the risk of being discredited before it has arrived in the organization at large.
- **Old Leadership Understanding**: Even when there are technical and project careers in most classic hierarchical organizations through which employees can take on lateral leadership roles, the term "manager" is often associated with disciplinary line responsibility. Who is a manager can be read from the organization chart. With the division of leadership responsibility into various technically and disciplinarily separated roles, this simple assignment is lost. If a team in the old structure saw itself assigned to a team leader, for example, it sees a whole bouquet of managers "above" itself in the new structure (see Fig. 3). If the involved managers lack understanding for the new role model, the opposite of what was intended with the change is achieved in everyday life: Instead of an expansion of self-responsibility and self-organization of the teams, there is an oversteering by managers acting in isolation.
- **Lack of Alignment:** The oversteering mentioned in the previous paragraph can result in a lack of alignment and clarity. One advantage of pronounced hierarchical systems is their ability to quickly establish alignment through directive control. Although this often creates silos along departmental boundaries, there is clarity within them about decision-making and escalation paths. In a distributed leadership model, this clarity is replaced by a complex interplay of different roles (see Fig. 4). This interplay requires firstly a certain practice in

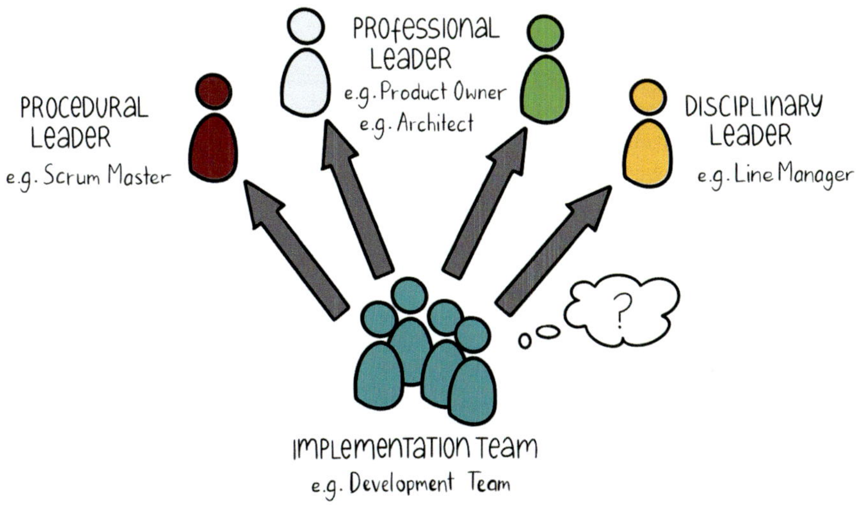

Fig. 3 Multiplicity of leadership roles in an agile context

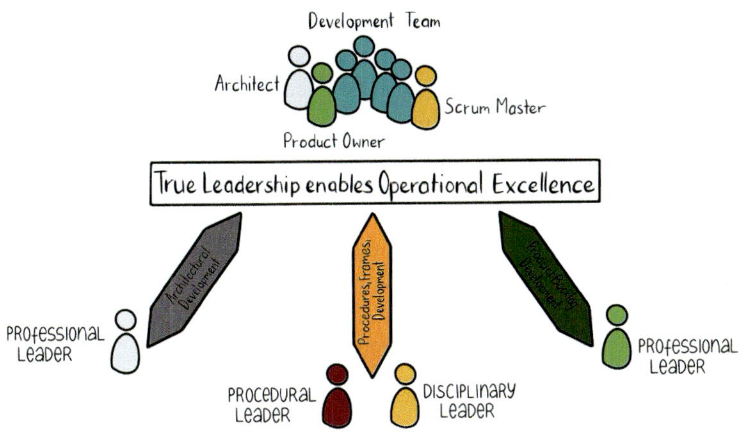

Fig. 4 The introduction of agile leadership models requires a change in leadership understanding

handling and secondly a good coordination structure, which must develop from the workflow structures and cannot be pre-planned in all details on the drawing board. As long as both are still developing, a kind of decision paralysis can arise in the perception of the participants, in which everything has to be coordinated with everyone and there is always another relevant stakeholder to involve. As a result, decisions are made too slowly or, in the worst case, not at all—often without the cause being comprehensible afterwards.

In assessing the stumbling blocks outlined above, a distinction can be made between the company and employee perspective: For companies, it is important to weigh up the risks that such a change in two dimensions poses to operations and the extent to which there is a risk of losing focus in management. Employees involved in and affected by such a transformation could particularly critical of the threat of (cognitive) overload and the loss of clarity in their working environment. Here, the diversity of people must also be taken into account. What one person welcomes as an opportunity for development, the other sees as an unwanted imposition of additional responsibility.

4 Solutions and Practical Tips

As a conclusion of the previous explanations, it should be reiterated that changing the organizational structure alone does not usually bring the desired effect. While a structural change can favor cultural change, it cannot bring it about. The behavioral changes of the executives should match this, either happening beforehand or immediately following. We take this into account in the following with a simple model that provides solution and practical tips for creating an adaptive and learning organization.

Figure 5 illustrates such an organization as a building, whose **foundation** forms a suitable work culture. The organization constantly evolves in the agile core cycle of building, measuring, and learning. Since culture cannot be dictated, but arises from the actions of the participants and continues to develop, agile working methods should have been successfully tested on a small scale before a company-wide change. The more positive basic experiences various participants and stakeholders can gather in this way, the denser and more resilient a network of culture ambassadors becomes, who develop a practical understanding of the advantages of agile collaboration in complex environments and their limits within existing organizational structures. If this also leads to the overarching realization that the organization as a whole needs a change in order to fulfill its purpose (better),

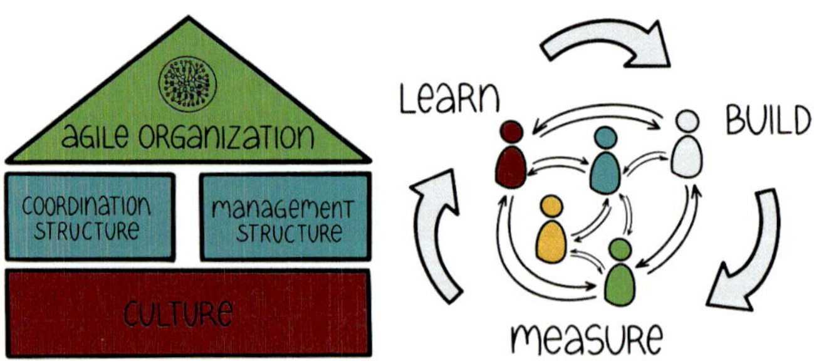

Fig. 5 The adaptive and learning organization as a building

the ambassadors can help as multipliers in the profound change process and be actively involved in its design.

On this foundation, the **actual organizational building** can now be erected, whose supporting pillars are coherent management and coordination structures. As described in the evolution model in the introduction, it is a great challenge to consistently bring agility to fruition in hierarchical structures established for other ways of working. With the introduction of an agile leadership model with separate professional and disciplinary leadership roles, the management structure is reorganized, which, however, brings its own problems in terms of coordination and alignment. Therefore, the coherence is crucial, for which we want to give some concrete implementation recommendations:

- A common understanding of the role and collaboration model can best be achieved through a **visualization of the process organization** from the perspective of the teams. Different perceptions of coordination requirements or role conflicts become transparent and can be clarified directly in the process.
- Coordination structures should be developed with the involved stakeholders based on **simple design patterns** and not predefined "on the drawing board". This ensures that only what needs coordination is coordinated. It is crucial to integrate all roles and decision makers into the process organization via suitable feedback loops. A concrete example of a simple and effective scaling via chapter structures can be found in (Schröder & Pilster, 2020).
- The **principle of subsidiarity** should apply between both pillars: The developed coordination and decision-making structures of the process organization should not overlap with those of the organizational structure. This requires a common understanding of all participants of disciplinary and professional leadership. The former should focus on organization, processes, and individual development, for example, and play virtually no role in everyday operations in order not to disturb the decision-making and escalation cascades in the process. The oversteering shown in Fig. 3 is thus counteracted.
- **Common goals** (and goal evaluations) make an important contribution to the alignment of the organization, especially during the transition. This strengthens the awareness of the bigger picture and does not fall victim to the (desired) focus of individual roles.

A decisive advantage of an organizational structure with separate professional and disciplinary leadership roles is its flexibility in terms of frictionless support of different process structures. Thanks to the decoupling of disciplinary leadership from everyday operations, process structures can be quickly and powerfully adapted to changed conditions. In the transition to such an organizational model, the organization can therefore initially focus on developing the role and collaboration model and set appropriate impulses to promote a suitable work culture. The process organization can then be developed iteratively and incrementally based on this and optimized in terms of coherence with the organizational structure. This way, the change is not planned for an unnecessarily long time on the "drawing board". On the other hand, the iterative further development in the process allows an appropriate pace of transformation that counteracts overload of the participants.

This continuous development should be anchored in the organization's everyday operations beyond the change process. Therefore, **the roof of the agile organizational building** consists of the principle of the learning organization, which lives the agile basic ideas of inspection, adaptation, and transparency at all levels and is thus adaptively aligned itself to the challenges of the future.

5 Summary and Outlook

If the introduction of an agile leadership model is successful, it not only makes organizations more competitive in the current environment, but also resilient to future changes in conditions. At the same time, it creates an environment for employees where they can develop more independently. Therefore, we are convinced that such models will increasingly gain importance.

References

Harari, Y. N., & Neubauer, J. (2015). *Sapiens: A Brief History of Humankind* München: Pantheon.

Kruse, P. (2010). *Wie die Netzwerke Wirtschaft und Gesellschaft revolutionieren.* Von YouTube: https://www.youtube.com/watch?v=ryiuuUKQJy0 (abgerufen am 23.10.2022).

Schröder, H., & Pfeiffer, U. (2022). Die Rückseite der Medaille – Psychologische Stolperfallen agiler Organisationsentwicklung. In J. Pilster, K. Bauer, & C. Brosig, *in_between Konferenzband 2022.*

Schröder, H., & Pilster, J. (2020). Agile Organisationsentwicklung bei TRUMPF: Herausforderungen, Erfahrungen, Erkenntnisse. In C. Gärtner, *Smart Human Resource Management.* Springer Gabler.

Shared Leadership

Arnd Albrecht

1 Introduction

The following will illustrate how shared leadership is characterized, what defines this leadership style, and why it is so often found in matrix and tensor organizations as well as in traditional, agile, and hybrid project management. Many experienced leaders refer to this leadership style as *state of the art*, as it positively contributes to the development of employees. The advantages and disadvantages as well as the implementation in practice are critically examined. The extent to which shared leadership differs from other leadership principles and why it will play a leading role in the future of the new world of work is explained in detail.

1.1 Causes for Shared Leadership as a New Leadership Style

Peter Drucker (1954) already shaped the image of a modern leader in the 1960s and was the first to develop the idea of a manager who acts integrated into the team up to the modern leadership term (Drucker, 2012): "*Leaders who work most effectively, it seems to me, never say 'I'. And that's not because they have trained themselves not to say 'I'. They don't think 'I'. They think 'we'; they think 'team'.*" *They understand their job to be to make the team function. They accept responsibility and don't sidestep it, but 'we' get the credit. This is what creates trust, what enables you to get the task done.*"

A. Albrecht (✉)
Munich Business School, München, Germany
e-mail: arnd.albrecht@munich-business-school.de

I. Knappertsbusch and G. Wisskirchen (eds.), *The Future of Work*,
https://doi.org/10.1007/978-3-658-45150-9_29

Only in the last 30 years has there been a call for a more parity-based approach. This is not least due to the increased co-determination rights of employees and the generally better situation in the labor market for certain groups of employees ("war for talents").

In a dynamic environment where not only new forms of work are emerging and agile work environments are demanded, but also new demands are being placed on leaders, new leadership models are necessary. Just 20 years ago, various leadership style models were developed depending on multiple factors such as organizational form, company size, business culture, etc. From this, various leadership models were derived that necessitate a change

- of the hierarchy (from pyramidal to flat)
- of motivation (from extrinsic to intrinsic)
- of the leadership style (from transactional to transformational).

Increasingly, it is found that such individual considerations are often too simplifying and do not sufficiently represent (economically) all business areas and (psychologically) all working people. The demand for more adequate leadership principles in highly complex project teams became loud, with old leadership patterns needing to be replaced by agile ones. In this process, the leadership culture and understanding of leadership have also changed (Albrecht, 2021). The distribution of responsibility has reached a new dimension: Shared Leadership.

1.2 Definition of Shared Leadership

While the common image of leadership was rather leader-centered (Bass & Bass, 1996), the concept of shared leadership developed away from the sole team leadership towards multiple and divided exercise of team leadership. Zhu and his colleagues (2018) identified three main features in their review that are found in most definitions of shared leadership:

1) A lateral influence on an equal footing,
2) an evolving team, and
3) that leadership and influence are distributed equally among team members.

According to Pearce and Manz (2005), shared leadership exists when all members of a team are involved in the leadership of a team. The two authors describe shared leadership as a process within a team that influences each other simultaneously, progressively, and mutually, with subsequent official and unofficial team leaders taking on the leadership role. Pearce and Manz aptly summarize that through shared leadership, employees are empowered for specific prevailing and future leadership tasks in teams.

1.3 Differentiation of Shared Leadership from Co-Sharing

Shared leadership is sometimes confused with or even equated to co-sharing (see the article "Job sharing in management - experiences and suggestions for practice"). Co-sharing always involves the division of a defined position with a defined job description. This means that in classic co-sharing, the position is divided between two people, either with an actual 0.5 FTE (Full Time Equivalent) per person or even a position with 2 FTEs. For example, the Lufthansa Group offers co-sharing (referred to as shared leadership on the website and in YouTube) for senior staff (Volkens & Fifka, 2019). Co-sharings of CEOs have not always been successful in the past (Sally, 2002), but under certain conditions, they may certainly have their advantages (Feigen et al., 2022).

1.4 Current Significance of this Form of Work

In Scandinavian countries, the Primus-Inter-Pares leadership style (Lewis, 2006) is widespread, as it corresponds to the Feminity parameter in Hofstede's cultural dimension MAS/FEM (Masculinity/Feminity, i.e., the dominance of the rather "male" versus the "female" values in a society or culture, or vice versa) (Hofstede, 1991) in a value-driven culture/society, which is still critically discussed (Erdener, 2013). Leadership here is parity-based. Grassroots democracy is important, everyone should and must be heard, mere egocentrically oriented competition is not supported. Responsibility, like work tasks, is shared among the members. A hierarchy is not practiced (Velten & Heggen, 2022). On the contrary: everyone is equal (Velten & Heggen, 2022). Only in case of a stalemate or non-consensus, or towards third parties, the overall responsible leader becomes visible—the Prima or "employee 'Primus inter Pares'" takes responsibility and leads the team (see Fig. 1). Otherwise, he or she remains largely unseen.

Currently, Shared Leadership is mainly found in matrix or tensor organizations. The latter corresponds to a matrix organization, but represents a three-dimensional structure due to different geographical allocation of team members. Through a non-disciplinary organizational structure, team members can only be led indirectly, i.e., functionally. Here, motivators rather than hygiene factors are applied

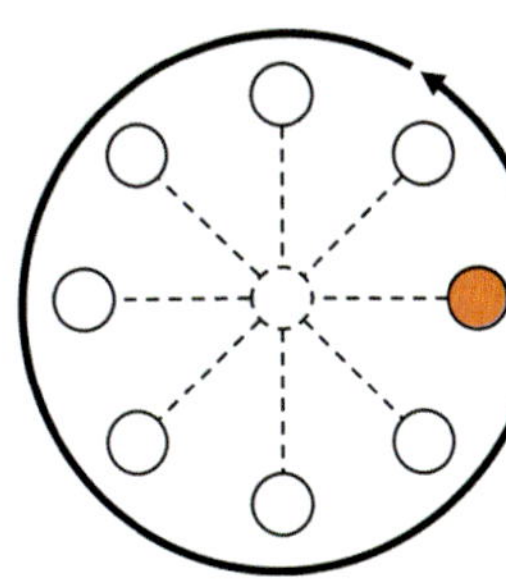

Fig. 1 Share Leadership Model based on the Scandinavian leadership style employee 'Primus inter Pares'. (Own representation)

(Herzberg, 1968), which require intrinsic basic motivation. Leaders are asked to create infrastructural conditions in which employees can both perform their actual activity and learn to take on leadership responsibility.

2 Advantages of this Form of Work

The advantages of the shared-leadership management style are clear. By involving all team members, a high team consistency and a strong sense of belonging are expected. Due to the variety of tasks and delegated responsibility, the motivation and willingness to perform are very high, which is reflected in high effectiveness (Small & Rentsch, 2010). Identification with the project and commitment to the company is also ensured (Girschik, 2020).

2.1 Shared Leadership as a Benefit for the Organization

Good exchange and flat hierarchy favor better knowledge and interface management within companies, thus promoting innovation while reducing the potential for conflict. This puts the focus on commonality, promotes the team spirit, and establishes a sustainable leadership culture (Wickert and de Bakker, 2019).

The shared leadership approach also leads to an increased sense of responsibility and ultimately strengthens the EVP (Employer Value Proposition), which is reflected in internal and external employer branding (Heskett et al., 2003).

2.2 Advantages of Shared Leadership for the Employee

The team around Crevani (2007) has comprehensively presented the advantages from four different perspectives: The leadership perspective, the employee's perspective, the organization's perspective, and the societal perspective.

2.2.1 Leadership Perspective

- Reduction of health risk (prevention of stress/burnout)
- More flexible design of work-life balance
- Backup and approval in decision-making
- Knowledge transfer from and into the team
- Generation of more joy in shaping work (motivation)

2.2.2 Employee Perspective

- Expectations of agile leadership forms (Shared Leadership) in the entire company
- Equal upbringing in western family cultures shape thoughts of equality

- Realization of democratic leadership in modern organizations

2.2.3 Organizational Perspective

- Requirement of multiple leadership responsibilities due to task diversification in business
- Improvement of communication of interface management
- Risk minimization for the development of suboptimal solutions
- Lower susceptibility in case of absence or departure of executives
- Building resilience through organizations and less stress for executives

2.2.4 Societal Perspective

- Reduction of the risk of power concentration of individual executives (Dark Triad)
- Increasing the chance for minorities to get into leadership positions

3 Challenges of this Form of Work

3.1 Challenge of Shared Leadership for Employers

The great challenge for employers is the acceptance of a new leadership model, as was already the case with the introduction of transactional to transformational leadership (Bass, 1996). It requires change management involving all stakeholders, including the approval of the management and every single employee. Like any change, this needs to be closely monitored and implemented with care.

It becomes even more difficult with bottom-up communication or even leadership parity approaches: In cultures where strong hierarchical leadership structures and styles exist, these proposals are met with very emotional (negative) reactions. This is why new organizational forms like holacracy have so far failed company-wide in corporations.

3.2 Challenge of Shared Leadership for Employees

For many executives, it was or is difficult to give up the supposed control and supervision of tasks and projects and thus the close monitoring of employees. One reason is the traditional culture through school/further education institutions, solving tasks alone. Delegating is the most difficult task for most executives!

Self-reflection (Self-Leadership) is one of the central building blocks, as shown for example in the Plena Leadership Model (Albrecht, 2021). Only when the executive is aware of their own motivation and person can they lead other people in a Shared Leadership format. Any personal doubt and lack of resilience can endanger a Shared Leadership approach, because the decentralized task distribution can lead to conflict potential in unbalanced personalities. Nordbäck and Espinosa (2019) were able to show that in very heterogeneous Shared Leadership teams, the disadvantages outweighed due to the uncoordinated meeting of different expectations and cultures.

4 Solutions and Practical Tips

4.1 Prerequisites and Implementation of Shared Leadership for Organizations

Shared Leadership requires even stronger intra- and interpersonal skills than traditional leadership styles, which Goleman (1998) summarized under the Emotional Quotient (EQ).

4.1.1 Intra-personal Skills

According to both the WHO (2020) and the World Economic Forum, the abilities to strengthen and optimize oneself are among the 10 most important competencies of the present and future!

Increasing empathy through listening without premature interpretations, asking for clarification in unclear conversations (grounding), and dialogue on an equal footing facilitate the execution of the Shared Leadership style (Albrecht, 2018).

4.1.2 Inter-personal Skills

In Shared Leadership, good communication skills are very important even in a virtual environment (Carson et al., 2016). Clear language, both verbal and non-verbal, is crucial. The creation of numerous communication platforms (Chat Portals, Dailys, Jour Fix, Monthlys, Quarterly Appraisals etc.) and the establishment of relationship-building activities (Socializing, Team Building, Workshops etc.) promote trust building.

In New Work or Work 4.0, the question of integrating AI (Artificial Intelligence) into teams is becoming increasingly important. It is difficult to estimate to what extent an AI will be recognized as a full-fledged team member or leader. The Shared Leadership leadership style may offer the only chance to integrate AI into teams and organizations.

4.2 Integration of Shared Leadership in Organizations

Early integration of current and future leaders in strategically designed leadership development programs favors acceptance. With optimal introduction, this novel approach can be represented in any work environment, as it is not about content or functional roles, but primarily about responsibilities.

Training Shared Leadership is not costly and can be quickly established internally by external trainers using the Train the Trainer concept. It helps internal trainers to train the necessary competencies for a Shared Leadership approach, the organization, and especially leaders. But also training on the job as a tandem with an experienced leader helps to learn the Shared Leadership concept.

However, it requires constant evaluation of the leadership style and a structural integration into the overall organization in terms of culture and operational processes.

Only in defined situations (crises, disagreements, decision weaknesses, and external communication to third parties) does the leader assume overall responsibility in the Shared Leadership team. But even this must be trained and understood when the situation requires suspending the Shared Leadership principle!

5 Summary and Outlook

The advantages of the new concept of Shared Leadership are obvious (Fig. 2). Nevertheless, organization managers and other stakeholders such as HR departments and leaders will have to do convincing and training work, especially in business and national cultures where a certain hierarchy exists.

In summary, Shared Leadership will not only establish itself as one of the leading leadership styles, but will gain even more importance:

- Firstly, the expected task solutions and thus the job requirements for employees will become even more specific, which makes functional leadership

	Topic	Undivided leadership	Shared Leadership
Agility	Flexibilization of tasks	☺	☺ ☺ ☺
	Increased communication requirements	☺	☺ ☺ ☺
Implementation/ costs	Increased training requirements	☹	☹ ☹ ☹
	Longer implementation of the transformation (change)	☹	☹ ☹ ☹
Motivation	Intrinsic: Strengthened sense of responsibility/leadership	☹	☺ ☺ ☺
	Extrinsic: Clear understanding of tasks and roles	☺	☹
Inclusion	Facilitated internationalteam building	☹	☺ ☺
	Integration of new employees and clients	☹	☺ ☺
Sustainability	Increasing loyalty / employer branding	☹	☺ ☺ ☺
	Open (error) culture	☹	☺ ☺ ☺

Fig. 2 Advantages and disadvantages of undivided leadership and Shared Leadership. (Own representation)

increasingly difficult, as the technical competence may not necessarily be united in the leader.

- Secondly, this will cause project teams to specialize even more and have to be led virtually due to ubiquitous availability. This increases the complexity of applying communication and resolving misunderstandings.
- Thirdly, the composition of project teams will become more heterogeneous. This affects both the onboarding and the inclusion of employees in trans-cultural and inter-generational teams.
- Fourthly, the requirement for a leader as a multi-project leader will become even more complex due to parallel projects, so that a classic leadership approach is no longer possible because the available resources for leading may not be sufficient and must be delegated.
- Fifthly, the binding of employees will be redefined by the dissolution of physical company structures towards flexible workplaces/forms: In the future, employer branding will also be characterized by responsible leadership, which is promoted by the Shared Leadership concept.

References

Albrecht, A. (2021). Zukunftsgerecht führen Plena-Leadership – die Synthese von Management Neurowissenschaft und Psychologie. Springer Gabler.

Albrecht, E. (2018). Business Coaching: Ein Praxis-Lehrbuch. Walter de Gruyter.

Bass, B. M. (1996). Anew paradigm of leadership: An inquiry into transformational leadership. U. S. Army Research Institute for the Behavioral and Social Sciences.

Bass, B. M., & Bass, R. (2008). The Bass handbook of leadership: Theory, research, and managerial applications. New York, NY: Simon & Schuster.

Carson, J.B., Tesluk, P.E., & Marrone, J.A. (2016). Shared leadership in teams: An investigation of antecedent conditions and performance. IEEE Engyineering Management Review, 44, 86–103.

Crevani, L., Lindgren, M., & Packendorff, J. (2007). Shared leadership: A post-heroic perspective on leadership as a collective construction. International Journal of Leadership Studies, Vol. 3 Iss. 1, 2007. 40–67.

Drucker, P. F. (1954). The Practice of Management. Harper & Row.

Drucker, P. F. (2012). Managing the non-profit organization. Routledge. 14

Erdener, C. (2013). Hofstede's MAS/FEM Dimension. Journal of International Business and Economics. 13. 141–146.

Feigen M. A., Jenkins M. & Warendh A. (2022). Is it time to consider Co-CEOs? Harvard Business Review 50–50(5).

Girschik, V. (2020). Shared Responsibility for Societal Problems: The Role of Internal Activists in Reframing Corporate Responsibility, Business & Society, 59(1), 34–66

Goleman, D. (1998). What makes a Leader? Harvard Business Review, 1998 Nov-Dec;76(6), 93-102.

Herzberg, F. (1968), Work and the Nature of Man. Staple Press

Heskett, J. L., Sasser W. E. Jr., & Schlesinger, L.A. (2003). The value profit chain: Treat employees like customers and customers like employees. The Free Press.

Hofstede, G. (1991). Cultures and organizations: Software of the mind. New York, NY: McGraw-Hill.

Lewis R. D. (2006). When cultures collide: leading across cultures (3rd ed.). Nicholas Brealey.

Nordbäck E. S. & Espinosa J. A. (2019). Effective coordination of shared leadership in global virtual teams. Journal of Management Information Systems 321–350.

Sally, D. (2002). Co-Leadership: Lessons from Republican Rome. California Management Review, 44(4), 84–99.

Small, E. E., & Rentsch, J. R. (2010). Shared leadership in teams. *Journal of Personnel Psychology*, 9(4), 203–211

Velten, J. & Heggen, R. (2022), Trust-based leadership and employeeship. Everyone is an employee, and some employees are leaders. Teamwork Forlag.

Volkens, B. & Fifka, M. (2019). Ready for Take-off: Wie die Lufthansa ihr Personal auf die Zukunft vorbereitet. Campus Verlag.

Wickert, Chr. & de Bakker, F. G. A. (2019). How CSR Managers Can Inspire Other Leaders to Act on Sustainability. Harvard Business Review Digital Articles, 1/10/2019, 2–5.

World Health Organization (2020). Life skills education school handbook: prevention of non-communicable diseases – Introduction. Geneva.

Zhu, J., Liao, Z., Yam, K. C., & Johnson, R. E. (2018). Shared leadership: A state-of-the-art review and future research agenda. J Organ Behav. 39, 834–852.

Job Sharing in Management—Experiences and Suggestions for Practice

Stephanie Dickes and Eva Grenz

1 Introduction

The labor market and the accompanying rising expectations of employees towards employers force the latter to rethink working hours and forms. Applicants can afford to be demanding today.

The retirement of the baby boomer generations will further exacerbate the shortage of labor (see the article "Shortage of skilled workers - myth or reality?"). These generations were often employed in companies for decades. Therefore, companies are threatened with a rapid loss of knowledge in the coming years if they do not take appropriate countermeasures.

A model that meets these challenges and offers solutions is job sharing. Job sharing means that a position is filled jointly by two employees. This work model is most often used in leading positions, hence the terms top sharing, co-sharing, and shared leadership (see the article "Shared Leadership").

In contrast to classic part-time work, job sharing does not automatically divide tasks, but they can overlap completely or partially. The working time models are also very different. The tandems together make up 100–200% of a classic planned position.

The current importance and design of this form of work varies greatly from company to company. While large corporations have already embraced job sharing, it is only slowly gaining ground in smaller companies. Interestingly, the

S. Dickes (✉) · E. Grenz
Allianz Beratungs- und Vertriebs-AG, Unterföhring, Germany
e-mail: stephanie.dickes@allianz.de

E. Grenz
e-mail: eva.grenz@allianz.de

I. Knappertsbusch and G. Wisskirchen (eds.), *The Future of Work*,
https://doi.org/10.1007/978-3-658-45150-9_30

founders of start-ups often work in job sharing. This shows that Generation Z has high demands for the compatibility of family and work or work-life balance and is realizing them.

2 Advantages of Job Sharing

Job sharing offers great advantages for employers both internally and externally:

2.1 Women in Leadership, Equality, and Diversity

If job sharing is offered to existing employees, it provides them with the opportunity to adapt their work to their lives without having to give up career opportunities. The employer can thus meet the various life cycles of the employees. The needs of the employees change over the course of a lifetime. By adapting to the needs of the employee, fluctuation can be significantly reduced. Especially the loss of highly qualified women hurts companies and has a negative impact on the female quota, especially at management levels. This "automatic" process can be significantly reduced.

Job sharing is also an investment in the issue of equality and diversity. If families are enabled to distribute work performance and thus income equally, care work in families can also be distributed accordingly. This could also help to mitigate the issues of gender pay gap and gender pension gap in the medium and long term.

2.2 Leadership Culture, Integration, and Collaboration

Many companies have grown and become successful through the decades of work by the "baby boomer" generation. These employees have a great deal of experience in the company and are carriers of specialist knowledge over years and decades. They often have internal knowledge (e.g., old programming languages, IT applications, product series, etc.) that is no longer documented in the company and therefore not available elsewhere. If this wealth of experience and knowledge is lost to companies in the coming years with the baby boomers, this will have negative consequences.

On the other hand, these employees are often used to a different work culture with strict hierarchies, high availability, continuity, etc. This often leads to tensions and conflicts with colleagues from generations Y and Z. Currently, often four generations are working simultaneously in companies (see the article "New Work and Generations") and it is important to bring out the strengths of each generation and each individual and to overcome boundaries. Also, more people in a company then have knowledge about certain topics. Thus, replacements and successors can be found more easily.

The answer to these challenges can be "job sharing". In this constellation, knowledge is passed on and exchanged. Understanding for the respective other generation can be created and conflicts can be reduced. Above all, however, everyone can contribute their strengths and learn from the other, thus achieving significantly better results for the company. Also, such a tandem is usually much better and faster at adapting to rapid changes.

2.3 Motivation, Performance, and Agility

Not to forget is also the effect on the willingness to perform and motivation of the employees. If they have the opportunity to adapt their working hours to their respective life situation, this allows those affected to achieve a better work-life balance. This gives them sufficient resources to fulfill their tasks and motivation can be increased. This increased motivation is clearly evident from the exchange with numerous tandems. If the employee can express his needs without fear of stigmatization in a trusting environment, a climate of psychological safety is created. In such an environment, peak performance can be achieved.

In a tandem, both parts usually bring different talents, strengths, weaknesses, experiences, educations, knowledge, etc. In our time with its rapid changes, different skills are constantly needed to master the challenges. Continuous feedback takes place, which is otherwise often neglected at management levels. Thus, a tandem can also develop very quickly.

In summary, job sharing makes the company more attractive, adaptable, and efficient as an employer. The employees benefit from the adaptation of work to their lives, which makes them more efficient and motivated. As companies, we need this realization and the attitude that we need to align ourselves much more with people in the future.

The aforementioned employer attractiveness is then played out externally when positions are advertised in whole or in part for job sharing. Especially people of generation Y and Z are usually very actively looking for flexible working time models, regardless of whether these play a role at the moment or should be available later. There is also a high sensitivity in the market regarding corporate culture (see the article "Corporate Culture - How the Culture of a Company Determines Success or Failure"). Since topics such as collaboration and transparency are emphasized in job sharing, this in turn allows conclusions to be drawn about the corporate culture.

At the same time, issues such as diversity, equality, equal pay, and much more play a role for a company. As mentioned at the beginning, it will become increasingly challenging to generate sufficient young talent from the younger generation and to keep them in the company. A very high employer attractiveness, which is also visibly played out externally, is essential here.

3 Challenges Regarding Job Sharing

Prior to the start of a job sharing tandem, numerous steps need to be completed to implement the model. As these take some time, a sufficient lead time of about three months is necessary. In particular, the tasks described below arise.

- Development of a basic concept for the planned job sharing, e.g.
  - what part-time shares are possible?
  - how can the working time be distributed, what options are there?
  - who belongs to the user/authorized group?
  - technical implementation in the personnel systems, regulation of legitimations especially for target agreements, evaluations, salary determination
- Making a corresponding works agreement, if non-executive employees are affected
  Discussion of the job sharing desire with the manager
- Finding suitable tandem partners, personal acquaintance and checking of the respective matches. The following questions are in the foreground:
  - Can I work well with this person?
  - Can we trust each other?
  - Can we adjust well to each other in our way of working, our expertise and our values?
- Development of a concrete suitable model by the two tandem parts:
  - respective part-time shares
  - Distribution of working time (e.g. division of the week or weekly change)
  - Period/duration of job sharing
  - Are both responsible for all topics or should topic areas be assigned?
  - Setting of annual goals (what applies to both, what is individual) and variable salary components by the manager
- Negotiation or discussion of this proposal with the HR department and the manager and contractual agreement in the employment contract

As soon as the prerequisites described above are met, the implementation can start. We describe below our own experiences and learnings that we have collected so far as a tandem in the management of a department of Allianz (Level—1 below the board).

A challenge that we consider unsolved in the large companies known to us—also outside our own—is the representation of job sharing for managers in the relevant personnel systems. The common personnel systems for large companies known to us do not yet offer sufficient possibilities to enable both job sharing partners access to personnel data, but only one disciplinary manager can be stored in the system.

The most important task of managers is the trustful cooperation with employees at eye level. This must not change through job sharing. Special attention must be paid to involving employees early on and taking them on the journey. Possible concerns about unclear responsibilities, delayed decisions or the right handling of personal issues need to be sensitively perceived and actively addressed, rather than tabooed.

An important key to the functioning of job sharing is that both members of the tandem are able to speak and make decisions at all times. The handovers must be smooth and routine. For the relevant stakeholders (colleagues, own manager, customers), it should make no difference who is currently "on duty". There should be no disadvantages compared to the classic model with one responsible manager. It is the task of the tandem to organize its accessibility and decision-making ability at all times, not that of the stakeholders.

It should not be underestimated that in traditional, successful companies a classic management model prevailed over a long period of time, for which there were usually no alternatives. If at all, there was rarely a reason for this. Careers ran over several hierarchical levels with extensive working hours, highest presence and a leadership figure at the top of each unit. Here we are entering cultural new territory and it may not be surprising that the joint perception of a management function in management is still viewed skeptically by one or the other, whether it can actually work in practice.

4 Solutions and Practical Tips

Above, we have described numerous tasks that need to be completed before the start of the tandem. In this regard, the exchange of know-how with other, already established tandems can provide valuable insights, from which success factors and stumbling blocks can be clearly identified in the planning phase. Already established tandems, especially in other companies, have relevant experience and are usually happy to share it. Active networking is required here! There are also various external coaches specialized in job sharing who can be asked for systematic preparation and reflection.

With regard to the technical feasibility of job sharing in management positions in personnel systems, there is an urgent need for action. Since, in our experience, there is still no demand-oriented standard solution available in the relevant HR software, continuous dialogue with the in-house HR and IT functions is essential in order to at least seek feasible ways and pragmatic solutions.

To maintain or build trust with the employees for the new leadership constellation, maximum openness, transparency, and feedback are indispensable. Any concerns, but also wishes, should be put on the table early on and not deliberately ignored. For this purpose, both individual discussions and joint team workshops are suitable. The principle must be that the job sharers ensure that the employees do not feel any disadvantages compared to the traditional leadership approach.

To ensure appropriate, competent action and decision-making ability of the tandem at all times, we consider a handover day per week, on which the tandem works together, to be indispensable. Job sharers must structure themselves very well and find a functioning, reliable rhythm with each other. A key success factor in this is transparent, clean documentation of relevant documents and meeting notes to seamlessly connect to the current work status. In the time windows when one of the two partners is absent and the other is on vacation, a colleague should be specifically tasked with the absence representation and this should also be transparent internally.

The cultural anchoring of job sharing by managers in the organization is indispensable for its lasting success. Cultural changes in companies generally require a convincing case for action, some patience, and influential promoters. The advantages of job sharing must be convincing all around: Not only the respective tandem should feel the benefits, for example, to devote sufficient time to private obligations such as childcare or care of relatives, but it must also deliver a noticeable value contribution for the employees to be led and the employer. This can consist, for example, in the fact that the development of creative, innovative projects in the tandem is much easier than in the traditional model, as different backgrounds and ways of thinking come together and mutually enrich each other. With job sharers, the individual working time is halved while the competencies, skills, and energy brought in for the task are doubled. Reliability, resilient mutual trust, the omission of personal vanities, and standing together even in case of mistakes are the prerequisites for acting credibly as a role model for job sharing.

5 Summary and Outlook

Based on the feedback from our employees, superiors, and clients, as well as our own experience, the model is well suited for use in management if it is oriented towards the criteria described. This is also reflected by numerous companies in other industries. The challenges mentioned can be managed without too great hurdles. In our company, we will continue to roll out the job sharing model, continuously evaluate it, and learn from it.

The flexibility of the working world will increase, as a recent study by Stepstone, one of the leading online job platforms from March 2022 (https://www.stepstone.de/wissen/the-silent-resignation) shows. Around 18,000 employees were asked about their expectations for future jobs and employers. 15 million employees in Germany think about changing jobs several times a week. And according to the study, they no longer want to do without these aspects in the job: flexible working hours, flexible working (e.g., home office), high work-life balance, and family friendliness. In the interviews for our management trainee programs, we experience this in the same way: It is the expectations for mobile working, professional time-outs (sabbatical), working from abroad (see the article "Work from anywhere - The free choice of workplace") and temporary part-time work that have changed the discussions at least since the pandemic. They now play an equally important role for qualified applicants as salary and benefits (see the article "Employer Branding on the Labor Market of the Future—What Must Companies Offer Workers?"), job security, and personally fulfilling work.

In addition, there is a significantly higher expectation of corporate culture: Values such as collaboration, transparency, and leadership at eye level are becoming increasingly important for applicants. Through job sharing, these values are sustainably strengthened and credibly lived in the company. An increasing number of such tandems can also shape and perhaps even change a company from within.

Job sharing increases employer attractiveness internally and externally and strengthens employee retention.

References

https://www.stepstone.de/wissen/the-silent-resignation (abgerufen am 16.10.2022)

Work Equipment and Further Education

Design Thinking Can Change the (Working) World—A Discussion of the Advantages, Challenges and Solutions of Applying Design Thinking on the Way to New Work

Amelie Kollhoff

1 Introduction

To understand how Design Thinking can assist in implementing and introducing New Work, let's first examine the definition and characteristics of the method.

How can one describe Design Thinking? Prof. Uli Weinberg, Director of the HPI School of Design Thinking, answered this question on the occasion of the 15th anniversary of the HPI School of Design Thinking as follows: "We had 15 years of time to come up with a short description but it never ended up to get one" (HPI-Digitalblog, 2022). This quote makes it clear: Design Thinking has many faces. Depending on how, how intensively, and where you apply Design Thinking, different levels of intensity and application or perspectives can be distinguished. Often, for example, Design Thinking is used as an innovation method that serves to solve complex problems. Others use Design Thinking as a toolbox or set of methods that provides a team with techniques and experiences during project work in a company. A large part of the Design Thinking advocates and users see it as a culture and philosophy (cf. Uebernickel et al., 2015, p. 16, 23). The Director of the HPI School of Design Thinking, Prof. Uli Weinberg, refers to Design Thinking, for example, as one of the best approaches to think and act in new ways in a digital world (cf. HPI-Digitalblog, 2022).

A. Kollhoff (✉)
neuearbeitszeiten, Hannover, Germany
e-mail: amelie@neuearbeitszeiten.de

I. Knappertsbusch and G. Wisskirchen (eds.), *The Future of Work*,
https://doi.org/10.1007/978-3-658-45150-9_31

2 Advantages of Design Thinking

As diverse as the understanding and applications of Design Thinking are, so are its benefits. I would like to introduce some positive characteristics in this chapter and show that certain parallels exist to the current understanding of the world of New Work.

The permanent integration of customers, or customer orientation, is at the center of Design Thinking and probably represents the greatest added value of this way of working (cf. Uebernickel et al., 2015, p. 22)—but possibly also one of the biggest differences compared to traditional development and change processes in companies. At the same time, the focus on the human factor is also a commonality with the current understanding of New Work.

The goal of Design Thinking is to capture, analyze, and understand people and their behaviors (Uebernickel et al., 2015, p. 52)—without judging or evaluating anything as right or wrong (cf. Brown, 2016, p. 33)—and to create solutions based on this. The behavior of customers and stakeholders is always the basis, so in the end, the customers and stakeholders decide on the result or success of a project—not the Design Thinking team, the management, or a project leader (cf. Uebernickel et al., 2015, p. 19). As a result, Design Thinking produces (only) results that are desired by the customers or are accepted after implementation (cf. Uebernickel et al., 2015, p. 22).

Another advantage and often also a parallel to the world of New Work is working with or following an iterative process. Instead of using the well-known waterfall principle and proceeding linearly, i.e., planning, executing, and completing a task (once) completely and then starting the next task, an iterative process is characterized by the fact that individual, consecutive tasks are combined into a cycle and this is run through several times to gradually approach the perfect solution (cf. Uebernickel et al., 2015, p. 25). The Design Thinking process according to Uebernickel et al. (2015) consists of the phases Problem Definition & Re-Definition, Need Finding & Synthesis, Idea Generation, Prototyping, and Testing. It is clear from the headings: Not only the iterative process of Design Thinking as such, but also the individual phases themselves represent a significant change in many companies compared to traditional and classic ways of working. In Design Thinking, for example, ideas are only generated when the team has previously developed a good and targeted question and has identified the needs and fundamental insights of the users through "Need Finding". Immediately after the idea generation, prototypes are created, which are then tested for their everyday suitability together with or by the users. With each new run-through of the cycle, one approaches the optimal solution and ensures customer orientation. The feedback from the customers and lived or reflected mistakes are the engine or the guarantee for the success of the project. Despite the increased repetition of the cycle, Design Thinking not only increases customer proximity, but also the speed and agility of a project (cf. Uebernickel et al., 2015, p. 20). In addition to the focus on people, the application of iterative processes and the increase in agility are also commonalities with the current understanding of New Work.

Further parallels are, for example, that value is placed on diversity[1] in team composition and space and workspace[2] adapt flexibly to the needs of the team (cf. Uebernickel et al. 2015,p. 222). All of this ensures that an optimal working environment prevails.

As a final advantage of Design Thinking, it should be mentioned that the method is not only limited to the development or optimization of products, but can also be applied to change processes and the strategy development of a company, i.e., also to the introduction of New Work.

3 Challenges Regarding Design Thinking

Since Design Thinking often differs significantly from traditional work methods and cultures, its application and introduction are usually associated with challenges that can inhibit or even prevent the potential unfolding of its advantages.

For example, in business practice, the team usually has to adapt to the available space or working conditions, rather than the workspace and conditions adapting to the team's needs.

Furthermore, there is often a strong culture of discussion and meetings in companies, and there is no room for experimentation. Companies often also lack the necessary optimism, which is a prerequisite for a positive attitude towards experimentation and the creation of prototypes. Optimism also requires confidence, and confidence is based on trust (see Brown, 2016, p. 62 f.). But exactly this trust, combined with freedom of action, is rarely existent in many companies—or at least does not last long. To successfully introduce and anchor Design Thinking and to benefit from its advantages, one needs perseverance, time, and patience. After a few weeks or months, one cannot expect a fundamental change in the work and thinking methods of the employees (see Uebernickel et al., 2015, p. 267)—neither in the topic of "Design Thinking" nor in the topic of "New Work".

Sometimes problems are overlooked that only arise while solving the problems that are immediately in front of one (see Brown, 2016, p. 153) or the complexity of the problem to be solved is a disruptive factor (see Uebernickel et al., 2015, p. 24). Also, the desired and necessary tolerance for failure is usually not prevalent in companies. It is of central importance that teams can—and are allowed to—make mistakes (see Brown, 2016, p. 59). Instead, there is a risk of falling in love with certain ideas, perfecting prototypes, and no longer acting objectively or customer-oriented (see Uebernickel et al., 2015, p. 32). Often in companies, ideas are also directly stifled before they can even unfold, or employees tend to anticipate the will of the executives (see Brown, 2016, p. 62). Instead, it is absolutely

[1] Not only in terms of expertise, but also in terms of personality type (cf. Uebernickel et al., 2015, p. 56).

[2] Physical and digital.

necessary that the so-called "silo thinking" is dissolved and teams share results and insights. Design Thinking is also ineffective if the optimal composition and diversity of the teams are not ensured or prioritized, because an important component of the success concept of Design Thinking is good teams (see Uebernickel et al., 2015, p. 56), which have freedom of action.

As you can see, most challenges are related to the prevailing corporate and innovation culture. Is tolerance for failure (really) lived? Am I allowed to experiment? And a—not to be underestimated—factor: Does management trust the method or is the "Design Thinking" project discontinued after just a few weeks or months?

So that you can instead generate sustainable successes and results with Design Thinking and also approach the world of New Work, I would like to introduce you to some solution approaches and tips in the next section.

4 Solutions and Practical Tips

4.1 For Beginners: Use Design Thinking as a New Work "Taster" Project

First, apply the method in individual areas of daily business, e.g., in the development of new products or an annual team workshop. Since Design Thinking possesses many characteristics often attributed to the world of New Work, such as the focus on people and their needs, your team will automatically experience the "New Work world" through the application of Design Thinking. The downside: Your New Work experience is limited to the general characteristics of Design Thinking and you forget the focus on your team—customer centricity is missing. Who are your stakeholders in the New Work world and what needs, problems, and desires do they have? Take it a step further for this.

4.2 For Professionals: Go YOUR (never-ending) way to New Work!—with the help of Design Thinking

Develop your personal world of New Work with Design Thinking and lay the foundation for sustainable change and improvement. The advantage: You define your own New Work characteristics based on the needs of the relevant stakeholders for you and also take into account the personal situation of your company. Create a center where the question is taken seriously: How must work be organized so that it is not forced and everyone does what they really, really want? And note: Frithjof Bergmann's concept of New Work assumes that people do not know what they want (see Olk et al., 2019). With the help of Design Thinking, you can find out exactly that.

4.3 Create the Perfect Team with a "we-feeling"—from Interns (m/f/d) to the Executive Floor

For Design Thinking and New Work to work, you must succeed in forming harmonious, optimistic, and diverse teams that feel part of a unit or pursue a common goal. Silo structures should belong to the past and instead, spaces should be created where teams can unfold and live freedom of action—and are also allowed to. It is essential that "everyone is in the same boat" and that there is also support from upper and middle management (see Uebernickel et al., 2015, p. 61). If the management's commitments are only lip service, the introduction and implementation of Design Thinking and New Work will be almost impossible (see Uebernickel et al., 2015, p. 267).

4.4 Be Open & Let Yourself be Inspired (Instead of Copying)

Open your eyes, because innovations and positive changes start with the right view (see Brown, 2016, p. 186). And yes, you can also build on the ideas of others, but "building" does not mean that you copy something one-to-one—for example from the competition, the market leader, or a start-up from Berlin. Because then you might create something with Design Thinking that is not aligned with your needs or the needs of your team, your customers, and the environment and therefore does not promise success or cannot promise it at all. Let yourself be inspired but stay open and be brave to ask yourself (always new) own questions—and to answer them (yourself).

4.5 Think, Live & Act always Customer-Centric

Never forget why and for whom you do what you do. That is: Never forget the stakeholders or the customers and align the organization, from strategy to the smallest processes, to them (see Uebernickel et al., 2015, p. 267). Go out into the world or as close as possible to the stakeholders and customers and separate yourself from purely theoretical considerations or the study of mountains of market data (see Brown, 2016, p. 181).

4.6 Experiment Instead of "carving in stone"

Let practice become routine instead of theory and interrupt one or the other discussion with a practical test. Establish a truly lived error culture and use feedback and reflection to continuously improve. Question yourself or the project, the benefit, the goal, etc., and use iterative processes for more flexibility and agility. This characteristic will not only promise you success in everyday Design Thinking projects, but also in the development of your own, suitable "New Work world".

4.7 Never stop!—and enjoy the Journey

Design Thinking does not aim for you to create something that lasts forever. Design Thinking also does not aim for you to go through the process (only) once and then be "done". Why?—The world is changing and so are the needs, requirements, and conditions of your company or the customers and stakeholders of your project. In addition, the goal of Design Thinkers is to constantly search for new, optimal solutions to problems. And you can transfer exactly this characteristic to the introduction and application of the concept of New Work. It's not about reaching a goal that is "carved in stone". Instead, it's about creating and maintaining a working world in which everyone does exactly what they really, really want at any time (see Olk et al., 2019). And that will probably be something different depending on the time, place, and person. So, the journey is our goal. And, if you enjoy the change journey, that is already the first step into your New Work world.

5 Summary and Outlook

Even in 2019, many years after the emergence of the "New Work", the originator of the concept, Frithjof Bergmann, had to note that what he originally understood by the concept was not really implemented in any German company (cf. Olk et al., 2019). Traditional work methods and cultures seem to fail in implementing the concept of New Work. The method and philosophy of Design Thinking, however, manage to change traditional work methods and cultures with its characteristics and advantages: lived error tolerance, iterative processes, more agility, diversity and the focus on people and their needs. Even companies that apply Design Thinking "only" for everyday processes, e.g., for the development of a new product, automatically benefit from these changed conditions. At the same time, the method can also be the basis for a company to define the concept of New Work for itself with a Design Thinking project.

Frithjof Bergmann only talks in his concept about creating a working world in which everyone does exactly what they really, really want (cf. Olk et al., 2019). However, what this working world looks like in concrete terms is not defined or cannot be defined at all; the individual needs of people are too different, and our world changes too much every day. This fact is often forgotten or ignored by many companies and instead supposed standard solutions are installed or copied.

My recommendation: Use Design Thinking to focus on your own company or the people of your own company and their needs, and thus be able to define and try out for yourself what fits best for you in the topic of "New Work".

The iterative process will enable you to constantly experiment with new ideas, improve them or possibly discard them, and thanks to the customer-centricity of

Design Thinking, it will also ensure that in the end exactly what fits is created: Your perfect "New Work (World)". Provided, you master the challenges and never stop striving for the optimal solution.

For me and many other advocates of the method, it is already clear: Design Thinking can change the (working) world. Now it's up to you; take the test! Try out the method and adapt your future work to your needs. I wish you a lot of success, but above all a lot of fun. Enjoy this wonderful transformation process!

References

Brown, T. (2016). Change by Design. Wie Design Thinking Organisationen verändert und zu mehr Innovationen führt. Vahlen.

HPI-Digitalblog. (2022, 15. September). Prof. Uli Weinberg about the importance of Design Thinking | Design Thinking ImpAct Conference 2022 [Video]. YouTube. https://www.youtube.com/watch?v=YsZM_MWSiAA (abgerufen am 17.10.2022)

Olk, J., Scheppe, M. & Wermke, C. (2019, 17. August). Warum New Work in deutschen Firmen nicht richtig umgesetzt wird. Handelsblatt. https://www.handelsblatt.com/unternehmen/management/interview-mit-frithjof-bergmann-warum-new-work-in-deutschen-unternehmen-nicht-richtig-umgesetzt-wird/24899568.html (abgerufen am 17.10.2022)

Uebernickel, F., Brenner, W., Pukall, B., Naef, T. & Schindlholzer, B. (2015). Design Thinking: Das Handbuch. Frankfurter Allgemeine Buch.

Requirements for the Workplace of the Future—Effective Collaboration and Innovation Through Activity Based Working

Leonie Kristina Stankewitz

"As for the future, your task is not to forsee, but to enable it."
– Antoine de Saint-Exupéry, French writer and pilot 1900–1944

1 Introduction

Various developments in the labor market present companies with a wide range of challenges. Competitive pressure and digital collaboration requires new ways of working. Collaboration and agile working are becoming key success factors for responding quickly and flexibly to changing needs and driving innovation. In addition, digitization and technical solutions make it possible to work from anywhere, so that hybrid collaboration has become part of everyday work (see Zukunftsinstitut 2021). These developments also place new demands on workplace design (see Figure 1). For example, workplace design must enable hybrid work or also create space for relaxation and rest in in the office (see Block et al. 2021). The importance of rethinking traditional workplace design is also shown by a recent study by the Fraunhofer institut für Arbeitswirtschaft und Organisation (IAO), in which only a small proportion of the employees are satisfied with their office design (see Bauer et al. 2021). The need for workplace redesign is not limited to the office. Since the Covid pandemic at the latest, working from home or third places such as co-working spaces have also become established (see Bockstahler et al. 2022). The same applies here: Effective and meaningful work can only take place in places that have the necessary environment and technology.

L. K. Stankewitz (✉)
designfunktion, Koblenz, Germany
e-mail: mail@leonie-stankewitz.de

I. Knappertsbusch and G. Wisskirchen (eds.), *The Future of Work*,
https://doi.org/10.1007/978-3-658-45150-9_32

New Work Trends	Requirements for workplace design
Collaboration	High level of interaction between employees, space for creativity and innovation (e.g. innovation hubs, open space, work café)
Work-life blending	Space for combining private and professional life (e.g. parent-child rooms, retreats for private telephone calls)
Hybrid working	Rooms and technical equipment for cross-location, digital collaboration (e.g. equipment with innovative conference systems, rooms for video conferences and digital workshops)
Agility	Support for flexible and interactive corporate cultures (e.g. use of one room for different activities, rooms and equipment for agile meeting formats)
Resilience	Space for relaxation and quiet work (e.g. quiet rooms, lounges, quiet workstations, break rooms for relaxation)

Fig. 1 Influencing factors of current New Work trends on workplace design. *Source* own illustration

A concept that is increasingly being used in practice is Activity Based Working (ABW) (see Elminger and Pistauer 2017; van Meel 2020, p. 89 ff.). Since each working activity involves different requirements for concentration, innovation, communication or interaction, the concept aims to provide the appropriate environments, equipment and technologies for all activities, thus ensuring employee satisfaction and performance (see Hoendervanger 2016; Hackl et al. 2017, pp. 122–123; v. Meel 2020, p. 13). Even though the concept of Activity Based Working is gaining more and more attention as part of the current New Work movement, it is not a newly developed idea. The origin can be traced back to the architects Phillip Stone and Robert Luchetti, who developed the idea in the USA in the 1970s and published it in 1985 under the title "The Office is where you are" (see Stone and Luchetti 1985). At the same time, similar concepts were being put into practice by companies like IBM (see Allen and Gerstberger 1973). In other areas too, it is not a new invention to perform our activities in an appropriate environment—this applies to the design of our homes as well as to the practice of various sports. For example, cooking in the bedroom works just as little as playing tennis in the riding arena. So why is Activity Based Working currently gaining so much importance? The reason for this is that it meets the requirements of sustainable workplace design to a particularly high degree.

2 Advantages of this Form of Work

Several studies show that, regardless of the approach, an appropriate workplace design has a positive impact on employee productivity and satisfaction. In particular, appropriate furniture, acoustics, room climate, and a sufficient number of meeting rooms play an important role (see Appel-Meulenbroek 2011; Bauer et al. 2021; Bauer et al. 2021a; IBA- study 2017).

However, the claim of Activity Based Working to create an individually tailored space for all necessary activities also brings two more essential factors for sustainable workplace design: the opening of the workspace (so-called open space) and the sharing of workplaces between different employees (see Eismann 2022, p. 174; van Meel 2020, p. 13). This means that workspace design based on the Activity Based Working concept can also offer innovative space solutions for hybrid work or spaces for agile meeting formats, for example, without neglecting the economic efficiency of a workspace (see Rolfö 2018a). Matching the available space and equipment to the different activities also ensures that employees can carry out their activities meaningfully and efficiently (see Elminger and Pistauer 2017, pp. 265–268).

In addition, the regular change of workplace and the flexible use of workspaces promote professional and informal communication and knowledge transfer within the team (see Eismann 2022, p. 181; Rolfö 2018a, p. 147) and also have a positive effect on employee satisfaction (see Hoendervanger 2016). Flexibility and the bundling of skills allow solutions to be found to complex problems at short notice, thus promoting the idea of agile working. Spontaneous conversations are also more likely, making the office an important place to work, as unplanned communication cannot be mapped via digital collaboration (see Bockstahler et al. 2022). Finally, studies have found that the high level of interaction and communication in Activity Based Working also has a positive effect on other factors, such as employees eating habits (see Arundell et al. 2018). This way of working may therefore also contribute to the growing importance of health management in companies.

Finally, the third key feature that distinguishes the "Multi-Space Office" from other large-space concepts it that the Activity Based Working concept ensures that employees can find rest and relaxation in the office in return for demanding co-creative processes and innovation work by integrating retreat rooms for concentrated work as well as recreation and break rooms. This is because the balance between development and relaxation is one of the most important drivers of satisfaction in workplace design (see Bauer et al. 2021). This also prevents employees from retreating to their home offices or to third places, thus ensuring regular personal interaction between team members (see Bockstahler et al. 2022).

3 Challenges of this Form of Work

Recent studies show that the opening of office spaces, disruptions caused by the movement of employees and observation at the workplace can have a negative impact on employee satisfaction, making areas or rooms for concentrated and undisturbed activities more important (see Appel-Meulenbroek 2011; Bauer et al. 2021; Rolfö 2018, p. 147). Too high occupancy density due to excessive optimization of the economic efficiency of an office space can additionally promote restlessness and discomfort.

In addition to the opening up of space, situational choice and the associated frequent changes of workplace also change the organization of work and require a high degree of self-organization from employees (see Eismann 2022, p. 189). Not only the right teams and skills must be assembled for each activity, but the appropriate workplace must also be selected.

In doing so, the right balance must also be struck between learning and experimenting, day-to-day operations, and adequate recovery time. All of this requires a high level of organizational skills on the part of the individual employee, as well as the ability to balance and prioritize personal needs, team and company goals, and compliance policies or other constraints. In the absence of measures to successfully manage and implement Activity Based Working, this form of work can lead to excessive demands, resistance, and demotivation (see Babapour and Rolfö 2019).

4 Solutions and Practical Tips

Workplace design according to Activity Based Working initially entails special requirements in terms of room design and workplace equipment. If these are not taken into account, this can lead to a decrease in productivity, dissatisfaction or even illness among employees (cf. Appel-Meulenbroek 2011). This is because the workplace design (system environment) influences the behavior of the people who work there and vice versa (cf. König and Volmer 2008, p. 49). If spaces are not used by people, they are worthless. If spaces interfere with people's ability to work, they are also ineffective. Spaces can therefore only develop their full power if we consider both as a unit (cf. Amstutz and Schwehr 2015). Therefore, in order to fully exploit the advantages of Activity Based Working, organizational and cultural aspects need to be considered in addition to room design and workplace equipment, both in the development and implementation of the concept (cf. Brunia et al. 2016). Four key success factors can be derived for a successful implementation of a sustainable workplace design in practice.

4.1 Consider Special Features in Workplace Design

When designing workplaces according to Activity Based Working, lighting, flooring and wall design must be used to create visual landmarks and structure the open space. Furniture must allow flexible use of the workplaces and storage space, such as lockers, must be integrated into the design to compensate for the loss of personal workspace and desks. In addition, acoustics and the provision of room-in-room solutions play a special role in order to avoid disturbing background noise, for example during phone calls, despite communication and interaction (cf. Appel-Meulenbroek 2011). Furthermore, modern telephone systems can significantly reduce the noise level and thus avoid disturbances. Finally, appropriate technologies must be provided when equipping workplaces. These include, for example, room booking systems, video conferencing systems and mobile devices (e.g. laptops, mobile phones) for the employees.

4.2 Align Workplace Design With the Organization

A detailed analysis of the work organization is a prerequisite for creating the right space offer for the activities actually carried out in the teams (cf. Rolfö 2018a, p. 146). This is because the business model, the competitive situation and the individual corporate culture determine how much agility and collaboration are actually needed to achieve goals and ensure future viability. To find this out, work diaries, employee interviews and workshops provide many helpful insights. The next step is to combine the results with the company's vision and goals to derive a comprehensive requirement profile for room design and workplace equipment, as well as other supporting organizational and management measures. Only through this comprehensive analysis companys can create workplaces in which the work results can contribute to the success of an organization.

4.3 Establish Goal Management Systems as a Decision-Making Framework

Working according to Activity Based Working requires a high degree of self-organization (cf. Eismann 2022, p. 189). However, to ensure that the employees activities contribute to achieving the company's goals, an overarching decision-making framework is needed. One option is to introduce a goal management system such as "Objectives and Key Results" (OKRs). OKRs are linked to the company's vision, mission statement and medium-term goals and specify measures for achieving goals at the operational level (cf. Lobacher and Jacob 2020, p. 115 ff.). Such a goal management system can also be an effective decision-making aid for prioritizing activities and thus a suitable choice of workplace, and reduce excessive demands or avoidance behavior on the part of employees. This ensures that forward-looking factors such as collaboration and agility are actually put into practice and can thus contribute to the future viability of a company. In addition, this also promotes informal exchange, as it is no longer the working time, but the effectiveness of the employees that decides on the evaluation of their work performance (cf. Eismann 2022, p. 190).

4.4 Structuring the Change Process

A fourth key success factor for leveraging the benefits of Activity Based Working is the guidance of the change process associated with the workplace redesign. Moving from traditional workplace concepts with fixed workplaces and individual or small group offices, opening the workspace and regularly changing workplaces is a major change. Workflows must be reworked and new technologies and communication channels must be used. A recent study also shows that only a minority (13% of respondents) actually use different work situations in practice (see Bauer et al. 2021). In addition to a possible lack of alignment of the workplace design to the employees needs, this can also be due to resistance and lack of experimentation in using the new space on the part of employees. Therefore, structured guidance of the change process through appropriate communication, appreciation of experimentation, and sustainable stabilization of the new way of working is essential. In addition, employees participation in the office design process increases satisfaction the chance to actually use different workplaces (see IBA study 2017). Setting rules, for example with regard to the use of different workplaces, can also increase the effective use of the new workplace concept. Again, this requires a participatory process with the actual users of the space (see Babapour and Rolfö 2019). In addition, the hypotheses made in the planning process should be regularly reviewed and, if necessary, subsequent adjustments made to the workplace design.

5 Summary and Outlook

In times of increasing uncertainty, competitive pressure and shortage of skilled workers, flexibility, innovation and employee satisfaction are critical to a company's future viability and success. In this context, workplace design becomes one of the key success factors: it must promote agile organizational structures, enable the connection of private and professional life, and create space for recovery. A workplace design based on the Activity Based Working concept allows all this without unnecessarily driving up the costs of providing suitable workplaces. Unlike to traditional workplace concepts and other open-space concepts, it creates space for collaboration and innovation, without neglecting the need for focused work, relaxation and informal interaction. At the same time, it provides the flexibility to to respond to changing conditions in the future. If companies succeed in connecting space and organization and supporting employees in self-organization, workplace design based on the Activity Based Working concept can make a significant contribution to the future viability and thus the success of companies.

References

Allen, T. J. und Gerstberger, P. G. (1973), A field experiment to improve communications in a product engineering department: The nonterritorial office, Human Factors, Jg. 15, Nr. 5, pp. 487–498.

Allmers, S. et al. (2022), On the Way to New Work, München 2022.

Amstutz, S. und Schwehr, P. (2015), Human Office: Arbeitswelten im Diskurs, Kompetenzzentrum Typologie & Planung in Architektur CCTP (Eds.), Luzern 2015.

Appel-Meulenbroek, R. (2011), An end-user's perspective on activity-based office concepts, Journal of Corporate Real Estate, 2011, 13. Jg., Nr. 2, pp. 122–135.

Arundell, L., et al. (2018), The impact of activity based working (ABW) on workplace activity, eating behaviours, productivity, and satisfaction. International journal of environmental research and public health, 2018, 15. Jg., Nr. 5, pp. 1005.

Babapour M. und Rolfö, L. (2019), Policies in Activity-based Flexible Offices-'I am sloppy with clean-desking. We don't really know the rules.'. Ergonomics, 62. Jg., Nr. 1, pp. 1–20.

Bauer, W. et al. (2021), Office Analytics: Erfolgsfaktoren für die Gestaltung einer typbasierten Arbeitswelt, Fraunhofer-Institut für Arbeitswirtschaft und Organisation (IAO), Stuttgart 2021.

Bauer, W. et al. (2021a), Raumpsychologie für eine neue Arbeitswelt, Fraunhofer-Institut für Arbeitswirtschaft und Organisation (IAO), Stuttgart 2021.

Block, J. et al. (2021), Zukunftskraft Resilienz – Gewappnet für die Zeit der Krisen, Zukunftsinstitut 2021.

Bockstahler et al. (2022), Homeoffice Experience 2.0: Veränderung, Entwicklung und Erfahrungen zur Arbeit aus dem Homeoffice während der Corona-Pandemie, Fraunhofer-Institut für Arbeitswirtschaft und Organisation (IAO), Stuttgart 2022.

Brunia, S. et al. (2016). Accommodating new ways of working: lessons from best practices and worst cases. Journal of Corporate Real Estate, 18(1), pp. 30–47.

Eismann, T. (2022), Understanding the Mechanisms of Activity-Based Workspaces: A Case Study, Environment and Behaviour 2022, Vol. 54 (I), pp. 170–210.

Elminger, M. und Pistauer C. (2017), Johnsen & Johnson: Better by Data – Workplace Innovation Studie, in: Bartz, M. et al (eds.), Unternehmen der nächsten Generation, pp. 257–276, Luzern 2017.

IBA-Studie 2017: Wohlbefinden im Büro, https://iba.online/knowledge/site/assets/files/3939/iba-studie_2017_web.pdf (abgerufen am 25.09.2022).

Hackl, B. et al. (2017), New Work: Auf dem Weg zur neuen Arbeitswelt, Wiesbaden 2017.

Hoendervanger, J. G. (2016),„Flexibility in use: Switching behaviour and satisfaction in activity-based work environments“, Journal of Corporate Real Estate, Vol. 18 Iss 1 pp. 48–62.

König, E. und Volmer, G. (2008), Handbuch systemische Organisationsberatung, Weinheim und Basel 2008.

Lobacher, P. und Jacob, C. (2020), Objectives & Key Results (OKR): Das agile Betriebssystem für moderne Organisationen.

Rolfö, L. (2018) Perceptions of performance and satisfaction after relocation to an activity-based office, Ergonomics, 61:5, pp. 644–657.

Rolfö, L. (2018a), Relocation to an activity-based flexible office–Design processes and outcomes. Applied ergonomics, 2018, 73. Jg., pp. 141–150.

Stone, P. J. und Luchetti, R. (1985), „Your office is where your are“, Harvard Business Review, Vol. 63 No. 2, pp. 102–117.

van Meel, J. (2020), Activity-Based Working Practice Guide, 2. Auflage, 2020.

Zukunftsinstitut (2021), Megatrend New Work, https://www.zukunftsinstitut.de/dossier/megatrend-new-work/ (abgerufen am 25.09.2022).

The Home Office: Achieving Productivity, Well-Being and Ergonomics

Lisa Rosa Bräutigam

1 Introduction

Even after the end of the mandatory home office in March 2022, almost a quarter of all German employees remained in the home office (see the article "Home Office: Perspectives, Challenges, Solutions"). The proportion of employees who regularly work from home only decreased minimally by 0.4 percentage points to 24.5% in the months that followed. "Apparently, companies and employees are permanently relying on home office," concludes Jean-Victor Alipour (in ifo 2022). What began as a forced temporary solution during the Covid pandemic, promising protection in times of crisis and often initially accompanied by a feeling of being overwhelmed, has long since established itself as the norm—and is now being continued voluntarily. Since then, the option of a workplace in one's own four walls has been perceived by many employees as an enrichment.

The statutory health insurance DAK-Gesundheit found in a panel survey in February and March 2021 with 4,814 respondents that the advantages of home office are mainly seen in higher productivity, more pleasant work, time gain and good compatibility with family life (DAK 2021). Ford et al. (2020) also found that employees working from home are relieved by lower expenses for things like commuting and gain time by eliminating commuting. In addition, some appreciate that "workplace politics" no longer play a role in their work environment.

Nevertheless, the switch to the home office also involves challenges and risks. Among other things, respondents see a lack of contact with colleagues, the absence of a suitable workplace and a high degree of distraction (DAK 2021).

L. R. Bräutigam (✉)
nuwo GmbH, Berlin, Germany
e-mail: lisa@nuwo.co

I. Knappertsbusch and G. Wisskirchen (eds.), *The Future of Work*,
https://doi.org/10.1007/978-3-658-45150-9_33

Only 10% plan to work almost exclusively in the home office in the future. At the same time, however, only a further 10% are willing to return to the office full-time. The vast majority welcome a model that combines both worlds and allows flexibility in the choice of workplace, with 33% wanting to do a quarter of their work and 47% half of it in the home office (ibid.). It can be assumed that work in the hybrid model will increasingly become independent of the workplace and, as a triad of home office, office workplace and third place, will not only meet the needs and wishes of employees, but also enable efficiency.

2 Advantages of an Ergonomic Home Office

Ergonomics, as the "science of human work", and in this context "the adaptation of working conditions to the human being and not vice versa", is defined by the Institute for Integrated Production Hannover (2022), founded as a non-profit society by the Leibniz University Hannover. According to de Macêdo et al., two essential advantages arise when work is adapted to the human being: "the first one refers to organizations and their performance such as efficiency, productivity and quality. The second objective is people-centred, focusing on safety, health, and comfort" (2020, p. 777). The factor of productivity, which is mentioned here as the first point, can be defined as "amount of work done per unit of time" (Ralph et al. 2020, p. 4931). Employees generally rate their individual productivity highly when they work from home, more precisely 50 to 65% higher than in the office (DAK 2021; Prinz 2021; Howington 2020). Prinz (2021) was able to establish a connection to the handling of technology, compatibility of work and family, and separation of work and private life.

Research on how this positive change is influenced by ergonomic home office equipment is still in its infancy. However, initial studies show a clear relationship. For example, Karakolis and Callaghan were able to demonstrate in a meta-analysis 2013 that the mere change from sitting to sit-stand workplaces has a huge impact on productivity. A positive correlation between ergonomics and productivity is also confirmed by Ralph et al. (2020) with a statistically significant value. Employees themselves also make this connection: In a study by Ford et al. (2020), 40% of 3634 respondents cited their home office equipment as a reason or at least a contributing factor for a more productive way of working. Based on estimates using the path coefficients of the structural equation models and the scales used by Seva et al. (2021) and Ralph et al. (2020), a factor of approximately 12 to 15% can be assumed.

The second, people-centred goal of ergonomics, according to de Macêdo et al., lies in "safety, health, and comfort" (2020, p. 777). These factors can be summarized in the general term of well-being, or also well-being. This is about the individual's subjective assessment of general quality of life (Görland & Kannengießer 2021). Researchers like Xiao et al. (2021) and Ralph et al. (2020) commonly distinguish between physical and mental well-being—and particularly physical complaints are often reported by home office workers.

In a survey of 843 university staff working from home, 40% reported moderate to severe complaints, including severe pain in the lower and middle back, moderate complaints in the eyes, neck or head, and complaints in the upper back and shoulders (Gerding et al. 2021). In a similarly designed study with 1135 respondents by Kotowski et al. (2022), problems in the upper back and shoulders (62%), lumbar spine problems (45%) and moderate to severe neck and headaches (49%) also predominated. In both of the aforementioned studies, more than a third of home office workers suffered from temporary discomfort in addition to the physical complaints (see Kotowski et al. 2022; Gerding et al. 2021). In many cases, it does not stop at isolated complaints: Musculoskeletal diseases are common in Germany and are the main cause of work incapacity at 13%, followed by mental illnesses at 17%. The former group of diagnoses alone accounted for 32.5 billion euros in lost gross value added in 2020, which corresponds to 0.9% of gross national income (see Federal Institute for Occupational Safety and Health 2022). Seva et al. (2021) point out that work-related musculoskeletal diseases (abbreviated: MSD) are responsible for 40 to 50% of the costs of all work-related diseases.

Xiao et al. (2021) dedicated their study with 988 participants to the question of which factors sustainably influence well-being in the home office. As a comparison value, they used, among other things, the number of new physical and mental health problems since the change from office work to home office activity. A higher level of physical activity, healthy food intake and a low consumption or even abstention from "junk food" as well as increased communication with colleagues were beneficial for the well-being of the surveyed employees. In addition, the establishment of a professional workplace becomes an obvious factor not to be neglected: In the context of the study, only 39% stated that they have a "good workstation" in the home office. Of the subjects in the group with poor or non-existent equipment, 50% suffered two or more new physical complaints during the study period, and 64% at least two new mental stress points, while the value for well-equipped employees was 20 and 34% respectively. Thus, good equipment reduces the risk of physical and mental problems in the home office by half.

3 Challenges Regarding an Ergonomic Home Office

Creating a workspace at home that ensures healthy and productive work is no easy task. While technical equipment such as laptops or headsets can be taken from the company's workplace to the home office, not all employees have the appropriate living space for their own office, let alone the financial means for or access to ergonomic furniture (cf. Mojtahedzadeh et al. 2021). A survey by Messenger et al. (2017) found that more than half of the 1508 respondents did not pay attention to ergonomics at their home office workplace according to their own statements, and 94% of employers did not fulfill their duty of care in this area. These are measures, alongside for example the assumption of internet fees or company training, that 30 to 50% of employees would like their company to take (cf. Ford et al. 2020; Ralph et al. 2020). Another study by Janneck et al. (2018) revealed that only three out of 41 respondents had ergonomic work tools available in their home office. At the same time, a third tried to create a health-promoting workplace on their own.

From a company perspective, there is a quite positive view of the hybrid change in the world of work, not least because of increased flexibility, satisfaction, and motivation of employees in the home office (DAK 2021). So where are the hurdles to also equip such an office ergonomically?

Setting up a professional workplace at home for employees is challenging for companies not only from a financial and tax perspective—considering the depreciation period of 13 years for the countless individual pieces of furniture distributed across private households. Legal certainty must also be ensured at home by complying with the numerous strict regulations and duties of care. In addition, the administrative processing ties up valuable resources of the HR and IT apparatus and is hardly feasible logistically, especially in a corporate environment. This is one reason why home office as-a-service providers have established themselves on the market to solve these problems holistically for companies.

4 Solutions and Practical Tips

A health-preserving workplace in the home office begins with movable seating furniture that allows dynamic sitting with changing sitting positions. The movable backrest and the seat surface should adapt to every body movement and give the upper body the necessary support. In addition to a significant increase in productivity, working at a sit-stand workstation, for example with a height-adjustable table, is also a key factor for physical and mental health (cf. Seva et al. 2021). From this it becomes clear that it is not the individual posture, but rather the change of this, that makes a difference. Based on this, Meyerhuber (2021) developed the following rule of thumb: 60% of the working time should be spent in dynamic sitting, 30% in dynamic standing and a further 10% should be used for movement (see Fig. 1). In addition, frequent short-duration standing up is recommended and static positions as well as entire standing breaks over 20 min should be avoided. There should be at least three to four of these posture changes per hour. Knowledge of how to correctly use and adjust the equipment also plays a central role.

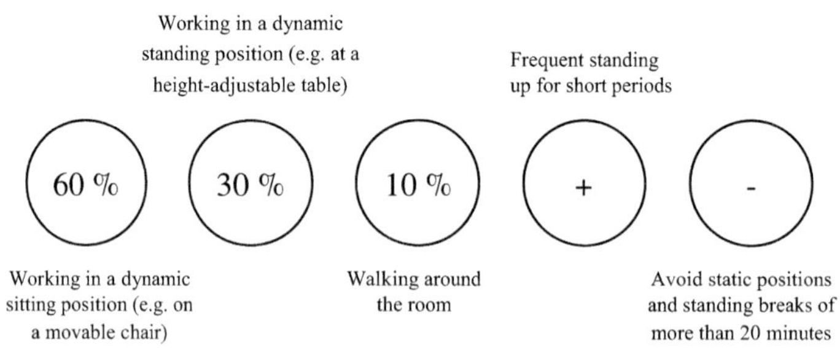

Fig. 1 Recommended movement in the home office, own illustration after Meyerhuber (2021)

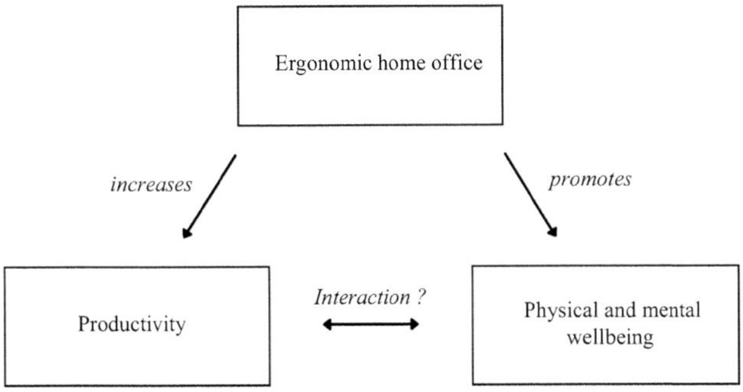

Fig. 2 Triad of ergonomics, productivity, and well-being, own representation

5 Summary and Outlook

The vast majority of employees are looking forward to a hybrid work model in the future, which combines the possibility of home office with the traditional office workplace. The design of a professional workplace is also essential in the home area, yet home office workplaces are still predominantly non-ergonomically equipped. Current research results show that, in addition to influencing factors such as exercise and nutrition, ergonomic equipment is crucial for maintaining the health and workability of employees working from home. Thus, providing an ergonomic workplace reduces the likelihood of physical and psychological illnesses by half. Specific movement and usage behavior are also decisive factors. Therefore, a fundamental triad of ergonomics, productivity, and the physical and psychological well-being of employees is assumed, which is illustrated in Fig. 2. The extent to which a concrete correlation exists between the individual variables should be further investigated in future studies due to the increased relevance.

Although employers, according to DAK (2021), also confirm the advantages of home office in terms of efficiency and productivity increase by 9-10%, the deficient condition of German home workplaces and their negative impact on the health condition of employees indicate a great need for improvement. In the coming years, it will be seen to what extent companies will take on these challenges, recognize the potential of ergonomics on productivity, and increasingly promote the well-being of employees strategically.

References

Bundesanstalt für Arbeitsschutz und Arbeitsmedizin. (2022). *Volkswirtschaftliche Kosten durch Arbeitsunfähigkeit 2020*. Bundesanstalt für Arbeitsschutz und Arbeitsmedizin (BAuA). https://www.baua.de/DE/Themen/Arbeitswelt-und-Arbeitsschutz-im-Wandel/Arbeitsweltberichterstattung/Kosten-der-AU/Kosten-der-Arbeitsunfaehigkeit_node.html (abgerufen am 29.10.2022)

DAK. (2021). *Digitalisierung und Homeoffice in der Corona-Krise – Update*. https://www.dak.de/dak/download/studie-pdf-2448800.pdf (abgerufen am 29.10.2022)

de Macêdo, T. A. M., Cabral, E. L. dos S., Silva Castro, W. R., de Souza Junior, C. C., da Costa Junior, J. F., Pedrosa, F. M., da Silva, A. B., de Medeiros, V. R. F., de Souza, R. P., Cabral, M. A. L., & Másculo, F. S. (2020). Ergonomics and telework: A systematic review. *Work, 66*(4), 777–788. https://doi.org/10.3233/WOR-203224 (abgerufen am 29.10.2022)

Howington, J. (2020). 2018 annual survey finds workers are more productive at home. *FlexJobs Blog*. https://www.flexjobs.com/blog/post/2018-annual-survey-finds-workers-more-productive-at-home/ (abgerufen am 29.10.2022)

Ford, D., Storey, M.-A., Zimmermann, T., Bird, C., Jaffe, S., Maddila, C., Butler, J. L., Houck, B., & Nagappan, N. (2020). *A Tale of Two Cities: Software Developers Working from Home During the COVID-19 Pandemic*. arXiv. https://doi.org/10.48550/ARXIV.2008.11147 (abgerufen am 29.10.2022)

Gerding, T., Syck, M., Daniel, D., Naylor, J., Kotowski, S. E., Gillespie, G. L., Freeman, A. M., Huston, T. R., & Davis, K. G. (2021). An assessment of ergonomic issues in the home offices of university employees sent home due to the COVID-19 pandemic. *Work, 68*(4), 981–992. https://doi.org/10.3233/WOR-205294 (abgerufen am 29.10.2022)

Görland, S. O., & Kannengießer, S. (2021). A matter of time? Sustainability and digital media use. *Digital Policy, Regulation and Governance, 23*(3), 248–261. https://doi.org/10.1108/DPRG-11-2020-0160 (abgerufen am 29.10.2022)

ifo Institut (2022, 05. September). *Nutzung des Homeoffice geht nur leicht zurück* [Pressemitteilung]. https://www.ifo.de/pressemitteilung/2022-09-05/nutzung-des-homeoffice-geht-nur-leicht-zurueck (abgerufen am 29.10.2022)

Institut für Integrierte Produktion Hannover. (2022). *Ergonomie am Arbeitsplatz ganzheitlich gestalten*. IPH – Institut für Integrierte Produktion Hannover. https://www.iph-hannover.de/de/impressum/ (abgerufen am 29.10.2022)

Janneck, M., Jent, S., Weber, P., & Nissen, H. (2018). Ergonomics To Go: Designing the Mobile Workspace. *International Journal of Human-Computer Interaction, 34*(11), 1052–1062. https://doi.org/10.1080/10447318.2017.1413057 (abgerufen am 29.10.2022)

Karakolis T., & Callaghan J. P. (2013). The impact of sit-stand office workstations on worker discomfort and productivity: A review. *Applied Ergonomics, 45*(3), 799–806. https://doi.org/10.1016/j.apergo.2013.10.001 (abgerufen am 29.10.2022)

Kotowski, S. E., Davis, K. G., & Gerding, T. (2022). Almost a year in: Virtual offices remained an ergonomic trouble spot. *Work, 71*(2), 319–326. https://doi.org/10.3233/WOR-211052 (abgerufen am 29.10.2022)

Messenger, J., Vargas Llave, O., Gschwing, L., Boehmer, S., Vermeylen, G., & Wilkens, M. (2017). *Working anytime, anywhere: The effects on the world of work*. Publications Office of the European Union, Luxembourg, and the International Labour Office. https://www.eurofound.europa.eu/publications/report/2017/working-anytime-anywhere-the-effects-on-the-world-of-work (abgerufen am 29.10.2022)

Meyerhuber, S. (2021). Strukturelle Voraussetzungen für gute Onlinekommunikation und -kooperation sowie Ergonomie am Arbeitsplatz. In S. Meyerhuber (eds.), *Sozial nachhaltiges Handeln in der Online-Kommunikation und -kooperation? Langzeitliches Homeoffice – Konfliktpotenziale und Lösungsansätze in digitalen Gruppen sowie für deren Leitung* (pp. 49–72). https://www.uni-bremen.de/fileadmin/user_upload/sites/artec/Publikationen/artec_Paper/228_paper.pdf (abgerufen am 29.10.2022)

Mojtahedzadeh, N., Rohwer, E., Lengen, J., Harth, V., & Mache, S. (2021). Gesundheitsfördernde Arbeitsgestaltung im Homeoffice im Kontext der COVID-19-Pandemie. *Zentralblatt für Arbeitsmedizin, Arbeitsschutz und Ergonomie, 71*(2), 69–74. https://doi.org/10.1007/s40664-020-00419-1 (abgerufen am 29.10.2022)

Prinz, W. (2021). Flexibles Arbeiten im Homeoffice – Analyse einer Langzeitumfrage. In M. Dohm, A. Große-Jäger, K. Rüffler, & J. Staff (eds.), *Expedition: Werte, Arbeit, Führung 4.0* (2nd edn., pp. 153–165).

Ralph, P., Baltes, S., Adisaputri, G., Torkar, R., Kovalenko, V., Kalinowski, M., Novielli, N., Yoo, S., Devroey, X., Tan, X., Zhou, M., Turhan, B., Hoda, R., Hata, H., Robles, G., Milani Fard, A., & Alkadhi, R. (2020). Pandemic programming: How COVID-19 affects software developers and how their organizations can help. *Empirical Software Engineering, 25*(6), 4927–4961. https://doi.org/10.1007/s10664-020-09875-y (abgerufen am 29.10.2022)

Seva, R. R., Tejero, L. M. S., Fadrilan-Camacho, V. F. F. (2021). Barriers and facilitators of productivity while working from home during pandemic. *Journal of Occupational & Environmental Medicine, 63*(1), 1065–1072. https://doi.org/10.1002/1348-9585.12242 (abgerufen am 29.10.2022)

Xiao, Y., Becerik-Gerber, B., Lucas, G., & Roll, S. C. (2021). Impacts of Working From Home During COVID-19 Pandemic on Physical and Mental Well-Being of Office Workstation Users. *Journal of Occupational & Environmental Medicine, 63*(3), 181–190. https://doi.org/10.1097/JOM.0000000000002097 (abgerufen am 29.10.2022)

New Work Requires New Learning

Joachim Giese and Claudia Suhr

1 Introduction

In the VUCA world, everything is constantly changing, at different paces, fluidly, disruptively—depending on the situation. Companies and the people who work in them must constantly update their knowledge and ability to act. This requires a willingness to learn and change, systemic thinking to solve complex situations and problems, and creativity, because existing knowledge of action is not suitable for solving future problems.

"New Work" is the answer of many companies to the change of work in progressing digitization. While the term "New Work" also aims at the structural changes in working life made possible by digitization, a part of it is also the acquisition of competencies through "lifelong learning". The term "lifelong learning" mainly refers to the difference between the current and the future necessary educational structure: In the past, school education and subsequent vocational training, studies or a combination of both were "sufficient". After that, one had "finished learning". Today, it is necessary for people to learn throughout their lives: Not only in school, vocational training and studies, but also continuously during their professional career until retirement. "Finished learning" no longer exists. Lifelong learning takes its place and requires a high degree of flexibility and willingness to learn and change from people. But how can the required level of lifelong learning be adequately addressed by companies? What opportunities are available within

J. Giese · C. Suhr (✉)
WBS TRAINING AG, Berlin, Germany
e-mail: Claudia.Suhr@wbstraining.de

J. Giese
e-mail: joachim.giese@wbstraining.de

I. Knappertsbusch and G. Wisskirchen (eds.), *The Future of Work*,
https://doi.org/10.1007/978-3-658-45150-9_34

working hours? How can different learning and personality types be addressed? Which digital learning formats are suitable and how should the human aspect be included in these plans? Can companies expect their employees to undergo personality development that corresponds to the company's goals?

While the good intention and the insight into the necessary investment are often present, it is often not possible or not allowed to take the workforce out of the daily business for a longer period of time to let them participate in further education. Here—analogous to New Work—"New Learning" is needed. This refers to professional further education that is offered during working hours and that opens up development opportunities that do not only focus on updating knowledge. This can be implemented through the use of Learning Content Management Systems (LCMS) and strategic competence management.

2 Advantages of this Working Method

Learning Content Management Systems accompany employees and managers during their time at work in their further development. Here, continuous development can be made possible. Either internally or externally hosted LCMS are tailored to the topics in the respective work areas. New, current knowledge as well as potential development are made possible during working hours.

What conditions must be met?

The keyword is strategic competence management. One or more strategic fields of action are assigned to sustainable goal planning, on which the goals are to be achieved. But to be successful there, a strategy-oriented analysis of the skills and competences that the employees and managers need is required. Here, specific measures can be taken to strengthen both technical and non-technical competences. The LCMS is set up in such a way that the required knowledge and necessary action competence can be built up in time. This is done through the feeding and sensible timing of learning opportunities that the LCMS provides to the employees. Driven by algorithms, the employees are encouraged to complete a certain development program within the next few days or weeks. In timely intervals, the employees can then deal with the new learning units during working hours under their own time control. An additional success factor is the accompaniment by cooperative and social learning in learning teams, which motivate and exchange each other.

This would solve the problem of optimally preparing the employees without them having to be away from their field of action for longer periods of time.

But another problem is exacerbated by digitization: The new knowledge has an ever shorter half-life. The time investment is hardly worth it anymore, because in the VUCA world, new methods are constantly emerging that could be used efficiently. Of course, it makes no sense to forego updating knowledge for this reason. The answer to this is an interesting other movement: Software systems like MS Office 365 update themselves and challenge the users to keep themselves up to date. Change thus becomes part of everyday work and it is the new "normal" to find innovations that were not prepared in long-planned and prepared training sessions. Instead of knowledge, the competence must be acquired to deal with this constant change. This applies exemplarily also to many other areas. People learn to live with changes and to perceive them as natural. The disturbing factor of an inserted "further education appointment" is thus more and more eliminated. Lifelong professional learning becomes a continuum. This is very good to represent, as long as it involves small steps of change and does not have a disruptive character.

3 Challenges of this Working Method

But what if the working and business world is suddenly changed by disruption? What if there are important software implementations that do not undergo automatic updates? How can we prepare people in the VUCA world to be ready to learn and change?

Here, a closer look at the previously mentioned strategic competence management is worthwhile. Competence includes current knowledge, ideally proven by a recognized qualification. Competence also includes professional action knowledge, i.e., experience gained from the application of knowledge. However, the most important aspect of competence is its focus on performance in the future. This is about people's personal success portfolio, so to speak, the basic equipment that every person carries within them to be able to act successfully even in unplanned, new situations. Especially in the unpredictable VUCA world, it is important to be equipped with good self-organization. What if experiential knowledge is no longer very useful because completely new situations arise? We remember the first months of the Covid crisis. There was no experiential knowledge on how companies could support their employees in the home office; how to deal with high levels of sickness absence and how to organize work on site in a health-conscious way. Those who had a willingness to learn and change, maintained good relationship management, and could think systemically were clearly at an advantage. But can we expect this from employees? Were these skills or the opportunity for self-development in the company seminar program? Mostly less so. And yet, strategic competence management is a central field of action for the HR departments of companies.

In the considerations of digitization, the term "skills" is currently most frequently encountered. The most diverse "future skills" are recorded, described, and presented as competence models for digitization. Here, there is often a mix of descriptions from general requirements ("future-oriented"), specific areas of action ("digital and media competence") and special knowledge such as programming languages or knowledge of database functions. Generally, it refers to what a person in the considered professional field of action must know, understand, and be able to do. It answers the question of WHAT needs to be done.

Furthermore, a distinction is made between "hard skills" and "soft skills". Hard skills describe the manifested, recognized knowledge, which is usually acquired in vocational training or universities. Hard skills have a professional action aspect and refer to a canon of knowledge that is assumed in the respective fields of expertise. This knowledge is usually acquired through recognized qualifications such as vocational training and degree programs. Perhaps they are called "hard competencies" because this knowledge is measurable and verifiable through exams: "You can rely on it". The answer to whether this is really guaranteed is important! In the education discussion, there is a large discourse about whether the transfer of "knowledge" into "successful action" is actually always guaranteed. It is not only about WHAT needs to be done, but equally about HOW it is done.

This is where the so-called "soft skills" come into the discussion. Soft skills are not so easily tangible and measurable. They cannot be tested and proven at one point in time under comparable conditions. They are "soft", fluid, and become visible in different situations in different ways. The term "soft skills" focuses on the abilities of self-organization beyond technical knowledge. Here, the question is answered of HOW something should be done. Soft skills are about the personal success portfolio. It arises from the personality aspect and is manifested through life and action experience.

Soft skills are competencies that become observable over time. Life and action experience cannot be acquired in short seminar days. In this sense, the "measurability" of soft skills is not present at a certain point in time, but requires a longer observation period. Another important aspect is that these are attributions. If a person has often been perceived as "competent" in the past, this will also be attributed to them for the future. The more people in their environment believe that the person in question is competent, the more the attribution is reinforced. Soft skills are therefore not as measurable as knowledge, they do not meet any objective criterion, but a consensus view of the participants emerges. However, this consensus view can be made visible with professional competence queries. This refers to self-assessments and external assessments that can be made based on questions about observable action. This also has considerable potential: It allows comparing the view of oneself with the view of others and deriving important development potentials from it. Nevertheless, the impossibility of objectively measuring competencies is a challenge for companies' personnel development. They face the challenge of adjusting to personality-related, not really measurable fields of action. This is often difficult in the business thinking, which naturally has to deal with numbers, data, and facts. In competence development, an attitude is required that builds trust in longer development periods.

Soft skills have a decisive advantage over hard skills: They are sustainable competencies. This is about working on one's own personal strengths. And people bring this potential every day and every hour and in every—even so novel—situation. But this exactly meets the requirements that companies and their employees face: Knowledge has an increasingly shorter half-life, processes change faster and faster with increasing digitization and there is no blueprint and no experiential knowledge for the newly emerging situation. So it is high time to think about how companies can accompany and strengthen their employees and managers to be able to deal with complexity and change. The required knowledge can, as described at the beginning, be provided time-efficiently via LCMS. This requires a team of curators and authors who bring this knowledge into digital learning formats. Finished learning units can also be purchased. However, the process of knowledge acquisition should be directly accompanied by measures that address the question of "how". Action competencies only ever arise in direct action, i.e., in the implementation and application of knowledge.

In conclusion, for the sake of completeness, it should be pointed out that competence is not the same as "responsibility". This term is often used synonymously. This comes from a time when a relevant education and qualification was sufficient for performing a job until the end of one's professional life and no targeted further development was necessary. Competence is also not exclusively the same as "knowledge". Both terms—"responsibility" and "knowledge"—denote manifested, completed states that no longer meet the requirements of adaptation to change. Therefore, the focus must be on the expanded concept of competence, which includes technical and experiential knowledge, but also covers the personal success portfolio of the actors.

4 Solutions and Practical Tips

To classify one's own actions and the handling of new facts, awareness of one's own values and attitudes is always required. For what else should guide action if there are no comparable reference situations? There may then no longer be a "we've always done it this way". The awareness of how to act; the attitude against which decisions are made—they will shape the impact of decisions. Therefore, processes should be initiated that make the values and attitudes of a company visible, develop them further and make them effective in practice. A simple example of why this might be important is the careful handling of personal data. Here, the ethical aspect of digitization becomes comprehensibly clear.

At the same time, a company that is dedicated to the individual potential development of its employees signals that it is interested in the human, personality-related level of personnel work. In general, when considering competence development, as far as it concerns the area of personality development, the ethical view must also be taken into account. If a company sets goals in strategic competence management that focus on the personal development of people, this goal setting can easily run the risk of making employees objects of the goal setting. This promotes a rather rejecting attitude of those affected, who rightly do not want to be personally instrumentalized. However, the development of personal competences can also be done subject-related. Then the invitation of personnel development to the employees would be to develop personally and individually preference-oriented for their own advantage. The characteristics of subject-related competence development should influence that people get offers to develop based on their own personality and their own strengths and weaknesses profile. The difference is clear: employees are not developed to be personally "aligned", but each person can consider their own strengths. This becomes very clear when considering the difference between introverted and extroverted personalities: Both types of personality have different strengths that they can use effectively. But both personality types will not always want to implement certain desired developments with joy. These differences can be referred to in mindful personnel development.

5 Summary and Outlook

In summary, it can be said that learning as pure knowledge transfer is outdated. It no longer meets the required adaptability to send employees to further training once or twice a year for a few days. And long-term educational measures to update knowledge outside the work context are not feasible for companies. Hardly any company will be able to afford to take employees out of their field of action for weeks and forego their productivity.

People must be supported in being able to manage a permanent change management with their self-control. We should above all aim to strengthen cooperative learning. Formats such as "working out loud", building knowledge in wikis, collegial advice and learning as a result of knowledge transfer should be promoted as much as possible. New Work is essentially characterized by specialists working together in different constellations. All routine work will be digitized sooner or later. What—for the time being at least—cannot be digitized is cooperation, intuition and value-oriented action. Here, collective learning and thus the further development of entire organizations is required. Cross-functional competences such as relationship management, cooperation and communication skills but also empathy will gain in importance.

Digitization will continue to drive our learning and development processes. All possible forms of collaborative, developing work in New Work also offer digital possibilities of collaborative, developing learning in New Learning. Adaptive, AI-supported learning platforms are already in development. Social development and digitization influence each other—visible for example in communication culture. Thus, with new digital possibilities, learning and development processes are also changed. The learning culture that results from this will again give new impulses for digital developments. As diverse as the working world of the future will be the learning world of the future. We see the developments in the offer of vocational education—be it further education institutes, universities or vocational schools—as an important impulse for the learning of the future as a whole.

Continuous Learning—The Importance for Companies and the Approaches of Continuous Learning in an Ever Faster Changing Working World

Simone Dogu

> *"Whoever always does what he can already do, always remains what he already is."*
>
> *– Henry Ford*

1 Introduction

The world of work is changing. The developments of the Covid pandemic make clear the benefits of digitized production processes, work and cooperation structures, and how helpful these can be in maintaining the operational capability of companies. They allow the continuation of operations and central work processes and offer the possibility to handle essential processes, customer inquiries, and work processes from other locations, such as the home office (cf. Hofmann, Piele & Piele 2020; Sostero et al. 2020). However, the possibilities of digital transformation were already a strategically highly relevant topic for companies, regardless of the industry, even before the pandemic began, as today's business environment is characterized by quick responsiveness to market changes, consideration of relevant trends, agile implementation of projects while simultaneously taking risks, in order to remain competitive in the market (cf. Binder & Hofmann 2021; Stifterverband/McKinsey 2018).

As part of digitization and automation, new job profiles will continue to emerge, and further training measures will change. All of this shapes the qualification requirements and the corresponding offers of vocational training and further education (cf. Binder & Hofmann 2021). The challenges are quite similar for all companies: it is necessary to develop new (digital) business models, open up new

S. Dogu (✉)
Mainz, Germany

I. Knappertsbusch and G. Wisskirchen (eds.), *The Future of Work*,
https://doi.org/10.1007/978-3-658-45150-9_35

markets, and make companies faster and more flexible using digital tools in order to be able to react to changes.

However, these innovations are only possible with employees who continuously adapt their qualifications to the changes in the environment in order to be able to realize new processes and forms of work. To build up these skills, a wide range of adaptation and advancement qualifications for the various job profiles and their tasks is required (cf. Deloitte Human Capital Trends 2017; Hofmann & Wienken 2020). The knowledge learned in school, during studies, or in training loses its timeliness and relevance over time. Due to the high innovative power and dynamics of digitization, this process is accelerated so much that the half-life of knowledge is getting shorter and shorter. This also means that the knowledge learned in vocational training or studies is not sufficient for an entire professional life, but must be regularly updated and adapted to the changing circumstances. This assigns a new meaning to learning as we knew it. In this context, terms such as *lifelong learning* or *continuous learning* have been established.

Terms like these two have received increasing attention in recent decades and have been increasingly taken into account in educational policy demands and concepts (cf. Becker 2012). The term *lifelong learning* developed from the 1960s onwards, initially with the aim of extending learning beyond the temporally limited phase of school, vocational, and university education. Nowadays, the goal should be to increase participation in education, to give all people more opportunities for personal, societal, and professional development according to their talents, and to help shape Europe as a location (cf. BMBF 2003).

By now, there are a multitude of concepts. Thus, *lifelong learning* and *continuous learning* are often interchangeable terms. Different terms may possibly be associated with certain conceptual orientations. In addition, there are translation difficulties at the international level.

To ensure a uniform understanding, this article will proceed from the following delimitation of terms:

The term *lifelong learning* focuses more on the individual person. Characteristic of the concept is that it puts the individual person with his or her learning biography more into the center of perception. It refers to someone who is long-term and voluntarily motivated to learn new skills or acquire new knowledge. A lifelong learner is someone who integrates learning as part of his or her lifestyle, even outside the professional environment.

In addition to *lifelong learning*, *continuous learning* has also been established. The term *continuous learning* refers to someone who is committed to learning new skills or knowledge, but is often used in a temporary or formal context, such as an additional seminar for the job to acquire new job-related skills.

2 Benefits of Continuous Learning

Continuous learning of employees is important for companies to remain competitive in today's global market. But what are the specific benefits of continuous learning for the company or for the individual?

2.1 Benefits of Continuous Learning for the Company

Companies that commit to continuous learning and provide the appropriate conditions can benefit from several advantages. These can be:

- Investment in the Future
  Future-oriented companies understand that the motivation and know-how of employees are the path to sustainable success. Continuous learning helps to achieve this goal.
- Sustainable HR Policy
  By investing in the skills and talents of their employees through continuous learning offers, companies create a pool of motivated and performance-oriented employees. This eliminates the time and cost of external talent acquisition.
- Targeted Promotion
  Organizations can control which (professional) content and impulses employees receive for learning. In this way, they can specifically promote their employees, which can contribute to achieving the company's goals, among other things.
- Option against Skills Shortage (see the article "Skills Shortage—Myth or Reality?")
  In a working world where every talent and employee is fought for, sophisticated and professional (further education) programs for continuous learning can be a competitive advantage over other companies.
- Increasing Employee Retention
  Many employees are also more satisfied when they have the opportunity to develop further. This means that turnover decreases and knowledge is not lost, but is retained within the company.

2.2 Benefits of Continuous Learning for the Individual

Not only do companies benefit from the opportunities of continuous learning. Employees can also derive their benefit from it and benefit from the continuous updating of knowledge or skills in both professional and private life.

- Additional training, seminars, or the development of skills can help support employees in their professional development, e.g., because they want to move into a new position.
- Investing time to learn a new skill or expand existing knowledge can enhance work performance and thus influence future promotions and salary development.
- Employees are given the opportunity for personal development, as additional knowledge can lead to new perspectives, which can also be applied outside the professional environment.

- In an ever-faster changing world, continuous knowledge building helps employees stay marketable. Knowledge about current trends and advances in their own professional environment helps them to be flexible and to change the work environment or even the company if necessary.
- Expansion of Personal Network
  Those who regularly participate in further education measures, both internally and externally, expand their network.

3 Challenges of Continuous Learning

There are various challenges to overcome when establishing continuous learning in the company.

For small and medium-sized companies, it is often a major challenge to create the appropriate organizational framework, as clear responsibilities for personnel development and further education are often lacking. Both managers and employees of these companies depend on easily findable and accessible offers. Further education advice offered by, for example, an external body can provide good services here (see Binder & Hofmann 2021).

In addition, it is necessary to delegate responsibility to the employees. The Bitkom Academy found in a survey of employees at all hierarchical levels that 70% see the responsibility for further education in the company with the employees (see Bitkom & HRpepper 2020). According to the Adult Education Survey (AES), however, only 40% participate in company further education (see BMBF 2019). To close this gap, further sensitization of all participants is needed.

Another challenge lies in the topic of further education costs. However, seeing further education only as a cost factor falls significantly short. Especially in the medium and long term, it is an investment in the organization and should be evaluated as such. All too often, further education budgets are cut or measures are limited as a result of economic problems. Given the worsening skills situation in various company areas (e.g., IT) on the German labor market, this should be carefully weighed up, because continuous, workplace-related, increasingly collaboratively organized learning puts every company in a good starting position to be able to cover competence needs from its own workforce (see Sung & Choi 2014; Zinke 2018).

4 Possible Solutions

Both companies and their employees should develop a new perspective on further education and learning, give it greater importance and establish it as part of the corporate culture.

Corporate personnel development will have to change significantly in the coming years. Its role will change from being a provider of training to a point of contact that provides employees and managers with guidance for their continuous learning. It is the employees and managers who are to be seen as the main responsible parties for lifelong learning and development (see Bauer, Hofmann, Korge & Reiners 2010). In addition, there is a significant shift in responsibility for the learning of employees: not the HR or further education departments, but the employees themselves or their managers are attributed a significant role in terms of lifelong learning and adaptability. Their task will be to manage this independently and self-organized.

The training formats also need to be adapted to the changed conditions. Instead of primarily relying on own and external teaching events (see Seyda & Placke 2020), other existing learning offers can be integrated. Today, there are already numerous digital learning platforms (e.g. LinkedIn Learning, Coursera, Udacity) as well as other quality-assured online courses (e.g. Massive Open Online Courses (MOOCs) from universities). But also possibilities like educational leave can be supported.

In some areas of vocational training, the use of new, innovative learning technologies such as Augmented Reality (AR) could be useful. In addition, vocational training needs extended forms of blended learning components as well as innovative forms of knowledge transfer, e.g. through digital, interactive workshop formats.

New content and formats for learning offers are necessary, but not sufficient. The training staff or trainers also need to be continuously further qualified in order to keep up with the methods and principles used, some of which are new, and to be able to convey them.

5 Summary and Outlook

The world of work has changed in recent years and will continue to do so. Vocational (further) education must keep pace with this. This results in the following areas of change:

Work and learning are increasingly merging. Learning becomes an integral part of work. It will become even more of a prerequisite than it is today that all employees independently maintain their own employability and every company maintains its ability to innovate. This means for both educational institutions and companies that they can no longer design their further education or learning offer independently of the specific work context of the participants. Rather, it must be made possible that learning can take place quickly and easily as needed, preferably even at the workplace.

New digital learning formats expand the understanding of further education, because it does not always have to be full-day training. Smaller learning units, such as knowledge nuggets on an online platform, make it possible to acquire new knowledge quickly, easily and tailored to needs.

If new forms of learning are enabled, it is the responsibility of all employees to use them. Under the premise that the employees know their further education needs and preferences best, they must become active themselves. In self-directed further education offers (e.g. asynchronous online courses, apps, self-organized learning groups etc.) they drive their learning forward independently. For this to succeed, they must be prepared and accompanied by the company.

Support for the learning process can come from internal learning companions, the HR department or direct superiors. In the future, the development of employees must become a central core task of leadership, because only with efficient, well-qualified employees can organizational goals be achieved. Managers must see themselves in the role of personnel development for their team. There is a lot of potential here for building strategic further education, also for companies without a (large) HR department (see Binder & Hofmann 2021).

The changes to the new learning offer also involve costs. As already explained, however, only considering the costs is too short-sighted. The focus should be on a medium or long-term view and thus the evaluation as an investment in the future of the company.

Ultimately, continuous learning and the development of employees is at least as much in the interest of the company as it is in that of the workforce. Without qualified, ready and capable employees, companies quickly lose touch in today's volatile world. A key task for maintaining competitiveness is therefore the continuous expansion of the qualifications of the employees.

References

Bauer, A., Hofmann, J., Korge, G. & Reiners, D. (2010). Länger leben. Länger arbeiten. Länger lernen. Unveröffentlichter Endbericht des Projektes. Stuttgart.

Becker, H. (2012). Politische Bildung in Europa. Bundeszentrale für politische Bildung, 6. November 2012, URL: https://www.bpb.de/shop/zeitschriften/apuz/148214/politische-bildung-in-europa/?p=all (Accessed: 22.08.2022).

Binder & Hofmann (2021). Neue Arbeitsformen – neue Weiterbildungsformen. In: Baron, S., Dick, P.-M. & Zitzelsberger (Hrsg.). Weiterbilden#weiterdenken. Den Strukturwandel in der Metall- und Elektorindustrie durch berufliche Weiterbildung gestalten. Bielefeld: Wbv Media.

Bitkom Akademie & HRpepper GmbH & Co. KGaA (2020). Weiterbildung 2025. Eine Studie von der Bitkom Akademie und HRpepper Management Consultants. URL: https://www.bitkom-akademie.de/sites/default/files/bitkom-akademie_studieweiterbildung-2025.pdf (Accessed: 27.07.2022).

Bundesministerium für Bildung und Forschung (BMBF) (2003): Lebenslanges Lernen in Deutschland – Finanzierung und Innovation: Kompetenzentwicklung, Bildungsnetze, Unterstützungsstrukturen. Bericht des BMBF für die OECD zu „Good Practice der Finanzierung des Lebenslangen Lernens“ im Rahmen des Projektes „Co-financing lifelong learning“. Bonn.

Bundesministerium für Bildung und Forschung (BMBF) (2019). Weiterbildungsverhalten in Deutschland 2018, Ergebnisse des Adult Education Survey – AES-Trendbericht. Bonn: BMBF.

Deloitte Human Capital Trends (2017): Rewriting the rules for the digital age. URL: https://www2.deloitte.com/content/dam/Deloitte/global/Documents/About-Deloitte/central-europe/ce-global-human-capital-trends.pdf (Accessed: 27.07.2022).

Hofmann, J., Piele, A. & Piele, C. (2020). Arbeiten in der Corona-Pandemie – auf dem Weg zum New Normal. Stuttgart: Fraunhofer IAO.

Hofmann, J. & Wienken, V. (2020): Führung in der digitalen Transformation, Ein Realitätscheck für mittelständische Industrieunternehmen. Stuttgart: Fraunhofer IAO.

Seyda, S. & Placke, B. (2020). IW-Weiterbildungserhebung 2020: Weiterbildung auf Wachstumskurs. IW Trends Vierteljahresschrift zur empirischen Wirtschaftsforschung, 47(4/2020), pp. 105–123. https://doi.org/10.2373/1864-810X.20-04-07.

Sostero, M., Milasi, S., Hurley, J., Fernández-Macías, E. & Bisello, M. (2020). Teleworkability and the COVID-19 crisis: a new digital divide? Sevilla: Europäische Kommission.

Stifterverband/McKinsey (2018). Future Skills: Welche Kompetenzen in Deutschland fehlen.

Sung, S. Y. & Choi, J. N. (2014). Multiple dimensions of human resource development and organizational performance. In: Journal of Organizational Behavior 35(6), S. 851–870.

Zinke, G. (2018). Berufsbildung 4.0, Erste Ergebnisse und Kernbotschaften zum veränderten Fachkräftebedarf aus dem Berufescreening. Bundesinstitut für Berufsbildung. Verfügbar unter https://kongress2018.bibb.de/wp-content/uploads/2018/06/forum_I_zinke_version_2_tag_2_final_dok.pdf (Accessed: 28.01.2020).

Digital Learning

Wibke Matthes

1 Introduction

1.1 Historical Development

The last 100 years of development in the working world have led to increasing automation, individualization, and digitalization. "In the face of this advancing societal transformation, competent handling of digital technologies and collaboration techniques becomes a central prerequisite" (Schröder and Winde 2018, p. 2).

Individualization, connectivity, knowledge culture, and New Work are megatrends of the future and they all include digital learning (Future Institute 2022). New technologies expand the realm of possibilities for working and learning in networks. However, the dissolution of learning spaces and increasing self-control also create new challenges and increasing complexity. Not only is our knowledge growing exponentially fast, but our handling of information is also changing (Future Institute 2022a). In the working worlds of the future, "the learner creates his learning processes need-oriented by using his network, by means of different methods, remix of various internal and external contents, and in exchange and co-creation with his learning peers, himself" (Foelsing and Schmitz 2021, p. 108). The future viability of companies in all sectors depends on the learning ability of their employees.

W. Matthes (✉)
Christian-Albrechts-Universität, Kiel, Germany
e-mail: matthes@zfs.uni-kiel.de

I. Knappertsbusch and G. Wisskirchen (eds.), *The Future of Work*,
https://doi.org/10.1007/978-3-658-45150-9_36

1.2 What Is Digital Learning?

Digital learning refers to learning with digital media (Zumbach 2021). It describes a learning format that changes what, how, with whom, when, and where we learn (Bils et al. 2019). What we can learn digitally is no longer limited to established education providers. How we learn digitally is heavily technology-driven and learner-centered. With whom we learn is independent of learning groups and time in the digital space. Digital learning does not only take place within formalized learning settings such as training and coordinated networks, but also occurs primarily informally (Schönfeld and Tillmanns 2021).

Digital learning is also to be understood as learning content and includes a set of knowledge, digital skills, and values (Winde and Klier 2021, European Commission 2022, Binkley et al. 2012). It aims to build a repertoire of competencies that employees should have across industries, disciplines, and tasks to be able to meet the digital change.

Digital competence is part of the Future Skills (Ehlers 2021) and includes the ability

- to retrieve, evaluate, use, and manage information,
- to assess information and communication technologies and to apply technology effectively and integrally,
- to communicate and interact effectively in the digital space,
- to analyze, evaluate, and create media and digital content,
- to ensure security in the digital space,
- to effectively solve problems in the digital space,
- to conduct projects digitally.

The most important learning contents of digital competence include information and data management, digital interaction, technological competence, data protection, and digital ethics (Schüller et al. 2021). For this, extensive knowledge, various skills, and values are important, which can only be hinted at here:

The knowledge level in digital competence includes knowledge about conceptual methods and various procedures in dealing with data, knowledge about sensitive data and their processing rules, as well as knowledge of the rules of digital ethics. This is supplemented by knowledge of theories, methods, and the possibilities and limits of digital communication and interaction.

At the skill level, employees should be able to capture, secure, organize, use, and efficiently manage information and data. They should be able to handle new technologies safely and be able to create interpersonal connections in the digital space. They should be able to communicate digitally effectively, collaborate, and solve virtual conflicts. To also act morally correctly, they should deal with questions of ethical boundaries of digitalization and handling of Big Data and preserve personality protection in the digital space.

In addition, there is a technical affinity as well as professional accuracy in dealing with data and data protection, an empathetic attitude towards the peculiarities of digital communication, and a digital mindset. Employees with high digital competence respect ethical values also in the digital space, have respect for the data and privacy of others, and have a reflective attitude towards questions of digitalization.

2 Advantages of Digital Learning

2.1 What Are the Benefits for Employers?

It is not enough to add digital learning as an "additional qualification" alongside the acquisition of professional competences in education and further training. The potential is much greater, as digital learning can offer many advantages for employers through individual tailoring, high scalability, and the ability to be provided independently of time. It creates motivating incentives for employees to continue their education independently and flexibly in the direct work context. Digital learning opportunities in the sense of New Learning provide space for continuous improvement processes, innovation, and habitualized competence development. If company management strategically aligns digital learning, the innovation performance, overall performance, and digital transformation of the company will increase in perspective (Dettmers et al. 2021).

Promoting learning individually among existing employees is a good way to achieve both qualification and the desire for new challenges, as almost 70% of respondents in a global study stated that "they do not have the necessary skills for a digital transformation" (Dell Technologies 2022). With digital learning, companies can quickly become learning organizations through cooperation and agility. Learning Analytics also provide insight into the learning progress and learning behavior of employees and enable targeted control and user centricity.

2.2 What Are the Benefits for Employees?

Five of the ten most important future competences are directly linked to digital learning: digital communication, digital application competence, digital strategy, virtual working, and basic technical understanding (Dettmers et al. 2021). Every second specialist and executive wants individualized development opportunities and more virtual networking formats. However, digital and individualized learning methods are used in hardly more than one in four companies (Dettmers et al. 2021). If employers were to invest in these, it would increase job satisfaction and could utilize the innovation power and positive design and transformation will and bring out the necessary skills. In addition, the change, which is sometimes perceived as overwhelming, would be countered by constructive changeability through digital competence development.

There are also some advantages from a learning psychology perspective, because, according to the Self-Determination Approach (SDT), it can enable the experience of autonomy, competence, and social inclusion (Ryan and Deci 2017, p. 3). If digital learning is made one's own (autonomy), self-directed and interest- and ability-guided (competence), and implemented with colleagues or other learners (social inclusion), it will bring the desired success.

If the company's learning offer provides enough such freedom, the approval of the works council should also be easier to obtain.

The use of digital learning can contribute to the improvement of working conditions, job satisfaction, and individual competitiveness.

Digital learning addresses the increasing diversity of the workforce. Reintegration measures after illness can be digitally supported and parents or caring relatives can be more easily integrated through digital accessibility of further training measures. Part-time workers also benefit from the use of digital learning materials, as these can be used independently of location and time.

Digital learning is possible sustainably without extensive travel and offers cost-saving opportunities for exchange and collaborative learning with colleagues from other locations, international partners, suppliers, customers, etc.

3 Challenges of Digital Learning

3.1 What Challenges Exist at the Micro Level?

At the micro level, it is necessary to confront the social distance in which digital learning takes place, because "working in a virtual environment changes how we interact with one another" (Neeley and Leonardi 2022, p. 64). Fundamentally, the first requirement is to establish a digital mindset individually. This means that all employees must learn to stay connected with each other even in the digital space. If learning is given into individual self-control, there is a risk that digital learning will lead to overload and inefficiency because it is not linked back to a common understanding of goals and procedures.

The diversity of digital learning offers can sometimes seem like an information explosion and can easily overwhelm. This causes stress and can provoke defensive reactions.

If employees fear that they do not have the necessary skills to be successful in a transformed workplace, there is a risk that they will reject the change (Dell Technologies 2022).

3.2 What Challenges Exist at the Meso Level?

At the meso level, the difficulty lies in embedding digital learning into the corporate culture in such a way that the company itself becomes a learning organization. Although there is a basic willingness to learn and "46.2% of respondents [want] targeted measures to close the skill gaps with suitable further training measures"

(IUBH 2020, p. 13), there are also employees who need more time to change habits and acquire new skills (Dell Technologies 2022).

So far, there seems to be no suitable learning culture in many companies. There is a lack of a learning environment "that enables agile and effective learning for everyone in the workforce" (IUBH 2020, p. 13). Especially in the digital space, the success of digital learning is lacking if there is a lack of individual self-organization or a curated and choreographed "learning experience" that ensures the quality and structure of learning offers so that learning can be transferred, secured, and networked into everyday work. Often, digital learning remains without close accompaniment by peers, managers, or coaches and therefore does not yet have a sustainable effect. If these conditions for successful didactics are not considered, learning effects fizzle out.

4 Solutions and Practical Tips

Learning, especially in the digital context, should be integrated into a learning ecosystem as an enabling space to avoid arbitrariness or inefficiency, or lack of connectivity and lack of contextualization. This enabling space is "a digital platform that arranges didactic, methodological, material, and media aspects in such a way that the probability for the desired development processes at all levels is made possible" (Erpenbeck and Sauter 2021, p. 87). This requires the collaboration of several interest groups and significant investments in the development of robust and dynamic training and further education systems for workers. The human resources development department should provide clear concepts for the development of digital competencies among employees in the short term and take on a curating, quality-assuring, and networking role.

The basic condition for the digital learning ecosystem is "a holistic design perspective that allows a sustainable framework for the interaction between people, learning formats, content, and technologies to be developed, so that a high degree of differentiation and adaptability is made possible" (Erpenbeck and Sauter 2021, p. 91). This should be enabled by time resources and a routine of networking to exchange learning results, by encouraging learners to pass on essential insights to interested colleagues. This requires appropriate framework conditions such as an intranet or lively internal social media (Neeley and Leonardi 2022).

To make effective investments, companies must provide well-coordinated, user-friendly, and flexible (digital) learning ecosystems. To do this, they need to better understand what skills are available, where the biggest skill gaps exist, which potential skills in the workforce are most in demand, and how suitable learning paths can be provided. It must be ensured that the system adapts to further change, because the canon of digital competencies itself needs ongoing review and context-related determination and further development. Thus, skills referred to as tech specialist skills today (e.g., data analytics, artificial intelligence, quantum computing, robotics) may count as general digital competencies tomorrow (Winde and Klier 2021). The digital learning offer should be able to respond to this.

5 Summary and Outlook

5.1 What Are the Key Findings?

The digital transformation is characterized by enormous speed. The rapid pace of change in tasks and skills means that the demand for updating skills is also growing.

Digital learning is to be understood as a learning format but also and even more as learning content. The latter is expressed in the digital competencies that encompass essential basic skills for working in the digitized world of the future and are important across all industries and fields of work.

The advantages of digital learning lie in the possibility of individual customization, high scalability, and independence from time and place.

The biggest challenges are to establish a digital learning culture in the company and to meet the increased demands for self-organization and complexity management.

The solution lies in the design of a learning ecosystem as an enabling space that anchors digital learning in a motivating, network-oriented, and self-directed routine in daily work.

5.2 What Can We Expect in the Future?

The megatrend of connectivity indicates that we will experience new worlds in the digital space, even into the metaverse, which could make digital learning the predominant form of learning. State education monopolies have long been under pressure. Whether university degrees will still matter in the hiring of employees in the future is already being questioned in many places today (Fuller et al. 2022).

The shortage of skilled workers will also continue to ensure that it becomes increasingly important to encourage the existing workforce to relearn and continue learning. And this can be better achieved through digital learning.

References

Bils, A., Brand, H., Pellert, A. (2019). Hochschule(n) im digitalen Wandel. Bedarfe und Strategien. Aus Politik und Zeitgeschichte 27–28:42–46

Binkley, M. et al. (2012). Defining Twenty-First Century Skills. In: Griffin, P., McGaw, B., Care, E. (eds.) Assessment and Teaching of 21st Century Skills. Springer, Dordrecht. https://doi.org/10.1007/978-94-007-2324-5_2

Dell Technologies (2022). Durchbruch. Durchbrechen der Barrieren für die digitale Transformation an der Schnittstelle zwischen Mensch und Technologie. April 2022. https://www.dell.com/de-de/dt/perspectives/breakthrough.htm (abgerufen am 07.10.2022)

Dettmers, S. et al. (2021). Future Skills – Future Learning. Eine Kooperationsstudie von Kienbaum Stepstone, Institut Kienbaum@ISM. https://www.kienbaum.com/de/publikationen/future-skills-future-learning/(abgerufen am 28.09.2022)

Ehlers, U.-D. (2021). Future Skills. Lernen der Zukunft – Hochschule der Zukunft. Springer VS, Wiesbaden. https://doi.org/10.1007/978-3-658-29297-3

Erpenbeck, J. & Sauter, W. (2021). Future Learning und New Work. Haufe, Freiburg, München, Stuttgart

European Commission, Joint Research Centre, Vuorikari, R., Kluzer, S., Punie, Y. (2022). DigComp 2.2. The Digital Competence framework for citizens: with new examples of knowledge, skills and attitudes, Publications Office of the European Union. https://data.europa.eu/doi/10.2760/115376

Foelsing, J. & Schmitz, A. (2021). New Work braucht New Learning. Eine Perspektivreise durch die Transformation unserer Organisations- und Lernwelten. Springer Gabler, Wiesbade

Fuller, J. et al. (2022) Skills-Based Hiring Is on the Rise. In: Harward Business Review, https://hbr.org/2022/02/skills-based-hiring-is-on-the-rise (abgerufen am 28.09.2022)

IUBH (2020). Digitalisierung und neues Lernen im Fokus. Trendstudie Upskilling. https://res.cloudinary.com/iubh/image/upload/v1615988600/Presse%20und%20Forschung/White%20Papers/Upskilling-Studie_Whitepaper_Juni2020_pbtcum.pdf (abgerufen am 29.09.2022)

Neeley, T. & Leonardi, P. (2022). The Digital Mindset: What it Really Takes to Thrive in the Age of Data, Algorithms and AI. Harvard Business Review Press, Boston

Ryan, R. M. & Deci, E. L. (2017). Self-Determination Theory: Basic Psychological Needs in Motivation, Development, and Wellness. Guilford Publications, New York, London

Schönfeld, J. & Tillmann, T. (2021). Lernhacks. Mit einfachen Routinen Schritt für Schritt zur agilen Lernkultur. Vahlen, München

Schröder, J. & Winde, M. (2018). Future Skills – Diskussionspapier 1: Welche Kompetenzen in Deutschland fehlen, September 2018, http://www.future-skills.net/download/file/fid/118 (abgerufen 28.09.2022)

Schüller, K. et al. (2021). Data-Literacy-Charta. Version 1.2. Berlin: Stifterverband

Winde, M. & Klier, J. (2021). Diskussionspapier 3: Future Skills 2021. 21 Kompetenzen für eine Welt im Wandel, https://www.stifterverband.org/download/file/fid/10547 (abgerufen 28.09.2022)

Zukunftsinstitut (2022) Die Megatrend-Map. https://www.zukunftsinstitut.de/artikel/die-megatrend-map/ (abgerufen 25.09.2022)

Zukunftsinstitut (2022a) Die Megatrends. https://www.zukunftsinstitut.de/dossier/megatrends/ (abgerufen 25.09.2022)

Zumbach, J. (2021). Digitales Lehren und Lernen. Verlag W. Kohlhammer, Stuttgart

Employer Branding, Employee Benefits and New Pay

Employer Branding in the Labor Market of the Future—What Must Companies Offer Workers?

Susanne Wißfeld

1 Introduction

The shortage of skilled workers has long been a reflection of a greater, general problem: the chronic shortage of workers across all economic sectors. This development has resulted in a labor market that is strong on its supply side - the amount of jobs available - but weak on the demand side, meaning that there are far fewer applicants than open positions. As talent pool continues to shrink, and the expectations of applicants for their future workplaces become ever more demanding, employers are faced with the necessity of a realignment of their employer positioning and branding. So how can employers meet the expectations and desires of talents and how can they tie employees to their company in the long term? Opportunities are offered by the concept of "New Work" in the form of clever employer branding.

What exactly constitutes an attractive, modern employer in the eyes of employees? Randstad studies on the employee-side expectations of jobs, career and the workplace highlight the increasing demands on employers. According to the Randstad Workmonitor (1st half 2023), both the desire for security and the desire for flexibility are increasing (see Fig. 1). The vast majority of employees place great value on job security (92%). A good salary is important to 93%. A further 86% want a good work-life balance. 77% consider flexible working hours to be important, while 59% want a flexible workplace. If the latter, i.e., remote work, is not possible in a company, that would be a reason for 40% of respondents not to accept a job there.

S. Wißfeld (✉)
Randstad Deutschland, Düsseldorf, Germany
e-mail: susanne.wissfeld@randstad.de

I. Knappertsbusch and G. Wisskirchen (eds.), *The Future of Work*,
https://doi.org/10.1007/978-3-658-45150-9_37

What is important to employees
and what are you satisfied with?

	Importance	Satisfaction
Salary	93%	69%
Work Life Balance	86%	71%
Flexible working hours	77%	53%
Flexible work location	59%	43%

Source: Randstad Work Barometer Graphic: Randstad Germany

Fig. 1 Job factors: Importance and satisfaction among employees (Randstad Work Barometer 2023)

In addition to working conditions, societal and ecological trends dominate the attitude of workers towards their job and their employer, especially among younger employees. Overall, 66% of German employees consider the values of their employer to be important. This affects trends such as sustainability and diversity, but also the purpose, or the meaning of work in the company. However, 31% say that their values currently do not match those of their employer. For 49% of Gen Z workers, this is a reason to reject a job offer. 38% of all German employees would reject a job offer if the company does not proactively strive for more sustainability.

In general, as the Randstad Workmonitor also shows, German employees have a positive attitude towards their jobs and employers. 52% feel connected to their current employer. More than two-thirds are satisfied with their salary and work-life balance (69% and 71%). Even on issues such as sustainability and diversity, the values of 69% of employees match those of their employers. But when it comes to flexibility, there is a gap. Only 43% express satisfaction with their current options for choosing the location of their workplace freely.

Overall, 34% of German employees are considering a change or are actively applying for open positions. What to do if the job is not the right one? Among all generations of employees, Generation Z are the most willing to act on their principles. 40% of 18- to 24-year-olds would rather be unemployed than unhappy in their job (Randstad Work Barometer 1st half 2023).

How can companies adapt to these changing conditions and create a future-proof employee experience that serves both the need for security and flexibility while enabling meaningful and sustainable work? This is no easy task for employers who want to successfully recruit and bind a dwindling pool of candidates (see the article "Shortage of skilled workers - myth or reality?").

The first step is to know the priorities and perspectives of their current and future employees. A solid business model, good internal communication as well as work models that are tailored to the individual requirements and needs of the employees, that is what matters. A solution that covers these aspects, combines efficiency with flexibility and puts people and their individual possibilities and perspectives at the center, is at the core of the concept of New Work.

New Work goes back to the theorist Frithjof Bergmann. According to the social philosopher, New Work is primarily about meaning, flexibility and independence—regardless of the industry. New Work is becoming more relevant as the entire world of work undergoes a significant structural change, driven especially by the megatrend of digitization (see the article "When digital meets demographic change - What opportunities and risks does digital transformation pose in a shrinking and aging working population?"). This change is moving towards people and their individual possibilities, desires and perspectives. This is exactly where employers need to start.

2 Advantages of Employer Branding

What makes a modern employer, based on the New Work principle, attractive in the competition for talent? As a collective term, New Work combines strategies and trends that characterize the working world of today and tomorrow. As a guiding principle, New Work defines a new form of collaboration that creates space for individuality and flexibility: a way of working that is tailored to the individual. And every individual has unique desires, perspectives, and possibilities.

An employer strategy based on New Work aligns with these requirements. Good salary and benefits, a positive working environment, flexible working, a long-term career perspective: What can we offer applicants and employees? How digital is our company? How are we positioned in terms of sustainability? What values does our company stand for? These questions are particularly in focus for employers with regard to the younger generations of workers.

Those who want to convince young talents as well as experienced employees rely on authenticity. Employers who promise outward what they cannot maintain within the company risk new employees quitting prematurely. Applicants who uncover weaknesses in the culture of their prospective employer during the interview may also immediately drop out. At the same time, companies are becoming increasingly transparent, particularly through social media. A negative comment, a poor rating can have a deterrent effect.

In addition, another factor affects the relationship between employer and employees. Since the Covid pandemic, trust and commitment between the two have suffered. Managing and caring for your own staff at a distance digitally is not always easy. This may have encouraged the willingness to change, which is also reflected in our Randstad studies (see above). On the other hand, with the rise of video interviews, the hurdle for applicants in applying for a job has significantly decreased. In short: Small mistakes, inconsistencies, or inattentiveness can cost companies new and long-term employees. Good employers pay special attention to their employees.

This is exactly where New Work has great potential. The idea of rethinking and realizing work is anything but "new". Nevertheless, the concept offers many opportunities, precisely because it encompasses many ideas and models as a collective term. The ideas behind New Work can also be interesting for areas outside the office environment, which is supposedly predestined for the New Work approach, since New Wor is not as a rule, but as a set of principles that can be applied in many areas of life.

how does New Work work in practice? Can production or logistics companies also benefit from it? As a work concept, New Work is not limited to the office area. It is also used in many areas of industry, promoted by digital progress.

How can I design every workplaces and the interactions in them in a way that ensures the inclusion of all employees? This question is paramount. Because everyone can make a contribution, everyone has a place. This mindfulness as a basic idea of New Work is important and especially crucial for the service industry.

This means taking responsibility for the workforce. To this end, managers need to show interest in each individual. What do employees need—different work shoes that fit better, or even a different place in the company where they can fully develop?

3 Challenges Associated with Employer Branding

When transitioning to a future-oriented employer concept, several areas of action are in focus: recruiting, onboarding, and career prospects within the company.

3.1 Where Should Companies Present Themselves to Candidates?

Where and how do companies present themselves? Applicants, as the Randstad Employer Brand Research 2023 study shows, increasingly use search engines and social media to seek out jobs and employers. Google and job portals are in the lead with 33% and 41% respectively. 23% of applicants use personal recommendations, while a further 15% use social media to find job offers. More than a quarter rely on the professional support of recruiting and personnel agencies when changing jobs (26%).

Companies, as the Randstad-ifo HR manager survey (Q1 2022) shows, primarily rely on external job postings (84%) in their attempts to find candidates. However, simply posting and then waiting for applications, without taking further steps to attract employees, today rarely yields the desired result. This is not surprising, as companies are often still not present in the places where candidates are active and looking for jobs. Companies are challenged to actively search for, approach, and convince candidates. However, this active sourcing strategy is only considered important by 38% of companies. The most important channel for this recruiting strategy is in fact the company's own workforce. A considerable part of employers have already received recommendations for suitable candidates by their own employees (77%).

3.2 A Direct, Personal, and Authentic Employer Appearance With the Help of the Company's Own Workforce

The internal employee network is excellently suited as a recruiting channel, as contact opportunities create a stronger personal connection to the candidates. Commitment, transparency, and genuine interest are essential. This increases the chances of success for employers in their efforts to bind talents to the company from the start. This bond is facilitated by the fact that the members of the company's own workforce act as brand ambassadors. Employees recommend the company as an employer because they enjoy working there, thus conveying a positive image.

Of course, the workplace also plays an important role. We at Randstad Germany have committed ourselves to the guiding principle of New Work with our new head office in Eschborn. "Multi Space" is the basic principle behind our idea behind the new, digitally oriented work spaces, which feature collaborative spaces and work surfaces, desk sharing, creative and focus zones as well as meeting spaces and rooms for discussion (see the article "Work is no longer a place to go - How the detachment from the office as a workplace creates opportunities for the development of our society and cities"). The organization aims at being together and working together, serving the overall purpose of open interaction across all areas and companies of our group. We use the flexible and creative possibilities of New Work in remote and presence. Our goal is to reinforce the individual with the collective strength of our teams through plenty of openness and opportunities for collaboration.

Because what really makes a company strong and appealing for applicants and employees is a good corporate culture. And this culture shines most clearly outward and inward when it is shaped in collaboration with the workforce. Team spirit needs just that: a team, a crew, a company that sticks together and appears together as a unit. New Work in the sense of the new social dimension of collaboration means just that: a new, more open interaction.

4 Solutions and Practical Tips

New Work should not be misunderstood as a rule. New Work is a principle, a maxim.

To know, to serve, to trust—this is our approach at Randstad, since our foundation. It already includes much of what is understood today as New Work. However, the concept can and should not simply be imposed on a company. Rather, each company must individually check which New Work approaches fit its own possibilities and working reality. Only in this way can a harmonious overall picture emerge, which the workforce then perceives.

Because the freedom associated with New Work can also raise concerns in the workforce. Especially because it is difficult to precisely grasp what is meant by the term. Therefore, a clear understanding and clear objectives are needed to successfully implement the concept in your own company. Only in this way can it ultimately help to position the company as attractive for application because, simply put, people enjoy working there and are active and successful in their work with fun and special commitment.

4.1 How Companies Develop a Future-Proof Employer Concept

A solid and authentic employer presence establishes reliability. And reliability creates trust. To build a convincing presence as an employer, there are some fundamental things that companies should consider. With these steps, they can get closer to their goal:

- **Analyze status: What is the state of the employer brand?**
  The first step begins with taking stock. Critically engage with the feedback from employees. The experiences of applicants as well as current and outgoing employees are valuable resources. From them emerges an overall picture of the company culture from the employee's perspective.
- **Set goals: What should be the aim of the company's employer branding?**
  By answering this question, target specifications for the employer brand can be defined. What is the current potential of initiatives? Where is there a need for optimization? The goal: to present the employer brand realistically and authentically and to confidently highlight one's own strengths.
- **Develop added value: Excite applicants**
  Successful employer branding emphasizes the factors that make the company unique. This sets an employer apart from the competition. Thus, a strong employer brand becomes the best argument for an application.
- **Create unity: Implement strategy across the company**
  Employer branding is a process. The aim is to unite the employer brand with the company brand. This works when the values as an employer are consistently anchored at all departmental and hierarchical levels.
- **Continuously improve**
  A good employer brand is not necessarily self-sustaining. What attracts talents today may no longer be convincing for the applicants of tomorrow. Companies should therefore regularly update their employer branding.

New Work is valuable and realizable at every workplace, whether in shift work or 9-to-5 jobs, and especially in production, logistics, and trade. Implementation means taking responsibility, being mindful and focusing on the people in the company. What can companies do to make their employees feel better? What can they do to ensure that the workforce can work productively and at the same time be flexible enough to respond to personal requirements in everyday life?

Flexible working is neither simply remote, nor is it limited to the home office. Individual solutions are key. Take the example of a city transport company that provides a good illustration of this principle. There, a team of cleaners autonomously scheduled their shifts. This allowed the employees to better organize their individual workday, reducing sick leave and significantly improving compatibility with family obligations. Agility (see the article "Agile Working") and self-determined work is also possible here, in logistics or shift work.

Successful companies rely on applicant-centered recruiting. This requires transparent and binding communication—also and especially during onboarding. Involve new employees early on. Team events, workshops, important news, all of this is important to keep new colleagues in the information loop before they start work. This conveys serious interest on your part and above all, you communicate that you are actively looking forward to the new employee starting with you. This shows employers that they take the probationary period very seriously, also in proving themselves as a good choice to the new employee.

Formats for internal exchange and internal communication strengthen cohesion. They provide space for exchange. What moves the workforce? Which positive examples of New Work shape the identity of the company as an employer and can be presented accordingly? Often it is small businesses that can represent the diversity of their workforce particularly credibly through their family-like interactions and should therefore actively promote this.

Because enormous potential lies precisely in this diversity. And the trend around diversity and inclusion now plays a central role in the world of work—rightly so. 76% of companies worldwide agree that diversity, equity, and inclusion are fundamental to attracting and retaining talent (Randstad Sourceright Talent Trends 2022). But there is still a need for catch-up in Germany. In the Randstad-ifo HR manager survey (2nd quarter 2022), we asked German HR managers to what extent diversity plays a role in recruiting. Only 9% stated that they pursue a diversity strategy in their search for staff. 8% of the other respondents plan to deploy such a strategy in the future.

Discussions concerning diversity are all too often lopsided, focusing exclusively on gender. But the concept of diversity is about much more. It's about openness towards workers with unconventional resumes and recognizing and promoting the potential in every employee. This approach tap into a pool of workers that had previously been neglected. What skills and experiences do colleagues over 50 bring that are valuable to the company? What work models offer opportunities for this group to integrate? In general: The internal mobility of employees is an important aspect. The aim is to accompany talents in the long term and to make them internal career changers who find their optimal place in the company.

This reorientation is not an easy task. Especially smaller and medium-sized companies often do not have a dedicated HR department. Bringing in expertise from an external HR consultancy can therefore help in this process. The aim of external HR consultants is not to impose a concept on small businesses, but to make more of the individual possibilities of the respective company with innovative ideas and tools.

5 Summary and Outlook

New Work does not mean doing everything differently. It's about strengthening strengths and utilizing existing resources. Good communication is key in this regard. Companies that transparently communicate the purpose and added value of their offerings and services show they offer jobs with meaning and fulfilment. Purpose is therefore primarily a question of how the company manages to convey its value to society both externally and internally. This could be an exceptionally good CO_2balance or a focus on appreciative interaction within the company. Meaningful in the sense of New Work is that which puts people at the center of the company's branding efforts.

References

Freuding, Julia und Garnitz, Johanna (2022). Randstad-ifo-Personalleiterbefragung – 2. Quartal 2022. Ergebnisbericht.

Randstad Arbeitsbarometer. 2023.

Randstad Employer Brand Research. 2023.

Randstad Sourceright Talent Trends Report. 2022.

Corporate Culture—How the Culture of a Company determines their success or failure

Arkadiusz Grontzki

"Coming together is a beginning, staying together is a progress, working together means success."

Henry Ford

1 Introduction

Many managements seem to be lost: Despite horrendous personnel expenses for recruiting activities, benefits programs internal development programs and many more, employees often do not remain for too long in their current job positions (Personio, 2022, p. 2).

Currently, each job replacement costs approximately €14,900 (Deloitte, 2019, p. 4). A lot of money, considered in the current time we are living in. In addition to the resource "time", "money" has also become a scarce commodity and it is crucial to be on the winning or loosing side in the market. Common reasons for a job change include dissatisfaction with the leadership in the company (1st place: 19%) and the lack of a positive employee experience (4th place: 13%). Even though salary (2nd place: 18%) and lack of promotion opportunities (3rd place: 17%) are mentioned (ibid., p. 8), dissatisfaction and negative experience have one thing in common: It is the result of a weak corporate culture. If the word composition is looked at individually, the words "company" and "culture" appear.

A **company** is "an economic-financial and legal entity [...], for which the hereditary economic principle is constituted" and characterized by a specific organizational structure (Gabler, 2019).

A. Grontzki (✉)
Berlin, Germany
e-mail: springer@arkadiuszgrontzki.de

I. Knappertsbusch and G. Wisskirchen (eds.), *The Future of Work*,
https://doi.org/10.1007/978-3-658-45150-9_38

The **culture** originally derives from the Latin "cultura" and initially describes agricultural activities. However, the Ciceronian interpretation understands the term as "human care through wisdom" to promote life as an individual as well as in the collective structure and to enable a dignified existence. If this image is transferred on organizations, they will have to balance and maintain the entrepreneurial interests on the one hand and the individual and collective interests on the other (Dormayer & Kettern, 1997, p. 50 ff., quoted from Perpeet, 1984, p. 22 ff.).

Corporate culture is thus an intersection of qualitative variables (e.g., values, attitudes, norms, and experiences) within a group of a company. It shapes and influences the perception, thinking, actions and feelings of these group members. The culture is partly reflected in (non-)verbal behavior (e.g., language, beliefs) and in objects (e.g., in documents such as work instructions, (leadership) guidelines, assignment of rooms in terms of location and size). For more in-depth insights, see the works of Sackmann (2017) or Dormayer & Kettern (1997). In short:

The distinction is made on the one hand based on cultural manifestations (e.g., artifacts such as uniforms) and (non-)verbal behavior (usually **visible** or **observable**) and on the other hand concerning the mindset in terms of beliefs and attitudes (usually **hidden** and **unconscious**). The second mentioned part is usually based on learned behavior and experiences, habits or affective anchors. A **cultural identity** is created (cf. Sackmann, 2017).

It should be clarified that corporate culture differs due to the uniqueness of companies. It is the product of various **subcultures** within organizations, which can be differentiated by reason of individual characteristics (e.g., gender, age) and/or organizational structure (departments, company affiliation, knowledge stocks). In these collective associations, own **rules** are usually developed to meet organizational requirements.

Corporate culture supports organizational members in their daily work by creating **order;** for example organization chart and job descriptions, from which tasks can be derived. This creates a kind of **orientation**, with which individual and collective behavior (partly unconscious reactions, mostly passive) as well as organizational actions (mostly conscious and proactive) are aligned with internal and external conditions. This cultural foundation creates a **stability** by establishing a common basis (e.g., communication, consistent thinking and action based on strategic goals). Additionally and finally, corporate culture conveys the **meaning** for the existence of each organizational member (cf. Sackmann, 2017, pp. 12 f. and pp. 59 ff.; Wirtz, 2003, p. 310, quoted from Wächter, 1990).

2 Advantages of a good Corporate Culture

With the incompletely listed characteristics of a corporate culture here, it becomes more clear that the culture has a significant influence on the performance of the organization's members and thus the company on the success or failure as well as on the survivability of an organization (Sackmann, 2017, p. 14; cited after Kotter & Heskett, 1992, p. 11 f.). However, for surviving under the constantly changing conditions as a company, an organizational resilience is needed (Hoffmann, 2016).

Only when the company identifies relevant changes in their environment (including market, society) in a timely as well as comprehensive manner and are able to initiate necessary forces to make a change in their own organizational thinking and action (Sackmann, 2017, p. 12), only then a lasting competitive advantage is created (ibid., p. 13; cited after Barney 1986 or 2002). This approach will be necessary regardless of whether in the sales or labor market. It is important to distinguish whether the culture was merely manifested in writing by management such as guidelines or is truly implemented as well as fully filled with life by every member of the organization in their everyday life (Sackmann, 2017, p. 13).

It should become clear that corporate culture is not developed with offering colorful mixed fruit baskets in the company's kitchen or with a foosball table. Culture means to implement, to grow, making mistakes and learning from them as well as to develop in a personal and in an organizational way. Culture affects everyone - regardless any hierachical position! Through allowing everyone in the company to participate, the so called **cultural identity** come to light (=develops), which will increase the urgently needed **employee retention**: "We grow, change and develop together - as employees, as managers and as a company". But here the sheep is separated from the goats. It is often assumed that employees only value only money and get their motivation from it - a deceptive assumption. But what employees do is to compensate for the lack of cultural life with steadily increasing their demands of their salary sums (Personio, 2022, p. 10). In allowing an equal participation of all organizational members not only encourages the intrinsic **motivation**, but also does it extend the entrepreneurial networking among each other, which boosts extensive synergy effects: In addition to individual knowledge, the collective knowledge base will expanded as well. Even the **organizational knowledge** can be sustainably preserved and further developed with a supportive information management tool.

3 Challenges in achieving an unique corporate culture

It should have become clear with the given informations that corporate culture and its elements cannot be simply manufactured like a product and that it is more than just a trendy term of the 21st century.

Even with the help of a well-founded strategy, the management can only prepare a common direction in organizational thinking and action. However, company specific measures (e.g., development programs, change management) can support a positive development.

Another fact is that informal organizational groups (so called subcultures) are difficult to control, as they develop their own rules. This is a normal process within an organizational context, but the management has to intervene, when subcultures affect the implementation of the desired corporate culture designed by the management.

Since many elements of corporate culture consist of **invisible** and **unconscious variables**, these must be (correctly) revealed on the first hand, before transferring them in a perspicuous way. If these two steps are successfully achieved, the performance of each individual organizational member and the company in general, but also the management of entrepreneurial fortunes, will be influenced positively. If the shown analyse and change process will not be established or will be limited to analyse and change specific elements, the positive urgently needed economic goals cannot be achieved at all or fragmentary. It shows that the development and implementation of a positive **cultural identity** is more essential then ever to achieve one important goal: a high employee retention rate. As a result of a unique corporate culture and a positive as well as supportive cultural identity a so called **organizational psyche** will be created, which can be seen as a entrepreneurial engine that influences the corporate efficiency and effectiveness in total.

In addition to the presented internal challenges, companies are surrounded by further serious obstacles: meeting with the VUCA environment. For some time now, the constantly accelerating competitive dynamics have come to fruition: organizations must expand their core competencies, give up business areas, need to realign their business purposes or even corporate within an (inter-)nationally network such as alliances. Particularly in the case of mergers or acquisitions (M&A) of institutions, serious mistakes still are made in regard with corporate culture. Mostly the diverse variables of corporate culture are not given any special attention in conceptual processes due to conscious or (less better) regrettable ignorance, because most elements of corporate culture are simply invisible to the eyes. Only visible, easily changeable elements are worked on and developed by the management. Above all, the "new-built" company is only given a new (mostly optical) layout within and after the M&A process, so that the management can simply "command" their employees to obey and adapt the new culture from then on. The successes of both companies, which have been merged, are carelessly set aside. From now on only the new values, a new thinking and new actions as well as the new company colors and layouts count. The new (old) management enforces to forget the previous—possibly decades-long—experiences and labels them as "no longer worthy", although these unique corporate culture elements were the most important values just "yesterday". This kind of procedure leads to a **cultural identity crisis** in many organizations and their members, which provokes unnecessary resistance that might interfere the implementation of the desired corporate culture, cause internal resignations and demotivation or raises staff turnover.

For many (whether management or employees), the own corporate culture is not always and fully conscious. This can be caused by the huge amount of information, an by an overtaxation, by a lack of competencies (e.g., reflection abilities, basic psychological knowledge) or simply by a lack of interest. If you look closer, it might gets clearer: If the highest-ranking members of an organization do not even know about how a corporate culture is structured and how it works, how can a group of people develope an unique fitting corporate culture, which is taking all the above mentioned internal and external variables into account, in order to derive suitable goals and measures for their own company? The question is: How can managers even recognize an incorrect alignment of the existing corporate culture in comparism with the internal and external requirements?

4 Solutions and Practical Tips

In order to develop and promote a unique corporate culture in the second step, it is necessary in the first step to create an **awareness** among all members in the organization. Corporate culture concerns everyone, regardless of hierarchical levels. Even the best ideas, concepts, and guidelines can be developed from the management, but if they are not implemented and animates by every organizational member, the plan of changing will fail. Due to Doppler et al. (2002) the above mentioned resistance or idleness can be classified as follows: Organizational members have a

1. lack of knowledge,
2. lack of understanding,
3. lack of belief (in the sense of support) or
4. lack of willingness (conscious resistance) or ability (lack of competencies, skills or abilities)

Before implementing a (new) corporate culture, special development programs are necessary to create the needed awareness. This includes in particular a common way of communication. "One cannot not communicate.", as Watzlawick et al. (2017) once said. This includes a culture of dialogue such as respect, honest feedback and trust, in executing employees, who form the base of every company. The knowledge of many employees e.g. in improving a design of a product or optimizing processes are often hardly taken into consideration by the higher management.

Furthermore, the management should take care that corporate culture is not only writen down on paper, but take action to support the growth of it by entrusting every member of the organization to fill it with life. Additionally to that, the management should mind a regular check up of corporate culture due to internal and external events. As a rule, this is not the case in many organizations, so that a high discrepancy between theory (Who do we want to be?) and practice (Who are we?) prevails. Corporate culture does not come to life when it is written down in words (often done by the managers), but if the management acts as role models, employees will trust in the (new) corporate culture and will act as role models too, to finally become corporate culture influencer. But the realtiy shows that in many organizations the loss of trust has already accumulated, which represents a further seemingly insurmountable obstacle in the transformation process.

In order to effect a successful change concerning corporate culture, it is important to critically review it due to external requirements and internal conditions. Additionally it is important to know, that the change process will take many years. Schreyögg and Geiger (2016, p. 346 ff.) advise a diagnosis and establishment of the actual state of the corporate culture in order to compare it with the desired target state. This review process reveals the actual potential of the company: The **organizational intelligence** (O IQ). According to Mendelson and Ziegler (1999), a long-term study in 17 countries revealed that cultural performance be determined based on five principles as well as there is a correlation between the organizational intelligence and the current company status such as profit or financial loss.

5 Summary and Outlook

"mizaru, kikazaru, iwazaru" is a well-known Japanese proverb and means: see no evil, hear no evil, speak no evil. More often, this saying is known as an image "The three wise monkeys". The management levels are indeed staffed with capable people, who carry different experiences and knowledge. But taking a closer look it becomes clear: The "soft" competencies and the possibilities in general improvement are not fully maxed out.

It's time for transformation, that means: Open the eyes and see, open the ears and listen, open the mouths and speak! It should have become understandable that the necessary changes will not be easy and are probably the only chance in winning the battle for talents. Due to the frequently changes of the external variables (e.g. society, markets, politics) the companies will have to change too. Besides the lack of talents (see the article "Shortage of skilled workers - myth or reality?") time and money as needed resources will be scarce too. But remaining in a state of shock will not help the company to survive. Corporate culture and its review as well as its frequently change process can be compared to a permanent construction site in form of a street, which is used daily. Any damage (focusing corporate culture in general) must be repaired immediately and in a sustainably way. Furthermore, science need to further explore the field of corporate culture by reviewing the current circumstances in order to develop sustainable business concepts. In particular, the Covid pandemic and digitalization (including years of home office stays) changed corporate culture internationally. The impacts and their consequences can only be seen "after the storm is over". Companies then will have to observe, if the employee retention sinks, stays stable or rises to understand. It will clearly show the company, if a solid cultural identity exists and the employees stay, because they are loyal.

It shows that a strong corporate culture thus not only ensures economical success, because processes can be designed, executed and reviewed in a flexible way. They also support an organizational thinking and action due to an exchanging coordination with each other, which assures a competitive advantage. This can only be achieved throughout the participation of all staff levels in a company and with the help of a positive, growth-oriented communication. It shows, that a strong corporate culture keeps the balance between individual needs, collective interests and economic requirements.

References

Deloitte (2019). *Fluktuation und deren Auswirkungen auf Unternehmen*, https://www2.deloitte.com/content/dam/Deloitte/at/Documents/consulting/at-deloitte-fluktuationsstudie-2019.pdf (abgerufen am 02.08.2022)

Doppler, K., Fuhrmann, H., Lebbe-Waschke, B. & Voigt, B. (2002). *Unternehmenswandel gegen Widerstände: Changemanagement mit den Menschen*. Frankfurt am Main: Campus. ISBN: 978-3593369921

Dormayer, H.-J. & Kettern, T. (1997). Beitrag B: Kulturkonzepte in der allgemeinen Kulturforschung – Grundlage konzeptioneller Überlegungen zur Unternehmenskultur. In E. Heinen & M. Fank (eds.), *Unternehmenskultur* (2. bearbeitete und erweiterte Auflage) (pp. 49–66). München: Oldenbourg Verlag. ISBN: 3-486-23108-1

Gabler Wirtschaftslexikon (2019). *Unternehmen*, https://wirtschaftslexikon.gabler.de/definition/unternehmen-48087/version-369159 (abgerufen am 02.08.2022)

Hoffmann, P.-H. (2016). *Organisationale Resilienz*. (1. Auflage) [E-Book, PDF], https://link.springer.com/content/pdf/10.1007/978-3-658-12890-6.pdf (abgerufen am 08.10.2022)

Mendelson, H. & Ziegler, J. (1999). *Survival of the Smartest*. New York: Wiley & Sons. ISBN: 978-0471295600

Personio. (2022). *Der große Wertewandel – Warum Sie Mitarbeiterbindung und Leistungsmanagement neu denken sollten*. https://hr.personio.de/hubfs/Personio_HR-Studie-2022_DE.pdf (abgerufen am 29.11.2022)

Sackmann, S. (2017). *Unternehmenskultur: Erkennen – Entwickeln –Verändern. Erfolgreich durch kulturbewusstes Management*. (2. vollständig überarbeitete und erweiterte Auflage) [E-Book, PDF], https://link.springer.com/book/10.1007/978-3-658-18634-0 (abgerufen am 08.10.2022)

Schreyögg, G. & Geiger, D. (2016). *Organisation. Grundlagen moderner Organisationsgestaltung*. (6. Auflage) [E-Book, PDF], https://link.springer.com/book/10.1007/978-3-8349-4485-6 (abgerufen am 27.06.2022)

Watzlawick, P., Beavin, J. & Jackson, D. (2017). *Menschliche Kommunikation*. (13., unveränderte Auflage) Göttingen: Hogrefe Verlag. ISBN: 978-3-456-85745-9

Wirtz, B. W. (2003). *Mergers & Acquisitions Management – Strategie und Organisation von Unternehmenszusammenschlüssen* (1., Auflage) (S. 311 ff.). Wiesbaden: Gabler Verlag. ISBN: 3-409-11994-9

Organizational Recovery—How Organizations Promote the Recovery of Their Employees

Laura von Gilsa

> *"The art of resting is part of the art of working"*
>
> *– John Steinbeck*

1 Introduction

Work is one of the strongest stressors. The effects of work-related stress are diverse and manifest in the short to long term in different areas such as work motivation, productivity, and health. Physical health can be affected, for example, in the form of high blood pressure, headaches, or sleep disorders; mental health can be affected in the form of anxiety disorders, depression, and exhaustion. Psychological impairments are steadily increasing and lead to high individual and organizational costs. Preventive measures for maintaining health reduce these costs, as recovery from work leads to increased well-being and higher performance (Steed et al., 2021).

A crucial factor in mental and physical health maintenance is recovery from work. Effective recovery is characterized not only by a high level of well-being but also by restoring work engagement and performance potential. However, sufficient recovery is increasingly difficult to achieve, mainly due to digitization, more flexible working conditions, and more permeable boundaries between work and leisure. In particular, constant availability, lack of disconnection from work topics, and high workload are associated with recovery impairments. Stressors at work lead to stress reactions, which in the short term manifest, for example, in acute fatigue, irritability, and/or lack of drive. In the long term, they can lead to

L. von Gilsa (✉)
Hochschule Fresenius, Frankfurt am Main, Germany

I. Knappertsbusch and G. Wisskirchen (eds.), *The Future of Work*,
https://doi.org/10.1007/978-3-658-45150-9_39

chronic impairments, such as persistent exhaustion, sleep disorders, and depressive moods. Effective recovery can prevent or at least reduce these strain consequences (Sonnentag et al., 2022).

2 Benefits of Organizational Recovery

Regardless of how good the working conditions are: Regular recovery from work is important to balance strains and resource consumption and to maintain motivation, health, and performance. Recovery is defined as a restoration process through which a person reduces their physical and mental strains caused by stressors and challenges and regains their individual well-being. Recovery can take place during the workday through micro and longer work breaks. Outside of work, recovery can occur in leisure time in the evening, on weekends, or during longer breaks such as vacations and sabbaticals (Sonnentag et al., 2017).

Recovery has benefits for individuals and organizations, as research results show various positive correlations with well-being and performance. For example, the feeling of recovery in the morning due to recovery processes in the evening positively correlates with self-perception of engagement and performance (Binnewies et al., 2009). But not only with self-perception, but study results actually show positive correlations between evening recovery and performance, e.g., in the form of positive customer interactions the next working day (Hur et al., 2020). Moreover, evening recovery also shows various correlations with variables of individual well-being and mood, such as higher vitality the next morning (ten Brummelhuis & Trougakos, 2014).

Recovery is a process that consists of activities and experiences. Recovery activities can take place anywhere and at any time, and examples include: sports, meeting friends, and pursuing hobbies. They are distinguished from other activities—such as household chores—by the fact that they are not experienced as a duty or burden. Recovery experiences are best achieved by disconnecting from work, relaxation, "mastery," and control over one's own leisure time. Disconnecting from work involves not thinking about work-related topics. Relaxation is characterized by low activation paired with feelings of inner peace, such as during mindfulness exercises. Mastering challenges ("mastery") includes activities that offer learning opportunities and/or build self-confidence (e.g., foreign language skills, performing a play). Control involves being able to autonomously design one's own leisure time according to individual needs (Sonnentag & Fritz, 2007). Additional work expands this taxonomy by the two factors of meaning/purpose and social belonging as further effective experiences (Newmann et al., 2014). Studies also suggest that specifically active (e.g., restaurant visits with friends) compared to passive leisure activities (e.g., streaming series) more strongly positively influence well-being (Kuykendall et al. 2020). Movement, e.g., through sports activities, also has a particularly effective impact on well-being (Calderwood et al., 2021).

However, the exact activities that contribute to recovery can vary inter- and intraindividually. For example, some people generally find child-rearing rather strenuous, while others can recover from work during it. And at the same time, the evaluations of these activities can also change depending on the situation (e.g., the children are in a bad mood or the social interactions at work were difficult) within people, so they are not fundamentally stable (Steed et al., 2021). It should also be noted that in recovery from work, not only work-relevant resources (e.g., autonomy) and stressors (e.g., workload) play a role, but also personal resources (e.g., self-efficacy) and stressors from private life (e.g., conflicts in the family). For successful recovery, it is therefore important that a person's recovery processes can be designed and experienced according to their individual needs (Wendsche & Lohmann-Haislah, 2017).

3 Challenges in Recovery

3.1 Recovery Paradox

Recovery promotes well-being, motivation, and performance. At the same time, well-being also stimulates recovery processes: for example, low fatigue at the end of the workday promotes physical activity in the evening (Sonnentag et al., 2022). However, the reverse is also true, leading to the so-called recovery paradox: recovery is particularly necessary when well-being is impaired—but precisely then, recovery processes are less likely, as individuals are too exhausted to motivate themselves for physical activities, for example. This paradox also applies to performance variables: on workdays that are perceived as successful and satisfying, recovery through switching off and relaxation is more successful than on workdays that went less well and where recovery would be even more important (Sonnentag, 2018). Studies also show that recovery processes in the evening are less likely when employees are exposed to many work stressors during the workday. Work stressors seem to particularly affect "switching off from work" and "relaxation" (Sonnentag et al., 2022). The problem with work-related stressors such as time pressure, poor customer behavior, and/or team conflicts is that they can only be avoided to a limited extent in regular working life. Organizations can influence some of the stressors that occur in everyday work, but many are little to no preventable. Therefore, it is all the more important to keep stressors as low as possible indirectly through modern work & office design, high person-job fit, and a healthy corporate culture. And on the other hand, to equip employees with diverse resources (such as autonomy, social support, stress management skills) and provide opportunities for recovery.

3.2 Changed Work Methods

Working from home and new technologies often lead to blurred boundaries between life areas. This promotes the trend to be "always on": especially teleworkers nowadays have the opportunity to be reachable at any time and thus constantly deal with work. Studies show that it is the engagement with work-related topics while surfing in the evening that is associated with exhaustion the next morning. Because surfing in combination with non-work-related topics is positively related to switching off from work (Liu et al., 2021). Switching off is harder to achieve when working from home, as for example, commuting and physical boundaries are eliminated. Studies also show that high "work-to-life integration" is positively associated with exhaustion and fewer recovery activities (Wepfer et al., 2018). When work is easily available, high self-control is necessary to avoid constantly working more than contractually agreed. However, if switching off is not or rarely possible, the stress level increases, performance decreases over time, and more and more work has to be done to manage the workload. This negative spiral affects recovery and thus well-being. Therefore, so-called "boundary management" is all the more important, so that an individually appropriate demarcation between work and leisure can take place. In some European countries, there is already the "Right to disconnect": For example, in Portugal, contacting employees after work is prohibited (Internat. Labour Organization).

4 Solutions and Practical Tips

4.1 Recovery During Work

4.1.1 Work Breaks

A effective strategy for recovery during work is regular breaks. It is recommended to take several short so-called micro-breaks, which can last only a few minutes, as well as a longer one of at least 30 minutes, e.g., in the form of a lunch break. Study results suggest that micro-breaks are differently restorative depending on the activity. For example, physical (e.g., walking), social (e.g., chatting with colleagues) and relaxing (e.g., surfing the internet) activities seem to have the greatest effect (Lyubykh et al., 2022). Lunch breaks that include relaxation, autonomy, and social contacts are also positively associated with performance and well-being (Bosch et al. 2018). Companies should provide conditions that enable their employees to engage in these activities. The effects of longer breaks—such as vacations/sabbaticals—on recovery usually fade within a month (Kühnel & Sonnentag, 2011). For this reason, it is advisable to allow employees to take regular short breaks instead of consuming their vacation days in as long units as possible.

Breaks work best with a so-called Person-Break-Fit: Because the break activities that match the currently existing individual needs are perceived as most restorative (Venz et al., 2019). Breaks that can also be freely chosen in terms of time are particularly beneficial. Break autonomy is therefore an important condition that allows employees to take breaks autonomously when they are needed. In addition, organizations should establish a healthy break culture that signals to their employees that breaks are allowed and even desired. In particular, managers should be encouraged to live a break culture, so that healthy break norms are implemented in the daily work routine of individual teams (Zhu et al., 2018).

4.1.2 Office Design

"Activity-based working" is a form of workplace design where employees can decide as often as possible when, where and how they work and take breaks. The special feature of this concept are so-called activity-related workspaces: e.g., focus rooms, meeting places, areas for social exchange and relaxation zones, which can be chosen depending on the activity and preference. The use of, for example, "concentration spaces" (to enable focused work), "breakout rooms" (e.g., with comfortable seating & lying areas for relaxation) and "vitality zones" (e.g., with table tennis tables for movement) is positively associated with well-being and performance (Kropman et al., 2022).

The ability to design and decorate one's own workplace according to individual preferences also has a positive effect on recovery. Decorative elements—such as plants, art, colors—as well as the view of greenery and the experience of nature are also beneficial. Recently, there has been increasing research on how exactly, for example, planting, natural areas and the view of greenery in office buildings can contribute to recovery (Bergefurt et al., 2022).

4.2 Recovery After Work

4.2.1 Availability

Switching off from work is one of the most effective recovery strategies. However, employees often feel that they have to be available at all times when technically possible. To prevent this, clear regulations and norms regarding availability can be established at the organizational level. Exceptions (e.g., emergencies) can be defined to contact employees outside of working hours. In addition, managers should be encouraged to implement these rules and act as role models, so that a healthy availability culture is actually lived. If availability arises due to overload or time pressure on the part of the organization, work design measures are recommended. The design and distribution of work activities are largely carried out by managers. For this reason, it is important to sensitize and possibly train managers who demonstrate the importance and implementation of health-promoting work design (Parker & Grote, 2022). Further suggestions for dealing with availability both at the individual and organizational level are: time and technical limitations (e.g., shutting down servers), prioritization (e.g., rotating emergency services), preventive avoidance (e.g., offering support in case of time pressure) and compensation strategies (e.g., allowing to reduce overtime) (Federal Ministry of Labor and Social Affairs, INQA).

4.2.2 Setting Boundaries

Organizational norms regarding the segmentation or integration of life areas are related to the individual's ability to switch off from work (Park et al., 2011). Organizations can, for example, promote healthy boundary management through training and company agreements. Company agreements should transparently include expectations regarding availability and working during leisure time. In particular, managers should be encouraged to set boundaries themselves in order to regularly switch off from work. Because they can establish healthy norms regarding availability and demarcation in their teams as role models and encourage their employees to implement them by setting an example. In addition, trainings for effective boundary management have proven to be helpful, especially for strengthening self-leadership skills, in order to be able to make a healthier demarcation of life areas (Haun et al., 2022).

5 Summary and Outlook

Recovery is a significant component for mental and physical health and therefore also relevant in the context of organizational health promotion. Organizations can support the recovery of their employees by promoting a corporate culture that encourages breaks, disconnection from work, and relaxation, as well as through a health-oriented office & work design. To ensure that recovery is actually permanently integrated into the (work) daily routine, it is useful to promote so-called "Recovery Mindsets & Habits" among the staff. This can be achieved, for example, by appointing & qualifying employees as recovery ambassadors, who regularly remind their colleagues of the topic using various methods and thus promote the implementation of recovery.

Organizational recovery will become even more important in the future: work intensification, shortage of skilled workers, acceleration, and an increasing number of mental illnesses are just some of the reasons why organizational recovery should be a mainstay in the corporate health management of companies.

References

Bergefurt, L., Weijs, M., Appel, R. & Arentze, T. (2022). The physical office workplace as a resource for mental health. Building & Environment. 1–18.

Binnewies, C., Sonnentag, S. & Mojza, E. (2009). Daily performance at work. J. Org. Behavior. 30: 67–93.

Bosch, C. & Sonnentag, S. (2019). Should I take a break? Int. J. Stress Manag. 26: 378–88.

Bosch, C., Sonnentag, S., & Pinck, A. S. (2018). What makes for a good break? A diary study on recovery experiences during lunch break. Journal of Occupational and Organizational Psychology, 91(1), 134–157. https://doi.org/10.1111/joop.12195.

Calderwood, C., ten Brummelhuis, L., Patel, A., Watkins, T., Gabriel, A. & Rosen, C. (2021). Employee physical activity. J. Manag. 47: 144–70.

Haun, V., Remmel, C. & Haun, S. (2022). Boundary management and recovery when working from home. German J. of HRM. 36: 270–99.

Hur, W., Shin, Y. & Moon, T. (2020). How does daily performance affect next day emotional labor? J. Occup. Health Psych. 25: 410–25.

INQA, https://www.inqa.de/DE/handeln/inqa-checks/selbstcheck-staendige-erreichbarkeit.html.

Kropman, D., Appel, R., Bergefurt, L. & Leblanc, P. (2022). Business case for a healthy office. Ergonomics. 1–17.

Kühnel, J. & Sonnentag, S. (2011). How long do you benefit from vacation? J. Organ. Behav. 32: 125–43.

Kuykendall, L., Lei, X. & Hu, X. (2020). Leisure choices and employee well-being. Appl. Psych. 12: 532–58.
Liu I., Ji, Y. & Dust, S. (2021). Fully recharged evenings?. J. Appl. Psych. 106: 990–1006.
Lyubykh, Z. et al. (2022). Role of work-breaks in well-being and performance. A systematic review. J. of Occup. Health Psych.
Newmann, D., Tay, L. & Diener, E. (2014). Leisure and subjective well-being. J. Hapiness Stud. 15: 555–78.
Park, Y., Fritz, C. & Jex, S. (2011). Relation between work-home segmentation and psych. detachment from work. J. of Occup. Health Psych. 16: 457–67.
Parker, S. & Grote, G. (2022). Why work design matters more than ever in a digital world. Appl. Psych. 71: 1171–1204.
Sonnentag, S. & Fritz, C. (2007). The Recovery Experience Questionnaire. J. Occup. Health Psych. 12: 204–21.
Sonnentag, S., Venz, L. & Capsar, A. (2017). Advances in recovery research. J. Occup. Health Psych. 22: 365–80.
Sonnentag, S. (2018). The recovery paradox. J. Appl. Psych. 88: 518–28.
Sonnentag, S., Cheng, B. & Parker, S. (2022). Recovery from Work. Annu. Rev. Organ. Behav. 9: 33–60.
Steed, L., Swider, B., Keem, S. & Liu, J. (2021). Leaving work at work. J. Manag. 47: 867–97.
ten Brummelhuis, L. & Trougakos, J. (2014). The recovery potential of intrinsically vs extrinsically motivated off-job activities. J. Occup. Organ. Psych. 87: 177–99.
Venz, L., Bosch, C., Pinck, A. & Sonnentag, S. (2019). Make it your break! Occ. Health. 3: 167–86.
Wendsche, J. & Lohmann-Haislah, A. (2017). Meta-Analysis on Antecents and Outcones of Detachment from work. Frontiers in Psychology. 7: 1–24.
Wepfer, A., Allen T., Brauchli, R., Gregor, J. & Bauer, G. (2018). Work-life boundaries and well-being. Journal of Business and Psych. 33: 727–40.
Zhu, Z., Kuykendall, L. & Zhang, X. (2018). Impact of within-day workbreaks on daily recovery processes. J. of Occ. & Org. Psych. 92: 191–211.

Implementing Physical Activity in the Workplace

Sara Scheltat

Any amount of physical activity is better than none, and more is better

World Health Organization

1 Introduction

The modern working world faces a shortage of skilled workers (see the article "Shortage of skilled workers—myth or reality?"), rising costs, and the lingering effects of COVID-19. Employees find themselves in a flexible yet demanding work environment, in need of a healthy and supportive foundation from which to perform. Since in many cases the human being is and remains the decisive performer in this environment, the human body can and must be this supportive foundation.

Physical activity (i.e., any body movement performed by skeletal muscles that requires energy expenditure) (World Health Organization, 2020) (hereinafter also **exercise**) is a key element in maintaining and optimizing human capabilities. Therefore, it is in companies best interest (ideally in collaboration with its employees) to promote employee participation in physical activity, in order to meet the challenges of the modern working world.

This article aims to investigate how promoting regular physical activity for employees can benefit companies, as well as addressing the challenges and solutions in implementing exercise programs.

S. Scheltat (✉)
MeisterAthletics LLC, Los Angeles, USA
e-mail: contact@meisterathletics.com

I. Knappertsbusch and G. Wisskirchen (eds.), *The Future of Work*,
https://doi.org/10.1007/978-3-658-45150-9_40

Using as broad and high-quality a data basis as possible, only findings from peer-reviewed studies and, with one exception, only meta-studies are used in this article. Unless otherwise noted, these studies refer to the units of energy expended (known as metabolic equivalents) as used by the World Health Organization (**WHO**). For the contextualization of the benefits of physical activity, current data from major health insurers in Germany were also evaluated.

2 Benefits of Physical Activity

Physical activity helps to lead a healthy and fulfilled life. The WHO recommends the following amount of exercise for adults between 18 and 64 years (World Health Organization, 2020):

- 150–300 min moderate[1] aerobic[2] exercise; or at least 75–150 min intense[3] aerobic exercise; or a combination of the two
- In addition, strength training[4] of all major muscle groups at moderate or higher intensity on two or more days per week

Studies show, however, that modern humans do not exercise enough; many are sedentary for the majority of the day. Research has long shown a correlation between prolonged sitting and an increased incidence of various diseases such as cardiovascular disease, cancer, back pain, and type 2 diabetes (Ekelund et al., 2016).

Unfortunately, in Germany, not even 60% of the population between 18 and 70 years reach the WHO recommendation for weekly physical activity (World Health Organization, 2022).

In particular, from a daily sitting time of over 6 hours, the risk of several life-threatening and/or chronic diseases increases significantly (Patterson et al., 2018). Higher amounts of sedentary behavior and its association with cardiovascular diseases and other poor health outcomes have been well-researched (World Health Organization, 2020). The effects of regular physical activity on the prevention and alleviation of symptoms of cardiovascular deseases (World Health Organization, 2020), even with existing risk factors such as smoking or obesity (Hamer &

[1] Physical activity performed between 3 and less than 6 times the energy consumption of the resting phase (World Health Organization, 2020).

[2] Rhythmic movement of large muscles performed over a longer period (also endurance training); this includes running, swimming, cycling (World Health Organization, 2020).

[3] Physical activity with at least 6 times the energy consumption of the resting phase (World Health Organization, 2020).

[4] Exercises that increase the strength, performance, endurance, and mass of skeletal muscles (World Health Organization, 2020).

Stamatakis, 2009), are also well researched.[5] In addition to classic aerobic and strength training, activities such as Tai Chi, yoga, or Qigong can also achieve the desired effects (World Health Organization, 2020).

Through focused support of physical activity for employees, companies can encourage the prevention of a variety of diseases and thus, employee sick days. In addition, regular physical activity can increase the performance and productivity of the workforce. The following will detail which sick days typically occur for selected diseases and will explain, based on peer-reviewed studies, how physical activity helps to avoid these sick days. Finally, current findings on performance and productivity increases will be presented:

2.1 Positive Impacts of Physical Activity on Cancerous Diseases

Fortunately, many types of cancer are curable today. However, cancer can lead to prolonged sick leave.

The Techniker Krankenkasse (**TK**)—one of the largest German health insurance companies—reports that companies in 2021 had to anticipate an approximate 97 days of work incapacity in the event of a female employee being diagnosed with breast cancer (Techniker Krankenkasse, 2022).

In the event of a colorectal cancer diagnosis, companies had to anticipate an average of over 43 days of absence in approximately 28% of cases (BARMER, 2022). Since these are average values, companies must also expect significantly longer sick leaves with such a diagnosis.

Regular exercise, especially in the intensive range, reduces the risk of developing breast or colorectal cancer by 10 to 20% (Physical Activity Guidelines Advisory Committee, 2018).

2.2 Positive Impacts of Physical Activity on Back Pain

Even seemingly less serious diseases can disrupt both the life and productivity of the individual employee and a team. The AOK —another major German health insurance company—states that in 2020, around 22% of all reported absences were due to diseases of the musculoskeletal system (AOK, 2022). In 2021, an estimated 26 million sick days were taken across Germany due to back pain (Techniker Krankenkasse, 2022). Companies had to expect 15 sick days per case of back pain; employees with disc herniations were absent for an average of 42 days (Techniker Krankenkasse, 2022). One can imagine, or perhaps has already experienced, the detrimental effects of prolonged absence on a team.

[5] No meta-study.

Regular exercise can prevent back problems. Existing pain, especially in the lower back, can be alleviated by various types of exercise (Burton et al., 2004). These are particularly suitable (Hayden et al., 2021):[6]

- Pilates exercises
- Muscle strengthening with a focus on the core muscles
- Stretching and flexibility exercises

The risk of further absences can thus be significantly reduced.

2.3 Positive Impacts of Physical Activity on Depression

Mental illnesses such as depressive episodes are unfortunately not uncommon among the workforce. Not only can they cause individual suffering and a decline in performance for employees, but this decline must also be compensated for by the rest of the team. Companies have to expect about *one sick day per employee per year*. Team members experiencing mental illness, however, were absent for an average of 67 days (Techniker Krankenkasse, 2022).

Research has long shown that aerobic exercise is well-suited to alleviating symptoms of mild to moderate depressive episodes. Recent studies show that strength training is also an effective treatment for depressive episodes (Gordon et al., 2018). About a quarter of those affected had significantly fewer symptoms or were even cured of symptoms in cases of mild to moderate depression after a supervised training program (Gordon et al., 2017, 2018). The following programs were suitable:

- Supervised training programs of up to 3 months
- Exercising 3 days per week
- Up to 45 min per training session
- Strength training and aerobic training were equally suitable (Gordon et al., 2017, 2018)

More active emplyees are also less likely to develop a depressive disorder than less active ones. Women benefit slightly more from such training programs than men (Gordon et al., 2018; Colcombe & Kramer, 2003).

2.4 Positive Impacts of Physical Activity on Performance

In addition to prevention or alleviation of ailments, physical activity is also suitable for increasing productivity and performance. Specifically, regular exercise

[6] This study did not examine the intensity of the training sessions.

at moderate to high intensity can particularly enhance concentration and even cognitive performance (i.e., among other things, processing speed and memory). This has been demonstrated for a variety of activities, including aerobic training, walking, strength training, and yoga (Physical Activity Guidelines Advisory Committee, 2018).

A 2003 study by Colcome and Kramer found the following (Colcombe & Kramer, 2003):[7]

- Training programs that last 6 months or longer have a greater effect on concentration and cognitive performance than shorter training programs
- Training sessions between 31 and 45 minutes are most effective
- The training should consist of a mix of aerobic and strength training

The effect (especially of the last point) is somewhat more pronounced in people over 55 years of age than in younger people (Colcombe & Kramer, 2003). In addition, regular exercise leads to a significant increase in energy and a significant decrease in fatigue or exhaustion. Sleep quality also improved significantly, even after a single training session (Physical Activity Guidelines Advisory Committee, 2018).

3 Challenges of Implementing Physical Activity Programs

Implementing a successful physical activity program requires a considerable spatial and temporal effort, which can be a challenge for companies. Once a program has been initiated, further measures are required—generally on an ongoing basis—to ensure the success of the program. In order to generate a measurable benefit for the company and its employees, programs should be designed for long-term engagement. They must not disrupt the company's operational processes or be incompatible with company goals, including short-term goals.

Assuming companies consider workplace diversity, designing a program that appeals to the majority of employees (and will actually be used) can present a challenge. Some employees prefer to exercise on their own time; some executives are reluctant to engage in athletic competition with their employees, for fear of losing authority. Some employees are uncomfortable with being subjected to performance pressure around physical activity in addition to their professional tasks.

The increase in workplace flexibility that resulted from Covid-19 (see the articles "Home Office: Perspectives, Challenges, Solutions, Hybrid Work" and "Work from anywhere—The free choice of workplace") presents a challenge: it is more difficult to offer physical activity programs that employees can regularly take

[7] This study did not examine the intensity of the training sessions. Only a distinction was made between aerobic training and strength training.

advantage of when they are working from home. An in-person training offer can only be accepted by those who are onsite during the session times.

The initial costs of implementing a program can also be challenging, especially before companies can predict or measure monetary benefits and other outcomes. Determining budget not only for program implementation but also program longevity can be difficult in the face of general cost pressure. Even when measuring the eventual success of physical activity programs, measurements can be complicated by questions of data protection and labor law.

4 Solutions and Practical Tips

Before launching a physical activity program, companies should analyze resources readily available within the organization, first offering quickly and easily accessible options for the short term. Simultaneously, companies can develop long-term plans for optimizing physical activity programming — incorporating, among other things, the diverse advantages of digital platforms and virtual training.

Though it can be a challenge in some ways, companies can also use the temporal and spatial flexibility developed in response to Covid-19 to their advantage. For example, when brainstorming spaces that could be repurposed for employee training sessions, a medium-sized company[8] noticed that part of their office space was no longer used regularly. In collaboration with the IT department, the company configured a booking system for the space, employees began taking regular yoga classes and organizing their own aerobic exercise sessions. The HR department then used the momentum of positive feedback to initiate a trial partnership with a nearby athletic club, most notably coordinating employee schedules with the athletic club's offerings.

To supplement this program, the company cafeteria prepared a takeaway meal on Mondays and Wednesdays, including a small snack for the trip to the club and a suitable meal for after training. Teams would meet in the cafeteria to pick up their "athlete's lunch" on their way to the club, where they would work with trainers on a strength training regimen.

If a company is planning future relocation, incorporating designated exercise areas in the planning of the new property would be even more preferable, especially for integrating physical activity into employees daily routines. Because the program needs to be accessible and functional to achieve longevity and reap long-term benefits, careful planning to determine the company's and employees specific needs is worth the investment. Budget allocations will determine the quality and/or quantity of the program in the medium and long term.

[8] Translated from the German term mittelständisches Unternehmen, meaning companies that employ fewer than 250 people and have an annual turnover of no more than EUR 50 million or an annual balance sheet total of no more than EUR 43 million.

Often, investments in expensive hardware (i.e. fitness areas or training equipment) do not make the biggest difference. Experience shows that in most cases, consistent everyday processes and coordinated schedules are the key contributing factors to program success. If not given enough time to exercise, employees under pressure will prioritize work, choosing to meet the short-term requirements of their work over exercising.

Given employees flexibility in the modern workplace, companies can take advantage of digital platforms and training formats. Some companies subsidize access to centrally booked and easily customizable apps with robust animated or recorded training modules. For particularly busy and/or highly paid employees, companies often book personal trainers, which can be in-person or virtual for flexibility. Employees receive a more tailored, individual training program with high temporal flexibility and no commute, from anywhere in the world.

In any case, when implementing physical activity programs, companies should engage consultants in exercise science, personal training, real estate, data protection and software solutions. Early and consistent involvement of internal HR and IT departments, as well as team leaders and management, is just as important. Ultimately, physical activity programs can only succeed with long term collaborative input from all parties involved.

5 Summary

Current scientific findings are clear: physical activity helps to reduce sick days and increase performance and productivity. The significant changes in the working world since March 2020 present both a challenge and an opportunity for innovation. Many companies are implementing focused physical activity programs for their employees. While expensive equipment may seem effective, a close look at the scheduling compatibility and accessibility of the program is imperative. External consultants are often indispensable; however, lasting success can only be achieved if the internal teams are involved from the start.

References

World Health Organization (2020) WHO guidelines on physical activity and sedentary behaviour

Ekelund U, Steene-Johannessen J et al (2016) Does physical activity attenuate, or even eliminate, the detrimental association of sitting time with mortality? A harmonised meta-analysis of data from more than 1 million men and women. The Lancet 388:1302–1310

World Health Organization (2022) Physical Activity Profile 2022 Germany

Patterson R, McNamara E et al (2018) Sedentary behaviour and risk of all-cause, cardiovascular and cancer mortality, and incident type 2 diabetes: a systematic review and dose response meta-analysis, Eur J Epidemiol 33:811–829

Hamer M, Stamatakis E (2009) Physical Activity and Risk of Cardiovascular Disease Events: Inflammatory and Metabolic Mechanisms. Med. Sci. Sports Exerc 41:1206–1211

Techniker Krankenkasse (2022) Gesundheitsreport – Arbeitsunfähigkeiten

BARMER (2022) Gesundheitsreport. Schriftenreihe zur Gesundheitsanalyse – Band 34

Physical Activity Guidelines Advisory Committee. (2018) Physical Activity Guidelines Advisory Committee Scientific Report. Washington, DC: U.S. Department of Health and Human Services

AOK (2022) Überblick: Gesunder Rücken. Available via https://www.aok.de/fk/betriebliche-gesundheit/gesunder-ruecken/ueberblick-gesunder-ruecken/ (abgerufen am 24.092022)

Burton A K, Balagué F et al (2004) COST B13 Working Group on Guidelines for Prevention in Low Back Pain. Chapter 2 European guidelines for prevention in low back pain Eur Spine J Suppl 2 136–168

Hayden J A, Ellis J et al (2021) Some types of exercise are more effective than others in people with chronic low back pain: a network meta-analysis. J. Physiother. 67: 252–262

Gordon B R, McDowell C P et al (2018) Association of Efficacy of Resistance Exercise Training With Depressive Symptoms: Meta-analysis and Meta-regression Analysis of Randomized Clinical Trials. JAMA Psychiatry 75(6):566–576

Gordon B, McDowell C et al (2017) The Effects of Resistance Exercise Training on Anxiety: A Meta-Analysis and Meta-Regression Analysis of Randomized Controlled Trials. Sports Medicine 47: 2521–2532

Colcombe S, Kramer A (2003) Fitness Effects on the Cognitive Function of Older Adults A Meta-Analytic Study. Psychol. Sci 14:125–130

With New Pay towards a Transparent, Fair and Participatory Salary Model—An Example from the Multi-Brand Company Celebrate Company

Steffen Behn

1 Introduction

When we think about salary, the economic perspective often comes to the forefront: that work is remunerated based on its value to the company. A few years ago, we asked ourselves a key question: How is the value of work determined in an increasingly complex and interactive world of work (Eichhorst & Linckh, 2019, p. 1)? We therefore completely restructured our organization: Rather than relying on traditional hierarchies, we embraced New Work principles such as self-determined action, situational leadership, and transparency and participation (Väth, 2016) are now at the forefront. This naturally lead us to question conventional salary models (Franke et al., 2019, p. 13).

For us, New Pay means a fair salary model based on performance—not on negotiation skills. Our unique New Pay solution outlines the shift to a new salary model where compensation is determined through peer feedback. Employees evaluate each other on how the professional performance and behavior of their colleagues has improved. This creates a transparent and fair process for determining salaries as much as possible. At the same time, New Pay is not a rigid model; it is fluid and should remain adaptable.

S. Behn (✉)
celebrate company GmbH, Hamburg, Germany
e-mail: steffen@celebrate.company

I. Knappertsbusch and G. Wisskirchen (eds.), *The Future of Work*,
https://doi.org/10.1007/978-3-658-45150-9_41

2 The Advantages of New Pay

One of the first questions we asked ourselves was: How transparent should the new salary model be, especially considering that transparency and open communication are core values of our company? Various studies indicate that full salary transparency (distribution transparency) has a negative effect on employee satisfaction due to unfavorable social comparisons (Card et al., 2012; Williams et al., 2006). In contrast, we consciously chose procedural transparency. Unlike distribution transparency, procedural transparency ensures that while individual salaries are not visible to everyone, the factors determining salary levels and the process of salary determination are clear and transparent (von Hülsen et al., 2020, p. 39). This approach aims to achieve several positive outcomes: increased employee motivation and performance (Franke et al., 2019, p. 58 ff.; Falk, 2014) as well as loyalty and recruitment of new employees (Trost, 2018, p. 277–278).

2.1 New Pay at the Celebrate Company: A Logical Consequence of New Work

New Pay was not a planned initiative for us but emerged from several factors:

Cross-functional Teams Self-organized, cross-functional teams make decisions independently. Each individual acting as a leader within their area of expertise. This shift meant that those responsible for salary increases lacked sufficient information. People who were department heads in the previous context and could make statements about the professional performance of their employees, suddenly no longer worked directly with their colleagues.

Transparency We began to question certain structures and processes. Thus, salaries within the teams were often opaque and unevenly distributed. Those who asked more often, received a salary increase more often. In addition, there are the differences in pay between genders for similar positions described by the gender pay gap. Moreover, gender-typical negotiation skills lead to men often achieving better results in salary negotiations (Voigt & Ruppert, 2018). However, negotiation skills were and are not a relevant soft skill for us and should therefore not be rewarded. Different leadership styles also often led to employees being evaluated differently depending on the leader. Moreover, these evaluations were often subjective, with little reference to current market data in the salary process.

Expectations There was no established process for employees to know when they could request a salary increase. In addition, there were no clearly defined expectations and criteria that employees had to meet in order to get a salary increase.

Contradictory Leadership Goals Ideally, reviews, i.e., the retrospective evaluation of past actions, should be separated from feedback, the forward-looking suggestions on how to do better in the future. However, leaders are required to evaluate performance when determining salaries. This conflicts with our leadership goals, as employee development remains our primary focus.

Based on these findings, we decided to rethink our salary model beyond the way we work. We then had discussions with several companies that had already introduced new salary models to define what is important to us in our own salary model. A particularly important factor for us was the connection of the salary model with our values.

2.2 From Self-evaluation to Peer Review to Feedback Discussion: The New-Pay process at Celebrate Company

The New-Pay model of the celebrate company consists of the following six different components:

2.2.1 The Competency Levels

We have defined nine competency levels across the company, independent of position and department. The focus is not on a person's resume or the number of years spent at the company, but solely on how far the person has progressed in their development. This means that managers do not automatically earn more than team members in the same field simply because of their position.

2.2.2 The Salary Curves

These competency levels are mapped to data-driven salary curves. Thus, for each level (on the x-axis), there is a specific salary (on the y-axis). The competency level is determined through Excel logic. Each chapter has its own exponential salary curve (see Fig. 1), which is based on market data. This external fairness, also known as market transparency, aims to ensure "appropriate levels and structures of salaries compared to typical market remuneration" (von Hülsen et al., 2020, p. 38). Factors taken into account included salary demands from applicants, salaries of competitors, data from friendly companies, as well as observations on general market development.

2.2.3 The Quantitative Peer Review

The assessment of an individual's development is conducted trough a questionnaire (see Fig. 2), which is filled out by both the person to be evaluated and eight colleagues. The questionnaire consists of two key questions: How has the person's/your own behavior changed? How have the results changed? This approach is designed to create a competency model based on the company's values and reflect expected behavior patterns at the individual levels. Additionally, both the person be ing evaluated and their evaluators answer a third question: At

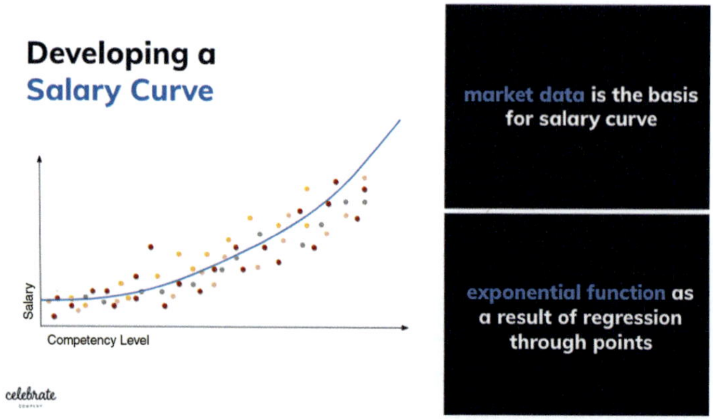

Fig. 1 Determining the salary curves

Fig. 2 The questionnaire of the peer review

which of the previously explained competency levels (1-9) do they see themselves or the other person. This ensures that the development assessment matches the competency level.

2.2.4 The "Excel Logic"

A salary model can be perceived as fair when it incorporates multiple factors such as performance or development. On the other hand, it can also be perceived as unfair and a simple model preferred, which only represents a few elements (Trost, 2018). Inititally, we developed a complex system, but it had the drawback of appearing as a black box to many employees. To address this, we simplified the model, integrating only a few key parameters to ensure clarity and transparency. The Excel logic thus consists today of comparing the evaluations of the peers and the self-assessment of the employees, adding them up and issuing a competency level with the corresponding salary based on this. This output then serves as a foundation for decision-making by the "Salary Council".

2.2.5 The "Salary Council"

What became clear in the course of time: That a human component was essential in the salary process to build trust. Therefore, a council was introduced (see Fig. 3), which receives both the self and peer evaluations as well as a decision-making basis that has resulted from the Excel logic. Initially, only the competency levels and their changes are discussed, and only afterwards is the salary checked based on the salary curves.

2.2.6 The Feedback Discussion

The final decision of the Council is communicated to the respective employees in the form of a report by the Chapter-Lead and explained and discussed in a feedback discussion.

2.3 Fair, Transparent & Value-oriented: What does New Pay bring for Employers and Employees?

Compared to our previous salary model, we have identified the following advantages:

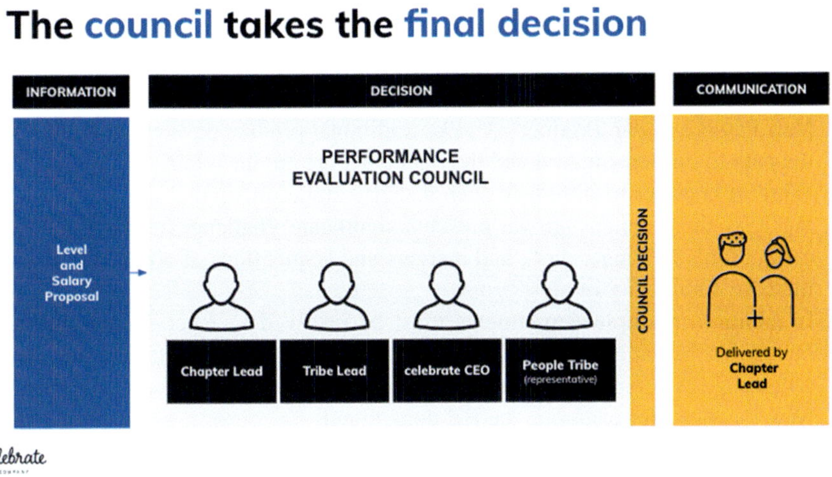

Fig. 3 The Salary Council

Peer-based In our earlier feedback processes, we had positive experiences with 360° feedback from colleagues. Thus, the evaluation of performance is not dependent on a single manager. Employees who frequently collaborate are often the best sources of insight regarding improvements in their colleagues' work.

Fair By aligning salaries with market data, we ensure that we offer competitive and fair compensation. At the same time, the salary curves and the continuous observation of the market allow employees' salaries to be increased without the extra effort of salary negotiations when market data shows that salaries in an entire industry are rising. This has already happened several times in the past.

Transparent The process is transparent and easy to understand, as it clearly outlines the elements relevant for salary increases. This procedural transparency has greatly enhanced the overall acceptance of the salary model overall.

Demanding & holistic The salary model reflects performance and is applied consistently across the company, using a uniform evaluation process.

Value-oriented Our salary model is deeply aligned with the company's core values, reinforcing the philosophy that a strong culture is the primary driver of growth.

3 Complexity, Relativity & Emotionality: Challenges of New Pay

Salary models are complex. Below, we outline the organizational, social, and technical challenges we faced during implementation.

3.1 Organizational Challenges

- New Pay is a "Lean Product": Unlike traditional product development methods, the path to implementation and the final outcome are uncertain.
- While it is easier to introduce such a salary model in smaller companies, scaling it as the company grows presents significant challenges. This is because certain tools no longer work and mergers and acquisitions of companies greatly increase complexity in most firms.
- In addition, multiple departments must be involved to meet specific requirements. Mathematicians, who determine the formulas for calculating the salary, will have a different perspective on the salary model during the development of New Pay than, for example, the HR department.

3.2 Social Challenges

- Salary models are inherently complex but should be as simple and understandable as possible for employees.
- "One does not talk about salary" is still a principle that many people have and complicates a transparent salary model.
- With a transparent salary model, care must be taken to ensure that certain aspects are indeed transparent. The rationale for adopting such a model must be openly communicated, along with the components that make up the salary structure (procedural transparency).
- Fairness is subjective: Two employees performing the same work and earning the same salary may have a entirely different perceptions of fairness (Ernst, 2021).

3.3 Technical Challenges

- Evaluations by colleagues can be distorted by the recency effect. Recent actions are more strongly remembered, leading to less consideration of past behavior.
- In our case, both the results and the behavior were relatively raised. Since most employees are unaware of the specific competency levels of their colleagues, simplifying the peer review process by only focusing on relative change was effective. A salary model that is based on absolute data, on the other hand, can better depict certain developments and can therefore be fairer. However, due to a lack of comprehensive data and the mathematical complexity involved, it is challenging to accurately track the development of all employees.

4 Solutions and Practical Tips

In the previous section, the challenges were sorted according to organizational, social, and technological aspects. For these three categories, the following describes how employers can meet these challenges.

4.1 Solutions for Organizational Challenges

If we understand New Pay as a flexible salary model that is constantly adapted to the needs of the employees in a constantly changing environment, it becomes clear that the mindset with which challenges are approached must also change. Companies need to foster the willingness to experiment with New Pay and constantly refine the model based new insights. This requires both a certain readiness to take risks and perseverance from company leadership to successfully implement and sustain New Pay.

4.2 Solutions for Social Challenges

What we also had to realize when introducing our New Pay model: The human factor plays a crucial role in salary matters. Especially for the comprehensibility of the salary model, the reasons for the introduction of New Pay and also the influencing factors on the salary should be communicated transparently and openly from the beginning. After all, the success of New Pay stands or falls with the acceptance of the employees. This acceptance can only be ensured through strategically planned and organized internal communication.

4.3 Solutions for Technical Challenges

Once the New Pay model has been introduced and has proven effective over time, companies may attempt to expand it by incorporating absolute data. Since the model becomes more opaque for the majority of employees due to the mathematical complexity, it should be ensured that the previous model is accepted. Changes should also always be accompanied by communication to create understanding.

Regardless of these specific challenges, employers should deal with two questions before introducing New Pay: What should be paid in the company? And what are the influencing factors? The answers are very company-specific and reflect the understanding of work and salary as well as the company values.

5 Summary and Outlook

With New Pay, some companies have taken on the sensitive issue of salary. Our salary model aims to serve as an example of what a modern compensation system can look like. Employees evaluate how the performance and behavior of their colleagues has changed. Through a combination of competency levels, salary curves, and an Excel-based logic that integrates peer reviews, a salary council decides on a salary increase, which is discussed in a personal feedback meeting. In this way, we have created a fair and transparent salary model that is applied across the entire organization and is aligned with our on the company values. As our working world is increasingly changing, our salary models will inevitably also change over time. New Pay encompasses all salary-related developments that arise within the framework of New Work, breaking down traditional organizational structures and thought patterns. Accordingly, the development towards New Pay is always closely linked to economic and social developments. Companies that want to pay a fair salary have the opportunity with New Pay to inspire more applicants and increase the satisfaction of their employees.

References

Card, D., Mas, A, Moretti, E. & Saez, E. (2012). Inequality at work. The effect of peer salaries on job satisfaction. *The American Economic Review*, 102(6), 2981–3003. https://doi.org/10.1257/aer.102.6.2981 (abgerufen am 06.12.2022).

Eichhorst, W. & Linckh, C. (2019). New Pay. Welche Anreize funktionieren überhaupt noch? *IZA Standpunkte*, 95, Institute of Labor Economics (IZA).

Ernst, M. (2021, 29. September). *Wertschätzung im Job geht nicht ohne faire Bezahlung*. Der Standard, https://www.derstandard.de/story/2000129795414/wertschaetzung-im-job-geht-nicht-ohne-faire-bezahlung (abgerufen am 06.12.2022).

Falk, A. (2014). Fairness and motivation. Fair treatment creates incentives, and is beneficial for workers and the firm, *IZO World of Labour*, 9. https://doi.org/10.15185/izawol.9 (abgerufen am 06.12.2022).

Franke, S., Hornung, S., & Nobile, N. (2019). New Pay. Haufe-Lexware GmbH & Co. KG.

Trost, A. (2018). Vergütung. *Neue Personalstrategien zwischen Stabilität und Agilität (S.* 273–308). Springer Berlin Heidelberg. https://doi.org/10.1007/978-3-662-57407-2_9 (abgerufen am 06.12.2022).

Väth, M. (2016). *Arbeit – die schönste Nebensache der Welt.* Gabal Verlag GmbH.

Voigt, M. & Ruppert, A. (2018). Follow-up-Studie: Gendertypische Verhandlungskompetenz und ihre Auswirkungen auf Gehalts- und Aufstiegsverhandlungen. *Working Paper Series: Business and Law*, 14. http://hdl.handle.net/10419/183109 (abgerufen am 06.12.2022).

von Hülsen, H., Feldkamp, T. & Koll, P. (2020). Vergütungstransparenz strategisch nutzen. *Controlling & Management Review*, 64, 34–41. https://doi.org/10.1007/s12176-020-0341-x (abgerufen am 06.12.2022).

Williams, M., McDaniel, M., & Nguyen, N. (2006). A Meta-Analysis of the Antecedents and Consequences of Pay Level Satisfaction. *Journal of Applied Psychology*, 91(2), 392–413. https://doi.org/10.1037/0021-9010.91.2.392 (abgerufen am 06.12.2022).

The Salary Guild: An Attempt at a Modern Salary Process for the Agile Company

Damla Nalbant

1 Introduction

Who earns how much and why? This question is constantly present in companies, yet it is rarely openly discussed how salaries are determined. Traditional salary negotiations leave many with the feeling that it's a game of poker: whoever bluffs best goes home with the highest salary, regardless of whether the performance is right or not. These actual and perceived injustices have a negative impact on motivation.

Basically, salary is a consideration for a service rendered. Dissatisfaction usually arises when the salary does not correspond to the level of performance. Conversely, it is hardly possible to increase motivation through higher financial compensation if other factors in the work environment do not fit. Sometimes a short boost in motivation is noticeable after a salary increase, but the original level of performance soon returns. According to Frederick Herzberg's two-factor theory of job satisfaction (Herzberg, 1998, p. 95), salary is only a hygiene factor or extrinsic factor: The salary itself prevents dissatisfaction at work, but it does not create satisfaction or higher motivation on its own. However, if something is wrong with this hygiene factor, if performance and salary do not correlate well, dissatisfaction arises. If the salary is too low in relation to the performance rendered, motivation is lost. Compensation systems should therefore include factors such as qualifications, professional experience, and remuneration adjusted to performance. In addition, it seems important to clearly define the gradation of salaries so that it is transparent according to which guidelines employees are classified. If such rules do not exist, there is a feeling of unfair treatment.

D. Nalbant (✉)
Wien, Austria
e-mail: damla.nalbant@borisgloger.com

I. Knappertsbusch and G. Wisskirchen (eds.), *The Future of Work*,
https://doi.org/10.1007/978-3-658-45150-9_42

In agile companies, traditional salary processes raise even more questions. When people work in a self-organized way, it is a contradiction that self-responsibility ends precisely on the subject of salary. The fact is that even in an agile organization, salary is an emotional issue. But the agile community has failed to answer the question of how salaries in an agile company are designed and negotiated. So far, there is no general solution for agile companies in the German-speaking world - not least because of the legal situation. For borisgloger consulting GmbH, we therefore looked for a way that is compatible with the laws but meets the criteria of agile performance management: The employees decide on their salaries, without annual talks with the management or veto right of the same. Agile means for us: The decision must lie with the teams, as one of the most important principles of the agile world is "ask the team". The associated process had to be iterative, i.e. recurring. In addition, we wanted to exclude any form of salary discrimination, so as many colleagues as possible should be able to have their say. Our "salary guild" model was launched as a pilot project in 2017 and has since become a fixed point in the annual cycle. Qualification, experience, and performance are taken into account through self-assessment on the one hand and through quarterly development talks in the respective team of the individual employees on the other hand. At the same time, everyone is involved in the evaluation system. The company clearly communicates which salary levels exist and according to which criteria the classification is made. This transparency in the decision-making process prevents the feeling of being treated unfairly in salary negotiations due to subjective parameters.

Guilds in general are dedicated to a specific topic and want to promote exchange and coordination among each other. The highest directive of guilds is to share knowledge, tools, or procedures with each other and thus promote learning in the organization.

The salary guild of borisgloger consulting meets once a year to evaluate the performances of individual employees and make salary decisions. The guild is staffed with new members every year. As a framework, the eight-member guild (which is 10% of the employees) receives a budget specification, guidelines from the management and the finance department, and the percentage value of the salary sum. For example, if the profit margin is 15% in one year, the managing director decides to make 7% of the personnel costs available as a budget for salary increases. This budget is divided proportionally into salary pots, to which the employees are assigned according to their performance.

Since borisgloger consulting is structured as a network of agile teams, the salary guild is composed of randomly selected representatives of these teams. This means that from junior to executive consultant, everyone has the same chance to participate in the guild. In addition, the Product Owners or the Scrum Masters of the teams supplement the guild. When staffing, care is taken to ensure a representative cross-section of the organization.

The Salary Guild meets each summer. Exempt from the agreed-upon evaluation scheme are individuals who have just negotiated their salary, have been with the company for less than six months, or have worked less than six months during the review period, for example, due to parental leave. In preparation, the Salary Guild meets one to two times in advance to determine the day's agenda, define the budget, and decide whom the process will apply to this time. The decisive meeting follows certain decision-making steps:

1. On the first half-day, the guild focuses on potential level jumps, for example, Junior Consultants can be promoted to Management Consultant. This is associated with a salary increase.
2. On the second half-day, it is decided who will reach the next level, what salary increases are associated with it, and it is discussed which individuals will not make a level jump but will receive a salary increase. For each employee, it is discussed to what extent the eight evaluation criteria are met, which were defined based on job and competence profiles as the basis for salary increases.

Whether and how these criteria were met is not (only) judged from the subjective perspective of the Salary Guild members. Each employee can make a self-assessment. In addition, all employees are advised to collect feedback from the organization using questionnaires at least four times a year. Ideally, the Scrum Masters of the teams have already discussed strengths and development steps with their colleagues in the context of a quarterly development radar conversation. Therefore, the Salary Guild has the feedback questionnaires, the self-assessments, and the results of the development radar conversations available as a basis for evaluation. If this continuous feedback was accepted and implemented by the employees over the course of a year, there are no more surprises in the assessment of performance and development - which can only be a snapshot. As a rule, external and self-perception coincide. Once the evaluation of all employees is completed, the results are set in relation to each other using the agile estimation method "Magic Estimation". This estimate serves both to determine the salary increase within a salary band and to decide on a possible level increase. The rule is: the higher someone is classified within a salary band, the less their salary can increase within the salary band, as development is expected. The goal is to develop into the next higher level. After all employees have been evaluated and those who are to receive a salary increase have been identified, the respective budget of the previously determined salary pots is distributed proportionally.

2 Advantages of this Form of Work

The implementation of salary guilds can contribute to greater transparency and fairness, which can positively affect satisfaction and thus motivation (cf. Nerdinger, 2014, p. 420). Recent studies confirm that employee participation in procedures and forms of variable remuneration based on performance can be an important motivational aid and is associated with increased productivity. Accordingly, behavioral experiments concluded that productivity can be increased by about 7% through employee participation, regardless of whether the co-determination actually resulted in greater fairness (cf. Fehr Advice, 2011). Similar results are also obtained from surveys of employees, with co-determination being particularly brought into play by HR managers as a decisive factor for employee motivation (cf. Sass, 2019, p. 56).

We wanted to know from the employees of borisgloger consulting whether they perceive the salary guild as a transparent, fair procedure and whether this has a positive effect on satisfaction. To this end, questionnaire-based interviews were conducted with 12 employees who participated voluntarily. The results were evaluated using Mayring's content analysis. It was also examined whether motivation has increased through the salary guild model, as studies have shown in connection with other models where employees were given a say.

2.1 Fairness and Transparency

Almost 60% of the respondents rated the salary guild as a "very fair" model, a third as "rather fair" and only one person as "rather unfair". 40% considered the salary guild to be "very transparent", 60% "rather transparent". In terms of job satisfaction, 60% were "very satisfied" and 40% "rather satisfied". In direct comparison with traditional salary negotiations, the salary guild scores as "very good" (60%) or "good" (40%).

Overall, the salary guild was primarily associated with transparency, which was consistently highlighted as a positive point in the interviews. The situation was similar with fairness: 10 of the 12 participants explicitly highlighted this as a central advantage. Conversely, lack of transparency and unfairness were associated with traditional salary negotiations. Most participants were familiar with traditional salary systems from their own experience and ranked the salary guild model between "rather fair" (approx. 45%) and "not fair" (approx. 18%). In the evaluation of traditional salary systems, the answer option "very fair" was not used, these were rated as "rather unfair" by 37%. At the same time, 60% of respondents considered traditional salary systems to be "rather opaque", 30% "rather transparent" and 10% "not transparent". Three people stated that they had dealt with bonus systems, one person had experience with employee equity participation and three knew forms of variable remuneration based on performance. These types of remuneration were consistently rated as "rather fair" (approx. 71%) or "rather unfair" (approx. 29%). Ultimately, the respondents agreed that the salary guild, compared to traditional salary negotiations, scores exclusively "very good" (60%) or "good" (40%).

The qualitative evaluation of the categories confirmed this result. The responses also addressed how important participation in the decision-making process is, as it is associated with fairness. One of the biggest advantages is that each case is viewed from different perspectives. In the case of the salary guild, the decision is made by a committee and not by a boss or a disciplinary superior. One interview participant put it succinctly: "If you are evaluated by one or two people, the result is always much more subjective than if you are evaluated by several people."

In this context, a democratic procedure was mentioned that could help to soften hierarchical structures. The salary guild was described as a "future-oriented procedure" that could "break rigid patterns" and distinguishes itself from traditional salary negotiations through flexibility and transparency.

2.2 Satisfaction

Indeed, the salary guild model is likely to have a positive effect on satisfaction. This results from the transparency and fairness of the procedure and thus confirms the results of well-known studies.

3 Challenges of this Form of Work

Possible disadvantages arise from the higher effort compared to traditional salary negotiations. It requires a relatively large planning effort to implement the system. Another uncertainty in the introduction or implementation could arise from the fact that it is a pilot project. Problems can, of course, also occur if the existing company culture is not optimally suited for the implementation of the model (for example, if there is a lack of trust in the company or the colleagues).

4 Solutions and Practical Tips

To meet the challenges, employee feedback is important. As soon as the salary guild's evaluations are completed during the conference, the group is asked whether everything has actually been objective. We pay attention to maintaining an open conversation atmosphere and there are always several people in the room. If someone feels that a member is not being objective, this is openly addressed and possible improvements are worked on.

Good preparation before switching to a salary guild model definitely pays off. Before implementing, you should familiarize yourself intensively with the procedure so that stumbling blocks can be largely cleared out of the way in advance. After each run, we thoroughly examine what is positive and less positive about the current state of the procedure. An important insight was that communicating the results to the employees requires a lot of sensitivity. A frequently expressed wish was to receive feedback promptly and to clearly identify strengths and development steps. This prompted us to determine at the beginning of the salary guild day which guild members will conduct the discussions with which employees. In this context, quarterly feedback is important: Serious conflicts usually arise after the salary guild's decision when there has been no consistent and open feedback for individual employees in the previous months. This creates expectations that can no longer be corrected.

For the salary guild meeting itself, the accompaniment by strong moderation is particularly valuable. This helps to keep an eye on evaluation pitfalls that guild members can fall into due to various biases.

Anyone who opts for a guild-like model should be aware that this work takes enough time. At least two days should be planned for the intensive phase of the assessment, in addition to thorough preparation. We also recognized that a guild meeting once a year is not enough. The salary guild must be part of a process, part of the dialogue and feedback discussions with the employees. Each of us can only really take feedback from the guild if we are aware of our own potential for improvement at the respective development level. And finally, only those who have once been part of the guild know how challenging and important this task is for the company. The more employees actively take responsibility for the process, the better the feedback process can become overall. Here it is important to give and use the design freedoms.

The salary guild requires an open culture. In companies with strong hierarchical decision-making structures, a rethink may have to take place first before a salary guild can be considered. Even in an environment characterized by mistrust and envy, the working climate and corporate culture should primarily be worked on. If the motivation of the employees has already reached a low point or motivation has to be "generated" through an authoritarian leadership style and the employees are not given any leeway, a salary guild will have a hard time.

Primarily, a salary guild model is suitable for organizations with an employee-oriented leadership style and a good culture of trust. Values come into play that not only play a major role in interpersonal relationships: appreciation, trust, responsibility, mutual help, and cooperation. The great advantage of a salary guild is that it can support and promote these values.

5 Summary and Outlook

It can be assumed that traditional compensation systems will lose importance in the coming years and will prove to be increasingly outdated. Modern organizations working according to agile principles will have to find ways to prevent frustration and demotivation among employees. It is necessary to develop models that take into account the principles of self-responsibility and self-organization and give employees a say. This is where the "salary guild" comes in, allowing the employees themselves to decide on their salaries in a participatory and iterative process. The salary guild, as initial attempts have shown, is perceived as a transparent and fair procedure. It promotes open communication and has a positive effect on employee satisfaction.

References

Fehr Advice (2011): Studie zur Mitarbeitermotivation: Je mehr Mitspracherecht im Unternehmen, desto höher die Produktivität. Abgerufen unter: https://fehradvice.com/blog/2011/03/09/studie-zur-mitarbeitermotivation-je-mehr-mitspracherecht-im-unternehmen-desto-hoeher-die-produktivitaet/ (abgerufen am 19.10.2020).

Herzberg, F. (1998): „Hygienefaktoren“ und „Motivationsfaktoren“. In: Kennedy, C.: 40 Vordenker und ihre Ideen. Management Gurus. Wiesbaden: Springer. pp. 95–97.

Nerdinger, F. (2014): Arbeitsmotivation und Arbeitszufriedenheit. In: Nerdinger et. al.: Arbeits- und Organisationspsychologie, Berlin, pp. 420–438.

Sass, E. (2019): Mitarbeitermotivation, Mitarbeiterbindung: Was erwarten Arbeitnehmer? Wiesbaden: Springer.

Company Participation—A Virtual Employee Participation Program (VSOP) Without Real Participation Rights as an Investment in Employees

Friederike Fritzsche

1 Introduction

Legally, virtual participation is a contractual obligation between the parties, which under certain conditions gives employees a claim to a payment.[1]

The employer must therefore create the specific legal criteria himself. He can decide under what conditions the employees have the opportunity to participate in the participation program. Virtual participation is largely unregulated to date and therefore offers a correspondingly flexible scope, which makes precise adaptation to the respective conditions possible.[2]

Within these conditions, a savings period is regularly set.[3] If an employee meets the requirements for participation in the program (so-called Cliff, e.g. certain period of company affiliation), the promised options are usually granted proportionally over a certain period of several years ("Vesting-Period"). This can achieve the goal of long-term employee retention. This "earning" of the options is in most cases solely due to the existing loyalty of the employee. However, there is also the possibility of linking to performance-related factors or a combination of performance and company loyalty. Here, a wide range of design options are allowed.

[1] *Bauer/Georgi/Weist*, Salamon Compensation Design, Employee Participation, Rn. 308; *Schönhaar*, GWR 2017, 293 (294).

[2] So also *Rödding/Jenderek*, Beck's Holding Handbook, Part B, Rn. 180.

[3] *Schönhaar*, GWR 2017, 293 (295).

F. Fritzsche (✉)
CMS Deutschland, Köln, Germany
e-mail: friederike.fritzsche@cms-hs.com

I. Knappertsbusch and G. Wisskirchen (eds.), *The Future of Work*,
https://doi.org/10.1007/978-3-658-45150-9_43

Following this vesting period, the question arises as to when the virtually acquired shares can be paid out. Typically, virtual participation, especially in the start-up scene, is linked to so-called exit events. The contractual obligation sets future scenarios in which the employee has the opportunity to convert the earned options. The aim here is to try to put employees on an equal economic footing with owners of ordinary business shares.[4] They should participate in the proceeds at an exit event (e.g. sale of the start-up by the investors, IPO of the company, merger process). The defined exit events can also be freely chosen in principle.

2 Advantages of Virtual Participations

2.1 Advantages for Employers

By designing an attractive participation system, the employer can attract and retain skilled workers in the long term, despite a comparatively low annual base salary. This is because the speculative nature of the participation and the associated chances for employees to achieve a high return can contribute to employees accepting deductions from their fixed salary.

Such participations are not uncommon, especially in the start-up industry. Especially in the first years after founding, financial resources may be lacking or the risk of uneconomical remuneration is high. Therefore, it is often difficult to pay highly qualified employees an appropriate salary that prevents them from moving to established companies or from signing an employment contract. Here, an additional participation in the company's success can help to compensate for an initially non-market-conforming annual salary.

In addition, participation can also contribute to employees being tied to their employer in the long term. Because with a steady increase in the company's value, the employee has a justified hope that his virtual participation will also become increasingly valuable over the years and that he will therefore refrain from changing employers. In particular, the design of strict "leaver clauses" within the participation program ensures that the employee must stay in the company in order to benefit directly from the increase in value. Otherwise, his participation in the program usually ends and he therefore has no chance of making a profit in the event of an exit.

Furthermore, a virtual participation program can be implemented with manageable financial expenditure. It can be introduced at any time and the employer does not initially have to provide any direct financial resources for this. Because unlike a real share participation, where the employees receive a direct financial value in the form of shares, the actual inflow of value of the options only occurs when the exit event occurs.

[4] *Weitnauer*, GWR 2022, 39 (42).

The employer can initially determine for himself what amount of money he distributes as options to the employees. Accordingly, it is possible to introduce the participation with a smaller amount of money. Even during an ongoing program, the employer always has the opportunity to roll out further self-contained programs in order to thereby expand the scope of participation. Unlike with real participation, he is not bound by formal hurdles, such as a notarial certification.[5]

2.2 Advantages for Employees

For the employee, the incentive is that he is economically involved in the success of his own work performance, depending on the size of the company. He can directly participate in the increase in value of the company and thus benefits twice from his work performance.

In contrast to real participation, the dry income problem is completely excluded in the case of virtual ones. With real participations, the problem is that the employee has to tax this inflow immediately upon receipt of the share. He pays taxes without receiving a direct return from which he could pay these taxes. This creates the risk that the employee cannot afford the participation and possibly taxed an option to a value that has significantly lost value at the time of the actual inflow (dry income problem).[6]

With a virtual participation, the advantage is that the employee is only considered to have received something for tax purposes at the point in time when he actually receives the value of his options.[7] The employee can pay the taxes from this direct return.

3 Challenges Regarding Virtual Employee Participation

Even though virtual participation is generally easier to implement than actual participation, the internal administrative and legal effort can also become significant. Especially depending on the size of the company, the administrative management of the program can lead to increased organizational effort. Legal issues are also partly complex. In particular, future financing rounds must be kept in mind, especially in the start-up sector. It should be ensured that the virtual shares of the employees do not become of little value due to a new financing round, thus posing the risk that the granted options become worthless in the exit event. The agreement of a dilution protection for the options can protect against this.

[5] *Schönhaar*, GWR 2017, 293 (296).

[6] See also https://www.capital.de/geld-versicherungen/klarna-mitarbeiter-zahlen-bei-beteiligungsprogramm-drauf-32637160.html, using the example of the Swedish start-up and payment provider Klarna.

[7] *Bauer/Georgi/Weist*, Salamon Remuneration Design, Employee Participation, Rn. 336.

Also, the employer will regularly not be able to set up a corresponding participation program alone and therefore will have to seek professional legal advice. Because the legal details of virtual participation are not yet secured to this day. Here, legal advice can help to illuminate the legally permissible gray areas within the framework of participation programs and to show design possibilities. However, a certain residual risk may remain, which can lead to legal disputes.

In addition, the employer should maintain the balance between his interests and those of the employees, so that the virtual employee participation program is also attractive for them and achieves the desired binding effect.

Virtual participation has a doubly speculative character. On the one hand, the employee cannot be sure of how much his options will be worth at the time of the exit event. It is possible that he will hardly make any profit here, as he is only transferred a chance of winning with the virtual participation. Secondly, there is the uncertainty of the exit event. Especially when scenarios are chosen that must occur (sale of the company) to justify the actual value inflow of the options, it may be that the exit event does not take place at all or much later than the employee expects. He has no influence on this.

Since this is a voluntary and predominantly still unregulated service on the part of the employer, he can adapt the conditions to his needs. The employer will often design the program in such a way that he binds the employee to the company for as long as possible. This restricts the employee in his free choice of workplace if he wants to secure the benefits of the virtual employee program.

4 Solutions and Practical Tips

When determining the objective of participation, a look at one's own employee statistics can be particularly helpful. There may be a shortage of applicants for higher positions, so an additional participation program can act as a lure to counteract this deficit. On the other hand, there is also the possibility of implementing the program in such a way that it counteracts high employee turnover in various positions. However, it is important to comply with the existing legal boundaries when selecting the circle of beneficiaries. According to case law, the principle of equal treatment in employment law must also be observed in the context of virtual participations. Therefore, employees cannot be treated differently without a valid reason.[8]

During the planning phase, the employer should carefully consider the conditions under which participation is subject. It is crucial to develop a legally structured concept that defines the circle of beneficiaries, the varying levels of hurdles on the path to achieving goals, and solutions for conflict situations, in order to ensure the goal of connecting the company and employees. Especially when the

[8] LAG Baden-Württemberg, judgment of 22.10.2021 – 7 Sa 26/21.

granting of shares is tied solely to company loyalty, the program can often be implemented quickly and without further effort, which can be advantageous from a cost perspective. If performance-related factors for earning the options are additionally linked, the contractual design of the program quickly becomes complicated (annual determination of performance targets, required regular performance evaluation). For this reason, the issuing company should carefully weigh up which hurdles the employee has to overcome in order to fully achieve his promised options in the end.

The conditions of virtual participation should also take into account the employee's premature departure from the company.

If an employee leaves before the end of the vesting period, it should be determined what happens to the options that have not yet been earned. It is usually agreed that these will be forfeited.[9]

In relation to the options already earned, a distinction is often made between Good-Leaver and Bad-Leaver scenarios. A Bad-Leaver scenario usually occurs when the employee is responsible for the departure (resignation, immediate dismissal for behavioral reasons, etc.). In other cases, a Good-Leaver scenario is spoken of. The relevant difference is the consequences at the time of departure. In a Bad-Leaver scenario, the earned options usually expire, whereas they often remain in a Good-Leaver scenario. Nevertheless, even in the case of a Good-Leaver scenario, the exit event must be awaited.

The completed forfeiture clauses in the context of the Bad-Leaver scenario make it more difficult for employees to terminate and therefore must be limited in time to be legally effective.[10] The specific deadline depends on the individual case and should generally not exceed 4 years.[11] Forfeiture clauses are also to be considered individually under the law of the general terms and conditions (allgemeine Geschäftsbedingungen). When evaluating them, the inherently increased speculative character compared to other special remunerations must be taken into account and lowers the requirement for the effectiveness of corresponding forfeiture clauses.[12]

The introduction of a virtual participation program is a measure that falls under the operational wage design and thus establishes a co-determination right of the works councils according to section 87 para. 1 no. 10 BetrVG. The employer sets the financial budget. The works councils exercise their co-determination right only within the framework of the distribution of the options, so that a works agreement is to be negotiated about these and about the further details of the participation,

---

[9] *Bauer/Georgi/Weist*, Salamon Compensation Design, Employee Participation, Rn. 333; *Schönhaar*, GWR 2017, 293 (295).

[10] *Bauer/Georgi/Weist*, Salamon Compensation Design, Employee Participation, Rn. 334; Schönhaar, GWR 2017, 293 (295); Schniepp/Giesecke, NZG 2017, 128 (133).

[11] *Schniepp/Giesecke*, NZG 2017, 128 (132).

[12] BAG, NZA 2008, 1066; *Hoefs*, Clemens/Kreft/Krause AGB-Labor Law, Special Compensation Systems, Rn. 37, 40; *Häferer/Burger*, NZA 2020, 143 (149).

such as the individual participation scope on a salary level, the leaver scenarios, and the duration of company loyalty.[13]

5 Summary and Outlook

With the introduction of a virtual employee participation program, the employer has the opportunity to bind its employees to itself in the long term and, by promising participation, to stand out from the competition in the job market. After all, the employee experiences appreciation through participation, which can lead to him delivering better work performance of his own accord and thus contributing to the company's success in the long term. However, the crucial point is that the employee refrains from changing employers.

5.1 Legal Outlook

Even though the Federal Labor Court has already decided in relation to real share participation that the labor law principles are to be interpreted from the perspective of the speculative character of the participation,[14] it remains open whether this statement also applies to virtual participation. Due to the new type of participation and the free design of the exit event by the employer, disputes before the German courts can be expected in the coming years. Until then, employers should weigh up the legal risks of protecting their own interests and the interests of their employees when designing the participation.

5.2 Battle for Talent

It can be assumed that the shortage of skilled workers will continue to rise in the coming years (see the article "Shortage of skilled workers—myth or reality?") and thus small differences can contribute to employee acquisition in the "War for Talents". Employers should therefore already consider what measures they will take to bind their talents to the company in the long term and to stand out from the competition in the battle for applicants. The implementation of a virtual employee participation program and thus direct participation in the company's success can play a decisive role in this.

[13] see for the real stock option, *Kutsch*, Munich Lawyer's Manual Stock Law, § 32, Rn. 108.

[14] BAG, judgment of 28.5.2008 – 10 AZR 351/07.

References

Aufsätze: *Katja Häferer/Franziska Burger*, Restricted Stock Units und Aktienoptionen – Aktuelle Entwicklungen bei Mitarbeiterbeteiligungsprogrammen, NZA 2020, 143; *Dr. Steffen Schniepp/Dr. Cordula Giesecke*, Virtuelle Anteile und AGB, NZG 2017, 128; *Dr. Tobias Schönhaar*, Ausgestaltung von virtuellen Mitarbeiterbeteiligungsprogrammen, GWR 2017, 293; *Dr. Wolfgang Weitnauer*, Mitarbeiterbeteiligung: „Echt" oder virtuell?, GWR 2022, 39

Kommentare: *Dr. Susanne Clemenz/Burghard Kreft/Prof. Dr. Krause (Hrsg.)*, AGB-Arbeitsrecht, 2. Auflage, Berlin, Hamburg und Stuttgart 2019; Dr. Kai *Hasselbach/Dr. Christoph Nawroth/ Dr. Adalbert* Rödding *(Hrsg.)*, Beck'sches Holding Handbuch, 3. Auflage, Düsseldorf, Köln und München 2020; *Dr. Erwin Salamon (Hrsg.)*, Entgeltgestaltung, Recht und Praxis maßgeschneiderter Vergütungsstrukturen, 1. Auflage, Hamburg 2019; *Dr. Matthias Schüppen/Dr. Bernhard Schaub (Hrsg.)*, Münchener Anwalts Handbuch Aktienrecht, 3. Auflage, Stuttgart/ München 2018

Sustainability, Social Responsibility and Diversity

Sustainability—Gamechanger for HR Work

Rupert Felder

1 Sustainability Stands for the Value Contribution "Human"

What characterizes sustainable human resources work? It is the criteria of a long-term orientation, across generations, it is the use of existing resources instead of constantly procuring and replacing new ones, it is the partnership-based, company affiliation that includes the whole personality and its contribution to the company's results.

In the sustainability debate, therefore, the contribution of HR is crucial. Why? Because—according to the theorem—human resource management is the sum of employee-related measures that are used to achieve the company's goals. Personnel is thus a central element of the company's management processes from research and development to purchasing, production, financing, sales, and service. Everywhere, the productivity factor "human" is relevant, in small, medium, and large companies. Sustainable human resources work, therefore, primarily aims at capturing the value contribution of personnel, its preservation, and expansion. This can make the value-added contribution through sustainable human resource management effective and "visible". And: Sustainability is increasingly becoming the "differenciator", the distinguishing factor that makes the difference in a candidate's decision.

Human resources work is not detached from constraints, it is rather embedded in a sometimes perceived as too tight corset of rules, laws, regulations, habits, and behavioral patterns. Precisely for this reason, it is necessary to know and classify the legal framework conditions and the history of sustainability.

R. Felder (✉)
Anwaltskanzlei Schork Kauffmann Wache, Karlsruhe, Germany
e-mail: rupert.felder@web.de

I. Knappertsbusch and G. Wisskirchen (eds.), *The Future of Work*,
https://doi.org/10.1007/978-3-658-45150-9_44

Currently, a world of labels, seals, certificates, and attestations is emerging. Sustainability seems to be only as good as it is visible, labeled, and stuck as a logo on the product. Do good and certify it so that customers and the public take note of the commitment. Self-commitment as an invitation to third parties. Caution is advised here.

2 From the "Honorable" Merchant to the ESG Criteria

To shape the future of work, it is worth looking back. Bona fides—the "Honorable Merchant" has a long tradition, starting from medieval Italy, regional trading companies to the Hanseatic League. The honorable merchants stand for responsible participation in economic life and wise management, from which the company and its environment benefit. An "Honorable Merchant" should be recognizable by the observance of virtues that respect long-term economic success without harming or opposing the interests of society. He thus operates sustainably. Cultivation and care instead of exploitation and predatory exploitation. Acting in the service of future generations and not just for the moment.

And Christian ethics and social teaching are older than all green thought games and the actual origin of the idea of sustainability. In economic history, this is an elementary chapter. Catholic social teaching is, after all, the pioneer of the social market economy, thus committed to balancing market forces; the dominance of the market and its mechanisms are ordered by social counterforces. Not only the capital factor, but also the human factor comes into its own, shaped by the experiences of predatory exploitation in early industrial situations.

The basis is the encyclical "Rerum Novarum" (1891), written by Pope Leo XIII, who is referred to as the "Worker Pope". But current impulses are also noteworthy: In 2015, Pope Francis published the encyclical "Laudato si". The document is considered an appeal to the historic climate conference in Paris the same year. "Laudato si" contains two central terms: "common good" and "modesty". The Paris Climate Conference has many predecessor events: the historic conference in Rio in 1992. As early as 1972, the report of the Club of Rome was published. Researchers examined the five fundamental factors that determine and ultimately limit the growth of this growth of the world population, agricultural production, the exhaustion of non-renewable resources, industrial production, and the generation of environmental pollution. So we should have known. Even more, in 1987 the report of the "Brundtland Commission" defined: "Essentially, sustainable development is a process of change (…)."

3 Sustainability Reports—The Structured Presentation of ESG

The obligation to prepare a "non-financial statement", also called a "sustainability report", is now specifically regulated by section 315 b HGB, which was inserted in 2017 with the Corporate Social Responsibility (CSR) Directive. The European

Commission regulates non-financial reporting obligations with the Nonfinancial Reporting Directive (NFRD). The non-financial report is part of the annual report and is integrated into it. A corporation that is a parent company (section 290 HGB) must expand its group management report to include a non-financial group statement.

Thus, the sustainability report, like the annual report as a whole, is subject to audit by external auditors. In section 289 c para. 2 HGB, the topics are listed in items 1 to 5: from environmental concerns to employee concerns to compliance with human rights and combating corruption. Companies are obliged to describe these topics and publicly disclose what they are specifically doing about these topics.

Many companies use these sustainability reports to describe current and upcoming projects in detail on these topics. Because: these reports are also aimed at customers, help to formulate the employer brand, and are objects of investigation for analysts and proxy advisors. The European Union now wants to tighten this further: The Corporate Sustainability Reporting Directive (CSRD) of the European Union is now in its draft form. Companies must adapt their CSR reporting processes for the reporting year 2023 to be uniform, transparent, and above all comparable. This means that the extension of reporting obligations for smaller companies is imminent.

4 Sustainability—Not without Regulation

In this context, the corset of paragraphs has become significantly tighter. The EU sets the precedent: prohibition of plastic, prohibition of combustion engines, reduction of CO2, and a tightening in nature conservation. The "Green Deal" of the European Union with far-reaching detailed specifications such as the "REACH Regulation", the EU chemical strategy or the EU supply chain requirement, have also led to an expansion of regulation. But also in the Stock Corporation Act and Commercial Code, there have been massive increases in regulations in recent years: the accounting regulations and self-commitments such as the German Sustainability Code or the Corporate Governance Code, for example, have been added.

The guiding principle of all guidelines and obligations are the 17 UN sustainability goals, the Sustainable Development Goals (SDGs). They are the core of the political objective of the Agenda 2030 of the General Assembly and were derived from the Millennium Declaration, which was adopted by the United Nations at the so-called Millennium Summit. The Millennium Summit (English: Millennium Assembly) refers to the 55th General Assembly of the United Nations, which took place from September 6 to 8, 2000 in New York. They are directed at everyone: governments worldwide, but also civil society, the private sector, and science.

To concretize the 17 goals, a catalog of 169 more detailed and measurable target specifications was adopted. Since July 2019, there has been a dedicated online platform for this, which prepares the current data for Germany for each of the 17 sustainability goals. For the sub-goal "Encourage companies, especially large and transnational companies, to adopt sustainable practices and to include sustainability information in their reporting", for example, the number of companies that publish sustainability reports is measured as a statistical size.

Regulations for the disclosure of sustainability efforts have been introduced: such as the additions in section 289c of the Commercial Code, in which companies must describe how they take into account employee concerns, with the information referring, for example, to the measures taken to ensure gender equality, working conditions, the implementation of the basic conventions of the International Labour Organization, respect for the rights of workers to be informed and consulted, social dialogue, respect for the rights of trade unions, health protection or safety at work. Companies are thus not only obliged to report the extensive keywords in the law, they must also act on them. If the description becomes a duty, then action is the minimum requirement.

5 The ILO Basic Principles and Core Labor Standards

The ILO basic principles have just been mentioned. The International Labour Organization (ILO), based in Geneva, is a specialized agency of the United Nations and is tasked with promoting social justice as well as human and labor rights. The ILO has four basic principles as a mandatory basis for member states. These four basic principles encompass the cornerstones for a sustainability orientation based on equality and equal opportunities.

Freedom of association and the right to collective bargaining—Workers have the right to organize themselves into trade unions without external interference. Trade unions have the right to conduct collective bargaining and to strike.

Elimination of forced labor—Everyone has the right to choose their work freely. Forced labor is prohibited. This includes all employment relationships in which work is enforced through violence or threats, such as slavery, debt bondage, and employment relationships where workers are imprisoned or threatened or their identification papers are taken away.

Abolition of child labor—Children have a right to protection from exploitation. Children before the end of compulsory schooling or under 15 years of age may not be employed. Dangerous or development-inhibiting activities ("worst forms of child labor") are fundamentally prohibited for persons under 18 years of age. For simple tasks, 13 to 15-year-olds may also be employed if national laws allow this and school attendance is not thereby prevented. The abolition of child labor also includes an obligation to create alternatives (school attendance, secured income for parents).

Prohibition of discrimination in employment and occupation—Everyone has the right to equal treatment regardless of race, skin color, sex, religion, political belief, nationality, or social origin. This also includes the principle of "equal pay for equal work".

These basic principles have found their elaboration in further provisions. Such as the Convention on Freedom of Association and Protection of the Right to Organize (1948, Convention 87), the Convention on the Right to Organize and

Collective Bargaining (1949, Convention 98), the Prohibition of Forced Labor (1930, Convention 29) and Protocol of 2014 to the Forced Labor Convention, the Abolition of Forced Labor (1957, Convention 105), the Equal Remuneration Convention (1951, Convention 100), the Discrimination (Employment and Occupation) Convention (1958, Convention 111), the Minimum Age Convention (1973, Convention 138) and the Prohibition and Immediate Action for the Elimination of the Worst Forms of Child Labor (1999, Convention 182).

For the legal sphere of the European States, the ILO standards lead to the corresponding directives, such as the Anti-Racism Directive (2000/43/EC), Employment Framework Directive (2000/78/EC), "Gender Directive" (2002/73EC), Directive on Gender Equality also outside the workplace (2004/113/EC). Compliance with these directives and documentation thereof is the basis for objective, verifiable, and transparent human resources work.

But sustainability is not a national issue and the legal sphere of the EU is not sufficient. Therefore, global efforts are necessary and relevant for globally operating companies. By anchoring in internal company guidelines (codes) and mandatory rulebooks (Code of Conduct), spheres of influence can be reached in all corporate branches. The Supply Chain Act does its part to apply the ILO standards (which have worldwide validity through the United Nations) in the countries of the extended workbench.

6 Self-commitment Through Labels, Codes, and Reports

In addition to legal requirements and internal company validity, self-commitments are a helpful way to document compliance with sustainability. Numerous labels are available to achieve a certain visibility with the compliance of the criteria and the use of the label. Companies are encouraged to practice good citizenship; this means good civic behavior in which a company respects laws, respects others, and integrates into the social community beyond its actual business activities. Compliance, the adherence to laws, has become its own business and legal term for the rule conformity of companies, i.e., law-abiding behavior in compliance with laws, guidelines, and voluntary codes.

The German Sustainability Code (DNK) is a standard for transparent reporting of corporate sustainability performance and can be used by companies and organizations of any size and legal form across all sectors. It was first formulated in 2011 by the Council for Sustainable Development, which was appointed by the Federal Government, and has since been further developed. The DNK makes corporate sustainability performance formally visible with its approximately 20 predefined criteria and is oriented towards the requirements of the Global Reporting Initiative (GRI).

Another example is the German Corporate Governance Code (DCGK). The preamble of the DCGK states literally: "The Code clarifies the obligation of the Management Board and the Supervisory Board to (…) ensure the company's existence and its sustainable value creation. These principles demand not only legality but also ethically founded, self-responsible behavior (model of the Honorable Merchant)."

According to section 161 para. 1 AktG, companies must make a declaration on the Corporate Governance Code (comply or explain) and document that they comply with the requirements ("Declaration of Conformity"). Even more: The remuneration structure of listed companies is to be aligned with the sustainable and long-term development of the company. "The remuneration of the members of the Management Board is to contribute to the promotion of the business strategy and the long-term development of the company." (Principle 23 of the DCGK)

7 Concrete Personnel Work in the Light of Sustainability

Compensation instruments are suitable for incentivizing sustainable business success—even beyond the scope of the DCGK. A multi-year horizon for achieving goals is intended to ensure that not short-term fireworks, but long-term oriented profit assurance have priority. Employee participation can also realize commitment to the company and thus sustainable engagement.

Health management has also long established itself as an instrument of mindfulness and balance. Work ability is the mental and physical ability of an employee, integrated into the work design and concrete leadership relationship, to successfully accomplish the assigned work tasks. The requirements should be in line with the performance capacity.

Finally, corporate health promotion according to section 20b SGB V is also a financial design element to promote actions. A "Works Well-Being Index" can analyze the situation of the workforce and reveal performance deficits. Last but not least, qualification impulses to maintain competencies are a contribution to sustainability and vocational training in the company is a (sustainable) investment in the future. Sustainability begins

Sustainability already starts with personnel selection to achieve long-term employer loyalty. And of course, travel policy and healthy nutrition are further elements of concrete personnel policy ideas. Picking up this thread and bringing it into an overall concept, that is the task for sustainable.

8 Outlook

The establishment of sustainability in the company initially requires a narrative. Similar to mission and vision, the central message must be tailored to the specific situation of the company's activities. The more challenging the business sector and the ecological burden of products and production processes, the more demanding the narrative. Derived from this, there is a need for a guiding principle for executives to fulfill their role model function. Standards and regulations further set the framework to define the maturity model for the establishment of sustainability in concrete personnel work. The social taxonomy planned for 2024 accelerates this process and forces even smaller and medium-sized companies to take a position with a sustainability report.

From Self to Sustainability—How Companies Can Succeed in Encouraging the Intrinsic Motivation of Their Employees to More Sustainable Action

Sophie E. Bochtler

1 Introduction

The fact that forward-looking companies today have a comprehensive understanding of sustainability, a sustainability strategy, or even align their entire corporate purpose according to sustainable criteria, is no longer a novelty.

But how do companies manage to motivate their employees to act more sustainably? To provide an answer, this article aligns the following terms: intrinsic motivation, autonomy, meaning, belonging, sustainability, and entrepreneurship—all with the aim of promoting more sustainable action among employees.

From external motivation to intrinsic motivation—a paradigm shift

The focus here is on promoting *intrinsic* motivation among employees, i.e., motivation from inner conviction and interest, not because of external reward.

Until the early 2000s, a perception dominated in which companies motivated their employees with the carrot-and-stick method. With the reward carrot in front of their noses, people were driven by management to achieve goals.

This now outdated perception of motivation originates from a view from the beginning of the twentieth century, in which companies were understood as machines. Thus, each employee had a function, was a specialist, everything ran hand in hand like in a production. The work to be done was possibly complicated, but not complex.

Since the end of the twentieth century, work in many industries, and thus also companies, has become increasingly *complex*. Today, these companies are rather understood as *organisms* in which people work together in reciprocal movements.

S. E. Bochtler (✉)
The House of Good, Hamburg, Germany
e-mail: sophie@thehouseofgood.de

I. Knappertsbusch and G. Wisskirchen (eds.), *The Future of Work*,
https://doi.org/10.1007/978-3-658-45150-9_45

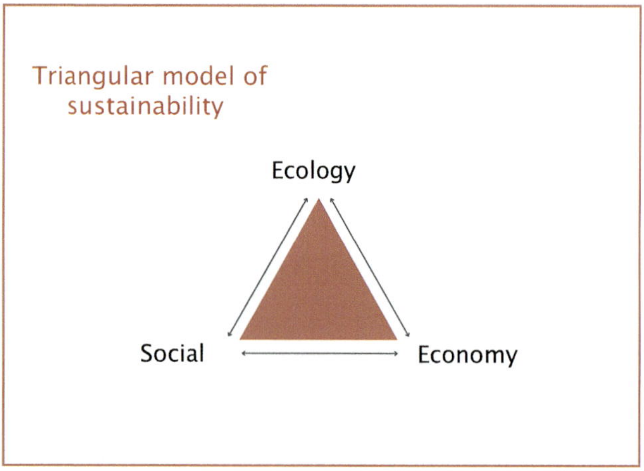

Fig. 1 The triangle model of sustainability, cf. German Bundestag (1994)

Employees are no longer just specialists, but generalists. It is no longer sufficient to focus on just one area. To understand complex strands, several areas of knowledge must interlock.

In the view that companies are *machines* with *complicated* processes, *extrinsic* motivation works well. Motivation researcher Dan Pink illustrates in his million-times viewed TED Talk,[1] that in this type of work a monetary incentive produces more performance.

But Dan Pink also shows that this view has long since become a thing of the past: *People in complex structures do not function according to extrinsic incentives, but through intrinsic motivation.*

He describes the achievement of intrinsic motivation through the AMP rule: Autonomy, Mastery, and Purpose. In particular, autonomy and purpose are important for this consideration in promoting motivation on the topic of sustainability. Both aspects require a corporate culture in which employees can develop accordingly. A corporate culture in which there is a comprehensive, a holistic understanding of sustainability.

The term sustainability is often mistakenly equated with CO_2 emissions, yet it has various meanings. For this article, two of the meanings are crucial:

1. On the one hand, the triangle model,[2] see Fig. 1: Only what meets all three criteria on a large scale is sustainable: ecology, economy *and* social.

[1] © TED Conferences: Title Dan Pink on the surprising science of motivation (2009), https://www.ted.com/talks/dan_pink_the_puzzle_of_motivation?language=de (as of: 30.11.2022).

[2] Based on the report of the Enquete Commission 1994, cf. German Bundestag (1994), p. 33 f.

It thus describes not only the simplified representation of an extremely complex reality, but also the mutual dependence.

Economy, environment, and social must therefore be in balance so that future generations are assured a life on earth.

2. Another important meaning of sustainability is long-term. Even before the term spread in environmental protection, the word was already used in a business sense. To sustain something, i.e., to be able to use it long-term over generations, to repair, maintain, and care for it.
   Long-term is a virtue in entrepreneurship that ideally is not only reserved for corporate decision-makers, but all employees can bring or develop.

2 Advantages of Intrinsically Motivated Employees

We humans have several basic needs, two of which are the need for belonging and autonomy. This means that we want to belong and at the same time live out our *self*—that is, decide independently what we do. The Riemann-Thomann model (Fig. 2) shows these two needs on opposite poles (here autonomy is initially titled as "distance", in the further course of this article the term autonomy is used).

In systemic coaching, this model is often used to describe the inner tensions of ambivalent feelings. *But what if we tried to connect these opposing poles and use the tension as an energy carrier?*

If we link this theory with the findings of Dan Pink, i.e., overlay two models, a guide for a win-win deal emerges: that intrinsic motivation for more sustainable action is promoted by meeting two basic needs, see Fig. 3.

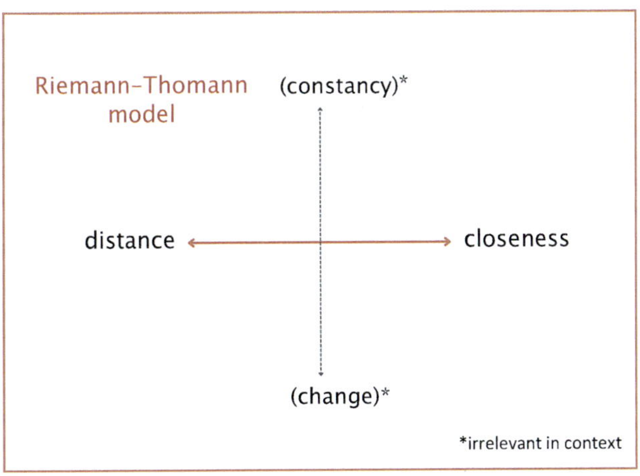

Fig. 2 The basic needs according to Riemann (1975) and Thomann (1988). (© Schulz von Thun Institute 2017)

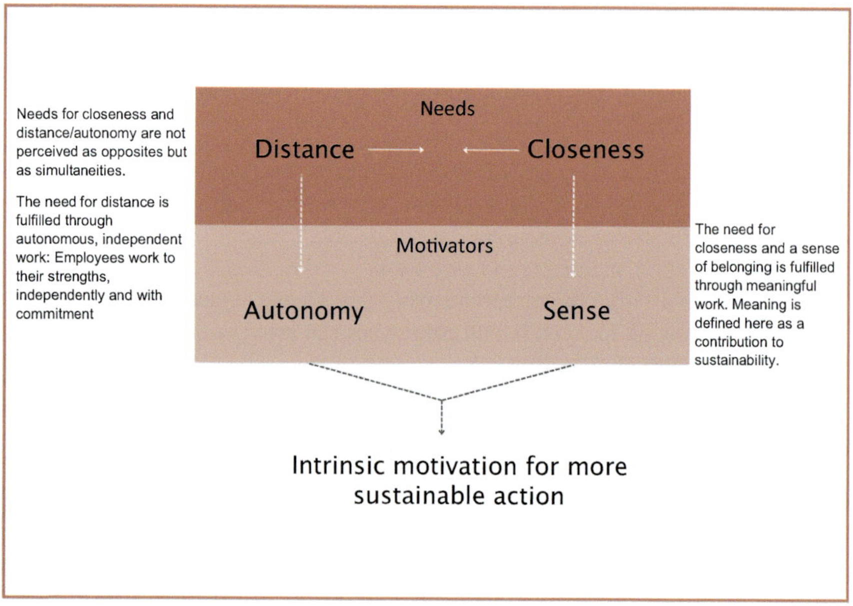

Fig. 3 Achievement of intrinsic motivation on the subject of sustainability. (own representation)

If companies give their employees the feeling of belonging to something bigger (*closeness & meaning*) and at the same time enable autonomous action (*distance & autonomy*) within a framework based on sustainable values, not only can the employees find fulfillment, but they can also increase the success of a company at the same time.

Because studies show that consumer companies that act sustainably are more successful with a 3% higher EBIT margin.[3] Sustainability costs more money in the short term, but is more profitable in the long term—an important factor!

In addition, employers who take sustainability seriously are more attractive in competition: 76% of employees cite sustainability as an important factor.[4] In the "War for Talent", i.e., the ongoing struggle for employees, this is essential.

For the Gen Z generation now flooding the job market, sustainability even has a special status: Sustainability at work is one of the most important factors for more than 25% of those surveyed. This makes sustainability more important to them than, for example, a quick promotion or a high level of responsibility.[5] This

[3] Study by LBBW, 2018 Burkert, Uwe: Sustainability pays off—Society and companies in transition., Landesbank Baden-Württemberg, 2018.

[4] StepStone and Handelsblatt Research Institute, Sustainability as an Attractiveness Factor, 2019.

[5] StepStone and Handelsblatt Research Institute, Sustainability as an Attractiveness Factor, 2019.

generation is now completing their school, training, and university degrees and is thus literally the *future of work*.

Finally, it is a fundamental opportunity: dealing with the intrinsic motivation of employees is not a process that stands alone. There is an opportunity here to set up the entire company for the future. Because, as will be explained in more detail in the following section, authenticity is a crucial factor in avoiding one of the pitfalls of sustainability: greenwashing.

Company decision-makers can therefore understand sustainability and intrinsic motivation as an opportunity to meet CSR criteria[6] based on values—because they want to, not because they have to.

3 Challenges for Companies in Implementing Measures for Intrinsic Motivation of Employees

Where there is an opportunity, there is often a challenge. The process of wanting to motivate people to act more sustainably cannot stand alone in corporate strategy. Companies that have not yet initiated this cultural change face high effort and resource use. This can deter company decision-makers, management, and works councils. Especially in a tense situation of skilled worker shortage and (psychological) overload due to pandemic, war, and inflation, implementing a strategy can seem overwhelming.

Not only overload can become difficult here, another challenge is resource allocation and thus the big money question. Yes, sustainability is expensive at first. However, viewing sustainability measures as an investment in the future, which may not generate tax-reducing effects through depreciation, but secure the long-term viability of the company, can help here.

Because this is a question of attitude, of mindset: how important do decision-makers in the company consider the issue of sustainability and its implementation?

In addition, the implementation can become uncomfortable for company decision-makers. Consequences must be drawn, employees who do not identify with the new company goals and their implementation may leave the company. Yes, even the company decision-makers, who determine the values and thus the orientation of the company, are confronted in this process with their own values and perceptions. This is personal and can be uncomfortable. The next feeling associated with the word sustainability is quickly guilt: We know what to do and do not change our behavior. This can lead to blockages and freezing—which is the opposite of motivating progress.

Finally, there is a major challenge that quickly becomes a trap: If the sustainability goals, which the employees should orient themselves towards, do not authentically fit the company, credibility is risked. And nothing is more fatal in

[6] Corporate Social Responsibility.

this context than practicing greenwashing. Even doing nothing is more authentic than proclaim goals that are unattainable or cover up other, non-sustainable products of the company.

In a perfectionist-oriented economy and society, it is difficult to expose weaknesses and vulnerabilities. But this economy and society is not separate from us, we are an inherent part of it. By changing our behavior, we also change the economy and society.

4 Solutions and Practical Tips

So what is needed in practice to *intrinsically motivate* employees to act more *sustainably*?

Following the models of Dan Pink and the Riemann-Thomann-model, it is about fulfilling needs: being able to create meaning, thereby feeling a sense of belonging and at the same time working independently. The following presents four possible action strategies:

4.1 Sustainability

It is essential to have a comprehensive understanding of sustainability and to define a sustainability strategy that fits the company's purpose. As highlighted in the previous sections, management should support and live this endeavor. The recommendation here is clearly not to strive for perfectionism, that's simply impossible. The authenticity mentioned above is crucial here. Small steps that are feasible instead of too big visions that cannot be fulfilled.

The UN's 17 Sustainability Development Goals provide orientation here (https://sdgs.un.org/goals). Professional consultations offer support in developing a strategy.

Possible questions could be: What approach to sustainability fits our company? On what values does our company base? Which of the 17 SDGs can we commit to?

4.2 Belonging through a Sense of Purpose

People like Greta Thunberg and Martin Luther King, are/were not successful with their ideology alone: They brought masses together. Striving together for something bigger connects—and connection creates belonging. To belong, to be seen, to be part of something.

In the corporate context, this means specifically: Including employees in sustainability projects, creating working groups to achieve sustainability goals, building communities and networks, defining purpose for departments, areas or for the entire company. Or aiming even higher: Offering only products and services whose purpose is sustainable.

Since the term *Purpose* has been established for several years and is also often misinterpreted, it is important to say that a similar trap exists here as with greenwashing. Beautifications, energy-charged slogans or cups with the credo printed as a hashtag are just as little "Purpose" as a ball pit or foosball table are New Work. Purpose should be translated with the word sense-making or *meaning* and accordingly profound should a process be designed.

It is important that employees are given the freedom (incl. the time) to be involved in the groups and processes and not decided top-down—the keyword here is belonging!

Questions here could be: What purpose, meaning does our company serve? What communities can we build? Which sustainability goals do we want to dedicate our purpose to? How can we create free spaces for employees so that they can engage in groups?

4.3 Autonomy

For employees to be able to work independently, two components are primarily needed: a trusting environment and the prerequisite that employees work in their strengths.

What a trusting environment looks like can be found in the remaining chapters of this book, as this is ultimately the definition of New Work: flexible working hours and locations, a new understanding of leadership, etc.

The concept of "strengthening strengths" emphasizes the potentials that are thereby unleashed. To ensure that employees work in their strengths, a comprehensive process is required, which should definitely be accompanied by experts. Even in recruiting, it can already be ensured that the right person joins the team: by having managers and teams go through the strengths-finding process in advance and thus being able to formulate which strengths should complement the team.

Structures and corporate cultures also play a role, promoting lateral movements, career changes, and specialist careers, and not exclusively rewarding leadership aspirations as career goals.

The right environment and the approach to strengthening strengths can not only offer employees autonomy but also satisfy another basic need: the feeling of appreciation. Moreover, employees who work autonomously also automatically think more entrepreneurially—and thus in the long term.

Possible questions here could be: Do our structures allow for autonomy? What is missing for employees to develop autonomously? What strengths do we need for which tasks?

4.4 Re-defining Success

One of the major problems of the economy in relation to sustainability is the focus on profit maximization. Goals and strategies are set up according to growth potential and profit opportunities, higher, faster, further. But: continuous growth is not possible without taking into account the potential finite nature of resources. Therefore, new benchmarks are needed to measure success.

The reality is that companies also want/need to make money in the twenty-first century. But there are now many options for doing business differently. One of them is the introduction of a different kind of controlling. Here, the Balanced Scorecard developed by Robert Kaplan and David Norton in the 1990s offers the possibility to make other factors besides profit measurable. Instead of the usual financial key figures, goals such as employee satisfaction and CO_2 emissions are added. Typically, success in a Balanced Scorecard is determined by four areas: Financial, internal processes, customers, and learning & development.

For those who want to go a step further, the concept of the Economy for the Common Good (ECG) is recommended. The ECG measures its balance with a point system, an alternative to the balance in the classic economy, and is based on four pillars: human dignity, solidarity and justice, environmental sustainability, and transparency and co-determination. 2000 companies from various sectors are already ECG-certified, the most prominent of which is probably the clothing brand Vaude.[7]

Questions on this could be: What prevents us from introducing a different measurability? How can we make our (sustainability) goals measurable? Green field approach: Why can't our company introduce the model of the Economy for the Common Good?

5 Summary and Outlook

In summary, an optimistic outlook can be attempted through a paradigm shift: to win the "War for Talents" and to still exist as a company in 20, 30, 40 years, companies must clearly position themselves. They must adopt a stance in which they act not out of scarcity, but out of abundance. In which they work towards sustainability not out of prohibitions and renunciations, but out of conviction. Such a company is a beacon in the thicket of the complex world. And who wouldn't want to be a beacon?

References

© TED Conferences: Titel Dan Pink über die überraschende Wissenschaft der Motivation (2009), https://www.ted.com/talks/dan_pink_the_puzzle_of_motivation?language=de (abgerufen am 30.11.2022)

Deutscher Bundestag, Bericht der Enquete-Kommission, Drucksache 12/8260 (1994)

[7] Economy for the Common Good Germany e. V.: Balanced companies and organizations (2022).

Burkert, Uwe: Nachhaltigkeit lohnt sich – Gesellschaft und Unternehmen im Wandel., Landesbank Baden-Württemberg, 2018

Schulz von Thun Institut (2017): https://www.schulz-von-thun.de/die-modelle/das-riemannthomann-modell

StepStone und Handelsblatt Research Institut, Nachhaltigkeit als Attraktivitätsfaktor, 2019

Gemeinwohl-Ökonomie Deutschland e. V.: Bilanzierte Unternehmen und Organisationen (2022) https://germany.ecogood.org/tools/gemeinwohl-berichte/ (abgerufen am 30.11.2022)

Strategic CSR Project Management in the Company

Paula Wernecke and Muskaandeep Multani

1 Introduction

CSR holistically deals with corporate responsibility for society.[1] Although it has only been increasingly—sometimes even inflationarily—integrated into corporate language in recent years, the origin of the first conceptualization dates back to the 1930s, when Barnard described the assumption of social responsibility for managers. After numerous scientific disputes, Bowen's 1953 understanding emerged that managers must use their concentration of power for a social contribution.[2]

The EU Commission defines CSR as "the responsibility of companies for their impacts on society".[3] Several crucial aspects are to be noted in this brief definition.

In coherence with the approach referred to by Elkington as Triple-Bottom-Line (TBL), companies must define and pursue not only economic goals but also social and ecological goals.[4] The fields of action thus include both direct effects of corporate action and indirect consequences, ranging from general working conditions to combating child labor to avoiding negative environmental impacts.

[1] *Meyer/Waßmann*, Research Papers on Marketing Strategy, p. 1.

[2] *Meyer/Waßmann*, Research Papers on Marketing Strategy, p. 3.

[3] *EU Commission*, p. 7.

[4] *Elkington* in: Henriques/Richardson, p. 3.

P. Wernecke · M. Multani (✉)
CMS Deutschland, Köln, Germany
e-mail: Muskaan.multani@core.se

P. Wernecke
e-mail: paula.wernecke@cms-hs.com

I. Knappertsbusch and G. Wisskirchen (eds.), *The Future of Work*,
https://doi.org/10.1007/978-3-658-45150-9_46

Furthermore, the term responsibility indicates a certain voluntariness of companies. CSR is not just about meeting legal minimum requirements, but about voluntary commitment to sustainability, defining one's own values and goals in this regard, and thus making a positive contribution to a sustainably acting society.[5] At the same time, there are numerous recognized principles and guidelines such as the ISO standard 26000 on social responsibility, the OECD guidelines, and the ten principles of the United Nations' "Global Compact".[6]

Furthermore, modern CSR understanding does not refer to the sole responsibility of decision-makers in the company, but to the connection to a company's vision and thus the responsibility of all participants.[7] This results in the necessity of multi-stakeholder management for companies.

Finally, these aspects result in the strategic component of CSR. CSR is not a short- or medium-term project. It goes hand in hand with the long-term, future-oriented vision of a company and must be embedded in the corporate strategy for effective implementation. CSR is thus a "strategic management tool" for companies[8] and must be distinguished from non-strategic CSR, where CSR activities do not relate to the business model.[9]

2 Advantages of this Work Organization

2.1 Win-Win Situation

According to Lantos, a key feature of strategic CSR is that both the company and society benefit, thus creating a *win-win* situation.[10] In other words,: the implementation of CSR action fields should not become a *trade-off* for companies with their growth and profit ambitions, but should be united with them and poured into a common strategy. Therefore, CSR is now also seen as a business case in companies, contributing to sustainable competitiveness.[11] Thus, a significant majority of 170 different studies that have examined the return on corporate investments in CSR activities suggest a possible relationship between *Corporate Social Performance (CSP)* and *Corporate Financial Performance (CFP)*.[12] However, there is still no evidence for a universal business case.[13]

---

[5] *Heblich/Gold*, p. 1.

[6] *EU Commission*, p. 8.

[7] *Schwerk,* p. 331.

[8] *Schwerk,* p. 331.

[9] *Meyer/Waßmann*, Research Papers on Marketing Strategy, p. 13.

[10] *Meyer/Waßmann*, Research Papers on Marketing Strategy, p. 13.

[11] *Meyer/Waßmann,* Research Papers on Marketing Strategy, p. 1.

[12] *Will/Hielscher,* Administrative Sciences, p. 220.

[13] *Schwerk,* p. 339.

Nevertheless, not only the business component, but the interplay of economic, ecological, and social benefits is crucial.[14] The *win-win* potential can thus be unfolded and used in the various categories and areas of a company. Examples include:

- Risk management: effective CSR monitoring can identify risks with financial consequences early on and initiate preventive measures that can minimize risks and increase profit margins in the medium and long term.
- Human Resources Management: CSR activities that promote the social component have an impact on the employer-employee relationship and can increase the attractiveness of a company and employee retention, thus bringing significant advantages in recruiting.[15]

From this perspective, CSR focuses on creating value for all participants and those affected, not the pursuit of selfish goals.

At the same time, however, companies are also under a certain pressure to take CSR measures in order to remain competitive. CSR activities that lead to a *win-win* are vital for companies because the alternative scenario can be a *lose-lose* scenario in the long term, not a *win-lose* scenario.

At the same time, CSR also drives innovation within the company. Thus, by strategically embedding CSR activities in their own value chain, innovative products, services, and processes can be identified and implemented.[16]

2.2 Strategic CSR Management as Risk Management

Even though risk management is already part of corporate governance and regulatory requirements are increasing at the same time, CSR management enables the identification and prevention of medium and long-term previously unconsidered risks resulting from ecological and social trends. Ecological trends include risks from energy or material supply, while personnel risks as a result of demographic change are among the social trends.[17] In general, CSR management aims to reduce risks in various areas such as in the operational process or in investments.[18] The implementation and execution of supplier audits, for example, are measures to reduce risk in operational processes by auditing suppliers for economic, ecological, and social minimum criteria in the audit.

---

[14] *Williams/Preston,* Journal of Corporate Strategy and Social Responsibility, p. 2.

[15] *Will/Hielscher,* Administrative Sciences, pp. 237 f.

[16] *Knoppe,* p. 18.

[17] *Loew/Clausen/Rohde,* pp. 62 ff.

[18] *Loew/Clausen/Rohde,* pp. 78 f.

3 Challenges of this Work Organization

3.1 Multi-Stakeholder Management

Strategic CSR management relies on the opinions and impulses of many, not just individual decision-makers in the company. In theory and practice, there are two models for answering corporate governance questions: the *Shareholder* model and the *Stakeholder* model.[19]

As the term shareholder model suggests, only the interests of the shareholders are taken into account here. The stakeholder model, on the other hand, pursues the approach of incorporating the interests of various stakeholders into a corporate decision by reconciling the different (often competing) interests.[20] Stakeholders of a company include all those who have a legitimate interest in the company: shareholders, senior positions and employees, suppliers, contract partners, representatives of local organizations, and many more. Accordingly, two central challenges for companies arise from multi-stakeholder management.[21]

Firstly, the stakeholders and their interests need to be identified. In the second step, companies face the mammoth task of reconciling the sometimes competing interests in order to implement CSR activities. While shareholders, for example, generally strive for short-term financial success,[22] employees prioritize better working conditions, such as better pay or a better working atmosphere. Frameworks such as ISO 26000 serve as a guide for a professional balance of these interests and for the design area of the respective stakeholders.

3.2 Key Performance Indicators

You cannot manage what you do not measure. The question of making CSR measurable has occupied science and practice as long as the topic of CSR itself.[23]

There is a large number of institutions, rating agencies, standards (e.g., ISO 14000 or ISO 26000), quality seals and certifications that provide guidance on how a company's CSR commitment can be measured. In the end, key figures and KPIs are custom work, depending on and in line with the topics identified as essential within the CSR strategy. They must be defined and operationalized individually.

[19] *Crifo/Rebérioux*, Journal of Governance and Regulation, p. 15.

[20] *O'Riordan/Fairbrass*, Journal of Business Ethics, p. 123.

[21] *O'Riordan/Fairbrass*, Journal of Business Ethics, p. 123.

[22] *Crifo/Rebérioux*, Journal of Governance and Regulation, p. 15.

[23] *Schwerk*, p. 339.

4 Solutions and Practical Tips

4.1 Step 1: Definition of the Company Vision and Values

The ideal-typical process of CSR management consists in theory of six steps, which partly interlock and must be taken in parallel.

Since the strategic integration of CSR is to be combined with the corporate strategy, the first step of the process is to define the vision, mission, corporate values, and goals. Almost every company has established a long-term vision, which is pursued, for example, under the name "Vision 2030". This is crucial for the later establishment of the CSR strategy, as it defines the success factors and shows which action fields are core topics for the company.[24]

4.2 Step 2: Materiality Analysis: Social Issues and Stakeholders

The second step involves a so-called materiality analysis, which aims to determine the priorities for CSR management by identifying the significant opportunities and risks of sustainability issues for a company, taking into account the interests of stakeholders, industry specifics, and the purpose of the business.[25] This makes it clear where a company can have a positive impact and where it must avoid negative impact. For example, the expectations and prioritization of the different stakeholders can be defined by identifying the core topics and challenges (*social issues*) through interviews.[26]

4.3 Step 3: Inventory Analysis of CSR Activities

In the third step, it is necessary to analyze what a company is already doing in the area of CSR. This creates a clear picture of the current situation in order to then derive measures for achieving the target situation.[27] It is crucial to check all areas of the company for *social issues*.

4.4 Step 4: Formulation of the CSR Strategy and Areas of Action

The core task in the fourth step is to define the CSR strategy in order to move from the current to the desired state. Companies define guidelines and policies

[24] *Meyer/Waßmann*, Research Papers on Marketing Strategy, p. 38.

[25] *Sawczyn-Müller/Krohn* in: Wagner/Roschker/Moutchnik, p. 7.

[26] *Schwerk*, p. 337.

[27] *Schwerk*, p. 337.

here. Integration into existing overarching guidelines is also conceivable.[28] In any case, responsibilities in guidelines and policies must already be formulated as part of the strategy. Furthermore, a resource allocation must take place, which shows any investment costs and personnel requirements to work on the identified areas of action. Regardless of where in the company the CSR strategy is defined, it is crucial that it complements the corporate strategy and corporate development and presents a coherent picture with it.

4.5 Step 5: Implementation and Communication of CSR Activities

The fifth step of the CSR process finally involves implementation. The measures defined for the different CSR areas of action are to be implemented in the company and the employees are to be trained accordingly. Two prerequisites must be met for successful implementation. First, a project plan is needed that defines the temporal progress. Under all circumstances, initiating too many measures at once, which lead to frustration and overwhelm, must be avoided. Second, clear responsibilities for the topics are needed. Even if there is a central CSR department in the company, those responsible for the individual areas of action for the respective area must still be defined to ensure *accountability*.

4.6 Step 6: Measurement and Reporting

The final step is to measure CSR activities on a regular basis to determine effectiveness, align with set goals, and if necessary, return to one of the previous steps. As outlined in the challenges to the metrics, defining numbers for the analysis of all relevant aspects—general as well as company-specific—is complex. Before setting up the metrics for controlling, companies must ask themselves why meaningful numbers are needed. The following questions serve as points of reference:

- Are the right measures being used and are they having their desired effect?
- What impact do CSR activities have on financial metrics and the overall success of the company?
- Do CSR activities meet the different expectations of stakeholders and can they be justified to them?
- How does the company compare with its CSR activities to competitors?
- What metrics can be used to communicate the successes of CSR management externally?[29]

[28] *Clausen/Loew*, p. 67.

[29] *Schwerk*, p. 340.

Based on these questions and the goals embedded in the CSR strategy, individual core areas must be identified and specific metrics set up for each area. For example, for the environmental area, measuring the energy saved from energy-saving measures may be relevant, or for the area of social responsibility, measuring the time invested in social projects. In the end, clear tasks and roles must be assigned so that the collected data is updated and tracked at a healthy interval.

5 Summary and Outlook

CSR has managed to move from the PR department to the C-level and work its way up to being part of the corporate strategy.[30] However, too many companies are still orienting themselves towards the legal minimum requirements and see their CSR commitment fulfilled by the preparation of the sustainability report. This can hardly be realized without CSR management. In the medium and long term, companies risk their sustainable development and competitiveness. By introducing strategic CSR management, companies establish CSR as a core component of their corporate culture and vision. For this, they must define a clear CSR responsibility in the company and set up a CSR strategy that, like the corporate vision, is long-term oriented.

References

Clausen, Jens/Loew, Jens, CSR und Innovation: Literaturstudie und Befragung, Februar 2009, abrufbar unter: https://www.4sustainability.de/wp-content/uploads/2021/06/Clausen-Loew_CSR-und-Innovation-LiteraturstudieundBefragung.pdf (abgerufen am 31.10.2022).

Elkington, John, Enter the Triple Bottom Line. In: Henriques. A. and Richardson, J., Eds., The Triple Bottom Line, Does It All Add up? Assessing the Sustainability of Business and CSR, Earths can Publications Ltd., London 2004, S. 1–16.

Europäische Kommission, Eine neue EU-Strategie (2011–14) für die soziale Verantwortung der Unternehmen (CSR), 25.10.2011, abrufbar unter: https://eur-lex.europa.eu/legal-content/DE/TXT/PDF/?uri=CELEX:52011DC0681&from=DE, (abgerufen am 31.10.2022).

Heblich, Stephan/Gold, Robert, Corporate Social Responsibility: Eine Win-Win Strategie für Unternehmen und Regionen, Januar 2008, abrufbar unter: https://www.researchgate.net/publication/42241763_Corporate_Social_Responsibility_eine_win-win_Strategie_fur_Unternehmen_und_Regionen (abgerufen am 31.10.2022).

Knoppe, Marc, CSR im Retail Management – Wertschöpfung oder Marketing-Gag?. In: Knoppe, Marc (Hrsg.) CSR und Retail Management: Gesellschaftliche Verantwortung als zukünftiger Erfolgsfaktor im Handel, Springer, Berlin 2015, S. 9–23.

Loew, Thomas/Clausen, Jens/Rohde, Friederike, CSR und Risikomanagement: Gesetzliches und freiwilliges Risikomanagement von Corporate Social Responsibility, abrufbar unter: https://www.4sustainability.de/wp-content/uploads/2021/06/Loew-Clausen-Rohde_CSR_und_Risikomanagement_2011.pdf (abgerufen am: 31.10.2022).

[30] *Elkington* in: Henriques/Richardson, p. 7.

Meyer, Margit/Waßmann, Jan, Strategische Corporate Social Responsibility. Konzeptionelle Entwicklung und Implementierung in der Praxis am Beispiel „dm-drogie markt“, Research Papers on Marketing Strategy 2011, S. 1–48.

O'Riordan, Linda/Fairbrass, Jenny, Managing CSR Stakeholder Engagement: A New Conceptual Framework, Journal of Business Ethics 2014, S. 121–145.

Schwerk, Anja, Strategische Einbettung von CSR in das Unternehmen. In: Schneider, Andreas (Hrsg.), Corporate Social Responsibility: Verantwortungsvolle Unternehmensführung in Theorie und Praxis, Springer Berlin 2012, S. 331–356.

Will, Matthias/Hielscher, Stefan, How do Companies Invest in Corporate Social Responsibility? An Ordonomic Contribution for Empirical CSR Research, Administrative Sciences 2014, S. 219–241.

Williams, Sarah/Preston, Diane, Working with values: an alternative approach to win-win, Journal of Corporate Strategy and Social Responsibility 2018, S. 302–319.

Mory, Linda, Dimensionen der internen CSR und dessen Wirkung: Ein empirisches Erklärungsmodell. In: Wagner, R., Roschker, N., Moutchnik, A. (eds) CSR und Interne Kommunikation. Management-Reihe Corporate Social Responsibility. Springer Gabler, Berlin, Heidelberg 2017.

Sawczyn-Müller, Angelika/Krohn, Caroline, Glaubwürdigkeit und Transparenz in der CSR-Kommunikation. In: Wagner, R., Roschker, N., Moutchnik, A. (eds) CSR und Interne Kommunikation. Management-Reihe Corporate Social Responsibility. Springer Gabler, Berlin, Heidelberg 2017.

Crifo, Patricia/Rebérioux, Antoine, Corporate Governance and Corporate Social Responsibility: A Typology of OECD Countries, Journal of Governance and Regulation 2016, Volume 5, Issue 2, S. 14–27.

ESG Components in Variable Compensation

Laura Matarrelli

1 Introduction

The abbreviation "ESG" (Environmental Social Governance) refers to a bundle of subject areas where sustainability plays a role in the company and thus forms part of its "Corporate Social Responsibility" (CSR). This is driven by the conviction that sustainability also lies in the responsibility of the economy and has therefore found its way into legal requirements and provisions in many places.

1.1 ESG Goals in Everyday Business

With the increasing demands for social and sustainably responsible corporate governance, companies of all sectors are currently confronted and therefore have to ask themselves how they can increase their sustainability balance. At the same time, the increased energy costs also give reason to promote sustainable initiatives. However, this can and will only succeed if these goals also reach the minds of the employees and internal decision-makers. One approach is therefore to start directly with the remuneration of employees and management and to take into account sustainability-related targets or benefits in variable remuneration. ESG-related criteria can, for example, be included in the agreed or company-imposed targets (so-called Key Performance Indicators, KPIs), the achievement of which influences the amount of short and/or long-term variable remuneration (Short Term Incentives, STI/Long Term Incentives, LTI).

L. Matarrelli (✉)
CMS Deutschland, Frankfurt am Main, Germany
e-mail: laura.matarrelli@cms-hs.com

I. Knappertsbusch and G. Wisskirchen (eds.), *The Future of Work*,
https://doi.org/10.1007/978-3-658-45150-9_47

Possible targets from the "Environment" area include, for example, the reduction of CO2 emissions, the improvement of energy efficiency, the proportion of renewable energies, the preservation of biodiversity or the reduction of waste. Important topics in the "Social" area can be employee satisfaction and development, diversity, inclusion, occupational safety or customer satisfaction. In contrast, in the "Governance/Corporate Governance" area, targets in relation to compliance, such as combating corruption and bribery, risk management, the implementation of whistleblower programs and sustainable supply chains play a role. The topics and targets are diverse and can have different focuses and structuring in every company and every sector.[1]

1.2 Legal and Economic Requirements

Although the consideration of such criteria in remuneration is not legally mandatory in many industries, recent developments in stock corporation law and increasingly strict regulatory and legislative requirements give a hint that they are taken seriously by political decision-makers at both national and European level. Thus, section 87 para. 1 s. 2 AktG was amended in the context of the law implementing the second shareholder rights directive (ARUG II) to the effect that the remuneration structure for board members of listed companies is to be aligned with a "*sustainable and long-term development of the company*". An identical formulation can also be found in the German Corporate Governance Code (DCGK; Principle 24 para. 3). This is predominantly understood to mean that the supervisory board must also take ESG-related aspects into account when determining remuneration.[2] These requirements have led to the fact that a large part of listed companies have incorporated ESG goals into the variable remuneration of board members, but also of subordinate hierarchy levels. According to an evaluation, 80% of DAX-40 companies currently have ESG criteria anchored in their bonus system as part of their remuneration systems, and ESG criteria are part of the long-term variable remuneration for 45% of the named companies.[3]

Additional requirements exist in particularly regulated industries, such as the financial market industry. Thus, financial market participants and financial advisors are obliged under Art. 5 of the EU Disclosure Regulation (VO 2019/2088/EU) to disclose on their homepage to what extent their remuneration policy is in line with the inclusion of ESG risks, even though the disclosure does not yet involve a specific requirement regarding the agreement of ESG targets in remuneration.

[1] See also Arnold/Herzberg/Zeh, AG 2021, p. 141 (143).

[2] Mückl, ArbRAktuell 2022, p. 303 (305); Arnold/Herzberg/Zeh, AG 2021, p. 141 (141); see also Reinbach, Capital online.

[3] Schmelter, ESG in Executive Compensation.

But supervisory authorities and legislators have also become active elsewhere. For example, the guidelines of the European Banking Authority for a sound remuneration policy of July 2, 2021,[4] the European Corporate Sustainability Due Diligence Directive[5] or the Corporate Sustainability Reporting Directive[6] lead to a significantly larger number of companies being confronted with reporting obligations on sustainability-related circumstances.[7] In addition, the much-discussed Supply Chain Due Diligence Act (LkSG), which came into force on January 1, 2023, provides for companies to operate comprehensive sustainability and environmental management.[8]

Furthermore, sufficient ESG compliance plays an increasing role for investors and proxy advisors as well as many other stakeholders (e.g. customers or suppliers). Investors expect, among other things, that ESG criteria have a significant influence on remuneration, are quantifiable, measurable and company-specific.[9] Customers are also increasingly conscious in their purchasing and avoid products with a negative social or ecological image. It is therefore in the companies' own interest to devote themselves to this matter and find ways to effectively (and not just on paper) manifest the topic of "ESG" in the corporate culture.

2 Advantages of ESG Remuneration Components

The benefits of incentivizing ESG goals for employees are clear. ESG-related issues, which the company has identified as relevant, become part of the employees' consciousness and play an increased role in everyday work when employees are also measured against them. Management and executives are motivated to align their strategies and decisions with the set goals, and affected employees feel compelled to ask themselves, for example, what impact their actions have on the environment in their daily work routine.

A management in which ESG goals may already be part of variable remuneration due to legal requirements can pursue the most progressive and ESG-compliant strategies, but these will only become a reality in the company when the other hierarchical levels also align themselves with them and implement them in day-to-day business. Against this background, the goals for different hierarchical levels should be linked as much as possible and be permeable in order to bring

[4] EBA Guidelines on sound remuneration policies under Directive 2013/36/EU.

[5] Directive (EU) 2024/1760 of the European Parliament and of the Council of 13 June 2024 on corporate sustainability due diligence and amending Directive (EU) 2019/1937 and Regulation (EU) 2023/2859.

[6] Directive (EU) 2022/2464 of the European Parliament and of the Council of 14 December 2022 amending Regulation (EU) No 537/2014, Directive 2004/109/EC, Directive 2006/43/EC and Directive 2013/34/EU, as regards corporate sustainability reporting.

[7] See also: Döring/Mayer, DB 2022, p. 31 (31).

[8] See Reinbach, Capital online.

[9] Schmelter, ESG in Executive Compensation.

about effective implementation. The company can then "claim" this effectiveness in implementing a corporate sustainability strategy and use it for advertising purposes. For example, the agreement of environment-related remuneration targets for employees who bear responsibility along the supply chain can be a measure to document compliance with the obligation to establish a risk management system according to the LkSG.[10]

Works councils present in the company, which must be involved in the introduction and design of variable remuneration systems, for example within the framework of their co-determination rights arising from section 87 para. 1 no. 10 BetrVG, are often easily convinced by the implementation of ESG components in compensation. This is particularly the case when the goals can be sensibly and comprehensibly derived from the company's sustainability strategy and the pursued goals appear achievable. The implementation of ESG goals in compensation also coincides with the general task of the works council to promote measures for operational environmental protection.[11]

3 Challenges of this Form of Compensation

Despite the aforementioned advantages and arguments for the introduction of ESG-related remuneration components, the concrete implementation does not lead to enthusiastic reactions in many companies. The abbreviation "ESG" and the topics hidden behind it are often perceived as very abstract by employers. "*What does this have to do with our company?*" "*Are these really problems that affect us?*" Such or similar lines of thought are often behind the perceived rejection and lack of creativity in implementation.

At the same time, the introduction and handling of ESG-related remuneration components pose some challenges. A topic typically perceived as difficult is the measurability of target achievement for ESG goals, which are often non-financial in nature. Employees sometimes only have a vague idea of what is specifically expected of them. At the same time, the determination of target achievement at the end of the performance period is then perceived as arbitrary when, in the absence of concrete points of reference, only a "*achieved*"/"*not achieved*" is ticked off in the result.

In addition, acceptance among the affected employees plays a crucial role. The introduction of ESG-related remuneration components appears particularly challenging when the individual feels that they have no influence on the achievement of the goal, for example because company-wide target sizes are used as a benchmark. The feeling of being measured against something that one cannot significantly improve through one's own performance can reduce motivation among

[10] Mückl, ArbRAktuell 2022, p. 303 (305); see also Reinbach, Capital online.

[11] See also Reinbach, Capital online.

those affected. The same applies to the formulation of completely utopian targets, which are taken from the company strategy without further reflection, but are presumably not achievable.

It is precisely at these or comparable points that works councils often criticize, who in this context have the interests of the employees in mind. A quick implementation of compensation concepts can fail or become very controversial against this background.

4 Solutions and Practical Tips

But how can one meaningfully and solution-orientedly meet the aforementioned challenges?

4.1 Good Preparation is "Half the Battle"

One of the most important points, in my view, is to take sufficient time for the introduction and implementation of ESG-related remuneration components and to carefully identify, with the involvement of relevant decision-makers, those topics where ESG issues play a role for the company. It is essential that people who are familiar with the operational business are involved in the decision-making process in order to establish a close connection to the field of activity of the affected employees and the company's products. For example, if ESG-related targets for short- or long-term variable remuneration are to be identified, these can have a completely different focus in the service industry than in companies that focus on the production of goods. Depending on the industry and business model, it may be advisable to focus on just one ESG target or to set several targets from the various ESG areas.

In order to anchor ESG targets at all noticeably in variable remuneration, they should make up a relevant percentage of the targets to be achieved. Recommendations from the area of compensation for board members provide a point of orientation and assume a weighting of ESG targets of 20-30%. Alternatively, there is the possibility of implementing an "ESG factor" in the sense of an additional multiplier in the calculation of variable remuneration.[12]

Since target agreements or unilateral target specifications are usually concluded/determined annually by the respective line manager of the entitled employee, it is necessary to provide the managers with the necessary know-how. They should not only be familiarized with the system of target-oriented compensation, but they should also be given a pool of possible company-specific subject areas from which the relevant targets can be derived. This can prevent individual

[12] See also: Döring/Mayer, DB 2022, p. 31 (32).

implementation from faltering and ultimately only abstract targets being agreed with the employees due to lack of knowledge or lack of creativity.

4.2 Measurability Creates Trust

In addition, it should be the goal of every company that wants to anchor ESG-oriented targets in compensation, that the fulfillment of the identified targets is also sufficiently measurable and quantifiable. The benchmarks for the degree of target achievement should ideally already be established when the targets are agreed upon and included in the target agreement (or the unilateral target specification).

This is of course easiest when the target specification is based on numbers (e.g. the proportion of electric vehicles in the responsible turnover or the proportion of sustainable funds in the portfolio). However, for a large number of targets, it is not or not immediately possible to put them into numbers. In these cases, the parties should agree on a way to make the achievement of targets measurable for themselves.

For this purpose, concrete reference points can be agreed upon, such as the number of completed projects in an ESG-relevant area or for a manager with personnel responsibility the employer rating on a specific job portal or the turnover rate in the team. Another alternative is the conduct of (anonymous) employee or customer surveys, the results of which are used as an indicator for the achievement of certain targets (e.g. employee or customer satisfaction, promotion of diversity in the team, etc.). In any case, the situation should be avoided where the assessment of target achievement depends solely on the discretion of the respective manager (unless this is desired for other reasons in individual cases). Otherwise, the desired acceptance of corresponding targets and their influence on variable remuneration will not be achieved among employees. In addition, intransparent target specifications or unclear measurability of target achievement can also have legal disadvantages for the employer and in the worst case lead to a 100% target achievement being legally assumed in the event of a legal dispute.

4.3 No "One Fits All" Solutions

Of course, the consideration of ESG targets in the manner outlined above is not sensible for all employee groups and hierarchy levels. It is particularly suitable for organs and employees in management positions below the board/management level, but also for employees in areas such as HR, IT and Sales. In many other areas, it is not common to pay variable target-dependent remuneration in addition to the fixed salary.

In addition, employees at lower hierarchy levels regularly lack sufficient influence on the achievement of ESG goals, so that an agreement of corresponding targets in the compensation context is little purposeful. For tariff employees in tariff-bound companies, there is the additional difficulty that changes to the compensation structure require a regulation with the union, unless it is a voluntary, above-tariff benefit of the employer.[13]

Nevertheless, employees in these areas do not have to be completely left out when incentivizing ESG goals. Possible are, for example, bonuses for participation in ESG training, the implementation of an energy saving project, the assumption of a mentorship or involvement in a social or environmental protection project. In the tariff area, this can be offered in the form of an additional bonus, which as an additional voluntary benefit does not conflict with the mandatory applicable tariff provisions.[14]

5 Summary and Outlook

It cannot be denied that the topic of ESG is gaining increasing importance in political and societal discussions. Although the strict stock corporation and regulatory requirements do not apply to all companies, it is essential for market participants of all sectors to face the new requirements and find strategies for integrating ESG goals into corporate reality. Against the backdrop of the numerous legal changes in recent months, it is expected that this trend will continue and the already existing corporate obligations will be further tightened or extended to more companies and sectors.

If the company decides to consider ESG components in the variable remuneration of its employees, the solution approaches presented above should be included in the considerations. It is advisable to define measurable targets tailored to the respective company, which lead to acceptance among the employees. If employees are motivated to achieve ESG-related goals, this can promote the company's sustainability strategy and better meet the expectations of the public, investors, and stakeholders.

References

Arnold, Christian/Herzberg, Julia/Zeh, Ricarda, „Vorstandsvergütung und Nachhaltigkeit“, AG 2021, pp. 141–148.

Döring, René/Mayer, Marius, „Environment – Social – Governance 2022 : ESG-Vergütungskomponenten in Arbeitsverhältnissen“, DB 2022, pp. 31–32.

Mückl, Patrick, „CSR, ESG und Abeitsrecht – Ein Überblick“, ArbRAktuell 2022, pp. 303–306.

Reinbach, Hubertus, „Warum sich Klimaschutz auch beim Gehalt auszahlen sollte“ in: Capital online, https://www.capital.de/karriere/warum-sich-klimaschutz-fuer-arbeitnehmer-beim-gehalt-auszahlen-sollte-32838402.html (abgerufen am 11.12.2022).

Stephanie Schmelter, „ESG in der Vorstandsvergütung“, https://www.wtwco.com/de-DE/Insights/2022/06/esg-in-der-vorstandsverguetung (abgerufen am 11.12.2022).

[13] See Döring/Mayer, DB 2022, p. 31 (31).

[14] So also Döring/Mayer, DB 2022, p. 31 (32).

Innovative Approach to Skills Shortage—With Solutions from Sustainable HR Management

Dina Barbian and Kerstin Knabenbauer

1 Introduction

1.1 Problem Statement

The shortage of skilled workers has been a concern for the German economy for decades and has intensified in recent years. According to DIHK (2022) and Hickmann and Koneberg (2022), every second company in Germany is already complaining about a shortage of skilled workers. Professions in the fields of social work, education, and care are particularly affected. There is also a lack of personnel in the crafts and among IT experts (see Fig. 1).

It is noteworthy that professions that are either predominantly male or predominantly female are particularly affected (KOFA 2019). Female-typical bottleneck professions are often societal services. Male-typical bottleneck professions, on the other hand, predominantly belong to the manufacturing sector.

Hickmann and Koneberg (2022) cite the demographic change in Germany as the main cause. One in five citizens in Germany is over 65 years old. In addition, Germany has a very low birth rate (Federal Statistical Office (Destatis) 2022). Approximately 60% of the work is done by less qualified people who can be replaced by digitization and automation. About 20% of employees are dissatisfied

D. Barbian (✉) · K. Knabenbauer
eco2050 Institut für Nachhaltigkeit – Institute for Sustainability GmbH, Nürnberg, Germany
e-mail: barbian@eco2050.de

K. Knabenbauer
e-mail: knabenbauer@eco2050.de

I. Knappertsbusch and G. Wisskirchen (eds.), *The Future of Work*,
https://doi.org/10.1007/978-3-658-45150-9_48

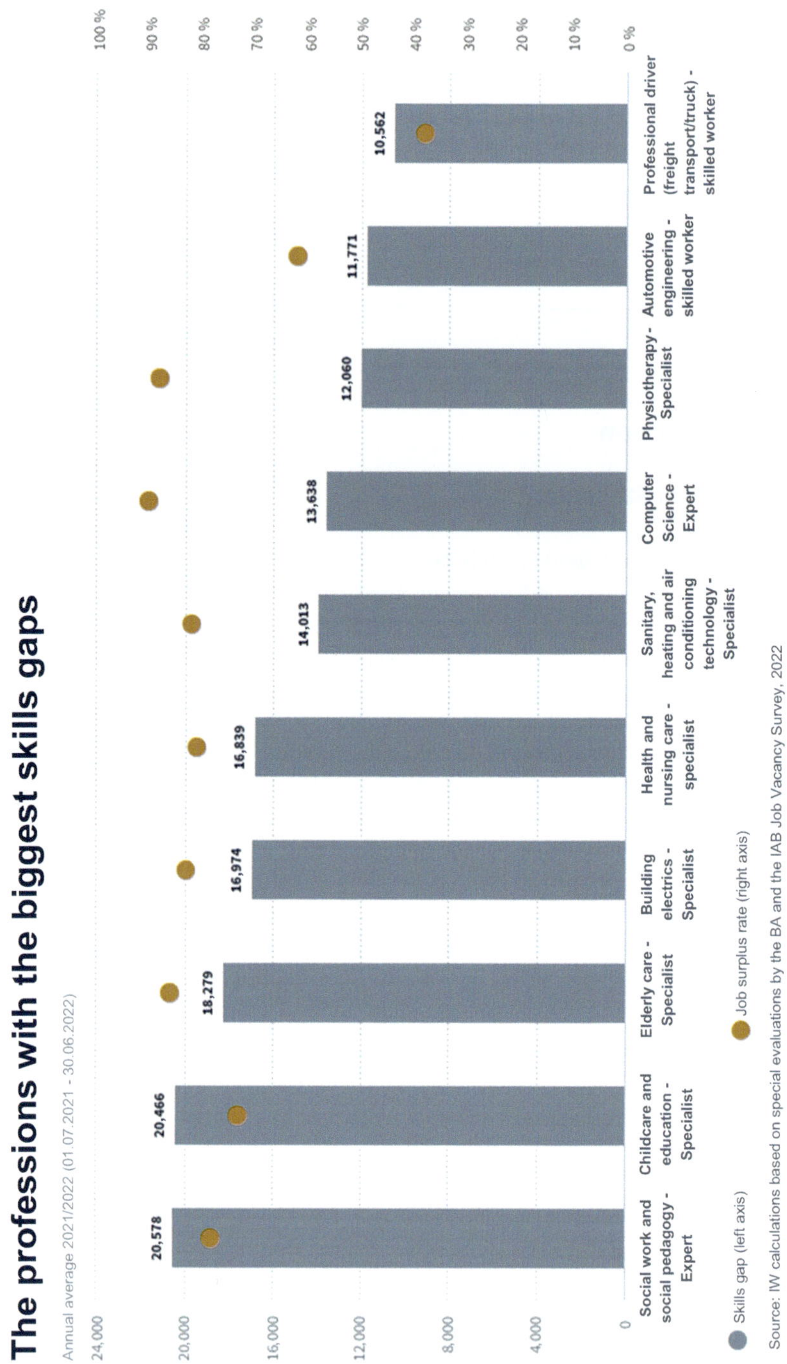

Fig. 1 Professions with a predominant shortage of skilled workers

with their job, increasing the likelihood of quitting. In a study (Raschka 2019), the most common reasons for quitting were not only dissatisfaction with salary (39.7%), but also a poor working environment (37.4%), unsuitable corporate culture (27.7%), lack of further training opportunities (25.2%), and a lack of work-life balance (25.1%). Thus, the shortage of skilled workers in Germany has both substantive and structural causes.

1.2 Sustainable Human Resource Management

The term "Sustainable Human Resource Management" (Sustainable HRM) has only established itself as a scientific discipline in the last 10 years. The contributions to the field include the study by Kurz et al. (2017) and the article by Maurer and Müller-Camen (2016). The latter refer to Cohen et al. (2010) and Ehnert and Harry (2012) in developing a definition. Accordingly, human resource management should not only have economic, but also ecological and social goals, reflecting the triad of sustainability (Economy + Ecology + Social) (Barbian 2001). Sustainable HRM creates skills, motivation, and trust among employees, and aims for the long-term health of the company's internal and external stakeholders (Cohen et al. 2010). According to this definition, health management, personnel development, and equality lead to sustainable human resource management.

It is also useful to consider the 17 Sustainable Development Goals (SDGs) of the United Nations (see Fig. 2). These were adopted at a UN General Assembly in 2015 and apply to all countries. The UN goals relevant to sustainable human resource management are "Good Health and Well-being" (SDG 3), "Quality Education" (SDG 4), "Gender Equality" (SDG 5), and "Decent Work and Economic Growth" (SDG 8).

1.3 Fields of Work of Sustainable Human Resource Management

Four fields of work emerge for sustainable human resource management (sustainable HRM, NHRM). Figure 3 shows the four areas in an NHRM matrix. The chapter "When digital meets demographic change - What opportunities and risks does digital transformation pose in a shrinking and aging workforce?" goes into more detail on the four fields of work.

Fig. 2 17 Sustainable Development Goals of the United Nations

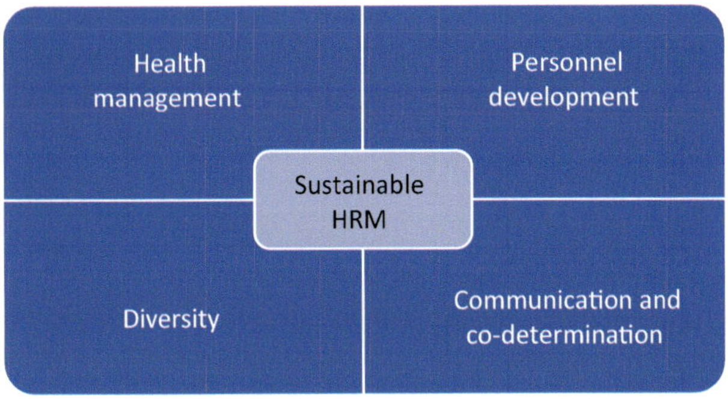

Fig. 3 The NHRM Matrix. (© eco2050 Institute for Sustainability)

2 Advantages of Sustainable Human Resource Management

The introduction of sustainable human resource management in companies is one way to contain the shortage of skilled workers in the long term. Those who want to be successful in business need the right employees who are capable of facing new challenges in the market. In addition to learned technical skills, transversal competencies play a major role. Transversal competencies include flexibility, adaptability, empathy, negotiation skills. These are usually not learned during (academic) education, but are part of learning processes in leisure activities or in extracurricular educational measures (KeyStart2Work n.d.). The successful assessment of transversal competencies serves as the basis for the selection and development of employees. There are now various synonyms for transversal competencies. According to Scharnhorst (2021), these are: key competencies, life skills, essential skills, twenty-first century skills, etc.

In addition to transversal competencies, it is also about reaching people who bring competencies, but are otherwise sorted out in usual application processes for various reasons. Often these people do not even appear in the labor markets. It is important to identify these hidden resources and integrate them into companies with suitable measures. Section 4.1.2 will go into more detail on this.

3 Challenges in Relation to Sustainable Human Resource Management

When implementing sustainable human resource management, the question arises as to how potential employees can be reached in the labor market who do not appear in the recruitment process? Fuller et al. (2021) conclude that sustainable human resource management enables the employer to find and win the hidden resources in the labor market for the company. The challenge here is how companies will succeed in establishing such a resource-oriented approach in the future.

4 Solutions and Practical Tips

The solutions include, among other things, the four fields of work mentioned in Sect. 1.3, which will be explained in the following. It is also important to adapt the recruitment process in the company.

4.1 Fields of Work in NHRM

4.1.1 Health Management

According to the Federal Ministry of Health (2011), occupational health management includes, among other things, a healthy diet, exercise, fitness offers, and courses for coping with stress situations. However, these measures only have a short-term effect on employee motivation. These measures only delay the natural decline in performance by three to four years (Ilmarinen and Tuomi 2004). A greater effect is only achieved when measures to improve working conditions are implemented in addition to health promotion. These include, among other things, corporate culture, leadership behavior, and ergonomic workplace design.

4.1.2 Diversity

According to KOFA (2019), diversity management describes "a holistic concept for profitable handling of personnel and cultural diversity in companies". This means that employees "can differ in terms of age, origin, nationality, gender, disabilities, health status, religion and worldview, sexual orientation, experiences, and numerous other characteristics".

An analysis by McKinsey (2020) shows that companies that take diversity seriously are more likely to be profitable. Heterogeneous teams perform better in the long term and deliver better results than homogeneous teams. Therefore, it is important to further strengthen the promotion of diversity among the competencies of the management and the executive board.

This includes identifying the hidden resources in society and integrating them profitably into companies. Table 1 provides a list of these groups of people.

4.1.3 Personnel Development

Successful personnel development is achieved by promoting competencies. Especially in today's fast-paced times, when changing competencies are in demand, not every employee in a company can bring the required competencies. Employers must also expect to get applicants who do not meet all the requirements for positions to be filled. Therefore, it is all the more important to pay attention to transversal competencies already at the time of hiring. The winners in the shortage of skilled workers are thus employers who are able to recruit employees with the

Table 1 Groups of Hidden Resources (Fuller et al. 2021)

Youths without education
No degree/Academic degree
Physical health problems
Mental problems
Physical disability
Addiction problems
Asylum seekers
Immigrants
Moved with partner
Childcare at home
Care of family members (parents, relatives)
Long-term unemployed
Seniors

transversal competencies required for their corporate strategy. These ensure with suitable training and education concepts that constantly changing requirements on professional competencies can be developed.

4.1.4 Communication and Co-determination

Another important aspect for sustainable personnel management is an open corporate culture that is based on transparency and co-determination. These points are an essential part of the Common Good Matrix (see Fig. 4) of the Economy for the Common Good, an alternative economic model.

COMMON GOOD MATRIX 5.0

VALUE / STAKEHOLDER	HUMAN DIGNITY	SOLIDARITY AND SOCIAL JUSTICE	ENVIRONMENTAL SUSTAINABILITY	TRANSPARENCY AND CO-DETERMINATION
A: SUPPLIERS	**A1** Human dignity in the supply chain	**A2** Solidarity and social justice in the supply chain	**A3** Environmental sustainability in the supply chain	**A4** Transparency and co-determination in the supply chain
B: OWNERS, EQUITY- AND FINANCIAL SERVICE PROVIDERS	**B1** Ethical position in relation to financial resources	**B2** Social position in relation to financial resources	**B3** Use of funds in relation to social and environmental impacts	**B4** Ownership and co-determination
C: EMPLOYEES, INCLUDING CO-WORKING EMPLOYERS	**C1** Human dignity in the workplace and working environment	**C2** Self-determined working arrangements	**C3** Environmentally-friendly behaviour of staff	**C4** Co-determination and transparency within the organisation
D: CUSTOMERS AND OTHER COMPANIES	**D1** Ethical customer relations	**D2** Cooperation and solidarity with other companies	**D3** Impact on the environment of the use and disposal of products and services	**D4** Customer participation and product transparency
E: SOCIAL ENVIRONMENT	**E1** Purpose of products and services and their effects on society	**E2** Contribution to the community	**E3** Reduction of environmental impact	**E4** Social co-determination and transparency

Fig. 4 Common Good Matrix (© Economy for the Common Good (ECG) 2022)

Under C4, co-determination and transparency within the organisation are mentioned. This includes, among other things, how employees can significantly participate in the processes of the company. If this happens to a high degree, they identify more strongly with the company. The likelihood that they will stay in their position increases. As a result, the company remains attractive to the employee.

4.2 Adaptation and Review of the Recruitment Process

In recent years, the application process has been continuously optimised. The latest innovations and technologies facilitate, improve, and accelerate almost every step of the process. However, the risk is that recruitment measures focus too much on stereotypical ideal candidate profiles and that candidates with valuable key competencies are not considered (OECD 2005). In a study by Weichselbaumer (2016), for example, it was found that female migrants wearing headscarves have to apply four times as often as Germans without headscarves to receive an invitation to an interview. Therefore, it is all the more important to adapt recruitment processes and make them non-discriminatory in every respect. Solutions are offered by digital recruitment systems, competency-oriented recruitments, and so-called blind hiring (anonymisation of personal data), which will be explained below.

4.2.1 Digital Recruitment Systems

With the help of automated processes or the use of machine learning, there is an opportunity to find hidden resources in the job market and integrate them into the company. This can be a good alternative to human-based personnel selection, as people are often driven by old habits. Digital recruitment processes in recruiting include, for example, sorting resumes to support executives in finding the most qualified candidate. These systems then sort out candidates who do not bring the required qualifications according to the job description in their resume (Fuller et al. 2021). However, the challenge here is also that digital systems are not programmed in such a way that they adopt "old recruitment patterns" and ultimately do not represent a real solution for finding suitable candidates.

Innovative solutions also include gamification recruitment tools offered via platforms. To determine suitable competencies of candidates, web-based applicant tests, questionnaires, and games are used to identify potential candidates (Landwehr 2020).

4.2.2 Competency-Oriented Recruiting

Another solution approach to finding personnel is competency-oriented recruiting, which deviates from the usual role-specific approach. The focus here is primarily on deciding who is suitable for a position based on transversal competencies. Factors such as education and previous professional experience play a subordinate role.

In the past, companies looked for, for example, a bachelor's degree and the applicant's last job title when hiring employees. However, today it is very easy to acquire and deepen skills outside of work without having a corresponding educational background. Therefore, competency-oriented hiring is a method for acquiring talents for hard-to-fill positions, where it apparently takes particularly long to find suitable candidates.

4.2.3 Blind Hiring

In blind hiring, applications are anonymized. This means refraining from mentioning personal data. The application only contains the qualifications and competencies of an applicant, based on which it is exclusively decided whether the candidate fits into the company and the vacant position. The recruiter should be made as "blind" as possible to prevent unprofessional, prejudiced opinions (Muñoz 2019).

5 Summary and Outlook

The introduction of sustainable human resource management offers great potential to curb the shortage of skilled workers in the company in the long term. The aim is to use the employees available on the labor market and in the company efficiently and sustainably. The authors come to the following conclusions:

1) Technical skills can be learned, but transversal core competencies often cannot.
2) Training and further education measures for technical skills in-house or together with educational partners must be increasingly organized.
3) Sustainability in human resource management means focusing on all four matrix fields (health management, personnel development, diversity, co-determination) both internally and externally.
4) Diverse and heterogeneous teams increase competitiveness if they are well managed, therefore continuous training and coaching for executives are necessary.
5) Existing recruitment processes should be reviewed and possibly adapted to avoid prejudices and old stereotypes.

References

Barbian D (2001) Ökonomie und Sustainable Development – Entwicklung eines Ansatzes zur Umsetzung von Nachhaltigkeit, Aachen

Bundesgesundheitsministerium (2011) Unternehmen unternehmen Gesundheit – Betriebliche Gesundheitsförderung im Fokus der kleinen und mittleren Unternehmen. https://www.bundesgesundheitsministerium.de/fileadmin/Dateien/5_Publikationen/Praevention/Broschueren/Broschuere_Unternehmen_unternehmen_Gesundheit_-_Betriebliche_

Gesundheitsfoerderung_in_kleinen_und_mittleren_Unternehmen.pdf (accessed on 14.10.2022)
Cohen E, Taylor S, Müller-Camen M (2010) HR's role in corporate social responsibility and sustainability. SHRM Foundation, Alexandria
DIHK (Deutscher Industrie- und Handelskammertag) (2022) DIHK-Fachkräftereport 2021 – Personalengpässe beeinträchtigen das Wachstum. https://www.dihk.de/de/themen-und-positionen/fachkraefte/beschaeftigung/fachkraeftereport-2021 (accessed on 01.10.2022)
Ehnert I, Harry W (2012) Recent developments and future prospects on sustainable human resource management: introduction to the special issue. Management Revue 23(3):221–238
Fuller J et al. (2021) Hidden Workers: Untapped Talent. Published by Harvard Business School Project on Managing the Future of Work and Accenture. https://www.hbs.edu/managing-the-future-of-work/Documents/research/hiddenworkers09032021.pdf (accessed on 14.10.2022)
Hickmann H, Koneberg F (2022) Die Berufe mit den aktuell größten Fachkräftelücken. IW-Kurzbericht 67/2022 vom 12.08.2022. https://www.iwkoeln.de/fileadmin/user_upload/Studien/Kurzberichte/PDF/2022/IW-Kurzbericht_2022-Top-Fachkr%C3%A4ftel%C3%BCcken.pdf (accessed on 01.10.2022)
Ilmarinen J, Tuomi K (2004) Past, present and future of work ability. In: Ilmarinen J, Lehtinen S (Eds.): Past, present and future of work ability. Helsinki
KeyStart2Work (oJ) Katalog für Transversale Kompetenzen als Schlüssel für die Beschäftigungsfähigkeit. https://keystart2work.eu/images/docs/o2-catalogue/O2_Katalog_DE.pdf (accessed on 14.10.2022)
KOFA (2019) Fachkräfteengpässe in Unternehmen – Fachkräftesicherung in Deutschland – diese Potenziale gibt es noch. KOFA-STUDIE 2/2019. https://www.kofa.de/media/Publikationen/Studien/Fachkraefteengpaesse_2019_2.pdf (accessed on 01.10.2022)
Kurz L, Jost L, Rabelt V, Ohlhausen P, Roth K, Simon D, Fiegel-Kölblin I (2017) Nachhaltigkeit im Personalmanagement. BMBF-Projekt „LeNa – Nachhaltigkeitsmanagement in außeruniversitären Forschungsorganisationen", Berlin. https://nachhaltig-forschen.de/fileadmin/user_upload/FactSheets_LeNa_Personal.pdf (accessed on 13.10.2022)
Landwehr J (2020) So funktioniert Gamification im Recruiting. https://employer.it-talents.de/blog/gamification-im-recruiting/ (acessed on 14.10.2022)
Maurer I, Müller-Camen M (2016) Nachhaltiges Personalmanagement. In: Doyé T (Ed.) CSR und Human Resource Management. Management-Reihe Corporate Social Responsibility. Springer Gabler, Berlin, Heidelberg
McKinsey (2020) Diversity wins – How inclusion matters. https://www.mckinsey.com/~/media/mckinsey/featured%20insights/diversity%20and%20inclusion/diversity%20wins%20how%20inclusion%20matters/diversity-wins-how-inclusion-matters-vf.pdf (accessed on 14.10.2022)
Muñoz A (2019) Anonymized Competency-Based Recruitment and Selection Process for Public Sector: A New Approach for Workplace Diversity and Equality. https://www.researchgate.net/publication/343470594_Anonymized_Competency-Based_Recruitment_and_Selection_Process_for_Public_Sector_A_New_Approach_for_Workplace_Diversity_and_Equality (accessed on 14.10.2022)
OECD (2005) Definition und Auswahl von Schlüsselkompetenzen. Zusammenfassung. Paris
Raschka B (2019) Die 8 häufigsten Kündigungsgründe. https://www.stepstone.de/e-recruiting/blog/die-8-haufigsten-kundigungsgrunde/ (accessed on 14.10.2022)
Scharnhorst U (2021) Transversale Kompetenzen – notwendig, erwünscht und schwierig zu erreichen. BWP 1/2021, pp. 18–23. https://www.bwp-zeitschrift.de/dienst/veroeffentlichungen/de/bwp.php/de/publication/download/17030 (accessed on 14.10.2022)
Statistisches Bundesamt (Destatis) (2022): Bevölkerung – Geburten. https://www.destatis.de/DE/Themen/Gesellschaft-Umwelt/Bevoelkerung/Geburten/_inhalt.html (accessed on 01.10.2022)
Weichselbaumer D (2016) Discrimination against Female Migrants Wearing Headscarves. https://docs.iza.org/dp10217.pdf (accessed on 14.10.2022)

New Work and Generations

Kira Marie Cremer

The older generation always says yes—but; the younger generation yes—so.

- Friedrich Wilhelm Viktor Albert von Preußen

1 Introduction

Currently, at least four different generations are active in the working world, which often poses challenges for companies (Jobst-Jürgens 2020, p. 15).

Not knowing how to deal with this challenge often leads to employees feeling misunderstood by employers, resulting in dissatisfaction at the workplace. This, in turn, often results in employees leaving the company.

But let us start from the beginning: Which generations are currently in the workforce? What differences and similarities do they have? What exactly does generation management have to do with New Work? And what is the current significance of the generation conflict for our working life?

Generations are usually divided into cohorts according to their birth years. In addition, there is the possibility to categorize them generatively, historically, and according to life stages. Since the most common classification is by birth years, I will use this classification in the following:

People born between the years 1946 and 1964 are referred to as the Baby Boomer generation. A large part of them occupy leadership positions in companies and also political positions (Jobst-Jürgens 2020, p. 16). They are thus decision-makers and currently have the greatest influence on our society.

K. M. Cremer (✉)
Quings, Hamburg, Germany

I. Knappertsbusch and G. Wisskirchen (eds.), *The Future of Work*,
https://doi.org/10.1007/978-3-658-45150-9_49

People born between the years 1965 and 1980 are referred to as Generation X. They also occupy leadership positions in companies, but still make up a small part of these positions.

People born between the years 1981 and 1994 are referred to as Generation Y. They are also known as Millennials and have already entered the professional world.

People born between the years 1995 and 2010 are referred to as Generation Z, although the classification here is not quite as clearly delineated. Some sources define the years as 2000 to 2010 (Esmailzadeh/Meier/Birkner/De Gruyter/Dietrich/Schwiezer 2022).

Now you know the classification of the generations. How many of these generations are employed in the company where you work? I would estimate that there are at least two. So there are already young and old people in your company. Because even if only Generation Y and Generation Z are in the company, the first generation is "old" and the second generation is "young". For this reason, I am reluctant to talk about young and old, as most people understand Generation Z and the Baby Boomer generation. People of middle age are often forgotten. It is interesting to understand what is associated with the words young and old.

New York author Marc Prensky refers to the younger generations as "Digital Natives" and the older generations as "Digital Immigrants", setting the boundary in 1980. If we rely on this, the Baby Boomer generation and largely also Generation X are considered "old" and Generation Y and Generation Z are considered "young" (Sueddeutsche 2020).

The Lucerne University of Applied Sciences highlighted in its generation management study which associations the respondents connect with young and old. In summary, the respondents associate the term "young" with the use of digital offers, flexibility and high learning readiness as well as high motivation but also rapid resignation in the absence of promotion. With the term "old", the respondents associate high loyalty and discipline, well-maintained networks and social competence as well as good dealings with people, but also high costs for companies (Hille, et al. 2019, p. 52).

In addition, the differences between the generations lie in their respective imprints. For example, Generation X is shaped by the fall of the Berlin Wall or Generation Y by the advent of the Internet. This individual imprint makes understanding the respective other generation difficult.

But there are also similarities: According to the study by Jobst-Jürgens, 72% of respondents strive for innovation, 80% want more recognition, 79% desire offers for personal development. And all this completely independent of generation (2020, p. 153–154).

In summary, you can see that different generations have different educational backgrounds and imprints, but similarities also unite them. If companies therefore focus on these commonalities, they create good conditions for high employee retention and thus prevent fluctuation (Gallup Engagement Index 2022, p. 13).

And what does generation management have to do with New Work?

Generation management, or genfluencing as we call it at QUINGS, focuses on these mentioned commonalities in the exchange of generations within companies and ensures a respectful, transparent, respectful and open interaction with each other. As a sub-area of age diversity, it is also a sub-point of diversity and thus an aspect of New Work. I am happy to explain this complexity with the help of the Megatrend Map from the Future Institute. Here, the New Work strand also includes the Diversity station, which includes age diversity and thus also generation management.

According to a study by the Lucerne University of Applied Sciences, the majority of employers consider generation management important, but need support in implementation. The surveyed companies rate the "investment in the promotion of knowledge transfer as particularly valuable" (Hille, et al. 2019, p. 6), but also see that young people still pass on their knowledge too little to older people. They also conclude that prejudices against the generations exist, which must be removed for a successful exchange (Hille, et al. 2019, p. 6).

2 Advantages of Generational Management

Just as the world of work continues to evolve, so too will the requirements of the various employees and thus the different generations. A fact on the side: The next generation is already on the starting blocks: Generation Alpha refers to all persons born from the year 2010 onwards (Welt 2021).

Strategic generational management makes it easier for companies to exchange within generations, ensures higher employee retention, and increases employer attractiveness for the coming years and generations, such as Generation Alpha. Of course, the expectations of the generations will change and today's generational management will no longer be the standard in about 10 years. Nevertheless, companies should now deal with the method and anchor it in their teams.

Results of a study indicate that employee retention and loyalty are higher the older the generation. Older people therefore leave a company less quickly than young people. So how do I now bind younger people to my company? The same study found that loyalty can also be increased by actively creating career opportunities and through good leadership. If companies ensure that younger people are offered career opportunities and leaders are trained in leadership, they also bind young people to their company (Angeli 2018).

According to the Gallup Engagement Index 2022, the willingness of employees to change decreases with high attachment to the company. With high attachment, only 10% of employees are actively looking for new employers. With no attachment, however, it is 28%.

A book published as early as 2014 with a new edition in 2021 by Prof. Dr. Martin Klaffke hits the nail on the head: "Specifically, [generational management] means adjusting to the expectations of Generation Y while not losing sight of the wishes of the established generations, especially the Baby Boomers" (Prof. Dr. Martin Klaffke 2014).

Almost 10 years ago, Klaffke saw the professional management of generations as a lever to strengthen employer attractiveness and also criticized at that time that companies pay too little attention to this instrument. Meanwhile, workforces or teams in terms of age have a positive effect on business success (Hille et al. 2019, p. 48).

To underline the importance of generational management once again, I would like to show you what happens when companies do not value the exchange of generations: The previously mentioned generational conflict arises. This is divided into the areas of relationship, things, roles, values, and power (Personalwissen.de 2022).

The greatest conflict potential is between Generation Z and the Baby Boomer generation due to strong friction points. These are, for example, result-oriented work and autonomy among the young and working according to time and the desire for security among the older ones.

According to the Gallup Engagement Index 2022, the medium-term willingness of employees to change is increasing dramatically and there have "never been so many" employees looking for jobs. Added to this is the increasing internal feeling of burnout, the decline in the importance of work (Gallup Engagement Index 2022, p. 9) and the generational conflict that both employees and managers have to deal with.

Jörg Tremmel is a political scientist, teaches at the University of Tübingen, and published his theory of generational justice as early as 2012. In it, he deals with the ruthlessness of older generations who do not think of the next generations in their actions and, for example, accumulate debt and destroy the climate, which has to be paid for by younger people. The fact that Generation Z takes to the streets, starts a movement like Fridays for Future, or mocks the Baby Boomer generation on the internet with the slogan "Ok, Boomer", is then probably self-explanatory. Not for nothing is Generation Z referred to as the "Generation Future" in the book "Gen Z for Decision Makers". And Hauke Schwiezer, one of the authors of this book, advocates that companies appoint a board member who is under 25 years old to remain competitive (Schwiezer 2019, Horizont).

But is the panacea simply to listen to Generation Z? No, because the wealth of experience that older employees bring to the table cannot be compensated for by the digital skills of young people. Knowledge transfer, an open mindset, and long-term and sustainable generational management are the key. How exactly this succeeds, what advantages, challenges, and best practices there are, and what my view of the future looks like, you can read in the next sections.

3 Solutions and Practical Tips

I would like to illustrate to you with an example how "simple" it can be to promote the exchange of generations:

Deutsche Bahn employs 336,278 people worldwide and 217,028 nationally, according to the company website on 20.10.2022 (https://www.deutschebahn.com/

de/konzern/konzernprofil/zahlen_fakten/mitarbeiter-6878564#:~:text=Weltweit%20arbeiten%20rund%20338.000%20Menschen,zentrale%20Anliegen%20der%20Deutschen%20Bahn.). Here too, four generations work under one roof and Deutsche Bahn, like other German companies, faces the challenges of a shortage of skilled workers, employee retention, and employer attractiveness.

DDN Hamburg has illustrated the case of Deutsche Bahn's generation management as a best practice on its own website (https://www.ddn-hamburg.de/ddn-Hamburg/Best-Practices-100138), from which I would like to quote the following: "Generation management is one of the dimensions of diversity that is actively addressed at DB." As described in previous lines, generation management is a sub-area of diversity, here referred to as "diversity".

"Differences are evident, for example, in attitudes towards work and leisure, in mentality, expectations of the employer, and in communication. This can lead to prejudices, misunderstandings, and conflicts." You notice, Deutsche Bahn has recognized that differences can have negative consequences if not properly communicated and clarified.

"Tools with an AHA effect, such as the stereotype film or the self-test for generation assignment, which playfully questions the self-image and external image, had a special effect." We often only understand how wrong we act when we look at situations from the outside and reflect on actions.

"Accompanying workshops make the managers fit for implementation." Generation management only bears fruit if the managers and employees pull together. Therefore, individual coaching of the managers is essential.

"As an employer, the railway also benefits from successful generation management, as it is an important prerequisite for knowledge transfer [...]." The most important thing about generation management is knowledge transfer. If knowledge is not exchanged and passed on among each other, no further development can take place.

"Multigenerationality has been incorporated into the HR strategy of the railway. The 'Generation Management' project has attracted attention, questioned age images, and contributes to mutual appreciation and understanding of the generations for each other." You see: Generation management is and will be part of every HR strategy and must not be pushed into the background. Deutsche Bahn has also recognized and implemented this (DDN Hamburg, 2022).

Of course, there are certainly employees who criticize this approach, suggest improvements, or consider it useless. However, on the whole, the study from Lucerne also shows that our working world needs generation management.

4 Summary and Outlook

You now know clear facts, unequivocal study results, and my personal assessment of the current development. In the final outline point, I would like to give you an outlook and also clearly illustrate my vision. For this, I use the term genfluencing, which I have defined and which, in my opinion, represents a more contemporary designation for the positive influence that generations can have on each other.

Imagine the following scenario: Two people of different ages, different origins, and different belief systems meet and start a conversation, BUT with their eyes covered. They therefore only hear what the other person has to say. I leave it up to you to assign characteristics to these people.

The conversation goes well, both exchange ideas, talk about their skills, find common ground, and establish a connection with each other. After about 30 minutes, the people are asked if they could work together. Both affirm.

The blindfolds are removed. Both people see each other for the first time and are asked (without speaking to each other again) if they could work together. Both hesitate.

Why?

We humans associate appearance with stereotypes, put people in boxes, and go through life with prejudices. If both people were not different in appearance, they would not have hesitated when asked the second time if they would work together. Because people like to work with people who are similar to them. This is known as the principle of similarity (Jimenez and Schallenberg-Kappius 2022). Therefore, people who are dissimilar to those in high positions have a harder time getting promoted. Women, people with disabilities, or younger people are just a few examples.

With the help of genfluencing, companies can not only increase their attractiveness and success, but they can also educate. They promote the exchange of generations, create acceptance for change, and open doors for people who would have a harder time in the world without this exchange.

Klaffke says that at its core, it will always be about differentiating between existing personnel and leadership tools and applying them more flexibly to meet the requirements of the individual employee generations (Klaffke 2014).

My conviction is that genfluencing not only has a positive impact on the world of work, but also on our society. An example: If people are trained in their communication at work and it is explained to them why, for example, we no longer say colored, what distinguishes older and younger people, or why some people use gender-neutral language, they take this knowledge to their families and friends and also provide enlightenment there.

This opinion is underscored by Hauke Schwiezer, who emphasizes that the shortage of skilled workers and the War for Talents should not blindly lead us into a youth cult, as it is about a new coexistence of generations in the future—not only in the world of work but also in our private environment (Schwiezer 2019).

So, in conclusion, I would like to say to you: Stay open to innovations, to people who are different from you, to visions, and to your colleagues. Open these doors. It will work to your advantage!

References

Angeli, Moriz (2018): Generationen-Management und Mitarbeiterbindung: Effekte und Maßnahmen

DDN Hamburg (2022): Respekt und gegenseitiges Verständnis – Generationenmanagement bei der DB. URL: https://www.ddn-hamburg.de/ddn-Hamburg/Best-Practices-100138 (abgerufen am 20.10.2022)

Esmailzadeh, Annahita/Meier, Yael/Birkner Stephanie/De Gruyter, Julius/Jo Dietrich/Schwiezer, Hauke (2022): Gen Z für Entscheider:innen

Gallup Inc, (2022) Gallup Engagement Index 2021 Deutschland

Hille, Anina Dr./Roos, Brigitte/Seiler Zimmermann, Yvonne Prof. Dr./Wanzenried, Gabrielle Prof. Dr. (2019): Generationenmanagement Studie – Arbeitsmarktfähigkeit im Alter Wissensaustausch und Zusammenarbeit zwischen Generationen Teil 2 – Großunternehmen

Jobst-Jürgens, Vanessa (2020) New Work. Was relevante Arbeinehmergruppen im Job wirklich wollen – eine empirische Betrachtung

Jimenez, Fanny/Schallenberg-Kappius, Judith (2022): Befördert werden die, die sich dafür am besten eignen? Warum das oft nicht so ist – und wie ihr eure Chancen erhöht. URL: https://www.businessinsider.de/karriere/psychologie-befoerdert-wird-wenig-nach-eignung-eher-nach-buddy-prinzip-b/ (abgerufen am 25.11.2022)

Klaffke, Martin (2014): Generationen-Management. Konzepte, Instrumente, Good-Practice-Ansätze

Kunath, Katharina (2021): Die „Generation Alpha“ steht vor ganz neuen Problemen. URL: https://www.welt.de/kmpkt/article234702378/Generation-Alpha-Diese-jungen-Menschen-folgen-auf-die-Generation-Z.html (abgerufen am 25.11.2022)

o.A. (2022): Generationen am Arbeitsplatz: Vorteil Generationenvielfalt. Die 5 gängigsten Konfliktarten im Unternehmen. URL: https://www.personalwissen.de/personalwesen/diversity/generationen-am-arbeitsplatz/ (Abrufdatum 20.10.2022)

Schenz, Viola (2020): Generationenkonflikt. Jung gegen Alt. URL: https://www.sueddeutsche.de/karriere/arbeit-generationen-konflikt-alt-jung-1.4831668 (abgerufen am 25.11.2022)

Schwiezer, Hauke (2019): Warum in jedem deutschen Unternehmen ein U25-Vorstand sitzen sollte. URL: https://www.horizont.net/marketing/kommentare/generation-z-an-die-macht-warum-in-jedem-deutschen-unternehmen-ein-u25-vorstand-sitzen-sollte-177076 (abgerufen am 19.10.2022)

New Work and Family—How Companies in the New World of Work Benefit from a New Family-Friendliness

Gabriel Rath

> *Hybrid work promotes family-friendliness, empowers employees, and ensures more diversity within a company.*
>
> *Anja Hendel, Managing Director Diconium*

1 Introduction

The compatibility of family and career has always been a massive challenge for many working parents. After all, 11.62 million families in Germany are constantly faced with the question of how to manage the organization of private and working life in an increasingly complex world.[1]

The fundamental differences between mothers and fathers, which are already evident in the fact that the employment rate of male parents is currently about 18 percentage points higher than that of women, reveal the acute need for action. In order to promote social justice in society and support families in their challenges in the new world of work, a new form of family-friendliness is urgently needed.

According to Duden, family-friendliness is what "serves the family (as a social group), is accommodating [and] promoting it".[2] It can give companies a clear competitive advantage by strengthening their own "recruitability". This is how bestselling author Gunter Dueck[3] describes the urgently needed ability of companies to find and retain talent in the new world of work.

[1] Statista.

[2] Duden.

[3] HR Today.

G. Rath (✉)
Rostock, Deutschland
e-mail: hi@gabrielrath.com

I. Knappertsbusch and G. Wisskirchen (eds.), *The Future of Work*,
https://doi.org/10.1007/978-3-658-45150-9_50

Family-friendliness was long considered just a label that companies liked to attach to their website to advertise themselves as an attractive employer. In a world of work of "9 to 5" and compulsory presence, this often merely concealed an attempt to enable mothers to re-enter the company after their parental leave. Even if the planned career path could not be easily continued with this. Or the theoretical possibility was considered that young parents could work from home if the child was sick. Many approaches remained superficial. Families, especially with several children, had to decide which part can make a career and which part takes more care of the family, because it was hardly possible otherwise. Due to the still existing pay gap between women and men, women in most cases renounced promising jobs. Companies took note of this, but rarely changed the structures.

Meanwhile, the worker shortage driven by demographic change (see the article "Historical Turning Point in the German Labor Market—How Demographic Change Slows Down Growth") has forced the economy to rethink. The employees traditionally viewed by management as "human resources" have been able to emancipate themselves significantly in the last 3 years. The macroeconomic understanding of organizations as machines increasingly changed to a new idea, according to which employees basically work together self-motivated, but are no longer reduced to their labor, but act as people with strengths and weaknesses and also serious personal challenges.

The perhaps well-intentioned family-friendliness of the past gradually gave way to a new family awareness that established itself in companies. HR departments renamed themselves "People and Culture" to take much more care of people than before, to see them in different phases of life, to appreciate and also to promote them. This family awareness is now not only directed at young parents, but equally at experienced employees, who can be enabled a positive work-life integration with flexible working conditions.

Family-friendly companies that take New Work seriously are committed to ensuring that work strengthens people and does not come as an additional burden. It includes proactively dealing with the needs and challenges of family members in the company.

2 Advantages of this Form of work

For decades, companies operated within the system of work organization conceived by the American engineer Frederick Taylor, in the sense of a machine. This was associated with the idea that employees needed to be extrinsically motivated and then controlled. However, the model of new work designed by the Austrian philosopher Frithjof Bergmann in the 1980s was based on the assumption that people want to act responsibly, so companies should only provide the framework and support them in answering the most important question. This question, which employees should ask themselves, was: What do I really, really want to do?

For families, the following questions also arose: How do I want to work? What does my career look like with children? How do I manage the daily jobs?

Companies that took these questions seriously could quickly develop a great advantage, as they could greatly strengthen the partnership relationship by supporting the employees, which the employees appreciated in return.

Basically, it can be stated today that organizations that focus on equality and personal responsibility can also gain a huge competitive advantage in the context of family, which consists in the fact that employees become actors and co-determiners from being mere executors. The responsibility for a lived family-friendliness in the future of work thus lies on both sides, who can together find a new way.

Employees who can plan and take risks themselves will not only find a flexible way to balance work and family. They will also "repay" the employer with organic loyalty. The culture of trust that gradually develops when the traditional model of "command and control" is also abandoned in leadership understanding pays off in employee retention, which in turn is the hardest currency in the shortage of skilled workers.

Especially young parents, who have to deal with major challenges such as finding a property, the right daycare or school place, and a suitable working time model, are not only grateful for an understanding of the employer, but also for active support. Companies thus become partners who not only exchange labor for wages, but are interested in the success of their employees' lives.

Interestingly, the emotional attachment of many employees to their employer has significantly decreased since the triumph of home office and mobile work since the spring of 2020. Teams that adapted to this and developed leadership as a new, individually tailored support offer, could do a lot for families who had to take care of the children's care during the lockdown, by designing the framework conditions flexibly. This not only increased employee satisfaction. In many places, the fluctuation in the company also decreased.

At the latest since the work trend of the "Great Resignation" in the USA, there is also increasingly talk in Germany of a growing willingness of employees to change. According to the XING willingness to change study 2022, in which employees in Germany, Austria and Switzerland were surveyed, 37% of Germans are considering changing jobs. That's 12% more than last year. A better work-life balance was given as a reason for a possible job change by 27% of those surveyed.[4]

Companies that intensively ask their employees about their wishes and ideas regarding their own work and the organization of the family therefore have an immense advantage in being able to proactively adapt to this. In the next step, this can also lead to employees who experience a new family-friendliness in the age of New Work talking positively about it on social media. They become corporate influencers who can positively fuel the company's employer branding (see the article "Employer Branding on the Future Labor Market—What Do Companies Have to Offer Workers?").

---

[4] Xing.

Works councils also generally support a newly lived family-friendliness, as it is about appreciation and co-determination of employees. Indeed, the topic is also important in the context of recruiting young talents. According to the "Future Talents Report 2022" by Clevis Consult[5] , the majority of young people stated that family-friendliness is a decisive factor in choosing a profession.

3 Challenges of this form of work

Organizations that now sustainably deal with the different challenges of employees in their life phases have to think about a new setting. Who should earn how much in the future? What is performance based on? Are the living conditions of young parents, who tend to sleep less, taken into account? And after all, what other benefits are there besides salary?

Developing an appealing and fair benefit model that can support families will be an important task. The new family benefits include, for example, workation models that allow families to combine vacation and work regardless of location (see the article "Working where others vacation—'Workation', a model with a future?").

A lived family-friendliness, which is reflected in some companies like Google in their own kindergartens and care offers, of course also costs money. You have to be willing to invest this. Otherwise, it ends at worst in the so-called #Familywashing, the mere claim to be family-friendly.

4 Solutions and Practical Tips

To embark on the path of new family-friendliness as a company, top management should first familiarize themselves with New Work and its possibilities. This is less about minor well-being assets like the famous fruit baskets. Rather, it's about asking employees what they need to be able to work successfully, and then taking seriously the needs and wishes of employees who are themselves family people.

In the form of a future workshop for families, a picture of the status quo in the company can be drawn together, on the basis of which a vision of a new family-friendly employer can be drawn. However, it's not just about the employer making family life easier with new flexibility and benefits. It's also about employees contributing to a "new way to work".

The results can be very different. For example, the XING parent company New Work SE developed a new family office at the "New Work Harbour" location in Hamburg's HafenCity. Young parents can bring their small children to work and keep an eye on them in a child-friendly office while they play with the toys.

[5] Clevis.

Another family-friendly approach in the context of new family-friendliness can be for employers to give their employees the opportunity to work in coworking spaces (see the article "Coworking Space as a third workplace"). Especially families who do not have a home office face the challenge of coordinating family and work in one place. During lockdown times, the additional task of homeschooling created a very demanding field for many families, which drove up stress levels. Therefore, the possibility of offering a third place (see the article "Third places—Third workplaces") is also a measure of corporate health management.

The Hamburg coworking space "work + play", for example, is considered one of the family-friendly coworking spaces that companies can book for their employees even for short periods of time. The children can simply be brought along, because "work + play" has developed a childcare program that relieves working parents.

In this way, companies can reduce the everyday stress of families. Here, companies can also offer special mindfulness programs for parents such as yoga classes and mindfulness circles.

Exchange with like-minded people remains important. In some companies like Telekom, parents have networked in communities and organize special offers for parents in consultation with the employer. These are also necessary, as the impending exhaustion of many parents due to the double burden of work and family organization often ends in burnout.

This also includes responsible handling of collaboration tools such as messengers, video conferencing and social intranets, which have become very popular in many companies since the Corona period at the latest. However, if an overzealous use of these tools gives the impression that constant availability is desirable, then companies achieve the exact opposite of family-friendliness at most.

In order to establish a new family awareness in the company, it is essential to work on this topic with the managers. They ideally embody the company's values in terms of enabling a balance between family and work and react understandingly when a child is sick and work therefore needs to be reorganized. Leadership will have to respond much more to the individual needs and situations of employees in the future and should support in successfully organizing family and work together.

In the case of pregnancy, the manager should signal early on that this does not have to interrupt the associated career. Early joint scenarios such as part-time work or job sharing (see the article "Job sharing in management—experiences and suggestions for practice") through new tandem models should be offered and discussed. It can also be helpful to generally deal with the model of the 4-day week (see the article "The 4-day week"), which has demonstrably increased employee satisfaction in the Rheingans management consultancy by improving compatibility.

To find your own way, it is also worth working with professional family-friendliness consultants. The father and educator Robert Casel, for example, founded Culturino, a tailor-made consulting offer that helps companies inspire their own employees through practically lived family-friendliness. He says: "Companies often still wait to strategically approach the topic of family-friendliness. It is fatal to hope that isolated measures will lead to real change," and advocates a holistic approach.

5 Summary and Outlook

As celebrated as the term "New Work" is in the media, it is still not taken seriously in many companies. Since it is fundamentally about responding to the needs of employees, and in our case parents, a change in the structure, i.e. the framework conditions, must become noticeable as a result. Companies that do not just want to stick a "Family-friendly Employer" seal of approval on their website to recruit more effectively, but actually value families, will be successful in the job market because they can earn a unique loyalty.

At its core, it's about nurturing relationships within the company, creating a culture of trust that can unfold in the long term. Those who invest in family-friendliness will not only visibly increase their own reputation as an employer of the future, they will also get satisfied employees who work together motivated and successfully, thus enabling the company's success.

References

https://www.clevis.de/future-talents/ (abgerufen am 02.11.2022)

https://www.duden.de/rechtschreibung/familienfreundlich (abgerufen am 02.11.2022)

https://hrtoday.ch/de/article/artgerechte-haltung-von-top-leuten-hr-festival-gunter-dueck (abgerufen am 02.11.2022)

https://de.statista.com/themen/5855/vereinbarkeit-von-familie-und-beruf/ (abgerufen am 02.11.2022)

https://www.new-work.se/de/newsroom/pressemitteilungen/2022-xing-studie-jeder-vierte-kuendigt-job-ohne-neue-stelle-in-aussicht%20zu%20haben (abgerufen am 02.11.2022)

The Future of Talent Management—How Women Make Careers Through Networks

Katharina Schleeberger and Katharina Klinge

1 Introduction

It has long been recognized that a balanced proportion of women in key positions is not only of demographic and moral-ethical relevance, but also promises a decisive competitive advantage for companies. In addition, the Second Leadership Positions Act has been making provisions for greater gender equality in executive and supervisory boards of large German companies since August 2021. In the context of "New Work", the targeted promotion of female talents therefore plays a crucial role for long-term successful personnel policy and corporate management.

Experience shows that the "talents" or "high potentials" make up about 10–20% of the company's personnel (Enaux & Henrich, 2010). If women made up 50% of this talent pool, this would be a good basis for parity-filled executive floors. But even these prerequisites have not yet led to the desired result.

Traditional methods of talent management focus on the identification, development, and placement of potentials in companies. With structured succession planning, potential successors for specific key and leadership positions are proposed and specifically trained for these positions. These conventional approaches, with their focus on vertical careers in traditional organizational structures, often no longer meet the requirements of global and flexible organizations (see Festing et al., 2017).

K. Schleeberger (✉)
Mülheim an der Ruhr, Germany
e-mail: kontakt@schleeberger.de

K. Klinge
Hochschule Macromedia, Berlin, Germany
e-mail: k.klinge@macromedia.de

I. Knappertsbusch and G. Wisskirchen (eds.), *The Future of Work*,
https://doi.org/10.1007/978-3-658-45150-9_51

The talents themselves are now demanding different support measures and want to shape their careers increasingly flexibly and self-responsibly (see Kienbaum, 2020). Thus, the responsibility for the individual professional career is increasingly shifting from the employer to the employee (Wingender and Wolff, 2019). This does not mean that they should be left alone. New forms of support are needed, such as promoting networks, creating visibility and maturity of talents, and the willingness to think more broadly about development paths (Kienbaum, 2020; Schleeberger and Möltner, 2021; Wingender and Wolff, 2019).

This is especially true for the promotion of female careers. Until now, a strong lever for sustainable change has been missing. With the new focus on the topic of "networking", real change can also succeed at the executive level.

In a professional context, networking is the active endeavor of individuals to build and maintain relationships with other people through social interaction. These people can provide access to professional resources and have the potential to support others in their work or career development (Forret and Dougherty, 2004; Wingender and Wolff, 2019).

Numerous research results prove that networking is positively associated with individual career success, as shown in indicators such as salary developments or promotions (Forret and Dougherty 2004; Wingender and Wolff, 2019, according to Langford 2000; Wolff and Moser 2009). In addition, due to economic and organizational developments, networking is becoming increasingly important not only for individuals, but also for the organizations as a whole (Wingender and Wolff, 2019).

Interestingly, there are significant differences between women and men in terms of networking approaches and results: On the one hand, women benefit less from networking, which is partly due to the fact that women are often excluded from important information, relationship, and support systems of their organizations (Haverbier and Weßels, 2016). On the other hand, women invest less in professional contact maintenance, for example in the context of social gatherings or events (Forret and Dougherty, 2001). One of the reasons is the negative attitude of many women towards networking. Women primarily associate networking with cliques and counteract this with the principle of performance as a typically female counter-strategy. Without appropriate self-marketing, however, women's performance often remains unrecognized (Haverbier and Weßels, 2016, according to Färber and Riedler, 2011).

This is where the authors come in: Female talents should be supported in recognizing, reflecting, and experiencing the added value of networking. In this way, they can use their potential for their career development, but also for the organization.

2 Benefits of Networking for Organizations and Talents

By focusing on the networking competence of female talents, companies achieve several goals. The overarching goal is to increase the representation of women in key positions with the ultimate aim of gender parity. While the relevance of networks for individual careers and corporate success has already been extensively proven, it has been shown that women invest less in networking activities and benefit less from networks. The targeted sensitization to and promotion of women's networking skills starts exactly there: It specifically supports women in advancing their careers through the establishment and maintenance of professional contacts as well as the enhancement of self-marketing competence in a responsible and strategic manner.

2.1 Benefits for the Organization

Promoting the networking competence of female talents serves the organization as a whole.

Internally, the talents can serve as connection points to bring teams together, initiate or accelerate projects, and promote collaboration within and between departments. Externally, well-networked employees can establish connections, recognize general and cross-industry trends, and bring new knowledge into their own company. As ambassadors of the company, they communicate the brand and increase the attractiveness of the company. Specifically for the recruitment of female specialists and executives, well-networked talents can develop positive radiance.

2.2 Benefits for the Talents

Female talents receive support in developing the critical networking competence as well as "start-up aid" for building their networks and thus independently assume the demanded responsibility for actively shaping their career paths.

This positive aspect is also supported by the results of the Kienbaum Talent Management Study from 2020, in which about half of over 1000 talents stated that they felt "too strongly confined by the "One-Size-Fits-All" development portfolio of their employer" (p. 2). Over 80% wished to shape their professional development themselves, to independently seek projects for their development and to network proactively.

3 Challenges in Promoting Networking Activities

3.1 Challenges for the Organization

Promoting external networking activities poses certain risks for organizations. After all, external networking automatically also increases the chances for interesting career perspectives outside the organization. The risk of high potentials migrating must be counteracted with correspondingly attractive internal development opportunities. Therefore, internal networking should be enabled and promoted by the organization just like external networking.

In both internal and external networking activities, the autonomy of the employees is paramount. There is little controlling intervention on the part of the organization. When members represent the organization externally, a framework of orientation is necessary that preserves the interests of the organization and ensures that it is represented in the best sense. Experience has shown that guidelines for external communication can also be useful in terms of data protection and compliance.

3.2 Challenges for the Talents

Talents who see talent management as a mechanism that automatically puts them in responsible positions must learn to proactively stand up for themselves. They should become visible with their own expertise in the organization in order to improve their own position. The relevance of networks is not yet apparent to everyone. The often prevailing classic vertical careers within the same business line may not have demanded these skills so far. A reserved or even rejecting attitude towards networking and the self-reliance and self-marketing required for it must therefore first be reduced.

Creating external visibility as an expert is also one of the challenges. In public speeches, interviews or discussion rounds, the less well-networked women are overlooked, especially in male-dominated areas. Here, it is important for the talents to position themselves as experts.

Another challenge for the talents is the perceived time expenditure for establishing and maintaining contacts in the network (cf. Sagebiel, 2016). The first successes only become apparent after a while and are often not clearly measurable. It can be difficult not to loose motivation along the way. In addition, the expansion and maintenance of networks is often neglected during time-outs for care work. Even in part-time roles, the concrete work result is often preferred to a less concrete activity such as an exchange in the network. There is a high risk that these talents will miss out on the next step in their career due to this purely performance-focused behavior.

4 Solutions for the Practical Implementation of Networks in Talent Management

Once companies recognize the relevance and competitive advantage of networking, concrete measures can be planned along the entire personnel and talent development cycle (see Fig. 1). Positive signals are sent here by research. This shows that networking is trainable (Wingender and Wolff, 2019) and as a result the professional optimism and the perceived career success of women demonstrably increases (cf. Ebner and Kauffeld, 2019).

The depicted personnel and talent development cycle schematically represents the occasions for development interventions in organizations. The cycle begins with the entry of employees into the company. This is followed by an initial analysis of existing skills and competencies in relation to the occupied function. This can be done through structured conversations or aptitude diagnostic tools. For about 90% of employees, this is followed by classic qualification with the aim of closing the gaps between the required and existing competencies. In addition to classic training, on- and near-the-job activities are often used. For 10% of the workforce, the analyses result in recognition as talent and associated additional development opportunities.

Experience shows that each phase of the depicted cycle, starting with the entry into the company, offers connections to the topic of networking. A structured step-by-step approach is essential when utilizing this potential in order to effectively counteract the described barriers. The following LINK Model therefore describes an approach that has already been successfully implemented in corporate practice

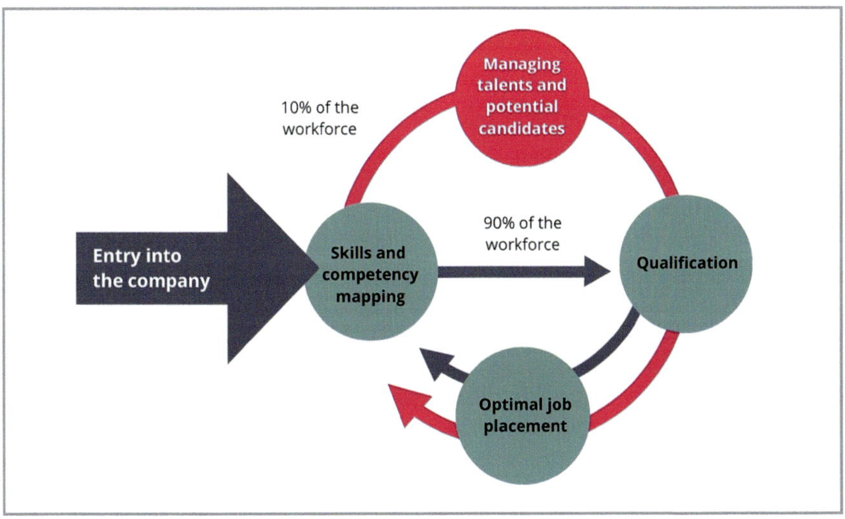

Fig. 1 Classic cycle of personnel and talent development. (own illustration)

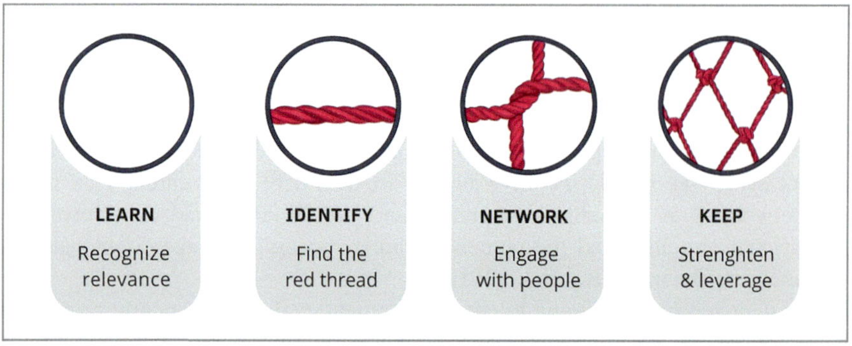

Fig. 2 The LINK Model: From the red thread to a sustainable network — Four steps to promote networking competence. (own illustration)

several times. Figure 2 first provides an overview of the individual steps to promote networking competence.

4.1 Learn — Recognize Relevance of Networking as an Investment in One's Own Career

In the first step, the organization is called upon to sensitize its female talents to the relevance of the topic. Women generally see networks as less useful in terms of their own advantage than men do (Haverbier and Weßels, 2016). Sagebiel (2016) points out that women in lower positions experience networking activities as time-consuming. However, if women are aware of the importance of networking, they use their time and resources specifically for this purpose. Thus, experienced female executives prioritize the topic of networking much higher than aspiring female talents. The earlier this awareness is present, the more efficiently these women can benefit from networks.

4.2 Identify — Find the Red Thread

Once the relevance of the topic of networking is established, organizations should support their talents in proceeding strategically. This is essential so that the talents can design their activities in the network in a targeted and time-efficient manner.

The concept of the "red thread" has proven to be highly relevant in business settings. Originally mentioned by the German poet Goethe in "Elective Affinities", the red thread stands for the motives and interests that run through one's own life. This analogy is perfectly suited in the context of networking to visually represent the following phases of networking competence.

The red thread is operationalized in this phase, among other things, by a so-called "elevator pitch". Here, the focus is on the addressee-appropriate formulation of one's own topics and goals (see also Wingender & Wolff, 2019, Janasz and Forret 2008). This is crucial for a concise self-presentation in social interactions. Once the red thread has been formulated, it is easier for the talents to get in touch with potentially interesting people.

The red threa" can be worked out and sharpened with formats from training, workshops or even individual coaching. The use of workbooks (for example, the netWORKbook® by Schleeberger, 2020) in self-study also leads to measurable successes.

4.3 Network — Engage with People

Regardless of the chosen development format, it should be ensured that the talents successfully interact within their internal company network. In this protected space, the self-presentation worked out in phase 2 can also be optimized. The organization benefits from strengthened internal connections that arise during this learning phase. Often, internal cooperations have emerged afterwards. Once the first internal interactions have been successful and the self-efficacy of the talents has increased, the exchange outside the company can follow. This can lead to interesting cooperations for the organization and promote future knowledge exchange.

4.4 Keep — Strengthen and Leverage Connections

In order to actually draw benefit from the networks for career development, this final phase is of critical importance. Even if female talents have diverse and helpful connections, using them often still requires considerable effort. As already explained, experienced female executives are much more successful in using contacts for their own benefit than aspiring female talents. These often want to continue to convince through strategies that have been helpful so far, such as performance and qualification. Without the appropriate self-marketing and the concrete approach to the network, the next career step will be much more difficult for these talents. However, if the network is experienced as positive and enriching, a supportive internal network can also be established for subsequent generations of female talents.

5 Summary and Outlook

Traditional, linearly planned talent management no longer meets today's requirements. The complexity, dynamism, and digitalization of the economy are constantly increasing. The expectations of employees regarding their own careers are also changing. A rigid talent management system orientated towards an "ideal worker" does not provide this flexibility.

Empowering talents in terms of network competence offers a so far hardly used and unique opportunity to respond flexibly to these requirements. Thus, career promotion through networks is a response to the organization's demand for flexible and self-responsible career development. Especially female talents can benefit sustainably from this. In this way, the female principle of "performance" is effectively supplemented by the component of "network competence".

If companies succeed in establishing positive cycles of supportive female network activities through the LINK Model, they move from reactive to proactive on an individual level. The individual red threads of future executives connect to form resilient networks. Increased employer attractiveness is just as much a consequence as an internal speak-up culture. In perspective, this approach serves as a crucial turning point for enhancing gender equality at management levels.

It is now up to companies to utilize the pioneering advantage and put these findings into practice.

References

Ebner, K. & Kauffeld, S. (2019). Laufbahngestaltung durch Karrierecoaching. In S. Kauffeld & D. Spurk (Hrsg.), Handbuch Karriere und Laufbahnmanagement (S. 759–784). Springer.

Enaux, C. & Henrich, F. (2010). Strategisches Talent-Management: Talente systematisch finden, entwickeln und binden (1. Aufl.). Haufe-Lexware.

Färber, C. & Riedler, U. (2011): Black Box Berufung. Strategien auf dem Weg zur Professur. Frankfurt am Main.

Festing, M., Harsch, K., Schäfer, L. & Scullion, H. (2017). Talent Management in Small- and Medium-Sized Enterprises. In D.G. Collings, K. Mellahi & W.F. Cascio (Hrsg.) The Oxford Handbook of Talent Management (S. 478–493). Oxford University Press.

Forret, M. L. & Dougherty, T. W. (2001). Correlates of networking behavior for managerial and professional employees. Group and Organization Management, 26, 283–311.

Forret, M. L. & Dougherty, T. W. (2004). Networking behaviors and career outcomes: differences for men and women? Journal of Organizational Behavior, 25(3), 419–437.

Haverbier, J. & Weßels, D. (2016). Erfolgsfaktor Netzwerk. Ansatzpunkte zur Förderung ‚weiblicher' Vernetzungsstrategien. In I. Welpe & G. Lenz (Hrsg.): Akademische Personalentwicklung – Wie der Wissenschaftsbetrieb Potentiale und Kompetenzen des Personals strategisch entwickelt (S. 248–261). Reihe Angewandte Genderforschung/Gender Research Applied, Band 7. Frankfurt: Peter Lang Verlag.

Janasz de, S. C., & Forret, M. L. (2008). Learning the art of networking: A critical skill for enhancing social capital and career success. Journal of Management Education, 32(5), 629–650.

Kienbaum (2020). Engaging Talent – Potenzialträger binden und entwickeln: Die Kienbaum Talent Management Studie 2020. https://www.kienbaum.com/de/publikationen (abgerufen am 09.09.2022).

Langford, P. H. (2000). Importance of relationship management for the career success of Australian managers. Australian Journal of Psychology, 52(3), 163–168.

Sagebiel, F. (2016). Männernetzwerke in den Ingenieurwissenschaften als Potenzial und Barriere für Ingenieurinnen. In U.C. Schmidt & B. Kortendiek (Hrsg.), Netzwerke im Schnittfeld von Organisation, Wissen und Geschlecht. Studien Netzwerk Frauen- und Geschlechterforschung NRW (Bd. 23, S. 104–116). Universität Essen.

Schleeberger, K. (2020). Natürlich vernetzt: Die Lernreise für weibliche Talente. Das Talentprogramm mit dem netWORKbook®. https://www.schleeberger.de/natuerlichvernetzt/ (abgerufen am 09.09.2022).

Schleeberger, K. & Möltner, H. (2021). Vier Mythen des Talent Managements. Personalwirtschaft, 2, 18–19.

Wingender, L. M. & Wolff, H. G. (2019). Die Rolle von Networking-Verhalten in der beruflichen Entwicklung. In S. Kauffeld & D. Spurk (Hrsg.), Handbuch Karriere und Laufbahnmanagement (S. 217–239). Springer.

Wolff, H.-G., & Moser, K. (2009). Effects of networking on career success: A longitudinal study. Journal of Applied Psychology, 94(1), 196–206.

GPSR Compliance

The European Union's (EU) General Product Safety Regulation (GPSR) is a set of rules that requires consumer products to be safe and our obligations to ensure this.

If you have any concerns about our products, you can contact us on ProductSafety@springernature.com

In case Publisher is established outside the EU, the EU authorized representative is:

Springer Nature Customer Service Center GmbH
Europaplatz 3
69115 Heidelberg, Germany

Batch number: 07946330

Printed by Printforce, the Netherlands